INTELLECTUAL PROPERTY RIGHTS
AND THE LIFE SCIENCE INDUSTRIES

Intellectual Property Rights and the Life Science Industries
A Twentieth Century History

GRAHAM DUTFIELD
Queen Mary Intellectual Property Research Institute,
University of London

ASHGATE

Published by
Ashgate Publishing Limited
Gower House
Croft Road
Aldershot
Hampshire GU11 3HR
England

Ashgate Publishing Company
Suite 420
101 Cherry Street
Burlington, VT 05401-4405
USA

Ashgate website: http://www.ashgate.com

British Library Cataloguing in Publication Data
Dutfield, Graham
   Intellectual property rights and the life science
   industries : a 20th century history. - (Globalization and law)
   1.Intellectual property 2.Patent laws and legislation
   3.Life sciences - Law and legislation 4.Life sciences -
   Patents
   I. Title
   346'.048

Library of Congress Cataloguing in Publication Data
Dutfield, Graham.
   Intellectual property rights and the life science industries : a 20th century history /
Graham Dutfield.
      p. cm.-- (Globalization and law)
   Includes bibliographical references.
   ISBN 0-7546-2111-1 (hbk. : alk. paper)
      1. Biotechnology industries--Law and legislation--History. 2. Intellectual property
(International law)--History 3. Life sciences--Research--History. I. Title. II. Series.

K1519.B54 D88 2002
341.7'58--dc21   2002028131

ISBN 0 7546 2111 1

Printed and bound in Great Britain by MPG Books Ltd, Bodmin, Cornwall.

Contents

List of Tables

List of Acronyms

AIPPI	Association Internationale pour la Protection de la Propriété Industrielle (International Association for the Protection of Industrial Property)
ASSINSEL	Association Internationale des Sélectionneurs pour la Protection des Obtentions Végétales (International Association of Plant Breeders)
BIRPI	Bureaux Internationaux Réunis de la Protection de la Propriété Intellectuelle (United International Bureaux for the Protection of Intellectual Property)
CAFC	Court of Appeals for the Federal Circuit
CBD	Convention on Biological Diversity
cDNA	Complementary (or copy) DNA
CGRFA	Commission on Genetic Resources for Food and Agriculture of the FAO
CIOPORA	Communauté Internationale des Obtenteurs de Plantes Ornementales de Reproduction Asexuée (International Community of Breeders of Asexually-reproducing Ornamental Plants)
COP	Conference of the Parties to the Convention on Biological Diversity
CPGR	Commission on Plant Genetic Resources
CRO	Collective rights organization
DBF	Dedicated biotechnology firm
DNA	Deoxyribonucleic acid
EPC	European Patent Convention
EPO	European Patent Office
ESTs	Expressed sequence tags
FAO	Food and Agriculture Organization of the United Nations
FDA	Food and Drug Administration
FICPI	Fédération Internationale des Conseils en Propriété Industrielle (International Federation of Industrial Property Attorneys)
GATT	General Agreement on Tariffs and Trade
GIPID	Global Intellectual Property Issues Division (of WIPO)
ICC	International Chamber of Commerce
ICT	Information and communications technology
IGC	Intergovernmental Committee on Intellectual Property and Genetic Resources, Traditional Knowledge and Folklore (of WIPO)
IP	Intellectual property

IPO	Initial public offering
IPR	Intellectual property right
ITC	International Trade Commission
IUCN	International Union for the Conservation of Nature and Natural Resources
MAb	Monoclonal antibody
MRC	Medical Research Council
MTA	Material transfer agreement
NBE	New biological entity
NCE	New chemical entity
NCI	National Cancer Institute
NGO	Non-governmental organization
NHS	National Health Service
NIH	National Institutes of Health
PBRs	Plant breeders' rights
PCR	Polymerase chain reaction
PhRMA	Pharmaceutical Research and Manufacturers of America
PLT	Patent Law Treaty
PMA	Pharmaceutical Manufacturers Association (former name of PhRMA)
rDNA	Recombinant DNA
RNA	Ribonucleic acid
SCP	Standing Committee on the Law of Patents (of WIPO)
SPC	Supplementary protection certificate
TBA	Technical Board of Appeal (of the European Patent Office)
TK	Traditional knowledge
TNC	Transnational corporation
TRIPS	Agreement on Trade-related Aspects of Intellectual Property Rights
UNCTAD	United Nations Conference on Trade and Development
UNEP	United Nations Environment Programme
UPOV	Union Internationale pour la Protection des Obtentions Végétales (International Union for the Protection of New Varieties of Plants)
USDA	United States Department of Agriculture
USPTO	United States Patent and Trademark Office
USTR	United States Trade Representative
WHO	World Health Organization
WIPO	World Intellectual Property Organization
WTO	World Trade Organization

Acknowledgements

During the writing of this book, it has been my pleasure and considerable good fortune to benefit from some of the brightest minds working in the field of intellectual property. In particular, I would like to acknowledge David Vaver and Peter Drahos.

Dwijen Rangnekar, with whom I have had many stimulating conversations over the years, referred me to some useful literature. Reading an article he recommended gave me the idea for this book.

André Heitz and Margaret Llewelyn gave me some helpful insights into plant breeding and the UPOV Convention, as did Paul Ong into genetics. Maiko Ozawa helpfully responded to my enquiries on the Japanese patent system. Eslah Stark managed to track down an English translation of the first German patent law and kindly sent it to me. Alan Story directed me to some valuable sources of information relating to the insulin patents. David Vaver, John Barton, Carlos Correa, Susan Sell, Christopher May, Keith Maskus, Pedro Roffe, Carl-Gustaf Thornström and Robert Lettington sent valuable comments on text I wrote that was partly or wholly incorporated into the book. Peter Drahos, Geoff Tansey and Tzen Wong read the manuscript and sent some helpful comments and suggestions. Frances Britain at Ashgate did a thoroughly professional job of preparing the manuscript for publication.

I must thank also the very helpful staff of various Oxford University libraries, the British Library and the WIPO Library.

The Economic and Social Research Council awarded me a research studentship from 1998-2001, which enabled me, while completing my doctoral thesis, to also make a start on the book with some financial security. Two awards graciously bestowed by St Peter's College, Oxford University, also came in handy at this time.

Finally, but most importantly, my wife Seok Yoon's companionship, enthusiasm and encouragement helped to make the writing of this book always a pleasure and never a grind.

Graham Dutfield

Introduction

A page of history is worth a volume of logic. (Oliver Wendell Holmes, past United States Supreme Court judge)

Intellectual property rights have never been as much in the news as they are today. Developing countries and civil society organizations rail against drug companies for charging exorbitant prices for treatments for patent-protected drugs to combat AIDS, a disease afflicting many African countries on a scale comparable to the medieval era Black Death. Indigenous peoples and advocacy groups supporting their rights condemn corporate 'biopirates' for making money out of their knowledge and claiming patent rights for 'inventions' essentially identical to knowledge acquired from tribal healers. Concerns are raised that patenting plants, animals, genes and gene fragments is not only immoral and even sacrilegious but may also be stifling innovation. And while the trend is towards ever stronger intellectual property right protection, increasingly determined efforts are made to buck the trend, as exemplified by Napster, the Open Source and Free Software movements, and the access to medicines and no patents on life campaigns.

What exactly is going on? It is not necessary to accept every criticism of intellectual property rights to locate behind the strengthening of these rights a worrying tendency for policy makers to embrace – on behalf of the citizenry – what Peter Drahos of Australian National University calls 'proprietarianism'. By this he means 'a creed which says that the possessor should take all, that ownership privileges should trump community interests and that the world and its contents are open to ownership' (Drahos, 1996: 202). The result is that the rights are getting unaccountably stronger and more expansive in their scope.

What are intellectual property (IP) rights? IP rights are legal and institutional devices to protect creations of the mind such as inventions, works of art and literature, and designs. They also include marks on products to indicate their difference from similar ones sold by competitors. Over the years, the rather elastic (and arguably misleading) intellectual property concept[1] has been stretched to include not only patents, copyrights, trade marks and industrial designs, but also trade secrets, plant breeders' rights, geographical indications and rights to layout designs of integrated circuits. Of these, patents, copyrights and trade marks are arguably the most significant in terms of their economic importance, their historical role in the industrialization of Europe and North America, and their current standing as major pillars of the international law of intellectual property.

1

Patents provide inventors with legal rights to prevent others from using, selling or importing their inventions for a fixed period, nowadays normally 20 years. Applicants for a patent must satisfy a national patent issuing authority that the invention described in the application is new, susceptible of industrial application (or merely 'useful'[2] in the United States) and that its creation involved an inventive step or would be unobvious to a skilled practitioner. Patent monopolies are extremely valuable for business.

Copyrights give authors legal protection for various kinds of literary and artistic work. Copyright law protects authors by granting them exclusive rights to sell copies of their work in whatever tangible form (printed publication, sound recording, film and so on) is being used to convey their creative expressions to the public. Legal protection covers the expression of the ideas contained, not the ideas themselves. The right lasts for a very long time indeed, usually the life of the author plus 50–70 years.

Trade marks are marketing tools used to support a company's claim that its products or services are authentic or distinctive compared with similar products or services of competitors. They usually consist of a distinctive design, word or series of words placed on a product label. Normally, trade marks can be renewed indefinitely, though in most jurisdictions this is subject to continued use. The trade mark owner has the exclusive right to prevent third parties from using identical or similar marks in the sale of identical or similar goods or services where doing so is likely to cause confusion. One of the main benefits of trade marks to the wider public is that they help to avoid such confusion.

Like many other systems of economic regulation, intellectual property rights have a history going back centuries. But the main IP rights like patents and copyrights took their modern forms and functions in the nineteenth century at a time when Europe and North America were in the midst of rapid industrialization.

Over the years, states have granted patents for a variety of public policy purposes, such as to encourage the immigration of craftsmen, to reward importers of foreign technologies, to reward inventors, to create incentives for further inventive activity, to encourage the dissemination of new knowledge,[3] and to allow corporations to recoup their investments in research and development. From a public policy perspective, each of these justifications is as legitimate as the others. Which is most appropriate for a country depends largely on its economic circumstances. Historically, and even today, the way patents have been justified in different countries has depended on the level of industrial development – and also to whom one speaks. Nonetheless, as with other forms of intellectual property (especially copyright), justice-based arguments for stronger and better enforced rights are also frequently deployed, and such claims can carry strong moral force. After all, many people would consider it just as immoral for somebody to copy an inventor's useful new gadget and claim it as his or her own as to similarly misappropriate somebody's new novel, song or painting.

Patents for inventions have their origins in Renaissance Italy. The Republic of Venice passed a patent law in 1474, whose underlying purpose was to attract foreign engineers with the incentive of a 10-year monopoly right to their 'works and devices' (Kaufer, 1980: 5–6). The next significant legislative development in patent law came in 1624, with the English Statute of Monopolies.[4] In reality, its primary purpose was to prohibit monopolies rather than to promote invention, and in passing the law the government hoped to encourage continental craftsmen to settle in the country (MacLeod, 1991: 891). Monopoly grants were declared illegal except 'the true and first inventor or inventors' of 'any manner of new manufactures within this realm' as long as 'they be not contrary to the law, nor mischievous to the state, by raising prices of commodities at home, or hurt of trade, or generally inconvenient'. Such inventors could acquire a patent or grant allowing up to 14 years' monopoly protection. Strict novelty was not required since courts interpreted the purpose of granting patents as being to introduce new trades to England whether or not they were 'novel' elsewhere in the world.[5] It is unlikely to be entirely coincidental that at this time England was less advanced technologically than both France and the Netherlands (Cornish, 1999: 111). The statute was amended several times but remained in force until 1977, an extreme case perhaps of what might be termed 'legal inertia'.

The original role of United States patent (and copyright) law was to implement Article 1 Section 8 of the Constitution, which empowers Congress 'to promote the Progress of Science and useful Arts, by securing for limited Times to Authors and Inventors the exclusive Right to their respective Writings and Discoveries'. US patent law, then, was not founded on a natural rights justification of intellectual property ownership. Rather, the granting of exclusive rights *for limited times* was regarded as being beneficial for the country in terms of scientific and cultural progress. It was intended from the start that the patent system should be accessible to all classes of society and not just to the rich and well connected (Khan, 2002).

Soon after independence, two patent laws were enacted. The first (in 1790) was quite progressive in that it rejected the English practice of awarding patents to local importers of foreign inventions (Khan and Sokoloff, 1998: 297). The second (in 1793) was rather less so, in that it forbade aliens from applying for patents (Vojáček, 1936: 123).[6] As a net importer of technology, the government saw no reason to allow patent rights to be enjoyed equally by US nationals and foreigners. A third law, the 1836 Patent Act,[7] was arguably the first modern patent law. It required all applications to be examined by the government patent office for novelty and usefulness. Although this law did not discriminate between US and foreign inventors with respect to the examination or the extent of rights granted, foreign applicants had to pay much higher fees, especially if they were British. Such discrimination was abolished in 1861 for nationals of countries whose laws were non-discriminatory towards Americans.

The German Patent Act (Reichspatentgesetz) of 1877 followed the US example by establishing an examination system. This made these two countries pioneers. Elsewhere, registration systems – which granted patents without the need to convince a specialist that the documentation submitted with the application described a genuine invention – were the norm. The term of protection was 15 years. In common with many countries today, it was possible to except inventions deemed contrary to public order or morality. Inventions regarding luxuries, medicines, articles of food or chemical products were prohibited.

Some European countries managed without a patent law for much of the nineteenth century. Switzerland had one briefly from 1799 to 1802, but only reintroduced it in 1888 (Dessemontet, 2000: 23). The Netherlands prohibited patents from 1869 until 1912. Looking further afield, while Japan's first patent law dates back to 1872, it also did without a patent system for some years later on in that century.[8]

As with patents, copyright's place of origin is Renaissance Italy, although the most famous early copyright law is probably the English Statute of Anne of 1710.[9] Early copyright law was associated with the interests of domestic printers rather than authors, and to some extent also with censorship. While its intent was both to prevent unauthorized printing, reprinting and publishing of books and writings and to encourage 'learned men to compose and write useful books', the Statute of Anne was primarily the outcome of a campaign by an association of printers (the Company of Stationers) to reassert its control over the English book trade, rather than a law to uphold the rights of authors. Nonetheless, for the first time in a statute, it did recognize that authors could be proprietors of their works (Rose, 1993: 4). This law provided a time-limited right to print and reprint books whose titles were entered in the register book of the Company of Stationers. According to the economic historian, Paul David (1993: 51), 'copyright law, from the beginning, has been shaped more by the economics of publication than by the economics of authorship'. Nevertheless, copyright law in continental Europe displayed much more concern for the artistic integrity of authors than did the Anglo-American copyright regulations. This is why some European countries use the term 'authors' rights' in place of copyright.

Copyright law took its modern form in the nineteenth century. The protection term increased, the law began to accumulate a wider range of subject matters, and international agreements began to proliferate, with the result that national standards became more harmonized, and opportunities to secure stronger protection of creative works in more countries were greatly enhanced. These trends have continued. With respect to subject matter, for example, UK copyright law had by 1988[10] been stretched to include literary and dramatic works (including computer programs), musical works, artistic works, sound recordings, films, broadcasts, cable programmes, typographical arrangements and computer-generated works. And protection was not only economic in nature, but, following continental tradition and the requirements of the Berne Convention for the Protection of Literary and Artistic Works, included authors' moral rights. Moral rights include the right of authors to be identified as such, and to object to having their works altered in ways that would prejudice their reputation.[11]

Historically, national copyright laws have generally been less friendly towards the interests of foreigners than have patent laws. This is because, while granting rights to foreigners was sometimes considered to benefit the country by encouraging the introduction of protected technologies, allowing foreigners to protect their literary and artistic works does not provide such obvious economic advantages (Cornish, 1999: 48, 50). For example, from 1891 until 1986, US copyright law contained a so-called 'manufacturing clause' which originally required all copyrighted literary works to be printed in the country. This was a protectionist measure intended to benefit American printers.[12]

While national IP regulations (in some countries) have existed for two or more centuries, the history of intellectual property at the international level really begins in the late nineteenth century with the formation in the 1880s of unions of mostly European countries for the protection of industrial property and literary and artistic works. Previously, the only instruments for international protection had been based on bilateral commercial agreements involving, again, mostly European countries.[13]

The process of expanded international IP regulation has continued since then to the extent of involving most countries of the world. In fact, the 1994 Agreement on Trade-related Aspects of Intellectual Property Rights ('TRIPS' or 'the TRIPS Agreement'), one of the main outcomes of the Uruguay Round of the General Agreement on Tariffs and Trade (GATT), indicates that the international IP regime has moved into a new phase. TRIPS, which is administered by the Geneva-based World Trade Organization (WTO), is of special importance in that it establishes enforceable global minimum (and high) standards of protection and enforcement for virtually all the most important IP rights such as patents, copyrights and related rights, and trade marks in one single agreement.[14, 15]

But there is much more to today's global IP regime than TRIPS. After all, the architecture of the global IP regulatory system has become increasingly complex, and includes a diversity of multilateral agreements, international organizations, regional conventions and instruments, and bilateral arrangements. In sum the international law of intellectual property in its present form consists of three types of agreement. These are multilateral treaties, regional and supranational treaties or instruments, and bilateral agreements. Of these, the agreements that affect the greatest number of countries are the TRIPS Agreement and some of the multilateral treaties administered by the World Intellectual Property Organization (WIPO), a specialized United Nations agency that is also located in Geneva, such as the 1883 Paris Convention for the Protection of Industrial Property and the 1886 Berne Convention for the Protection of Literary and Artistic Works.

Most multilateral IP agreements are administered by WIPO, but there are some important non-WIPO treaties such as UNESCO's 1952 Universal Copyright Convention, the 1961 International Convention for the Protection of New Varieties of Plants (the UPOV[16] Convention), and of course TRIPS.

Regional agreements and instruments include the 1973 European Patent Convention, the 1998 European Union Directive on the Legal Protection of Biotechnological Inventions, the 1982 Harare Protocol on Patents and Industrial Designs within the Framework of the African Regional Industrial Property

Organization, and the 2000 Andean Community Common Regime on Industrial Property. Some of these, such as Chapter 17 of the North American Free Trade Agreement, are components of trade agreements rather than stand-alone IP treaties.

Bilateral agreements include those which deal specifically with IP, and trade or investment agreements covering a range of topics including intellectual property. A recent example is the 2000 Free Trade Agreement between the United States and Jordan, but there are many others.

Why Another Book on Intellectual Property Rights?

This book aims to provide a historical perspective that will give readers a more informed view of some of the current debates on intellectual property rights than a purely contemporary analysis allows. But it tries to achieve much more than this, not only helping to make the present situation more understandable, but, in investigating the transformation of IP rights over the years in ways allowing for the enhanced protection of the fruits of life science research and development, providing a comprehensive understanding of the forces driving such transformation, including the extent to which big business influences IP regulation in the life sciences field and the strategies that are used to mediate this influence. More broadly, the book offers a case study of historical change in a specific area of economic regulation, which is intellectual property rights.

Why the life sciences? First, the applied life sciences constitute one of the two major high-technology fields expected to underpin the global economy of the twenty-first century, and whose advancement has justified many of the most radical and controversial changes to IP regulation in recent years. Second, the accusation that patents were always meant to protect ingenious new devices and not chemicals, drugs or living things is often made by critics who use this point to argue that patents are fundamentally inappropriate, and that big business, in lobbying for such changes, has perverted the patent system for its own ends. This allegation requires closer investigation. But there are several other reasons why the subject matter of this book should interest scholars interested in economic history, business history, economic regulation, and of course intellectual property rights, as well as policy makers engaged in trade and industrial development in the developed and developing worlds.

This history of the life science industries tells the story of the emergence and global dominance of transnational research-based corporations operating in a range of industrial sectors and product markets. It also recounts how these corporations have affected and been affected by the development of intellectual property law not just recently but going back over a century, and have helped to shape the IP regimes in many countries and internationally in very fundamental ways that today's policy makers ought to be aware of.

More specifically, the book compares the international patent regimes of the late nineteenth century and the late twentieth century and seeks explanations for the differences in the emergence and globalization of industries which specialize in elucidating, synthesizing, manipulating and commercially exploiting the molecular properties of microorganisms, plants, animals – including humans – and other organic raw materials. These are referred to as 'the life science industries'. Among the main prerequisites for the existence of these industries were the late nineteenth-century advances in organic chemistry in several western European countries, especially Germany. Many of the companies involved were from the start among the heaviest users of the patent system, both domestically and abroad, and some were able to influence the development of patent law in their respective countries. Even so, one country – Switzerland – had no patent system at the time its first chemical companies were established, and only introduced a patent law *after* these firms had rapidly turned the country into a major producer and exporter of synthetic dyestuffs.

There are several reasons why the rapid emergence of west European firms set up around that time to develop synthetic dyestuffs derived from coal tar is of historical *and* current significance. First, although it was not the beginning of the chemical industry – arguably the first science-based industry – this period is associated with the first appearance of the corporate research laboratory. German companies such as Bayer, Hoechst, BASF and AGFA were pioneers in in-house research and development in which teams of scientists collaborated to solve technical problems in the development of collective innovations. Among other things, this marked a decline in the economic importance of independent amateurs, inventor-entrepreneurs, small firms and countries that had tended to rely on 'practical tinkering' and were thus rather slow in moving into organized industrial research and development (von Tunzelmann, 1995: 186). As it turned out, the first mover advantages of the first research-based companies were tremendous and enduring.

Second, chemical analysis and synthesis paved the way for a fruitful marriage between the synthetic dyestuff industry and microbiology that provided a huge impetus for the modern pharmaceutical industry. Third, some of the largest life science corporations that dominate the chemical, pharmaceutical and agribusiness sectors of the modern global economy are direct descendants of the original late nineteenth-century European synthetic dyestuff companies like the German ones just mentioned and also Swiss firms like Ciba and Geigy. A study of this period should reveal how far and in what ways such firms influenced IP law at national and international levels. It should also show the extent to which IP rights have helped them to achieve and sustain their present status as major transnational corporations. Fourth, the synthetic dyestuff industry provides an interesting example of how countries appeared to benefit from adopting a strategic approach to designing their patent systems in which the companies themselves were involved, and how others were harmed by not doing so. This has present-day relevance, since it suggests that today's developing countries have much to gain from a global regime that affords them an equivalent amount of freedom, and a great deal to lose from one that unduly restricts their room for manoeuvre.

A twentieth-century history of IP rights and the life science industries must include plant breeders' rights and the seed industry. Until recently, this industry evolved quite separately from the dyestuff and pharmaceutical firms, and tended to resort, not to the patent system, but to alternative systems referred to as plant breeders' rights (PBRs) or plant variety protection (PVP). It is through a combination of advances in biotechnology and new possibilities for interindustrial sector business synergies that firms producing medicines, agrochemicals and seeds nowadays have found it convenient to shelter under the same corporate umbrellas.

The title of the book requires an explanation. It is a history neither of intellectual property nor of the commercial life sciences. In fact, it is a history of a relationship between two phenomena, the first of which is the evolution and globalization of two particular intellectual property rights, which are patents and plant breeders' rights. The second is the 100 years of advancement in industrial chemistry and life science capabilities starting with the invention of synthetic coal tar-based dyes and culminating (so far) in an ever-widening range of genetically modified organisms, therapeutic proteins and, of course, Dolly, the world-famous cloned sheep.

The historical period covered in the book does not exactly fit conveniently within the period from 1901 to 2000. In fact, it is longer than 100 years, and longer still than other historical accounts, such as Eric Hobsbawm's 'short twentieth century', which only gets under way in 1914 and finishes as early as 1991 (see Hobsbawm, 1995). However, given that most of the events described take place between the former two years, it is not inappropriate to subtitle this book as it is. In fact, nearly all of the events covered take place between around 1880 and 2000, and most of them after 1900. Besides, pharmaceuticals and seeds are very definitely twentieth-century industries.

Changes in IP law at the international level have, over time, moved mostly in the direction of more and stronger private rights, and have been almost entirely driven by domestic and regional-level changes in just two parts of the world, which are the United States and western Europe. Most of the new developments in the international system during the century first came into being within those two areas, were subsequently adopted elsewhere and gradually became part of international law as well. It is hardly surprising that the most economically dominant countries have influenced the development of international IP law far more than the poorer nations have. But such an observation cannot fully explain how the international IP system has come to take the form it has, nor whether, why or how far one should be concerned about it.

For many who wonder about the implications of current IP trends, it may be far from obvious that looking back into the past can shed much light on present-day realities. But history can explain a great deal about the present situation. Being guided by a historical perspective may better equip us both to evaluate recent changes to the IP regime *and* to develop our own proposals for change.

It is convenient for some to believe (or at least to argue) that IP rights are created and amended to solve new problems created by technological developments that mean existing systems need reform, replacement or the addition of new IP categories. But there is every reason to doubt that policy makers have ever been able to shape and reshape such powerful economic rights in a dispassionate, informed and objective manner even when they have wanted to. After all, the full economic effects of a particular IP structure are difficult if not impossible to predict, and powerful economic actors are bound to take a keen interest in the decisions of these policy makers when there is so much at stake, and to seek to influence change. In addition, the complex and technical nature of IP regulation means that policy makers must depend on outside experts. These are likely to be practitioners with their own agendas and biases.

History should not only enhance our understanding of the political economy of past *and* present-day systems; it also should tell us much about the interplay and relative influence of such factors as developments in science and technology, interest group lobbying and path dependence.[17] With respect to the latter, David (1993: 44) argues that *only* history can explain the existence of many apparent anomalies:

> Although the history of intellectual property rights in the West is replete with instances of redefinition and reinterpretation in response to pressures to accommodate or advance the economic interests of those most affected by the laws, many of the structure's gross features continue to reflect the remote historical circumstances in which they originated. These legacies from the past should not be ignored, nor should their problematic aspects in contemporary contexts be minimized.

History should shed light on the various public policy purposes that IP rights have officially been used to promote. More specifically, looking to the past should help answer two sets of important questions. First, do present-day arguments used to support changes favouring industry have some historical basis? And if so, does this make them legitimate? Or are they no more than synthetic and self-serving pretexts for expanded rights that do not consider the interests of the public? Second, to what extent have the basic tenets of patent law remained the same, such as that substances existing in nature are discoveries and cannot therefore be patented? Or have they changed over time? And if they have, are the reasons purely technical? In particular, it is necessary to see whether the line drawn between the patentable and the unpatentable is objective and stable or whether the criteria for distinguishing between the two are vulnerable to interpretative 'capture' by special interest groups *and actually are captured*. Finally, history should help us to understand whether complaints about 'inadequate' IP standards in developing countries are fair and principled or unjust and hypocritical.

It is clearly important to know if the shaping and reshaping of IP rights over time have tended to serve private economic interests at the expense of the public. But whether such subversion of the IP regime is the norm, the exception, or even a falsehood put about by conspiracy theorists, the findings of this book should be useful both for those making policy and for those who seek to understand how policy is made. At the very least the book is likely to make a strong case that the onus should be placed on those promoting changes to IP regimes to explain to the public how they will benefit.

There is another excellent reason to trace the history of patent law. This is to investigate whether developed countries benefited during their industrial revolutions from being free to tailor their patent systems to suit their development needs in ways that international IP rules preclude present-day developing countries from also doing. While the British industrial revolution falls mainly outside the period covered and in any case has been the subject of other studies (for example, Coulter, 1991; Dutton, 1984; MacLeod, 1988; Sherman and Bently, 1999), the book should nonetheless provide some helpful observations about countries that industrialized after Britain. These may provide lessons for those trying to predict the effects of IP rights on countries industrializing today.

One should not overstate the case that history matters. After all, the world has changed considerably in the last 100 years. Nonetheless, the point made many decades ago by Justice Holmes, a past US Supreme Court judge, that 'a page of history is worth a volume of logic', while undoubtedly exaggerating the benefits of historical insight and underestimating those of logical analysis, seems otherwise to be a useful principle to bear in mind when seeking ways to better understand IP regulation.

Structure of the Book

Chapter 1 explains why intellectual property rights are increasingly important in today's global economy and how IP regulation has changed over recent decades in ways that respond to this heightened importance. The chapter also identifies those particular changes which have triggered controversy and provoked a proliferation of published critiques and opposition movements.

Chapter 2 treats intellectual property rights as a field of economic regulation and evaluates a number of currents within economic regulation theory. The purpose of doing so is to identify the approach likely to be most useful for understanding intellectual property law and policy. This chapter explains why the use of new institutionalism is a very useful analytical approach for investigating and understanding why such IP rights as patents and plant breeders' rights have come to take the particular forms they have, what the implications may be for the general public, and why it is that, while some creative individuals and groups enjoy strong legal rights to their innovations, others do not. Applying new institutionalism to IP rights helpfully deters us from assuming that IP regulation necessarily creates 'win–win situations' that provide gains for all and losses for none. It also encourages us to expect that private interest groups will play important roles in driving change in intellectual property as in other areas of regulation where the economic stakes are high. It is argued, then, that new institutionalism is useful for investigating the evolution of IP rights over time at national and international levels and for explaining how their present structures were arrived at. It should be added that new institutionalism requires us to treat with scepticism the increasingly common but intellectually vacuous claims that improving IP rights necessarily entails strengthening them. Readers turned off by theory should persevere with this chapter. It has been kept reasonably short and strenuous attempts have been made to avoid alienating readers with the sort of esoteric discourse that is popular in social science writing.

Chapter 3 is a descriptive overview of the historical development of patent law from the late nineteenth century to the beginning of the twenty-first. The account begins in the 1880s, at a time when national patent laws in the industrializing nations of western Europe and North America were beginning to take their present forms but were still quite varied, and when these countries undertook to negotiate rules for an international patent regime. It explains the ways in which national patent regimes varied during the late nineteenth century and the economic conditions that made an international patent convention (that is, the Paris Convention) necessary from the viewpoint of the countries involved. After discussing the situation in the late nineteenth century, the chapter provides an overview of changes made to national and international IPR laws and systems relating to life science innovation up to the present time.

Having compared the international patent regimes of the late nineteenth century and the beginning of the twenty-first, we go on to seek explanations for the differences between them. The next five chapters apply the analytical framework outlined above and presented in Chapter 2 to patents and plant breeders' rights at the national (Chapters 4–7) and international levels (Chapter 8). The intent is to see how far organized interest groups representing the main users of the patent and PBR systems have driven the evolution of these rights. If such interest groups turn out to have played a dominant role historically and in the present day, we ought to question whether the result is necessarily a good thing for society. After all, patents and PBRs are public policy institutions. IPR-owning firms and business associations should certainly have a say in how these systems are designed and reformed, but other interests, such as non-IP rights holding firms, independent inventors, the public sector and consumers ought to be represented as well. Inevitably, the focus is mainly on the dynamics of change in those countries which were in the forefront of patent and PBR evolution – the USA, the UK and Germany and, to a lesser extent, France, Japan and Switzerland. These chapters delve at some length into the relevant science and technology, and also into the technicalities of patents and PBRs. They also discuss the appropriateness of these IP rights with respect to the life sciences at a fairly detailed level, essential for anything more than a superficial account of how and why the life science businesses and IP regulation changed over the century, and the problems that have arisen in consequence.

Chapter 4 traces the history of the synthetic dyestuff industry whose appearance and development were inextricably linked to advances in organic chemistry. Scientists working in the world's first industrial research and development laboratories not only synthesized thousands of new chemicals on an unprecedented scale but also succeeded in copying some highly complex chemicals that had previously existed only in nature. The most successful dyestuff firms converted themselves also into the first pharmaceutical companies. Several interesting lessons emerge from the story told in this chapter. For example, countries that designed their patent regulations strategically seemed to do better than those that did not. Also interest groups tended to be very much involved in such regulatory design.

Chapter 5 investigates how the evolution of patent regulation has affected, and been affected by, the emergence and advancement of the pharmaceutical industries of Europe and North America. It begins by describing the main scientific and technological advances in the area of pharmaceuticals during the twentieth century up to the biotechnology era (which is covered in the following chapter). It then traces the development of the pharmaceutical industries of Europe and North America over that period, bearing in mind the role of patents. In particular, it aims to address three questions. First, how did pharmaceutical corporations use patent law and other IP rights to maximize returns from their research and development investments? Second, what did corporations do when they found patent systems to be inadequate in furthering their interests? Third, how successful were their attempts to change patent systems? This is a big subject to cover in one chapter and, for reasons that should become apparent, the focus is on the most important firms, the main types of pre-biotech therapeutic product, especially the sulphonamides, the antibiotics and the cortico-steroids, and the following countries and regions: the USA, Germany, Switzerland, the UK and Europe (including two overlapping jurisdictions, which are the European Patent Convention and the European Union).

Chapter 6 logically follows the previous two, yet its focus is very different. Rather than tracing the historical development of a particular industry, it concentrates on a set of technologies used by several industries that are collectively referred to as biotechnology, and whose development benefited tremendously from many of the scientific advances described in Chapters 4 and 5. In fact, if the synthetic dyestuff industry is a 'parent' of the modern pharmaceutical industry, it is something like a 'grandparent' to biotechnology, not so much because of the longer chronological gap, but because biotechnology has a larger number of disciplinary forebears. But, as this chapter will make clear, it is misleading to talk of a biotechnology industry as if it is a discrete industrial sector. Rather, there are dedicated biotechnology firms (henceforth DBFs) that do nothing but biotechnology, and other companies, universities and public research institutes that do biotechnological work but do not specialize in it. Business had very little to do with the initial development of biotechnology, yet, once business became interested in biotechnology, it did not take long for the issue of patentability to emerge and provoke tremendous controversy. Since the early 1980s not only have the number of biotechnology patents increased exponentially, but the subject matter boundaries dividing the patentable from the unpatentable seem to have been pushed back so far that they no longer appear to exist. Increasingly, many scientists, including some who work in the private sector, are expressing their concerns about this situation. And, from the start, political opposition has come from those who oppose the idea that a scientist can invent a microorganism, plant or animal, or that a company should be able to claim monopoly rights over such 'inventions'.

Chapter 7 shows that the seed industries have a history which until recently was quite separate from the dyestuff and pharmaceutical firms. It is through a combination of advances in biotechnology and new possibilities for interindustrial sector business synergies that firms producing medicines, seeds and agrochemicals have been brought together under the same corporate umbrellas. Therefore, of necessity, the chapter breaks with the chronological order of the narrative to show how and why the seed industries of North America and Europe emerged and then established sui generis IP rights that specifically addressed their needs.

Having traced in the previous chapters the spread of strengthened patent rights and the development of a system for plant varieties, as well as their standardization at regional and international levels, Chapter 8 investigates the process by which such changes were globalized through the Agreement on Trade-related Aspects of Intellectual Property Rights. It was not enough for life science-related business interests that the changes described in Chapters 4–7 were restricted to North America, western Europe and Japan. They wanted to globalize these raised intellectual property standards so that they could secure the same levels of protection anywhere in the world. As this chapter shows, when they realized in the mid-1980s that they had the power and influence to achieve this, they got to work. TRIPS was the result. This is not to say that the TRIPS Agreement they got was exactly the same as the TRIPS Agreement they wanted. Nonetheless, that there was such an agreement at all was due in large part to an effective alliance consisting of representatives of the life science industries and those of other industrial sectors, which was built first in the USA and then extended to western Europe and Japan.

WIPO continues to play a pivotal role in promoting harmonization and ever-stronger IP protection through the conventions it administers and the technical assistance it provides to developing countries. Nonetheless, the WTO has for the time being become the lead institution for regulating global IP standards of protection and enforcement. Consequently, the WTO and TRIPS have been the main target for civil society organizations and networks campaigning in support of the right of developing countries to design their own IP systems free from what they regard as inappropriate and inflexible rules imposed from outside. One might add that many of these groups have some fundamental concerns regarding intellectual property more generally. Chapter 9 assesses the importance and impacts of countervailing pressures emerging from such groups, from intergovernmental forums like the Conference of the Parties to the Convention on Biological Diversity and the Commission on Plant Genetic Resources for Food and Agriculture of the Food and Agriculture Organization of the United Nations, *and* from increased activism by developing-country negotiators at the WTO. While it is difficult to imagine TRIPS and the international IP regime more generally in the near future incorporating or being affected to any great extent by the demands of these resisters, one cannot be completely certain about this. Besides, some countries have already introduced IP-related measures that seek to integrate some of these demands in their national laws. Significantly, the USA and Europe are actively responding to the backlash by sidestepping the WTO and negotiating 'TRIPS plus' IP and free trade agreements directly with developing countries. In addition, WIPO has embarked on a process to harmonize substantive patent law. Harmonization is likely to entail making the patent systems of the world like each other, using those of Europe and the USA as the models.

Chapter 10 closes this book by providing a discussion on the role and importance of patents and plant breeders' rights in the advancement of the applied life sciences and the commercial success of the life science industries. The chapter is primarily an attempt to answer – albeit tentatively – the question of whether a patent-free world would have generated as many cures and other welfare-enhancing products as the patent-infested twentieth century we ended up with.

Notes

1   It is important to note that 'intellectual property' does not lend itself to any precise definition that would satisfy everybody. Indeed, a recent document published by the World Intellectual Property Organization expressed some quite reasonable scepticism about its validity:

> Intellectual property, broadly conceived, may be seen as a misnomer, because it does not necessarily cover 'intellectual works' as such – it covers intangible assets of diverse origins, which need not entail abstract intellectual work; nor need it be defined and protected through property rights alone (the moral rights of authors and the reputation of merchants are not the subject of property, under a civil law concept). (WIPO, 2002: 9)

2   Although usefulness appears to be a less demanding requirement, it is possible for a claimed invention to pass the test of industrial applicability in Europe but to fail the usefulness test in the USA. As Alain Gallochat, an advisor to the French Ministry of Technology explains (2002: 5): 'one can imagine a product or a process giving an answer to a technical problem, or involving steps of technical nature, but without any utility: such an invention, patentable according to the European system, shall not be patentable according to the American system'.

3   The idea that patent applicants should disclose their inventions and that the dissemination of technical information and not the finished product alone is the inventor's part of the 'bargain' was introduced into patent law from the late eighteenth century following an English legal decision (see Merges, 1997: 657).

4   Officially, 'An act concerning monopolies and dispensions with penal laws and the forfeitures thereof'.

5   A 1602 court case (*Darcy* v. *Allin*) determined that 'the introducer of a new trade into the realm, or of any engine tending to the furtherance of a trade, is the inventor' (in Webster, 1844: 756). A 1691 patent dispute (*Edgeberry* v. *Stephens*) clarified that:

if the invention be new in England, a patent may be granted though the thing was practised beyond the sea before; for the statute speaks of new manufactures within this realm; so that if they be new here, it is within the statute; for the Act intended to encourage new devices useful to the kingdom, and where learned by travel or study, it is the same thing. (Hayward, 1987: 118)

6   From 1800, foreign residents who had applied for US citizenship were also allowed to apply.

7   Officially titled 'An act to promote the progress of useful arts, and to repeal all acts and parts of acts heretofore made for that purpose'.

8   The 1872 patent law was revoked after just one year. Another patent law was passed in 1885. Until 1899, protection was available only to Japanese nationals (Vojáček, 1936: 161).

9   Officially, 'An act for the encouragement of learning, by vesting the copies of printed books in the author's or purchasers of such copies, during the times therein mentioned'.

10 By virtue of the Copyright, Designs and Patents Act 1988.

11 These are often referred to respectively as the right of paternity and the right of integrity.

12 Admittedly, the clause was weakened over the years. But when President Reagan vetoed a four-year extension in 1982 in the face of an unfavourable GATT panel ruling and complaints from Europe, Congress disregarded the ruling and overruled Reagan.

13 A total of 69 bilateral industrial property-related conventions to protect the rights of foreigners were signed between 1859 and 1883 (Ladas, 1930: 54–7). All parties to these conventions were either European, North American or Latin American, but the vast majority were European countries.

14 These also include geographical indications, industrial designs, layout-designs of integrated circuits and protection of undisclosed information (trade secrets). Among the few IP rights excluded from TRIPS are utility models and plant breeders' rights (although plant varieties must be protected whether through patents or by an alternative system such as UPOV-style PBRs, or a combination thereof).

15 Prior to the TRIPS Agreement, the main IP conventions played the biggest role in the worldwide adoption of national IP systems sharing common standards. However, the conventions still allowed these systems to vary widely. So, when 33 developing countries joined the Paris Convention for the Protection of Industrial Property and 25 joined the Berne Convention for the Protection of Literary and Artistic Works during the 1960s and 1970s, this did not mean that national IP systems would begin to look like each other. In fact, because these new members were allowed to have a say in the further development of the conventions, harmonization was unlikely to go too far if it meant they would have to adopt high standards of protection before they thought they were ready.

16 From the French name of the organization administering the Convention: Union Internationale pour la Protection des Obtentions Végétales.

17 Path dependence refers to a situation in which apparent anomalies result from decisions made in the past intended to fulfil objectives or solve problems that have become irrelevant. Once the feature in question becomes established it can persist when no longer necessary (or even when sub-optimal from an economic efficiency perspective) and exert a strong influence on the evolutionary trajectory of a given institution, technology, law or economic system.

Chapter 1

Intellectual Property in the Global Economy: High Stakes and Propaganda Warfare

The competition of industry has become a competition of intellect. (Lord Lyon Playfair, British pro-free trade liberal, 1852)

At least three-quarters of the industrial wealth of the United States is based directly or indirectly upon patent rights. (*Scientific American*, June 1925)

Information is not merely an organizing concept for the technologies and disciplines of the twenty-first century. It is a central feature of the international economy. Indeed, the protection of information 'value-added' in products is one of the key elements in the foreign policy of the developed world. (James Boyle, Duke University, 1996)

High Stakes

For most developed countries, the contribution of advanced technologies to economic performance in terms of manufacturing value added and exports has increased substantially since the early 1970s. One reason is the incessant and increasing pressure on businesses and national economies to be competitive. This puts a premium on innovation and creativity aimed at developing new products and services and at differentiating existing ones from those of competitors. Perhaps the most important of these advanced technologies are information and communications technology (ICT) and those based upon the applied life sciences. Both have multiple industrial applications and are of interest to companies operating in a wide range of product and service markets. So, in addition to the commercial interests responsible for innovating in these fields, such as software, telecommunications, and pharmaceutical and biotechnology companies, many other business sectors deploy these technologies, including producers and providers of computers and other electronic goods, music, television programmes, films, printed works and financial services to name a few.

Technological change creates new opportunities for private appropriation, but also poses new challenges. One of these challenges is the threat of free-riding, which certain new technologies may facilitate. IP protection helps to maximize

17

these opportunities while minimizing the risks. This is why many companies operating in all the above sectors hold large intellectual property portfolios protecting products and services developed through the deployment of these technologies. Indeed, for such businesses, the high market value of their goods and services may be due largely to such IP-protectable intangible inputs as technical knowledge and artistic creativity or attributes like reputation and distinctiveness. Such businesses assert these rights with great determination. After all, developing, applying and benefiting commercially from such inputs and attributes can involve enormous research and development (R&D) and marketing expenditures. Moreover, despite the knowledge-rich corporations' market dominance, they are also highly vulnerable. While the marginal cost of manufacturing such goods as software packages, compact discs and videos is extremely low, so is the marginal *and fixed* cost of copying them. Multiple reproduction of these goods requires only low-cost equipment and minimal technical know-how. In countries where IP rights such as patents, copyrights and trade marks are unavailable or enforcement is weak, imitators can quickly and inexpensively copy these products and sell them at home and in other countries where effective IP protection is also weak. Similarly, plant-breeding companies can find their non-hybrid plant varieties being sold without their consent. Even though entry barriers for generic drug firms are higher, in that competent chemists need to be hired and bulk production will require more expensive equipment than for, say, software and compact disc piracy, the free-riding problem that research-based drug companies face is also potentially serious.

Among the most dominant businesses in the world today are the so-called 'life science corporations'. A major consequence arising from the emergence of this type of business is that the ownership of life science-related technologies and new products is becoming ever more concentrated. A handful of corporations operating in different life science sectors managed to amass a valuable stock of technologies and products, not just developed in-house but acquired from elsewhere, and in the process have become global megacorporations. Such life science giants as Novartis, AstraZeneca, Aventis and Pharmacia, which hold dominant positions in two or more industrial fields and have annual turnovers higher than the gross national products of individual countries, did not result from internal growth alone. Their enormous size actually results largely from mergers, acquisitions, joint ventures and strategic partnerships involving companies in such sectors as chemicals, seeds, processed foods and dietary supplements, toiletries and cosmetics, and pharmaceuticals.

There has been a tremendous consolidation of patent ownership and global market shares in the hands of a small number of these corporate giants. According to the United Nations Development Programme (1999: 67), the 10 largest corporations in the main life science sectors now dominate global markets to a very high level. They control 32 per cent of the $23 billion commercial seed industry; 35 per cent of the $297 billion pharmaceutical industry; 60 per cent of the $17 billion veterinary medicine industry; and 85 per cent of the $31 billion pesticides industry. Even these figures do not tell the whole story. For example, the market for treatments of particular diseases may be completely controlled by only one or two companies. Burroughs Wellcome at one time sold the *only* anti-AIDS drug, AZT (a substance that the company had not even invented but whose therapeutic use it had a patent on). Heavy market concentration in industrial sectors whose products are vital to the lives and livelihoods of many people is bound to have implications for economies and societies throughout the world. These implications relate generally to development policy options and more specifically to access to technologies and to important products, including those that can save lives.

IP regulation has been far from unresponsive to the increased pressure on businesses to be creative and innovative and the desire of national governments to foster competitiveness. From the 1960s and 1970s, developed-country IP regimes began to undergo radical changes. These changes, which appear to be continuing, were of three kinds. The first of these was the widening of protectable subject matter. The parameters of protectable subject matter have been expanded, and there has been a tendency to reduce or eliminate exceptions. Examples include the extension of copyright protection to computer programs as if they are literary works, the application of patent protection to cover business methods, computer programs, life forms, cell lines and DNA sequences, the removal of exclusions on product patents for drugs, and the extension of trade mark protection in some countries to include sounds and smells. The second change was the creation of new rights. Examples of new systems created during the late twentieth century included plant breeders' rights, rights to layout designs of integrated circuits, and rights related to copyright such as performers' rights. The third change was the progressive standardization of the basic features of IP rights. For instance, patent regulations increasingly provide 20-year protection terms, require prior art searches for novelty and examinations[1] for inventive step (or non-obviousness) and industrial application, assign rights to the first applicant rather than the first inventor,[2] and provide protection for inventions in a widening range of industries and technological fields.

These developments in IP law, all of which began in Europe or North America, are spreading to the rest of the world, and at an accelerating pace. Consequently, national IP regimes throughout the world are becoming increasingly held to harmonized minimum standards of protection. These, however, remain a long way from uniform law, a situation that some countries and interest groups hope to remedy in the coming years.

But the changes were not introduced gradually over time even in the developed world. For example, until the 1960s, several west European countries (for example, France, Belgium and Italy) still granted patents on the basis of registration (Robbins, 1961: 219).[3] Moreover, several developed countries lifted the bar to patentability on pharmaceutical products only in the 1960s or 1970s. And other important expansions in protectable subject matter are even more recent (such as the patenting of animals and DNA sequences, and the sui generis protection of integrated circuit layout designs and of databases). At the same time, a few developing countries moved in the reverse direction. For example, in the late 1960s and early 1970s, Brazil and India passed laws to exclude pharmaceuticals as such from patentability (as well as processes to manufacture them, in Brazil's case).

One could argue – as many do – that these trends are necessary responses to technological change. While there is undoubtedly some truth in this, there is no reason to suppose that the appropriate response by policy makers should always be to strengthen existing rights, to reduce or eliminate exceptions, or to create new ones. Such approaches may indeed be necessary in certain cases where the IP systems available are inappropriate for new types of creative work or technology or become inadequate for protecting existing types because, for example, new technologies make mass copying easier. In other cases, weakening rights might be a more appropriate response to some instances of technological change. For example, in some industries there may be a fall in the average life cycles of new products. This has in fact happened with semiconductor products. And in others again, average research and development costs for an industry might decline. In such cases, the protection available may well turn out to be excessive to the point of being dysfunctional in the sense of stifling competition with over-high barriers to market entry, and raising the transaction costs of follow-on innovation or even blocking it completely. This seems to happen with the patenting of genes and gene fragments.

More fundamentally, it is far from self-evident that the existence of strong IP protection is a precondition for the transformation of developing-country economies into developed ones. In fact, it is impossible with any certainty to calculate the long-term impacts of TRIPS on developing countries and their populations. It is possible that, ultimately, every country will benefit. But this is pure speculation. We can be certain, though, that developing and least-developed countries will incur short-term costs in the form of administration and enforcement outlays and rent transfers, and that these will outweigh the initial benefits. The cost–benefit balance will vary widely from one country to another, but in many cases the costs will be extremely burdensome. According to a recent World Bank publication, 'if TRIPS were fully implemented, rent transfers to major technology-creating countries – particularly the United States, Germany, and France – in the form of pharmaceutical patents, computer chip designs, and other intellectual property, would amount to more than $20 billion' (World Bank, 2001). Stated baldly, and if the assumptions on which the research is based are reliable, this means that TRIPS represents a $20 billion plus transfer of wealth from the technology importing nations – many of which are developing countries – to the technology exporters, few if any of which are developing countries, that may or may not be outweighed by future gains.

Propaganda Warfare

The potential economic and social repercussions of IP policy making are tremendous, and the stakes have never been higher than they are today. Increasing numbers of people have begun to recognize this. Consequently, despite their long history, public interest in IP rights worldwide has reached unprecedented levels. And as an ever-wider range of interest groups seeks to influence public opinion and national and international policy making, debates become ever more polarized and adversarial. Pressure on countries to introduce ever-stronger levels of protection has provoked a backlash. This has taken various forms, including a huge and growing volume of critical propaganda produced by civil society organizations, and well coordinated political campaigning on numerous fronts around the world, from Geneva, Washington and Brussels to rural India, the Amazon and the Australian outback. Academics have also entered debates on intellectual property policy.

It is no exaggeration to say that there is a propaganda war going on. As with other wars, the truth is likely to be a casualty in the face of the selective deployment of truths, untruths and unsubstantiated assertions, which are the conventional weapons of such conflicts. At one end of the political spectrum are those who argue that strong IP protection and enforcement is indispensable for a modern economy, and the stronger the better. At the other end are those who – if their rhetoric is anything to go by – consider that IP rights are just another device by which the rich make themselves richer and the poor poorer, and may even be unnecessary to foster innovation anyway. Most critics (the present author included) are not anti-IP at all, but are sceptical of many of the claims deployed to justify ever-stronger protection, especially when the changes advocated are to be globalized so that all trading nations of the world must accept them.

Three recent closely related developments are responsible for galvanizing the increasingly heated debates on IP rights, at least with respect to the life science industries.[4] The first development was the so-called 'seed wars' which broke out in the early 1980s with the Food and Agriculture Organization of the United Nations providing the main battlefield. It was sparked off by a number of civil society organizations based in North America and Europe, and some influential individuals. They believed that IP rights were having a malign influence on agriculture in both the developed and developing worlds. In particular, they blamed IP rights for helping to cause genetic erosion, for legitimizing the unfair exploitation by developed countries of the genetic resources of developing countries, and for encouraging the takeover of national seed industries by a small number of powerful transnational corporations.

The second was the successful attempt of the USA, Europe and Japan, supported by business associations representing transnational corporations, to place IP rights on the GATT Uruguay Round agenda, and then to force through an agreement covering a wide range of IP standards going far beyond the original aim of preventing counterfeiting of trade-marked goods and piracy of copyrighted works.

The third development was the 'patenting life' controversy. This was triggered in the USA by the 1980 Supreme Court decision in *Diamond* v. *Chakrabarty* that living things may constitute patentable inventions, and in Europe in the late 1980s by the European Commission's drafting of a directive on the protection of biotechnological inventions.

Political opposition and critiques have highlighted several problematic aspects of extending patent law into this area. These include, first, the moral significance of treating as property such 'inventions' as plants, animals, microorganisms and – in some jurisdictions – functional or structural components of life forms including gene sequences, proteins and cell cultures (see, for example, Beyleveld and Brownsword, 1993; Bruce and Bruce, 1998; Drahos, 1999a); second, the way that these patents appear to overturn some of the basic groundrules of patent law, such as that substances existing in nature are discoveries and cannot therefore be patented; third, the possibility that basic research may be discouraged when overly broad patent claims are allowed, which may also overlap with claims in other patents, and biotechnology research tools such as gene sequences are privatized through the patent system (for example, Heller and Eisenberg, 1998); fourth, that allowing patents on life forms supports the practice of 'biopiracy' (for example, Baumann *et al.*, 1996); and fifth, that patents on plants and plant breeders' rights infringe the basic right of farmers to freely dispose of harvested seed as they see fit, including to sell it (for example, Verma, 1995).

This expanded interest in IP rights is echoed in an increase in academic writing beyond the disciplines of law and economics where the subject has traditionally been confined, exposing IP systems to ever more critical examination. In fact, since the late 1980s, the intellectual property literature has proliferated and expanded, being supplemented by contributors from such disciplines as sociology (for example, Buttel and Belsky, 1987; Kloppenburg, 1988), anthropology (for example, Brush, 1993; Coombe, 1998; Greaves, 1994; Strathern, 1999), international relations and political science (for example, May, 2000; Sell, 1998), moral and legal philosophy (for example, Drahos, 1996; Sterckx, 1997), ethnobiology (for example, Posey, 1990) and economic history (for example, David, 1993; MacLeod, 1988, 1991). Critical political and academic works have focused on various issues, but mainly on the inherently protectionist motivation behind TRIPS (for example, Bhagwati, 1998), concern for the environment (for example, Cameron and Makuch, 1995; Yamin, 1995), the rights of indigenous peoples (for example, Brush and Stabinsky, 1996; Posey and Dutfield, 1996), the general interests of the developing countries (for example, Correa, 2000), food security and the rights of farmers (for example, Mooney, 1979, 1996; Shiva, 1996; Tansey, 1999) and on the high prices of life-saving drugs in developing countries (for example, Oxfam, 2001).

This increased critical attention and activism unnerves business associations and patent professionals that have hitherto been regarded by policy makers as *the* experts on intellectual property, and who have generally treated improving IP rights as making the rights they provide more exclusive, broader in scope and less territorially delimited. Now they are having to compete for influence with other individuals and organizations who are much more sceptical about IP rights, and whose expertise they tend to disdain. Such disrespect is becoming less and less justified. Several civil society organizations have closed the expertise gap and some can match if not exceed the technical capacity of some of these pro-strong IP lobbyists. A good example is Médecins Sans Frontières, but there are others. They have done this not only by hiring staff to concentrate full-time on intellectual property, some of whom are trained in intellectual property law, but also by using consultants including academics with decades of legal experience, and who may be referred to as 'counter-experts'. The outcome of this competition for influence is by no means a foregone conclusion.

Notes

1　Albeit with some exceptions, even in Europe. For example, the Netherlands, which used to apply very high inventive step standards, has stopped examining patent applications since 1995.
2　The USA is the only country still to have a first-to-invent system (as opposed to first-to-file).
3　In France pharmaceutical patents were examined for novelty from 1960. Novelty examinations for other types of invention were phased in from 1968 (Lynfield, 1969: 205).
4　Here I limit the discussion to those developments most relevant to the subject matter of this book. Other factors are responsible for the emergence of the Free Software and Open Source Movements (see Lessig, 2001; Moody, 2002).

Chapter 2

Intellectual Property and Regulation Theory

For years I thought what was good for our country was good for General Motors and vice versa The difference did not exist. Our company is too big. It goes with the welfare of the country. (Charles E. Wilson, President of GM, 15 January 1953)[1]

The readiness of legislatures and international institutions to grant ever stronger intellectual property protection to private elites is readily explainable in terms of theories of public choice, regulatory capture and institutionalist approaches that factor power into their explanations. (Peter Drahos, Australian National University, 1999)

The political economy of reforming intellectual property law to accommodate new technologies creates a particularly perplexing dilemma. From the standpoint of a political economist, the opportunity for comprehensive reform is most propitious before interest groups form around a new technology. Unfortunately, policymakers usually do not have sufficient understanding of the path of such technology and the implications for an appropriate intellectual property regime during this nascent stage of development. Policymakers thus are left in the awkward position of either creating a regime before they adequately understand the problem or waiting until the contours of the problem emerge, at which point economic interests have vested, and reform, if it is possible at all, is severely constrained. (Peter S. Menell, University of California, Berkeley, 1994)

Regulatory Theory and IP Rights

The patent and PBR systems are more than just pieces of legislation. They consist of the relevant statutes, rules and regulations plus the government agencies, courts and professional people involved in interpretation, implementation and enforcement. Understood thus, it is convenient to view either system as a form of government regulation in the sense that the definition, allocation and enforcement of property rights are per se regulatory. For the purposes of this book, a broad understanding of regulation is adopted that encompasses all state activities intended to manage the national economy.

One may accept the public interest approach that public servants in democracies strive to regulate in the public interest independent of the influence of special interests, and are successful in doing so; or one may be sceptical that this really

25

happens, at least in the case of the patent system. Either way, the patent and PBR systems are ostensibly public policy regulatory institutions and as such may reasonably be judged according to how far they further the public interest (while admitting that 'the public interest' is hard to define).

The public interest approach 'holds that the state acts in the public interest to tackle market imperfections. Public officials thus translate public preferences into legal regulatory institutions and elected legislatures direct such officials in pursuit of the public good. Those pressing for regulation, on such a view, act as agents for the public interest' (Baldwin *et al.*, 1998: 9). This perspective has been challenged by other approaches and concepts that seek to explain how and why governments, legislatures and bureaucracies come to act as if the public interest is identical to that of powerful commercial interests *whether or not this is really the case*. In colloquial terms, these alternatives attempt to answer the following question: how does 'what is good for General Motors' – or in the context of this book, say, for Pfizer – become construed as being 'good for America'?

Interest group analyses of economic regulation[2] draw on a number of schools of thought. What they have in common is the expectation that private interests will dominate regulatory processes and outcomes, that the regulators will, or that there will be mutually beneficial collusion between them. Whether or not the outcome is in the public interest, it will be presented as if it is. Two prominent schools of thought are public choice and institutionalism, including the so-called 'new institutionalism' and its antecedent versions. Both schools claim to offer insights into dysfunctional institutions including regulatory agencies and processes, as well as providing theoretical support for interest group 'regulatory capture' as a useful concept. Public choice extends rational choice utility-maximizing assumptions about individual motivation to the behaviour not just of regulatory agencies but also of legislatures. Institutionalism can hardly be said to constitute a single theory. It has become an assemblage of theoretical approaches (see Black, 1997: 54; Goodin, 1996: 2; Peters, 1999), some of which are complementary, and some much less so. Law, economics, political science, sociology, economic history, anthropology and public administration are all disciplines in which versions of the new institutionalism have been developed. It is probably most true to regard institutionalism as a body of theories, since there is a wide divergence in interpretations of the word 'institution', and fundamental differences in assumptions about human motivation, behaviour, cognitive capacity, and about how far reality is or is not socially constructed. It is useful to look at the way scholars from this broad church have analysed government regulation as it relates to the definition and allocation of property rights, and then to see how far their insights might be relevant to IP rights. For reasons that will become apparent in the discussion below, I intend to adopt the new institutionalist approach.

Why do we have Patents and Plant Breeders' Rights?

Before going further, the following question needs to be addressed: if patents and PBRs can legitimately be analysed as regulatory institutions, then what is their function? IP rights ostensibly exist primarily to benefit society. But this does not tell us much about the ends they are meant to serve, or how these ends ought to be achieved. In general terms, IP rights – especially patents – are tools for economic advancement that should contribute to the enrichment of society through (i) the widest possible availability of new and useful goods, services and technical information that derive from inventive activity, and (ii) the highest possible level of economic activity based on the production, circulation and further development of such goods, services and information. In pursuit of these aims, inventors are able to protect their inventions through a system of property rights: the patent system. Once these rights have been acquired, the owners seek to exploit them in the market-place. The possibility of attaining commercial benefits, it is believed, encourages invention and innovation.[3] But, after a certain period of time, these legal rights are extinguished and the now unprotected inventions are freely available for others to use and improve upon. Enhancing the society's capacity to generate such useful goods, services and information by itself is one means of achieving such ends (and may, it could be argued, be a sufficient end in itself). But it is not the only means. After all, these could also be imported, and legal incentives could be created for such importation, as they were in the past.

Perhaps the most benign way to interpret the modern patent and PBR systems[4] since the nineteenth century is as a regulatory response to the failure of the free market to achieve optimal resource allocation for invention and innovative plant breeding. This is consistent with the public interest approach according to which states intervene to resolve market failures. As Paul Geroski puts it, 'patents are designed to create a market for knowledge by assigning propriety rights to innovators which enable them to overcome the problem of non-excludability while, at the same time, encouraging the maximum diffusion of knowledge by making it public' (Geroski, 1995: 97; see also Arrow, 1962: 619). This explanation for patents assumes that knowledge is a public good. This notion was nicely articulated by Thomas Jefferson who wrote in an oft-quoted letter that the 'peculiar character' of an idea is that 'the moment it is divulged, it forces itself into the possession of everyone, and the receiver cannot dispossess himself of it', and also that 'no one possesses the less, because every other possesses the whole of it'. He then went on to explain that 'he who receives an idea from me, receives instruction himself without lessening mine; as he who lights his taper at mine receives light without darkening me'.

Patents are temporary exclusionary rights. Such rights can be converted into market monopolies if the invention so protected results in a commercial product. The public goods explanation for patents posits that the possibility of acquiring such rights encourages both investment in invention and the research and development needed to turn inventions into marketable innovations. Information about the invention as revealed in the patent and by the invention itself is, into the bargain, diffused throughout the economy. In this context, it is helpful to conceive of a patent as a contract between the holder and the government on behalf of the citizenry. The holder receives an exclusive right over his or her invention in exchange for the payment of fees and – which is much more important – for disclosing the invention for others to learn from. Without a patent, the inventor would have no incentive to disclose it. This would be a loss for society if such lack of protection left the inventor with no alternative but to keep it secret. Such an alternative is a feasible option in several technological fields including biotechnology. But it is also true that many kinds of product would upon examination readily betray the invention[5] that brought it into existence.

As for the creation of markets for knowledge, it might be useful here to explain why these are considered beneficial and how patents are thought to bring them into being. The explanation relates to the common situation that many patent holders are poorly placed to exploit their invention in the market-place. Take the case of a creative but small company lacking the funds to develop and commercialize new products based upon its inventions. If such products are desirable for consumers, failure to commercialize would be a loss for society. But if the company owns a patent, a wealthier company may wish to license or buy the patent, secure in the knowledge that the invention is legally protected. And if the invention were kept secret, how would bigger companies know about it? The disclosure of patent information makes it possible for prospective users to find inventions of interest and then to approach their owners.

However, several studies (for example, Merges and Nelson, 1990; Scotchmer, 1991) have undermined such public goods-based justifications of patents on the grounds that they are based on an oversimplistic assumption that innovations are discrete and independent, whereas in reality they tend to be cumulative and dependent (Menell, 1994: 2646). Moreover, reproducing them may depend on tacit knowledge which cannot easily be documented in written form, such as in a patent specification, and is therefore available only to the innovator. Also, as is sometimes pointed out, other means of appropriation are not only possible but may be more effective in some cases than patents. These include marketing, customer support services, reputation and the advantage that comes with being first to bring innovations to market (see Levin *et al.*, 1987). Apart from – and partly because of – the fact that intellectual works are not necessarily public goods, it is extremely difficult if not impossible to determine an optimal level of protection for achieving an optimal allocation of resources for inventive activities. The difficulty for policy makers is further compounded by the task of ensuring that protection is effective but not so strong as to unduly restrict the freedoms of follow-on innovators.

One of the reasons that patents are so controversial is that the IP incentive, as far as it actually works, functions by restricting use by others of the protected invention for a certain period. Yet follow-on innovation by others is more likely to happen if use is not restricted. Thus a balance between private control over the use of technical information and its diffusion needs to be struck. Where the line should be drawn is very difficult to determine, but its ideal location will vary widely from one country to another. In countries where little inventive activity takes place, free access to technical information may well do more to foster technological capacity building than providing strong private rights over such information. In fact, technological capacity building may at certain stages of national development be best achieved by requiring foreign technology holders to transfer their technologies on generous terms rather than by trying to encourage domestic innovation by making strong legal rights available to all.[6] This suggests that developing countries should be careful not to make the rights too strong until their economies are more advanced. Historical evidence indicates that several present-day developed countries, rightly or wrongly, took such a policy decision in the past.

In short, patents and other IP rights are intended to balance different aims and interests in order to achieve certain public policy goals most effectively. Striking an optimum balance is extremely difficult for the reasons given earlier. IP rights can be underprotective, but they can also be overprotective. It is important to understand, though, that balancing the interests of present and future creators, of users of intellectual property and of the public is not just a matter of economic calculation – it is an inherently political exercise.

Regulatory Capture

The concept of regulatory capture goes back at least to the mid-1950s, but one of the early seminal works is George Stigler's 1971 article, 'The Theory of Economic Regulation'. The basic assumption upon which his capture model is based is that firms, like individuals (including politicians and bureaucrats), are motivated by utility maximization. The only difference is that for firms utility means profit, while utility for civil servants or politicians is likely to be non-monetary. Given the unique powers of the state to 'prohibit or compel, to take or give money' (Stigler, 1971), firms can be expected to try to use the state to increase their profitability. Four likely means to this end are to seek monetary subsidies, to control market entry of rival firms, to restrict substitute products and services while supporting complementary ones, and to fix prices. Bearing these assumptions in mind, Stigler argued that regulation tends to be acquired, designed and operated for the benefit of industry and with the collusion of the relevant state agencies. This is only to be expected in view of the likely information asymmetries between the regulated and the less informed regulators. If there is nothing for regulators to gain from correcting this imbalance, they will simply leave things as they are. This is likely to be the usual state of affairs. 'One may expect the regulators and those regulated to end up in a common strategy after playing the regulation game a couple of times. Both would agree on a regulation policy that would remain stable over time, with maximization of their joint interests in stable and predictable outcomes' (Lane, 1995: 122). Thus the public interest is bound to become subordinated to these joint interests. In contrast to the public interest approach, then, regulation is not about achieving economic efficiency at all, but about distributing income from some sectors of the economy to others. The winners are likely to be the special interests (firms, regulators and politicians) and the losers the weaker and/or more dispersed interests such as consumers.

Stigler also attempted to establish which particular industrial sectors will have most influence over legislative processes in the regulatory sphere. He predicted that, even though outcomes satisfying the interests of larger industries will impose greater costs on society than will satisfying those of smaller industries, and persuasion will therefore be relatively expensive, the former industries will still be the more influential because of their greater resources. Smaller industries can only influence political process in certain circumstances, for example if they are concentrated geographically.

It is hard to see regulatory capture as anything other than a bad thing. Privileging private interests over those of the public in relation to a public policy instrument can hardly be justified. Yet private and public interests do not have to be in mutual opposition: 'it surely is bad for regulators to believe that "what's good for General Motors is good for America": but it is also undesirable for regulators to believe that "what's bad for General Motors is of no consequence to America"' (Makkai and Braithwaite, 1998: 185). So even if it can be shown that a national patent or PBR law was reformed in accordance with the proposals of certain influential firms and industries, one should not take as a given that, because these firms subsequently benefited from the changes, their intervention was harmful to the interests of the public or bad for the rest of the economy. And we should not be indifferent to complaints from domestic firms about proposed changes to patent or PBR laws if we cannot be sure that such changes will benefit the rest of society.

Another way that regulatory agencies are said to be captured by industry is linked to a phenomenon known colloquially as 'the revolving door'. This idea was popularized by the US consumer rights activist and former presidential candidate Ralph Nader. He argued that capture was a consequence of both employment of former business executives by regulatory agencies and, more importantly, the aspirations of regulators to move to more lucrative positions with corporations they used to regulate.

Apart from the revolving door, another regulatory capture tactic is to coopt experts that are potential rivals for influence. In a book published in 1978 and aimed at industry executives, the authors gave the following advice to their readers:

> Regulatory policy is increasingly made with the participation of experts, especially academics. A regulated firm or industry should be prepared whenever possible to co-opt these experts. This is most effectively done by identifying the leading experts in each relevant field and hiring them as consultants and advisors, or giving them research grants

and the like. This activity requires a modicum of finesse; it must not be too blatant, for the experts themselves must not recognise that they have lost their objectivity and freedom of action. At a minimum, a programme of this kind reduces the threat that the leading experts will be available to testify or write against the interests of the regulated firms. (Owen and Braeutigam, 1978: 7, quoted in Millstone, 2002: 182)

Both models of regulatory capture can be criticized. Taking Stigler's model first, four criticisms can be made. First, as with all rational choice models, it may be contested by those who argue that rational utility maximization hardly does justice to the complexities of human behaviour, motivations, capacities and incapacities (North, 1990: 17, 20). Second, the empirical evidence is inconclusive (Lane, 1995: 124). Third, contrary to what Stigler assumes, it is not single economic interests that capture an agency but coalitions containing groups whose interests may be quite various (Majone, 1996: 30–31). Fourth, Stigler's theory treats economic interests and resources as fundamental, but pays little if any attention to the regulatory agencies or processes, except as the institutions for translating private interests into public policy. In fact the institutional and behavioural characteristics of these agencies and their political environment are both likely to be important in explaining changes in regulations and regulatory policy. Both Stigler's theory and the public interest approach tend to ignore this fact or at least to treat it as insignificant.

With respect to the revolving door model, while such movements of personnel are undoubtedly common, a 1998 publication that reviewed a number of studies found a weak correlation between the phenomenon and regulatory capture. The authors also commented that the revolving door might not be a bad thing in every case:

> The best regulatory culture is one where regulators are tough and absolutely committed to maximising the policy objectives that lie behind the law while at the same time being flexible ... If mutual understanding by each side of the legitimate concerns of the other is the stuff of a healthy regulatory culture, then the revolving door might have positive effects. (Makkai and Braithwaite, 1998: 185)

But rejecting these particular approaches does not mean rejecting regulatory capture as a useful concept. The case for regulatory capture in the IP context (or any other) does not require humans to be rational utility maximizers in all situations. Undeniably, humans are not rational all the time. And in certain regulatory domains government and non-state actors do collaborate in terms of design, implementation and enforcement. Given the highly technical nature of IP regulation and the increasingly common perception within government trade and industry departments that, the larger the size of IP portfolios held by domestic firms, the better it is for the national economy, patent and PBR law are likely to be cases in point.

Public Choice

Public choice is consistent with the concept of interest group pluralism, which holds that political society comprises multiple interest groups and coalitions of them competing for political power and influence, and ultimately taking control of regulatory systems. From outside the government, other interest groups also seek to influence the system to their advantage. But public choice scholars tend to expect politicians and bureaucrats to have a stronger bargaining position than any single outside interest group and to pursue their own interests rather than those of the general public. Most public choice accounts supplement Stigler's thesis rather than contradict it. Public choice is likewise founded on the rational choice model according to which humans are treated as if they are self-interested rational utility maximizers. Such maximization is assumed to be an achievable aspiration. Essentially, public choice is the application of rational choice to politics and government.

Public choice does not necessarily preclude altruism in public life. Nonetheless, it tends to encourage a cynical attitude towards public servants and politicians. Public choice rejects two basic conventional political science tenets. These are the 'organic conception of the state' and 'the view that government officials (legislators, regulators, bureaucrats, etc.) seek to act for the common good or in the public interest' (Mercuro and Medema, 1997: 85). Unsurprisingly, public choice scholars generally have a negative view of regulatory rule making and implementation.

Nicholas Mercuro and Steven Medema (1997) divide public choice theorists into two groups. What they call the 'homo economicus' branch tends to analyse regulation, legislatures, political parties or theories of bureaucracy, adopting the conventional microeconomic utility-maximization paradigm. The 'contractarian' or 'catallaxy' branch focuses more on processes of exchange in the political and economic arenas. It departs from the homo economicus paradigm in rejecting the judgment of effective public policy on the basis of an objective and external calculation of efficiency. Rather,

> The appropriateness or correctness of a public policy (or legal change) is *not* the improvement in an independent, observable assessment of allocative efficiency, but is instead agreement – consensus among the group. In a sense, a policy is fair because the individuals in the society unanimously adopted it; they did not adopt it because it was a priori 'fair'. (Ibid.: 96)

Although adherence to public choice does not require one for consistency to be right-wing, public choice scholars provided intellectual support for 'new right' policies of deregulation, privatization and rolling back the state from the late 1970s. But there are also normative public choice theorists who do not consider the overexpansion of regulatory functions and budgets, and the capture of regulatory agencies and processes by special interests, to be inevitable. To these scholars, modifying incentive structures so as to discourage short-term and inefficient strategies may be politically feasible goals (ibid.: 85, 94).

The applicability of public choice to the sphere of IP regulation is somewhat limited. First, as with Stigler's theory, it depends on the assumption of rational utility maximization, which is useful to an extent, but has serious limitations in its explanatory power. Second, the subjects for analysis are usually legislators and bureaucrats rather than outside interest groups. Third, the depiction of such people tends to be overly cynical. And fourth, public choice accounts generally assume that the bargaining power of outside interests is relatively weak compared to that of politicians and bureaucrats. In fact, given the technical nature of IP regulation, outside interests are likely to be much better informed that most policy makers, and will thus be strongly placed to influence change.

Institutionalism

Institutionalism has its origins in the work of certain US economists of the late nineteenth and early twentieth centuries, such as Thorstein Veblen, Robert Hale and John Commons (for example, see Veblen, 1923; Hale, 1923; Commons, 1934). Economic institutions were central to their analyses of the economic system. Diverging from orthodox methodological individualism, what united the 'old' institutionalists was the idea that economic behaviour is conditioned by the institutional environment just as institutions are shaped by economic behaviour. Furthermore, conflicts are inherent to economic relationships. Resolving these conflicts requires the appropriate structuring of institutions.

One of the most important of these institutions was property rights. The state plays an active role in defining, allocating and enforcing these rights, or providing the legal and administrative infrastructure to allow owners to enforce them. So for those who wonder 'what is the government doing when it "protects a property right"', Hale's response is that 'passively, it is abstaining from interference with the owner when he deals with the thing owned; actively, it is forcing the non-owner to desist from handling it, unless the owner consents' (Hale, 1923: 471). Any changes to rights structures have distributional repercussions throughout the economy. Existing beneficiaries may have their rights strengthened, weakened or eliminated. New beneficiaries may appear. And those who are excluded may find their duties, responsibilities and liabilities increased further. Analytically speaking, economic efficiency cannot be separated from the question of distribution. 'Rights determine the distribution of income and wealth, which in turn determines the efficient solution to be reached. But at the same time, the specification of rights, and the resulting efficient outcome, structure the future distribution of income and wealth in society' (Mercuro and Medema, 1997: 119).

Nonetheless, economic efficiency is unlikely to be considered a key objective for those interest groups most involved in designing rights structures. In a comment on property rights, Drahos points out that, 'for the institutionalist, the property rights that actually emerge in the market place are not necessarily efficient, for the simple reason that those with the capacity to shape the design of property rights may be more interested in rents than efficiency' (Drahos, 1999b: 149–50).

The old institutionalism was criticized from the 1950s on various grounds, but generally because it was descriptive and insufficiently theoretical (Scott, 1995: 5). The main critics were behavioural and rational choice scholars. In response, a number of scholars, such as March and Olson (1984), in arguing for the continued relevance of institutional approaches, advocated a 'new institutionalism'. New institutionalism is quite varied, as is the number of ways 'institution' is defined. Two central tenets of the economic version (sometimes referred to as neoinstitutional economics or new institutional economics) are (i) that individuals are far more constrained in terms of their abilities to maximize utility than many rational choice models tend to assume, and (ii) that, in view of the central position of institutions in the economic system, appropriately designed institutional structures can help enhance the wealth of society (Mercuro and Medema, 1997: 130). New institutionalism, then, is both analytical and normative.

Two areas of institutionalist thinking appear especially applicable to IP rights. First, there is a body of economic scholarship which focuses on property rights and treats them as state-regulated institutions. How the state structures these property rights has potential impacts not just on right holders but on the economy as a whole. Second, several institutionalist analyses of interest groups can help one to understand how such groups are formed and constituted, and the factors which make some groups influential and others less so.

Douglass North of Washington University and Thráinn Eggertsson of the University of Iceland are two eminent institutional economists with a strong interest in property rights. According to North (1991: 97), institutions are 'the humanly devised constraints that structure political, economic and social interaction'. In his earlier work, North accepted the basic functionalist explanation of property right formation and definition, which is that the rights are created to fulfil a need once it becomes cost-effective for a community or society to do so.[7] Eggertsson calls this 'the naïve theory of property rights' because it seeks to explain the structure of property rights without considering political and distributional factors (Eggertsson, 1990: 249). In his later work, North distanced himself from the naïve theory because of its failure to account for inefficient property rights, and attributed such perverse rights structures, among other factors, to the influence of vested private and governmental interests. Eggertson's 'interest group theory of property rights' posits that 'the basic structure of property rights is determined by the state and reflects the preferences and constraints of those who control the state' (ibid.: 79). Complementary to this theory is his interest group theory of regulation, which seeks to explain 'unintended side effects of regulation' that arise from transaction costs, asymmetric information and the fact that changes in property rights structures create winners and losers. These side-effects not only redistribute wealth but may in some cases lower economic growth indices.

Where the new institutionalism is helpful is in the way it treats property rights not as a priori rights but as state-granted rights. The state enjoys the formal powers to grant these rights, restructure them, supplement them and take them away.[8] But the state may not be in the best position to design the rights to achieve the most desirable outcomes. At the same time, it becomes very clear that, however rights are defined and allocated, the opportunity sets of everybody else are potentially, and for many people actually, affected.

To what extent may such perspectives be relevant to *intellectual* property rights? On the face of it, treating inventive knowledge as analytically comparable to scarce finite 'things' such as land and non-renewable resources is wrong. New knowledge is constantly being generated and is theoretically inexhaustible. Therefore, one might argue, granting property rights over newly created valuable intangibles can harm nobody; nor are others affected when the legal incidents of these rights are changed by statute or a new juridical interpretation, whether or not influenced by self-interested interpretive custodians.

Put simply, the position of IP right holding firms is likely to run like this: we invented something useful. It did not exist until we brought it into being. It is not something from the intellectual commons that we have appropriated. Our exclusive rights to use and market the invention do not incur any cost on society or intrude on any legitimate interests of other inventors or rival firms however strong these rights are. How could they, if it is our creation?

This position is almost certainly fatally flawed. There are several theoretical and practical grounds for responding sceptically to those who argue that defining, redefining and assigning intangible property rights in the form of patents and PBRs cannot diminish the legitimate rights, freedoms and interests of others.

First, both patents and PBRs are winner-take-all systems. The winner is the first to file an application.[9] In theory this need not be the first inventor or breeder. If an earlier or simultaneous inventor or breeder did not publish details of the invention or make an earlier application, he or she will have no rights to the invention or variety and will have a legal obligation to respect the rights of the right-holding inventor or breeder (assuming the application is subsequently awarded).[10]

Second, compared to real property, the boundaries between one person's legally enforceable intellectual property and another's tend to be extremely fuzzy and are more likely to overlap. Initially, the scope of a patent is determined through an examination by trained specialists. Later on, courts may decide to adjust the boundary line or even remove it. Ideally – to quote Greg Aharonian, who runs an e-mail patent news service – the 'fence' that is a patent claim 'should be no bigger than the thing you've invented. In particular, the fence shouldn't be extended to existing inventions that are quite close or the same' (quoted in Stix, 2001). This requires patent examiners and the courts to place the fences in the right place so as to keep the invention from intruding, not just on inventions that are someone else's property, but on the public domain of knowledge that is nobody's property. But the intangible nature of intellectual property means this can be an extremely difficult task and a very expensive one. Consequently, users of the patent system must be prepared to spend a great deal of money. Acquiring a patent is expensive enough, but the costs of asserting it in the courts and defending it from competitors are likely to be astronomical. This makes the system much more accessible to larger companies than to small firms and individuals. For this reason, and also because of the fuzzy nature of patent right boundaries, incentives exist for companies, especially the big ones, to perform various kinds of opportunistic behaviour. One can expect, for example, that large corporations may sometimes seek to free-ride on the intellectual property of smaller firms, independent inventors and traditional healers that cannot afford to take legal measures to stop them. They may speculatively accuse small businesses of patent infringement, safe in the knowledge that these firms will be so frightened of legal action that they will agree to pay royalties and even withdraw their competing products from the market. Firms may deliberately file excessively broad patent claims in the hope that at least some of these will slip through the examination system and be allowed. In addition, those firms able to submit large numbers of patents are likely to consider it a sound commercial strategy to file multiple applications to block off areas of research from competing inventors and companies. While some might claim there is nothing wrong with doing this, it is not a strategy that is equally available to all companies. And it may unfairly restrict the commercial opportunities of firms that could never afford to do the same thing. As for PBRs, the less rigorous novelty criterion (compared to patents) and the absence of a prior art search may encourage bogus applications for what are really landraces or other extant varieties. Evidence exists to suggest this sometimes happens (see Dutfield, 2000: 53).

Third, many individuals and communities have fundamental objections to the patenting of living things. Some hold that the 'creation' and patenting of life forms by laboratory scientists is 'playing God', and therefore sacrilegious. For example, in Pope John Paul II's message for Lent in 2002, he pronounced:

> The beginning of life and its marvellous development ... is a gift. And because it is a gift, life can never be regarded as a possession or as private property, even if the capabilities we now have to improve the quality of life can lead us to think that man is the 'master' of life. The achievements of medicine and biotechnology can sometimes lead man to think of himself as his own creator, and to succumb to the temptation of tampering with 'the tree of life'.[11]

Others find such patenting immoral on animal welfare grounds (d'Silva, 1989: 48). In short, ownership of a patent on such life forms is deemed by such people to be fundamentally wrong. One does not have to agree with all such sentiments to accept that inclusion of living organisms in the domain of protectable subject matter may conflict with the deeply held values of many members of society, and that these values deserve respect.

Fourth, patents and PBR certificates protect inventions and plant varieties that are considered to be new according to criteria which can justifiably seem arbitrary, inflexible and reductionist to many non-western societies. By contrast, the knowledge of indigenous communities tends to be treated as part of the global intellectual commons until it has been scientifically validated. Although it should not be possible for a scientist to acquire a patent or PBR merely by describing, say, a shaman's herbal formulation and demonstrating its efficacy with some test results, or taking a traditional folk variety and passing it off as a new one, such abuses do happen.[12] This is not only exploitative, but also, by commodifying what the community concerned may deem to be sacred, can also cause great offence.

Fifth, while new knowledge is indeed constantly being generated and is therefore inexhaustible in theory, business sectors may encounter stages of development where they run into innovation bottlenecks. As it gets harder to come up with genuinely new ideas and applications, one can imagine firms in such sectors becoming ever more creative in finding ways to extend the monopoly protection they already enjoy over existing products, thereby delaying the entry of old inventions into the public domain. Where the law allows this, drug companies, for example, may adopt strategic patenting practices to successfully delay price-reducing competition from generic firms, to the detriment of the latter companies and of course those who would benefit from cheaper medicines.

Finally, in a general sense, one can argue that like all systems of property rights the institution of patents and PBRs affects all non-right holders. Every single person except the patent or PBR holder has a duty to observe the rights granted. Of course only a limited number of individuals and organizations are in market competition with the owner. But if the patent makes it possible to charge a monopoly price for an important product such as a cure for cancer, then many more members of society are directly affected. If an association of major IPR-holding entities successfully lobbies in favour of stronger rights (arguing perhaps that only 'intellectual pirates' and unscrupulous consumers will suffer), it can be predicted that more people will be affected more deeply.

Paul Doremus gives support to the view that IP rights are regulatory institutions that clearly affect the opportunity sets and freedoms of right and non-right holders, and are thus bound to be the focus of interest group competition when reforms are being considered (Doremus, 1996): 'IPR ... are a form of adversarial regulation. IPR rules distribute costs and capabilities among competing groups that are in a zero-sum relationship (as opposed to policies that regulate individuals or groups for their own individual or collective benefit).' Moreover,

IPR reform potentially affects not only the interests of prospective rights holders and related users, but also the interests of long-standing right holders, whether or not they are in economically related arenas. Accordingly, one would expect the politics of IPR reform to be shaped considerably by the classic organizational characteristics of affected groups

– their structure (concentrated or dispersed), their cohesiveness (cooperative or conflictual), and the general nature of the policy cleavage (within an industry or between industries).

The prominent intellectual property scholar Robert Merges agrees on the usefulness of the new institutional economics approach: 'property rights, firms, institutions, governments: all of these are the subject of extensive study by social scientists operating within the NIE framework. It is time to integrate the study of IP rights into this framework ... here finally, is an economics literature that makes thorough sense for our field' (Merges, 2000: 1877).

In the face of so much basic uncertainty about patents and PBRs, new institutionalism (and common sense?) leads us to expect interest groups seeking to secure 'interpretive custody of the patent system' to resort to propaganda and myth-making (Drahos, 1999a). Interpretive custody may be taken to refer to a situation where an interest group, or a collection of such groups acting together, has achieved acceptance in government and society as authoritative, definitive and exclusive explicators of a particular issue. Alternative views may not necessarily be absent completely but, to be influential, these unconventional voices will need to find forums in which their way of construing or framing the issue makes their interpretations more persuasive.

This interest group propagandizing may take three forms. First, it may treat as self-evident what should require proof. Second, it may make threats about what will happen if the rights being demanded are not granted. Third, it may link IP rights with positive ideas and resist or disparage less favourable linkages made by opponents that could be turned into reasons to limit the rights. As Jessica Litman of Wayne State University, author of *Digital Copyright* (2001: 79), observes, 'if you're dissatisfied with the way the spoils are getting divided, one approach is to change the rhetoric'. We need to find out how far this 'interpretive custody' accurately depicts reality, and to what extent the use of unsubstantiated assertions, threats and framing bias[13] have been effective in achieving changes to the international system. Let us consider each of these strategies in turn and come up with some preliminary conclusions.

With respect to the former, economists have been largely unsuccessful in determining what an optimal patent system (or any other IP system) should look like. Bearing such a fundamental uncertainty in mind, the new institutionalist approach leads one to predict that companies and patent professionals will seek to convince policy makers that the huge gains for society to be made from strengthening patent rights are so obvious that there is no need to prove they will be achieved.

As for threats and falsehoods, at least as far as economic regulation in its broadest sense is concerned, Eggertsson (1990: 147) finds:

Sometimes regulations are initiated outright by special-interest groups, or special interests may capture the regulatory process.... Part of the strategy for minority interest groups is then to spread false information about the costs and benefits of the regulatory measures. For example, it is commonly argued that the absence of regulations will bring one or more of the following: *destructive competition* (among airlines, in the stock market), the *elimination of desirable cross-subsidies* (no more service to small communities by airlines or trucking), *excessive risk and harm to consumers* (electrocution of users if terminal telephone equipment is supplied by other than a national monopoly).

It seems reasonable to expect such misinformation spreading in the IP sphere. The new institutionalist approach encourages us to seek out – and expect to find – cases where interest groups attempt to convince governments that rejecting their proposals will result in negative outcomes. These might include, for example, the relocation of companies – or redirection of their investments – to other countries, and the weakening of the country's competitive position in terms of its ability to generate innovative activity, or to attract direct foreign investment or technology transfers.

When it comes to framing bias, we need to bear in mind that both patent and PBR law are linked to other areas of law and policy. One would expect propagandists for strong systems to portray these connections, or create new ones, in ways that place patents in a positive light. Where this is more difficult to achieve, these propagandists will either deny the link is a negative one or say there is no link at all. Their opponents, of course, are likely to seek to do the opposite. For example, one can expect a pharmaceutical company to argue that a strong patent system[14] is totally consistent with a good system of public health care. But if we take as an example the case of a cure for a lethal disease we could easily provide an opposing argument. The demand for such a medicine is likely to be high if no alternative treatments are available. If the company believes that most of the patients are willing and able to pay a very high price to prolong their lives, it will make sound commercial sense to set a high price even though poorer patients unable to afford the drug will die. Critics might argue that the company concerned should be required to ease the financial burden on poor patients by licensing the patent to bring in competition and thereby lower prices. In short, patent law should be responsive to public health emergencies by allowing compulsory licensing or unrestricted parallel importing, especially in developing countries where the proportion of poor patients will be much higher. How might the company respond? It is likely to argue that to finance the development costs of drugs aimed at the diseases of the poor, large profits need to be made from successful drugs. Therefore, the company would argue, strong IP rights are entirely consistent with good public health. Another example is the link between the patenting of life forms and morality. Companies will certainly find it convenient to argue that patent law has nothing to do with morality. Opponents of 'patenting life', on the other hand, consider there to be serious moral implications.

So far we have made a case for treating the patent and PBR systems as regulatory institutions, and outlined some strategies that interest groups might adopt to achieve regulatory capture or interpretative custody of them. We need now to identify and describe the relevant interest groups, and the regulators and regulatory processes.

The main interest groups are of course the patent and PBR-holding organizations, since they have the biggest direct economic stake in any redefinition or reallocation of rights. Of these the large chemical and pharmaceutical firms have usually been among the most powerful and determined, although the biotechnology and computer industries have become influential stakeholders in recent years (Doern, 1999: 49). Seed companies were the main private interest groups in terms of PBR protection, though many such firms are no longer independent.

In most economic sectors there is unlikely to be an industry position as such vis-à-vis strong versus weak IP protection. Owners of intellectual property are likely to require access to the property of other owners, so firms often find themselves in the position of licensees as well as owners. And patent and PBR interest groups are far from being homogeneous either in the extent of their interests or in their power to effect or resist change. Strong IP rights may involve costs as well as benefits for many firms. One can expect generic pharmaceutical manufacturers to oppose extensions to patent terms for pharmaceutical products. Conventional (that is, non-biotechnology) crop breeders may be very concerned about applying patents to plants since the UPOV research exemption benefits industrial breeders using conventional methods. And public sector researchers and even pharmaceutical corporations may be opposed to the 'driftnet patenting' of basic research tools such as DNA sequences (which is probably why this matter is now taken seriously by policy makers and patent offices).[15] Even large firms have to figure out how to balance their interests as patent owners with their interests in licensing those held by other institutions, and in navigating through what may be a veritable jungle of patents held by competitors, some of which may be extremely broad in scope and even of doubtful validity.

During the twentieth century, patent holders in the developed countries increasingly tended to be corporations rather than independent inventors. The interests of large firms may be very different from those of smaller firms and these individuals. Therefore one can expect competition for influence over the patent and plant variety systems by groups with conflicting interests. Disparate economic power among interest groups may go a long way towards explaining which ones interact most advantageously with politicians and regulators.

The wider public undoubtedly has a stake in the patent and PBR systems. Nonetheless, consumer groups in the developed countries have in the past hardly been involved in the shaping of law or policy. Bruce Doern of Carleton University in Ottawa describes consumers in this context as being a 'weak, diffused, virtually voiceless interest' (1999: 46), although he cites the health sector as a possible exception in some countries, since health ministries are sometimes more sympathetic towards patient interests than towards corporate ones. The wider significance of IP rights is also becoming clearer to many people outside the patent community, and increasingly patents and PBRs are becoming more widely debated.

Collectively, pro-patent and PBR interest groups may be conceived of as a community or a collection of communities. The term 'patent community' was coined by Drahos (1999a). It consists of 'patent attorneys and lawyers, patent administrators, and other specialists who play a part in the exploitation, administration and enforcement of the patent system. They form a community by virtue of their technical expertise and general pro-patent values. Regular users of the patent system (like the pharmaceutical companies) might also be said to be part of this community'. Members of the patent community speak the same language and share basic assumptions about patent law. As Susan Sell of George Washington University sees it (1999: 175), 'IP lawyers are socialized to promote the *protection* of IP, and uphold the ideology of private property rights'. And because IP lawyers in government departments and patent offices tend to share such a commitment, 'there is no neutral or objective group of civil servants in a position to counterbalance private demands'. Patent community members bear technical knowledge that most opponents and sceptical governments cannot match. According to Sell, 'to a certain extent IP law is reminiscent of the Catholic Church when the Bible was in Latin. IP lawyers are privileged purveyors of expertise as was the Latin-trained clergy. IP law is highly technical and complex, obscure even to most general attorneys' (1999: 174). Many of them have an obvious economic stake in the system, but some do not, particularly those from academia. With enormous economic power of some members arrayed alongside the 'objective' expertise of others, it would be surprising if one particular perspective on patent law did *not* become the conventional wisdom within regulatory agencies and processes, government trade and industry departments, and throughout society. Understood this way, the patent community is not just an economic interest group but an 'epistemic community', a term used by the political scientist Peter Haas (1999) to refer to 'networks of professionals who share common normative and causal beliefs, accept common truth-tests and are engaged in a common policy enterprise'. The same can be said for PBR law.

Another way to conceive of the array of interest groups promoting pro-IP values in government and throughout society is as a policy network which operates nationally, regionally and now globally, and which includes the public and private sectors. It is well known that patent communities and/or members of such communities combine internationally to form both transnational lobby networks and specific organizations. In addition to individual firms, there are four types of pro-IP organization that seek to influence IP law and policy at the international and national levels. The first are what may be referred to as multi-sector business associations for which IP is one of several issues they work on. These include the International Chamber of Commerce and the Union of Industrial and Employers' Federations of Europe (UNICE).[16] The second are the single or multi-sector business associations that are dedicated to promoting the IP interests of the firms they represent. These include the Business Software Alliance and the International Intellectual Property Alliance. The third are the single-sector business associations that are concerned with several issues, including IP rights. These include the Pharmaceutical Research and Manufacturers of America (PhRMA),[17] the European Federation of Pharmaceutical Industries and Associations (EFPIA), and the Association Internationale des Sélectionneurs pour la Protection des Obtentions Végétales (ASSINSEL).[18] The fourth are expert associations that are not inherently business-related, but which give support to IP systems by such means as advising policy makers, training, capacity building and propagandizing. Generally, they favour high standards of protection. These associations include the Association Internationale pour le Protection de la Propriété Industrielle (AIPPI),[19] the Fédération Internationale des Conseils en Propriété Industrielle (FICPI), and the Max Planck Institut für Ausländisches und Internationales Patent, Urheber und Wettbewerbsrecht (Max Planck Institute for Foreign and International Patent, Copyright and Competition Law). Undoubtedly, quite a number of individuals are members of – and may hold senior positions in – more than one of these associations. It can safely be assumed that these organizations will collaborate to promote their shared interests. More controversially, perhaps, one could include the World Intellectual Property Organization, whose role is to promote IP rights worldwide and is involved in training, capacity building, and to provide a forum for the negotiation of new norms, including international treaties.

Table 2.1 provides a simple typology of such interest groups with examples of some of the more prominent organizations. It is not always easy to place organizations in the categories. For example, while the International Intellectual Property Institute claims to be non-partisan, it receives funds from the private sector and is headed by a former Commissioner of the United States Patent and Trademark Office who was also previously a professional lobbyist for the Business Software Alliance.

Treating interest groups as collectivities should not blind us to the important role that individual policy entrepreneurs can play in terms of identifying and defining problems, and devising policy solutions in response. Developing such solutions may involve introducing new concepts and arguments, producing innovative proposals for framing demands, and selecting promising forums in which they can be introduced. It is likely that such policy entrepreneurs will exist in the IP policy arena.

Regulation involves four distinct areas of action (Hancher and Moran, 1998: 148). These are the design of general rules, the creation of institutions responsible for their implementation, the clarification of the exact meaning of a general rule in particular circumstances, and the enforcement of the rule in those circumstances.

In the case of national patent regulation, statutes provide the basic rules and create the implementation agencies, which are the national patent offices.[20] These agencies are then made responsible for interpreting these rules. In individual cases, the patent examiners are charged with determining whether or not the claims submitted in a patent application fulfil the criteria of novelty, industrial application and inventive step. Their work may be assisted by a handbook which clarifies the

Table 2.1 The patent and PBR communities: some key actors

Single-sector business associations	Multi-sector business associations	Expert associations
Association Internationale des Sélectionneurs pour la Protection des Obtentions Végétales – ASSINSEL	International Chamber of Commerce	*Association Internationale pour la Protection de la Propriété Industrielle – AIPPI*
Business Software Alliance (USA)	Keidanren (Japan)	*Fédération Internationale des Conseils en Propriété Industrielle – FICPI*
European Federation of Pharmaceutical Industries and Associations (EFPIA)	Union of Industrial and Employers' Federations of Europe – UNICE (Europe)	*Max Planck Institut für Ausländisches und Internationales Patent, Urheber und Wettbewerbsrecht (Germany)*
Motion Picture Association of America (USA)	*International Intellectual Property Alliance (USA)*	*Chartered Institute of Patent Agents (UK)*
Pharmaceutical Research and Manufacturers of America – PhRMA (USA)	*International Intellectual Property Institute (USA)*	

Note: Organizations dedicated to IP issues are in italics.

rules so that they are applied in a standardized manner. But agencies do not always just implement rules made elsewhere. In some jurisdictions, they may take a more activist role. For example, in February 1997, the US Patent and Trademark Office unilaterally announced that discovered expressed sequence tags could be patented and with only minimal disclosure of their function. In June 1999, the Administrative Council of the European Patent Office decided by itself to use the European Union Directive 98/44/EC on the Legal Protection of Biotechnological Inventions as a 'supplementary means of interpretation'.

Courts also have an important role to play in patent regulation. They may interpret the rules in ways that may bind patent offices. Furthermore, they are normally the final arbiter of disputes over the appropriate scope of specific patent grants. Courts also have the power to legally enforce patent rights, though patent owners also play a major enforcement role both indirectly and directly by monitoring the commercial activities of rivals, and through litigation, threats of legal action and out-of-court dispute settlement. In a very real sense, companies are not just customers of the regulatory system; to a greater or lesser extent they too are its designers, funders,[21] interpreters and even its enforcers.

Evidently, while national patent (and PBR) offices are the main implementation agencies, a number of regulatory spaces are available to be contested. These include patent offices, the government departments in which they are located, the politicians that oversee them, and the courts. But there may be others, such as competition regulators. Indeed, the term 'regulatory space' may be more appropriate than 'regulatory capture' in the patent and PBR system cases (see Hancher and Moran, 1998). Their decentralized structures within the state suggest it is extremely difficult for any one interest group to capture the whole system.

Power, Propaganda and Forum Shifting[22]

The perspective presented in this chapter so far leads one to surmise that (i) national patent and PBR systems are likely substantially to reflect the interests of large, powerful and well-organized interest groups more than those of small weaker ones; (ii) stronger and more expansive rights will be introduced if this enables powerful groups that already have a foothold in relevant regulatory spaces to further entrench their economic dominance;[23] and (iii) that consequent gains for such groups will negatively affect other groups and possibly consumers as well.

If these propositions are correct, what would lead most countries of the world to accept an agreement such as TRIPS, which requires national IP standards to be pitched at a level which developed countries themselves have only recently reached, and which is likely to lead to unintended consequences, some of which may well run counter to their development interests? Essentially, three approaches are available to the dominant nations to achieve such an outcome. These are coercion, propaganda and forum shifting.

The dominant interest groups among patent communities in developed countries include many transnational corporations that would benefit greatly from an international system with high standards of protection. In such a case, their task would be to convince their national governments that the interests of the country are best served by raising standards globally so as to create a level playing field that prevents free-riding, especially in developing countries. These governments, if suitably impressed, may then pressure individual developing countries to raise their standards of protection or enforcement, collaborate with other like-minded governments to propose a multilateral treaty, or pursue both strategies. Such activist governments may either use their economic dominance to bully developing countries or adopt a more subtle approach, arguing that raising the standards will benefit all countries, in effect to persuade them that 'what's good for Pfizer is good for the world'. Naturally, for transnational corporations headquartered in countries like the USA and the various European countries, there is much to be gained from building strategic alliances with firms sharing the same interests in these other countries. After all, the costs of doing so are likely to be vastly outweighed by the potential benefits.

Braithwaite and Drahos explain that forum shifting encompasses three main strategies: 'moving an agenda from one organization to another, abandoning an organization and pursuing the same agenda in more than one organization' (2000: 564). While the tactic is easier for the strong to adopt than the weak, success is not necessarily a foregone conclusion. Bringing IP rights out of relatively esoteric forums such as specialized United Nations agencies like WIPO and into international negotiations dealing with more mainstream issues like trade is likely to attract the interest of other well-organized non-governmental actors such as environmental pressure groups and lobby group networks which have experience in related issues and are likely to take a more sceptical, if not hostile, view of IP rights. Moreover, the possibility for economically weak but well-organized opponents to take advantage of forum shifting or even to play the forum-shifting game themselves cannot be discounted, especially as the number of available forums increases.

Notes

1   In E. Knowles (ed.) (1999), *Oxford Dictionary of Quotations*, 5th edn, Oxford: Oxford University Press.

2   Lane (1995: 119) divides public regulation into two categories: economic regulation and product regulation. The former involves entry conditions and price controls. The latter comprises a set of regulations stipulating how various types of goods should be produced and delivered.

3   Invention and innovation are not interchangeable words. Invention is the first step in the development of a marketable new product or process. Innovation comes afterwards. Joseph Schumpeter's well-known definition of innovation (or what he calls 'carrying out new combinations') comprises '(1) The introduction of a new good.... (2) The introduction of a new method of production ... which need by no means be founded upon a discovery scientifically new.... (3) The opening of a new market.... (4) The conquest of a new source of supply of raw materials.... (5) The carrying out of the new organization of any industry ...' (Schumpeter, 1983 [1934]: 66). Innovation connotes newness but it is possible to argue that an innovation for one company or national economy may not necessarily be innovative to another. Ernst *et al.* (in Mytelka and Tesfachew, 1998: 1–2) make this point when they define innovation as 'the process by which firms master and implement the design and production of goods and services that are new to them, irrespective of whether or not they are new to their competitors – domestic or foreign'.

4   Most of the analysis here deals with patents, but much of it applies also to PBRs. One exception is the information disclosure element, which is not relevant to PBRs.

5   In this context I am using the word 'invention' to refer to the act of bringing a new thing into existence rather than to the thing itself. Elsewhere in this book I use the word to refer to one or the other, or to both. The particular meaning should, I hope, be clear from the context.

6   This point applies to those developing countries that have attained a reasonable capacity to adopt and benefit from such technologies. Countries with very limited capacity have little to gain from free access to technologies.

7   In a well-known exposition of the functionalist explanation of property rights, Harold Demsetz (1967) argued, with some supporting empirical evidence, that property rights are created when, as a result of changes in relative prices or technology, it becomes more beneficial to establish and enforce them in spite of the costs of doing so than continuing without them.

8   According to William Roy of University of California, Los Angeles (1997: 11):

> Contrary to classic liberalism, there are no inherent or natural 'property rights.' The conception of inalienable or natural property rights existing prior to society or history may have been an effective ideology for creating capitalism, but it has clouded the historical analysis of what specific rights, entitlements, and obligations govern economic relations. Rather, the content of property relations is historically constructed and must be explained, not taken for granted.

> But accepting this point and treating property rights as state-granted rights does not, in my view, require us to deny a role for such notions as desert or fairness in guiding their design.

9   Except in the United States.

10   The power of this argument is one reason why US politicians are so reluctant to convert the US patent system from first-to-file to first-to-invent. First-to-invent means the legitimate right holder is always the first inventor. First-to-file means the right may not necessarily go to the first inventor if another claimant to the same invention applies first.

11   'Message of the Holy Father for Lent 2002' – (*http://www.vatican.va/holy_father/ john_paul_ii/messages/lent/documents/hf_jp-ii_mes_20020205_lent-2002_en.html*).

12   To give just one example, for as long as anybody knows the Xhomani San (Bushman) people of the Kalahari Desert have eaten parts of a local plant called hoodia to stave off hunger and thirst during their hunting trips. South African scientists working at South Africa's Council for Scientific and Industrial Research (CSIR) learned about the Xhomani people's use of the plant, did some experiments, and claimed this use of the plant as their own invention. In fact, the CSIR has filed patent applications in about 100 countries claiming ownership of the process of obtaining the active ingredient of this plant and its analogues and derivatives, as well as their use 'for the manufacture of medicaments having appetite suppressant activity'. Nowhere in the patent documents are the Xhomani people even mentioned. While it could be argued that first describing the mode of action in chemical terms may deserve to be considered as inventive, several other patents relating to traditional knowledge do not even go this far and seem to appropriate traditional knowledge with virtually no additional intellectual input at all.

13   This psychological concept was first applied to the analysis of the patent system by Drahos (1997).

14   Here I take 'strong' to refer to the extent of enforceability of the rights and to indicate the absence – or at least relative lack – of exceptions to patentability by subject matter or technological field.

15   Not even all biotechnology firms favour such patenting. For example, Ron James, Managing Director of PPL Therapeutics of Dolly the sheep fame, criticized the patenting of cDNA and ESTs at an April 2001 conference hosted by Edinburgh University that the author attended.

16 Note that some such organizations may be 'associations of associations' (for example, IIPA).
17 Founded in 1958 as the Pharmaceutical Manufacturers Association.
18 ASSINSEL was founded in 1938. In May 2002, ASSINSEL merged with the International Seed Federation (FIS) to form the International Seed Federation (ISF).
19 AIPPI was founded as early as 1897.
20 The European Patent Office also acts as an implementation agency in those countries that are member states of the European Patent Convention.
21 In North America and Europe, patent offices are increasingly expected to become financially self-sufficient. The danger is that examiners will be pressured to prioritize patent quantity over quality.
22 This term is borrowed from Braithwaite and Drahos (2000). The same phenomenon is often referred to elsewhere as 'forum shopping'.
23 However, in countries where such groups prefer a weaker system of rights such as in many technology-importing developing countries, it is possible that the rights will be relatively weak, perhaps weaker than they had been when they were colonies of European imperial powers.

Chapter 3

The Emergence of Modern Patent Law

It is probable enough that the patent laws will be abolished ere long. (*The Economist*, June 1869)[1]

Patent Law in Europe and North America in 1883

In the late nineteenth century the most economically powerful and technologically advanced countries in the world were Great Britain, the United States, France and Germany. Although these and a number of other countries in Europe and the Americas had patent laws, they were quite different from each other. And it was generally quite difficult for inventors to secure effective patent protection in foreign countries.

The first multilateral response to this situation came about in 1883 in the form of the Paris Convention for the Protection of Industrial Property. At that time there were five key areas of variation among patent systems. These were interpretations of novelty, the length of protection terms, the treatment of foreign applicants, the issue of whether or not patents needed to be 'worked' domestically, and exceptions to patentability. Let us look at each of these in turn.

Interpretations of novelty varied widely in nineteenth-century patent laws. In some countries (for example, France, Turkey and Italy) inventions could not be patented if there were prior knowledge, use or publication anywhere in the world. In most other countries (for example, the USA, Germany and Belgium) only unpublished foreign use or knowledge did not destroy novelty.[2] But in Britain only 'public manufacture, use or sale in England' invalidated patent applications for lack of novelty (Ladas, 1930: 26–7). Philip Grubb, a corporate patent lawyer, helpfully refers to these different conceptions of novelty respectively as absolute novelty, mixed novelty and local novelty (1999: 54).

There were no standard protection terms. The longest period of protection was provided by the USA, where patents were for 17 years.[3] France and Germany awarded patents for 15 years. British patents had a duration of 14 years, but the protection term of foreign inventions previously patented abroad automatically ended upon the expiry of the foreign patent even if this was less than 14 years.

By the 1880s it seems generally to have been accepted that countries ought to treat patent applicants equally and not discriminate against foreigners. Even so, the rules were often uncertain and national treatment was by no means a universal principle with a meaning shared by all trading nations (Evans, 1996: 150).

There were wide variations concerning regulation of local manufacture or use (that is, the 'working') of patented products or processes. In some countries (such as the USA) patent holders were under no obligation to work the invention or even to commercialize it. In others, rival manufacturers could apply for a compulsory licence if the patent holder refused to work the invention or license it willingly. In some others (such as France), merely importing a patented product would lead to revocation of the patent.

In the USA and Great Britain no classes of inventions were explicitly excepted. Elsewhere exceptions were usually indicated in the statutes. The most common of these appeared to have been medicines and foods (as in France and Germany). This was largely because private (especially foreign) monopolies for such basic essentials were considered to conflict with the public interest. Such a view has deep roots in European society, and persists in the patent laws of some developing countries such as India. With respect to drugs, protection may have been denied also so that the public would not be deceived into thinking that, because an ineffective or dangerous drug had been patented, its use had been endorsed by the government (Lewers, 1922: 530). In addition to explicit exceptions, implicit ones existed in all jurisdictions. Courts and patent offices determined (or simply assumed), as they sometimes do today, that certain categories of invention were unpatentable even if the patent statutes in force made no actual reference to them. They may have been considered as falling outside the definition of an invention provided in the legislation, or granting patents for such inventions may have been deemed to be against the public interest.

Because the differences between national laws were so great, there was little expectation that harmonizing national laws through a single convention was achievable. But there was broad understanding that certain common principles and administrative procedures should be agreed upon. Even so, the efficacy of patents was by no means universally accepted, even by industry, and from about 1850 to 1875 opposition to patenting in Europe was so strong that its future was in serious jeopardy (Machlup and Penrose, 1950). Britain came close to abandoning its patent system in the early 1870s, largely because of the free trade lobby (Coulter, 1991). The pro-patent case was undermined by the impressive economic and technological advancement of Switzerland and Holland, which did not have patent systems (Dutton, 1984: 29; Schiff, 1971). As for Germany, such was Chancellor Bismarck's scepticism that patents had anything to offer his country that, without some highly effective lobbying, the establishment of the patent system there might well have been delayed by many years (Kronstein and Till, 1947: 767; Machlup and Penrose, 1950: 4).

Two things should be clear from this brief survey of patent law history and politics. First, patent systems were established ostensibly to fulfil public policy objectives relating to economic and technological progress. Second, these laws were bound to vary as a result of the different developmental opportunities and aspirations of countries, the perspectives of interest groups most able to influence legislatures, the absence of political pressure for harmonization and path dependence.

Patents, Industrialization, Trade and Protectionism

It is impossible to understand the development of patent law and the decision to establish an international patent convention at this time without reference to the following four factors: the European and North American industrial revolutions, the expansion of international trade and investment, national trade and development policy, and the economic recession of the late nineteenth century.

From around 1770 to 1870,[4] Britain experienced an industrial revolution characterized by rapid economic growth and technological advancement that was to make the country the world's leading economic power. These phenomena were experienced in other areas of Europe and in North America, but to a much lesser extent, at least initially.[5]

British manufacturers sometimes complained that the patent system enabled foreigners unfairly to acquire information about cutting-edge technologies by reading patent specifications. Interestingly, such complaints are echoed in more recent (and ultimately unsuccessful) objections by many companies to changes in US patent law providing pre-grant publication of specifications (for example, see Trudel, 1995). But it is possible that these concerns were exaggerated because until 1852 the patent administration system was chaotic, and patent specifications were not very detailed. In fact, patents were not subjected to any kind of examination, so many would probably have been fraudulent (Coulter, 1991: 24). As it was, even registering a patent was a bureaucratic nightmare, at least according to one account by Charles Dickens that, while fictional, was presumably based on fact.[6]

By the 1880s, several European countries had experienced industrial revolutions of their own, as had the USA. The leading industrial sectors in Europe and North America at the time were textiles, iron and steel, mechanical engineering, electrical engineering, chemicals (first heavy chemicals, then organic chemicals and synthetics), and food processing. These were to be accompanied – or in some case superseded – by motor vehicles and electronics from around the turn of the century (von Tunzelmann, 1995: 150–57). Competition between countries and firms within these countries became particularly intense as catch-up with Britain (in some technological fields) was achieved by more countries, export markets grew and foreign direct investment increased. The biggest and most successful firms expanded by adding value to their products through the application of specialized technical knowledge, and secured domestic and international markets through the acquisition of patent rights. Swiss and Dutch companies, even those which opposed a domestic patent law, acquired foreign patents in countries to which they exported their products (Schiff, 1971).

West European and North American national economies expanded rapidly during the hundred or so years leading up to the Paris Conference and, for much of the time, except from the early 1870s, when there was an economic recession, trade and investment expanded at an even greater rate. Industrial transnational corporations emerged from the mid-nineteenth century. At first these were mostly British companies which invested first in the Americas and later in Australia and Africa. US and then continental European companies followed soon after. Britain remained the largest source of overseas investment until the First World War (Dicken, 1998: 20–21). Given these circumstances, it is hardly surprising that Britain and the USA were early proponents of an international patent convention.

From the late eighteenth century and for most of the nineteenth, infant industry protectionism rather than open trade was usually considered to be the best strategy for industrializing countries like the USA and Germany to catch up with Britain. Both countries actively sought to industrialize and diversify so as to compete more effectively with other countries, especially Britain, and were highly successful in doing so.[7] France adopted a mercantilist high tariff policy until the 1850s, but became more open thereafter. In 1860, the Cobden–Chevalier Treaty between France and Britain reduced trade barriers, introduced the most-favoured-nation principle to international law and was succeeded by a proliferation of bilateral free trade agreements. But at the same time, the USA reverted to protectionism after a 30-year period of greater liberalization (Kenwood and Lougheed, 1999: 66). This was considered necessary to finance the Civil War, but tariffs and duties remained high until just before the First World War.

Concerns about infant industries were not the only protectionist motivation at this time. The revival of nationalism, the economic depression of 1873 to 1879, and the huge influx into Europe of Russian and American grain combined to unite agricultural and industrial interests with politicians favouring the preservation or restoration of trade barriers. The major European powers – Britain excepted – responded with protectionist policies to safeguard their domestic industries and raise revenues. In 1879, Germany introduced tariff protection for agriculture and from the same decade allowed price-fixing cartels to proliferate (von Tunzelmann, 1995: 171). France, Italy and Switzerland introduced and then strengthened tariff protection from around this time. From 1880 to the eve of the First World War, only Britain, Denmark and patent-less Holland remained as free trade nations (Kenwood and Lougheed, 1999: 72). Clearly, when the Paris Convention was opened for signature, free trade ideology was far from being ascendant in Europe or in North America.

An issue which remains as controversial today as it was during this period is the relationship between patents, protectionism and free trade, and economic development. Does supporting free trade mean opposing patent rights or the opposite? Should countries seeking to catch up with the most developed countries adopt protectionist policies and oppose patent rights? In fact, the way that European and North American governments and industrialists responded to these questions varied.

Patents are essentially a market intervention impeding the operation of free market competition by prohibiting the unauthorized use, manufacture, sale and import of products or processes identical to the protected one. Holland was pro-free trade and abolished its patent system. Britain came close to following its example. Whether or not patents appeared to be inherently consistent or inconsistent with free trade depended on the language used to describe patents. This was well understood by propagandists pro and contra patents and free trade.

Opponents of patents denounced them as anachronistic and unfair monopoly privileges that should be dispensed with. J. Geigy-Merian, founder of a Swiss chemical firm that later merged with Ciba to form Ciba-Geigy and an opponent of an 1882 attempt to revise the constitution in order that a patent law could be enacted,[8] was particularly vitriolic: 'patents are a paradise for parasites ... Patent protection forms a stumbling block against the development of trade and industry.... The patent system is a playground for plundering patent agents and lawyers' (quoted in Hobbelink, 1991: 99).[9]

According to the economists Fritz Machlup and Edith Penrose in a well-known article published half a century ago (1950: 9),

> The strength in nineteenth century Europe of the movements against privilege and monopoly and for free international trade was such that the ideological linking of patent protectionism with tariff protectionism and of patent monopoly with monopoly privileges in general tended to help the opponents and to weaken the defenders of the patent system. It was strategically essential for the latter to separate as far as possible the idea of patent protection from the monopoly issue and from the free-trade issue.

Despite the association between patents and monopoly privileges, it was common also during this era to justify private property in terms of natural rights.[10] So supporters of the patent system could sometimes adopt proprietarian positions that were quite extreme. For example, Lysander Spooner, the American nineteenth-century libertarian who apparently first introduced the term 'intellectual property' to the English-speaking world argued that scientists and inventors should enjoy a permanent property right in their ideas (see Spooner, 1855, 1884). The USA was probably most supportive of the rights of patent holders (including opposing working clauses) even while the patent controversy was casting serious doubt on the future of patent law in Europe. Courts and legislators in that country tended in Lockean fashion to equate private property rights with freedom, and also with the fostering of economic growth (Ely, 1992).[11] This view was not universally held in the twentieth century. Up to the 1980s, it was common for courts to be suspicious of the system and its users, at times even equating patent rights with the most rapacious forms of monopoly capitalism. But the idea that governments should not interfere with the rights of patent holders has also been an enduring one.

Although he was writing in 1950, a patent lawyer called John Dienner (1950: 620) vividly conveyed the philosophy behind the US patent system, not only of his age but of this earlier era, when he explained:

America is the only country in the world that ever trusted the plain ordinary citizen with a private monopoly – the patent. In America, the basic concept is that what a man invents he is entitled to monopolize for a limited time by a patent. The patent is his property. He can do with it as he pleases, so long as he doesn't use it to break the law or injure the public by misuse of it. The patentee need not 'work' his patent if he doesn't want to. When he makes his application, the Government examines his claim, and if it is found worthy, he gets his patent. No snooper is allowed to look at it, and file an opposition to put him to trouble, delay and expense before he can get it. No tax collector knocks on his door some fine day and says, 'Pay me or your patent expires.' No competitor hauls him into court or before the Commissioner of Patents and says, 'You are either not working your patent or not doing a good enough job if you are producing it, and you must let me into your market. I will take away your market from you.' No Government official will say, 'You haven't worked your patent for five years, so I am cancelling it.'

The fact that the examination system sought to filter out the spurious inventions may have helped give prestige to patent owners and to the system itself which must have appeared more meritocratic than those of Europe. But perhaps the basic underlying reason was the prevalent idea that technological advancement was best achieved by creating strong private rights over inventions and creative works, as well as the broad assumption that holders of these rights would not abuse them (Kronstein and Till, 1947: 771). Until around the mid-1870s, even those European governments which regarded patent monopolies as necessary still believed the rights had to be strictly regulated in the public interest. But as the century came to a close opinion gradually shifted towards the US view, which contained elements of both instrumentalism and proprietarianism.

Continental patent laws that mandated domestic manufacture on pain of revocation or the possibility of compulsory licensing were tariff-like instruments that blocked foreign competition (Anderfelt, 1971: 65). This is one reason why pro-free trade economists tended to dislike patents. But once protectionism became popular with governments, the possibility of revocation or compulsory licensing in the case of non-working not only did much to ensure the survival of patent law in Europe but also made agreement on an international convention possible. This is because such a provision weakened the position of those who viewed patents as mercantilist monopoly privileges (Wegner, 1993: 17).

The Paris Convention for the Protection of Industrial Property

We have seen that the nineteenth century experienced tremendous industrial and technological development in Europe and North America as well as an explosion of international trade and increasingly intensive competition between these nations. Existing markets expanded as a result of economic growth and rising populations. New overseas markets opened up through trade, investment and, of course, colonialism., and European firms encountered increasing competition in their home territories from foreign rivals. It is not difficult, then, to see why these countries would favour an international patent system allowing their companies to acquire secure protection in foreign markets. But these realities do not explain why the international system appeared when it did.

The first proposal for an international patent convention can be traced back to the 1851 Great Exhibition which took place in London. Queen Victoria's consort Prince Albert is sometimes suggested as being the first public figure to propose such an agreement (Beier, 1984). Although his proposal was not taken up, the prestige of hosting such an exhibition forced the government to respond to concerns from domestic manufacturers about foreign visitors pirating their inventions. Not only did Parliament pass a temporary law protecting all unpatented exhibits during the exhibition, it also set up a committee to study the patent system, which resulted in some fundamental amendments to the British law a year later (Coulter, 1991: 39).

But the main catalyst was the 1873 International Exhibition of Vienna, one of several international exhibitions that took place during the mid-to-late nineteenth century. These were highly prestigious events, and to newly industrializing countries they provided opportunities to acquire international acclaim for their recent scientific and technological achievements.[12] Unfortunately, they also created possibilities for visitors to copy the exhibits.

Responding to concerns expressed by several governments, the Austro-Hungarian government introduced temporary IP protection for foreign exhibits with effect to the end of that year, and agreed to sponsor an international patent congress during the exhibition (ibid.: 175). While both measures had first been proposed by the US government, the lobbying efforts of a group of Austrian and German patent attorneys and engineers helped to ensure that the congress took place (Beier, 1984: 2; Gaultier, 1997: 18).

The event was attended by 244 participants from 13 countries.[13] The German-born British industrialist William Siemens (brother of Werner Siemens, founder of the Siemens corporation, who also participated and reappears in the next chapter) was elected congress chairman. However, while pro-patent views dominated the congress, it was not only the Swiss and Dutch delegates that were anti-patent. In fact, one of the six elected vice-presidents denounced patents as being 'irreconcilable with the progress of modern times, and with free trade' and 'a substitute of the privileges offered by the trade guilds' (Coulter, 1991: 175). Nonetheless, the three resolutions adopted by the congress indicated a majority view in favour of patent protection. The first propounded the principle that 'protection for inventions is to be granted by the legislatures of all civilized nations'. The second provided a series of elements for an effective and useful patent law which included compulsory licensing in the public interest (Coulter, 1991: 176). It was agreed that non-working should not be grounds for revocation if the patent had been worked in another country and if nationals could acquire a licence. The third resolution recommended that national laws be harmonized by means of an international agreement. This was the first public call for an international industrial property convention. The congress's Preparatory Committee was turned into a Permanent

Executive Committee charged with seeking to implement these resolutions, including the convening of future congresses as appropriate. Paradoxically, this proposal for an international agreement was acceptable to some of the strongest anti-patent campaigners, at least in Britain. Why? One explanation is that an international system was the only thing that made a domestic system tolerable to such people, since it did at least purport to create a 'level playing field' for competition with foreign rival firms (ibid.).

The next congress took place five years later, during the 1878 Paris International Exposition. As the earlier congress had been dominated by Austrians and Germans, this one was dominated by French delegates, who made up 60 per cent of the almost 500 delegates (ibid.: 178). Interestingly, while the congress took the project for an international convention a major step forward, French influence and perhaps growing protectionism in response to the recession resulted in some contradictory and controversial outcomes. So, while the natural property theory was accepted as the justification for patents, the action of revocation of those not worked locally was supported in favour of compulsory licensing as at Vienna. Agreement on the principle of national treatment was reached without controversy. On the other hand, a French resolution opposing compulsory prior examination of patent applications was adopted despite its unpopularity with many delegates from the other 10 countries represented. A Permanent International Committee was set up to draft an international industrial property convention. The committee's draft of a 'Project for an International Union for the Protection of Industrial Property' was circulated by the French government. In response, 19 governments sent delegations to the 1880 Paris Patent Conference. The conference adopted a draft convention which was finally approved (with some small changes) and opened for signature at a follow-up conference also in Paris three years later.

The founder members of the union created by the Paris Convention for the Protection of Industrial Property were Belgium, Brazil, France, Guatemala, Italy, Netherlands, Portugal, El Salvador, Serbia, Spain and Switzerland. Great Britain, Tunisia and Ecuador joined within a year. Ironically, while the USA and Germany were notable absentees, two founder members (Netherlands and Switzerland) were without a patent system. The USA did not join the Paris Union until 1887, and Germany not until 1903. However, both countries thereafter became consistently strong advocates of the international patent system.[14]

The Convention established the Paris Union for the Protection of Industrial Property, which consisted of all member states, and whose International Bureau was located in Switzerland. This institution merged with the Berne Union for the Protection of Literary and Artistic Works in 1893 to form the Bureaux Internationaux Réunis de la Protection de la Propriété Intellectuelle (BIRPI), which in 1970 was transformed into WIPO.

The most important patent-related matters dealt with in the Convention concerned national treatment, the right of priority and rules relating to local manufacture. National treatment is the right of foreign citizens to be treated the same as nationals with respect to legal rights and remedies. Swiss manufacturers, therefore, could not be denied patent rights in other Paris Union countries simply because patents were not available in Switzerland. National treatment was and continues to be one of the pillars of international IP law.

An applicant for a patent in one member state was permitted a six-month period from the date of the first application (the priority date) to file for patents in other countries. During this period the applicant could prevent third parties from applying for a patent on the same invention. Moreover, subsequent applications during this period could not be invalidated on the grounds of prior registration, publication or working by a third party. The USA and Germany, both of which granted patents only after examination, were unhappy with this provision. According to US practice, priority began from the date of publication of the patent, not of its filing. The German government felt that the priority period should be 12 months, since it often took at least that length of time for patents to be granted (UK Board of Trade, 1901). While such technical matters affected the decisions of these countries to delay joining the Union, strategic considerations are likely also to have been involved.

The Convention made no reference to compulsory licensing and stated that patents could not be revoked solely on the grounds of importation from a member state to the country where the patent was granted. However, members were otherwise free to require patents to be worked. This provision was a compromise that allowed importing as long as there was also local working. Since then, 'two fundamental principles [of the Paris Convention] have remained virtually unchanged: (i) that importation will not entail forfeiture; and (ii) that member countries may pass legislation to mandate local working within the patent granting country' (Halewood, 1997: 253–4).

On the other hand, the Convention made no reference to three important areas of variation among national patent laws, indicating a lack of consensus. These were, first, the matter of whether national patent institutions had to examine patent applications or could serve merely as registration offices; second, the term of a patent; and third, exceptions from patentability on the basis of industrial or technological fields, or of morality concerns.

So was the Paris Convention a blow for free trade, a protectionist device or a concession to free trade that was palatable to governments only because they had already taken steps to close their economies and thus render the Convention's national treatment provisions harmless to domestic industry? To Friedrich-Karl Beier (1984: 2), 'the anti-protectionist characteristic of the Paris Convention's international protection renders it an important instrument of the free market economy'. As we have seen, to many people at the time, neither the Convention nor patent law generally had an 'anti-protectionist characteristic' at all. Whether it does or has the opposite character remains a controversial question, depending as it does on the perspective of the observer. For example, a representative from a developing country who considers his or her nation has benefited from being able to copy or export foreign inventions may regard being prevented or restricted from doing so as a protectionist restraint, or alternatively as an undesirable free trade measure that conflicts with the need to allow infant industries to flourish. Somebody promoting the interests of a developed country may well take an opposite view of the international patent system, arguing that it helps establish fair rules of the game for otherwise deregulated international trade and creates the secure property rights needed to encourage intensified cross-border transactions in goods, services and technologies.

It is probably truest to say that providing patent rights is protectionist in the sense that competition is constrained during the life of a given patent. But it is pro-competitive if it encourages the patent holder's competitors to be innovative; even more so if it successfully encourages innovation throughout the economy. So while a patent is itself a protectionist instrument, a patent *system* can be a pro-competitive institution if on balance it results in higher levels of innovation than would otherwise occur. As for the Convention, there are reasons to believe that the protectionist measures implemented by many countries at the time meant they could join the Union with confidence that their emerging industries would not be overexposed to foreign competition.[15]

It is interesting to note that this historical debate about whether patents are a form of protectionism or not continues to this day. Many commentators supporting the interests of developing countries believe they are. For example, the enthusiastically pro-free trade economist Jagdish Bhagwati (1998: 78–80) criticized TRIPS on two grounds: first, that it will increase financial transfers from poor to rich countries in the form of royalties and licence fees, thereby further impoverishing the former and enriching the latter nations; and second, that it is protectionist because it allows developed countries to impose sanctions on countries that fail 'adequately' to respect their companies' IP rights. According to Paulo de Almeida of the Brazilian Foreign Ministry (1995), the establishment of a global IP regime via the GATT Uruguay Round was an act of technological protectionism by the developed countries which will impose huge economic and social costs on many developing countries. This view is shared by many advocates of developing country interests.

Patent Law at the End of the Twentieth Century

Patent law has come a long way in 120 years. National systems are still varied, but those of the industrialized countries are much more standardized. During the course of the twentieth century, most developed countries relaxed the more onerous working requirements, and during the 1960s and 1970s those countries that still excluded pharmaceutical products from patentability decided to allow them. These countries included France (from 1960), Ireland (1964), Germany (1968), Japan (1976), Switzerland (1977), Italy and Sweden (both 1978) and Spain (1992).[16] However, plant varieties are still expressly excluded in Europe, and the patentability of biotechnology products and research tools continues to be highly controversial.

Some new IP rights have been created, such as the PBR systems adopted to implement the UPOV Convention which came into being during the 1960s (see Chapter 7).

As for the rest of the world, prior to TRIPS many independent former colonies already had patent laws, though often these were inherited from their erstwhile colonial rulers. While many middle-income countries had continued with some or all of the exceptions that most of the developed countries had abandoned 10–20 years previously, a large proportion of low-income countries had few of these. In fact only India, China and Vietnam excepted pharmaceuticals, food products *and* chemicals, reflective of a mixture of pragmatism and, at least in the case of the two latter countries, of both ideological and cultural hostility to Western formulations of intangible property.[17]

My account of the changes that took place gives special attention to the three most important agreements relevant to the content of this book, and to five issues. The agreements are the Paris Convention, the European Patent Convention and the TRIPS Agreement. These merit our attention because of the vital role they have played in norm creation, standard setting and the harmonization of national systems. The five issues are as follows: the shifting balance between instrumentalism and proprietarianism; the patenting of life forms, other living material and natural substances such as DNA; compulsory licensing; exceptions to patentability; and perceptions on the relationship between patents and free trade and protectionism.

The Paris Convention

Since 1883, the Paris Convention has been revised six times, most recently in 1967, and its membership has expanded tremendously, including many developing countries which joined in large numbers during the 1960s and 1970s. These revisions (though not necessarily all provisions within them) have tended progressively to strengthen the rights of IP owners. This is hardly surprising when we consider that groups like AIPPI[18] and the International Chamber of Commerce[19] were active participants in most of the official revision conferences that took place during that century.

Apart from the extension of the priority date for patents to 12 months, the main substantive differences between the 1883 version and subsequent ones have been to do with working and compulsory licensing. While the 1883 version stated that 'the patentee shall remain bound to work his patent in conformity with the laws of the country into which he introduces the patented objects', subsequent revisions have strengthened the rights of patent holders in this respect, principally by providing for compulsory licensing as a sanction for non-working, albeit without completely excluding the possibility of revocation. According to the current text of the Convention, 'a compulsory licence may not be applied for on the ground of failure to work or insufficient working before the expiration of a period of four years from the date of filing ... or three years from the date of the grant of the patent, whichever period expires last'. Such a licence must be non-exclusive and non-transferable, and an application for one 'shall be refused if the patentee justified his inaction by legitimate reasons'.

The periodic changes to the text dealing with this issue reflected a continuing conflict between two groups of countries. The first group consisted mainly of the most advanced industrialized countries who considered it unreasonable and unrealistic to require patent holders to set up manufacturing facilities in every domestic market. In taking such a stance, they were supported by AIPPI, which has for long opposed compulsory working. The second group was made up mostly of much less industrially advanced countries seeking to protect their emerging industries. Supporters of the latter position increased in number during the 1960s. This was because many newly independent countries joined the Paris Union, and these tended to be much less interested in using IP rights to generate their own technologies than in acquiring useful technologies from foreigners. But attempts by developing countries in the late twentieth century to reverse the strengthening trend at the international level were completely unsuccessful.[20] In fact, it was when these countries decided to use their numerical strength to revise the Paris Convention to further their developmental interests that lawyers and businesses in the USA came up with the idea that a comprehensive agreement on IP rights should be negotiated in the GATT Uruguay Round rather than under WIPO's auspices (see Chapter 8).

The Paris Convention has never explicitly required that chemical substances (including of course drugs) be patentable. This is not surprising given that the Convention has always avoided the controversial and potentially divisive question of stating what is or is not patentable subject matter. Nonetheless, the fifth revision conference, which took place in Lisbon in 1958, discussed the issue and adopted a resolution recommending that member countries study the possibility of doing so.[21] Considering how influential it was, AIPPI must surely have been behind this resolution. According to the head of the US branch of AIPPI who attended the Conference,

> No amendment of the Convention was adopted on any point which was not the subject of a resolution by the AIPPI, though in some cases the text adopted differs in some respects from the AIPPI text. A number of proposed amendments of the Convention voted for by the AIPPI failed at Lisbon by the opposition of countries represented particularly by officials of the Patent Office only. On the other hand, resolutions of the AIPPI which were not adopted by it unanimously did not fare well. (Kemman, 1961: 741)

The Convention on the Grant of European Patents (European Patent Convention)

The importance of the European Patent Convention, which was signed in 1973, extends well beyond the confines of the European continent. Some of its provisions have been incorporated into the TRIPS Agreement, and it has served as a model for legislation in other parts of the world. The Convention has the effect not only of facilitating patent coverage throughout the various European national markets, but of significantly harmonizing patent law in the various national jurisdictions. Consequently, the EPC marks the most important stage thus far in a (so far incomplete) harmonization process that began in the late 1940s as an initiative of the Council of Europe and was then also taken up by the European Economic Community (as the European Union was then called) shortly after its creation in 1957 (see Beier, 1981; van Empel, 1975; Stein, 1964).

By the end of the 1950s, the Council of Europe accepted the unfeasibility of creating a single Europe-wide patent office and of unifying the various rules, procedures and principles existing in each country in one single step. Therefore three patent conventions were adopted as intermediate measures, the most important being the 1963 Convention on the Unification of Certain Points of Substantive Law on Patents for Invention.[22] According to one informed view,

> The original intention of the Convention was to give industry a greater degree of certainty about whether it could secure protection for any given invention on a broad geographical basis. Otherwise it could be faced with a situation in which, for example, drugs could be produced in Italy, where there was no patent protection, and then sold to the National Health Service in Britain, where the Crown claimed the right to use inventions without regard to any patents granted if such use was for the benefit of the community as a whole. (Groves *et al.*, 1993: 18–19)[23]

The preamble indicates that another of its objectives was to 'contribute to the creation of an international patent'. Given that the European Patent Convention contains language borrowed from the above Convention, some of which was included also in TRIPS, one can conclude that it was to a large extent successful. The Convention had to accommodate wide differences in national patent rules relating to pharmaceuticals, food, agriculture and horticulture while encouraging states to harmonize their rules within a realistic time frame at the level of the most expansive rights available at that time in any one country. Thus contracting states were allowed to reserve the right 'not to provide for the grant of patents in respect of food and pharmaceutical products, as such, and agriculture or horticultural processes', but for a limited time only (10 years). Both Italy and Switzerland took advantage of this option. On the other hand, parties were not required to grant patents in respect of

> (a) inventions the publication or exploitation of which would be contrary to ordre public or morality, provided that the exploitation shall not be deemed to be so contrary merely because it is prohibited by a law or regulation; (b) plant or animal varieties or essentially biological processes for the production of plants or animals; this provision does not apply to microbiological processes and the products thereof.

The terms 'essentially biological' replaced 'purely biological' from an earlier version of the text. The Council's Committee of Experts on Patents, that was responsible for drafting the Convention, changed the wording to broaden the exclusionary language to embrace such 'essentially biological' processes as varietal selection and hybridization methods even if 'technical' devices were utilized to carry out the breeding processes (Bent *et al.*, 1987: 66–7). The singling out of microbiological processes and products was made at the suggestion of AIPPI, which pointed out that microorganisms were commonly used in well-established industrial activities such as brewing and baking (Bent *et al.*, 1987: 66). These terms are important because of their incorporation into the European Patent Convention and the TRIPS Agreement.

With its large membership, the Council of Europe was not the ideal forum either to intensify European patent law harmonization or to negotiate a Europe-wide system. The initiative was thus taken by the then six-member European Economic Community (EEC), whose overriding interest in patent law appears to have had more to do with the Treaty of Rome's objective of a common market than with a desire to promote innovation in Europe. The main concern here was that the territorial nature of patent protection could hinder the free flow of goods. Therefore, rather than to harmonize the national patent systems, it was felt necessary to create a unitary patent system with EEC-wide coverage to operate alongside the national systems, and which in time would render them obsolete.[24] Another motivation that was of particular interest to industry (and still is) was to reduce the costs of obtaining Europe-wide patent protection. Not surprisingly, then, businesses including those from the chemical industry 'led or at any rate urged on primarily by German interests' pressured national governments to work towards the creation of a European patent system (Robbins, 1961: 220).

The Draft European Patent Convention was published in 1962, but, while the EEC's small membership made it an ideal forum to draft such a convention, most European countries were not members. This meant it was hardly an appropriate institution to develop a Europe-wide system, even excluding the Eastern Bloc countries. For several years, very little progress was made under the EEC's auspices. This situation changed in 1968, when the French government broke the deadlock by proposing not only a community patent system, but also a separate non-EEC convention to be drafted with all interested European countries. France, which was anticipating a substantial increase in the volume of foreign applications, was concerned that its registration system would handicap its domestic industries. The authorities feared that companies would have to check for themselves the validity of vast quantities of unexamined patents held by competitors, and that this would became increasingly burdensome for them. Setting up a European patent office responsible for examining every application would avoid this.

This proposal was accepted by other governments and led to a conference in May 1969 at which 17 countries were represented. Two drafts of the European Patent Convention were published in 1970 and 1971. Interested non-governmental organizations (NGOs), including those representing potential users of the proposed system, were invited to give their views on each draft at hearings. In 1972, a complete draft was agreed and submitted to governments and, a year later, at a Diplomatic Conference in Munich, the EPC was adopted. The Community Patent Convention was signed in 1975, but has still not been implemented.

The EPC allows a single patent application to be filed with an institution known as the European Patent Office (EPO), where it is examined.[25] Effectively, an EPC application is a bundle of national applications in the chosen countries. Enforcement is a matter for national courts, and it is perfectly possible for a patent to be invalidated in one country but to remain in force elsewhere. The EPO has an appeals system consisting of various boards, the most important being the Enlarged Board of Appeal. While their judgments are not legally binding, national courts tend voluntarily to accept their authority (Paterson, 2002: 131).

With respect to the substantive aspects of patentability, the EPC adopts and builds upon those contained in the 1963 Convention. Thus, although 'invention' still lacks definition, some clarification is provided through specific mention of 'non-inventions', which are '(a) discoveries, scientific theories and mathematical methods; (b) aesthetic creations; (c) schemes, rules and methods for performing mental acts, playing games or doing business, and programs for computers; and (d) presentations of information.' As for exceptions, Article 53 repeats those of the 1963 Convention while making them mandatory rather than optional, stating that

> European patents shall not be granted in respect of: (a) inventions the publication or exploitation of which would be contrary to ordre public or morality, provided that the exploitation shall not be deemed to be so contrary merely because it is prohibited by law or regulation in some or all of the Contracting States; (b) plant or animal varieties or essentially biological processes for the production of plants or animals; this provision does not apply to microbiological processes or the products thereof.

'Essentially biological' continues to lack a precise and genuinely scientific meaning (Funder, 1999: 569), though the EPO has attempted to clarify its application. According to the EPO guidelines for examiners,

> The question whether a process is 'essentially biological' is one of degree depending on the extent to which there is technical intervention by man in the process; if such intervention plays a significant part in determining or controlling the result it is desired to achieve, the process would not be excluded.

And the EPO Technical Board of Appeal in a 1995 case (*Greenpeace* v. *Plant Genetic Systems NV*) affirmed that 'a process ... comprising at least one essential technical step, which cannot be carried out without human intervention and which has a decisive impact on the final result' is not essentially biological and would thus be patentable. On the other hand, conventional plant and animal-breeding methods and other techniques such as artificial insemination would not be (Warren-Jones, 2001: 122).

Computer programs as such and methods of medical treatment are also excluded. The mandatory nature of the plant varieties exception came about because most European countries had by this time opted to adopt sui generis systems of plant variety protection based on the UPOV model (see Chapter 7). Chemical and pharmaceutical products are patentable, though individual countries had the right to exclude them for the first 15 years of the EPC's operation (from 1977 until 1992). The EPC defines novelty in absolute (as opposed to local) terms. Thus Article 54 states:

> An invention shall be considered to be new if it does not form part of the state of the art. The state of the art shall be held to comprise everything made available to the public by means of a written or oral description, by use, or in any other way, before the date of filing of the European patent application.

Article 54 diverges from past practice in many European countries (and in the United Kingdom until 1977) where local novelty was the rule. This means that only prior publication or use in the country where the patent was being applied for would destroy novelty. This should be contrasted with the USA, which continues with a mixed novelty rule that recognizes knowledge held abroad but not locally as prior art only if it has been published. Japan had such a mixed novelty rule until 1999.[26]

Article 63 establishes a patent term of 20 years from the filing date. This is repeated in the TRIPS Agreement and is now the global standard. Why 20 years and not, say, 15 or 25 years, and for all industrial sectors? This is an example of political convenience trumping economic logic. When governments undertake to harmonize regulatory standards it may be politically difficult for any of them to accept levels less favourable to powerful interest groups than the present ones. This is especially the case when, as in IP rights, the economic stakes are so high for private industry. The progressive strengthening of domestic IP standards results from the lobbying pressure of interest groups which stand to gain economically the most. Governments will usually find it more politically palatable to raise IP standards than to lower them, since opponents are unlikely to be so well-organized or resourced. Since the minimum patent term in Europe – as apparently elsewhere – was 20 years, it was expedient to choose this term rather than a lower one.

As for the decision to make patent terms equal for all industries, economic rationality also had nothing to do with it. After all, product life cycles within different industrial sectors can vary tremendously. For example, semiconductor products now have an average life cycle of only 12–16 months (Hall and Ham, 1999: 41), which is likely to be a shorter period than the time it takes for a patent to be granted. In the pharmaceutical sector the situation is very different. Aspirin, for example, recently celebrated its centenary, while many other health products may be marketable for several decades. But as Doern explains (1999: 46), interest group politics may not provide the complete explanation either. As he sees it, a standarized term 'would preserve the notion that IP was indeed an area of real framework law which applied across the economies of member states and did not constitute a form of sector-specific "industrial" policy which it would be if many sectoral-based periods of protection were possible'. In a similar vein, Robert Merges argued in a submission to a US Senate Committee that the raison d'être of the patent system would be undermined if the rights granted varied according to specific industries:

> Patents issued every day for devices ranging from the proverbial mousetrap to superconductors and man-made organisms ... In the eyes of the patent system ... all inventors are created equal ... Indeed, it is this equal treatment which distinguishes a true patent *system* from a series of *ad hoc* awards to inventors. (Merges, 1996: 1315)

The TRIPS Agreement

In 1986, the contracting parties to the General Agreement on Tariffs and Trade (GATT) adopted the Punta del Este Declaration, which committed GATT parties to 'clarify GATT provisions' relating to IP rights and counterfeit goods and to 'develop a multilateral framework of principles, rules and disciplines dealing with international trade in counterfeit goods'. By 1989, these limited aspirations had expanded quite considerably as developing countries dropped their earlier resistance to a substantial agreement on IP rights that would form a package of agreement covering various trade issues such as agriculture, textiles and services.

On the face of it, this is puzzling, especially when we consider that several relatively industrialized developing countries had revised their patent systems a decade earlier in order to facilitate imitation by their domestic firms in the interests of strengthening national self-reliance, and were hardly enthusiastic about reversing these reforms (Roffe, 2000: 404–5). Be that as it may – and this is a matter we explore further in Chapter 9 – the TRIPS Agreement is now the key multilateral agreement promoting the harmonization of national IP regimes. Its intent is to guarantee minimum standards rather than to harmonize the substantive laws of patents, copyright and the other IP rights. But the effect of TRIPS will be to make national IP systems more similar to each other.

While the original purpose of an agreement on IP rights at the Uruguay Round was to prevent the trade in counterfeit goods, these two words were deleted from the title of the Agreement. In fact, the resulting agreement turned out to be much more ambitious than this. It also became more ambiguous in its aims. Indeed, the official goals of TRIPS are not at all clear. The preamble affirms the desire of member states 'to tak[e] into account the need to promote effective and adequate protection of intellectual property rights', while 'recognizing the underlying public policy objectives of national systems for the protection of intellectual property, including developmental and technological objectives'. There is little doubt that 'effective' implies enforceable. But whether IP protection is adequate depends largely on what the systems of rights are supposed to achieve. Dealing with counterfeiting is clearly considered important. Its main importance lies in the fact that the trade in counterfeit goods is what makes intellectual property most clearly trade-related. The preamble indicates that members recognize 'the need for a multilateral framework of principles, rules and disciplines dealing with international trade in counterfeit goods', and yet the objectives as stated in Article 7 make no reference to the eradication of counterfeiting. Rather, TRIPS is explicitly aimed at promoting public policy objectives, the nature of such objectives presumably being left to national governments, though technological development is given priority. Article 7 states that the protection and enforcement of intellectual property rights should contribute to the promotion of technological innovation, and to the transfer and dissemination of technology; and be to the mutual advantage of producers and users of technological knowledge, and in a manner conducive to social and economic welfare and to a balance of rights and obligations. The addition of this language was made, not surprisingly, at the insistence of a number of developing countries.

This suggests that TRIPS is intended to stimulate technological advancement, thereby giving greater priority to economic development than to the eradication of the trade in counterfeit goods, which was the original idea of having such an agreement. Better still, it acknowledges the need to strike a balance so that the interests of the public, the producers and the users of technological knowledge are all promoted and in ways that enhance social and economic welfare. In addition, Article 8.1 allows member states implementing their IP regulations to 'adopt measures necessary to protect human health and nutrition, and to promote the public interest in sectors of vital importance to their socio-economic and technological development'. These measures are not obligatory but, again, they highlight the socioeconomic welfare implications of IP rights.

In reality, this rather positive interpretation of the Agreement is probably naïve. This pro-development language is the price developed countries paid to make TRIPS possible, which is otherwise very favourable to their interests. In any case, ensuring that the rights and obligations of these producers and users are well balanced and best support the social, economic and developmental objectives that governments intend their IP laws to pursue is extremely difficult to achieve, particularly considering that much of the data available is inconclusive, and that policy makers must depend on the advice of experts and stakeholders with vested interests that may not really be compatible with such lofty aspirations. Moreover, the proviso that the measures mentioned in Article 8.1 be consistent with the provisions of TRIPS appears to narrow their possible scope quite considerably.

By virtue of Article 3, members accept the principle of national treatment, while Article 4 upholds the principle of most-favoured nation. This means that any concession granted by one member to another must be accorded to all other members 'immediately and unconditionally'. So if country A agrees to take special measures to prevent the copying of the products of a company from country B, but turns a blind eye when the company is from country C, D or E, such inconsistency of treatment will violate this principle. Although this principle of international trade law dates back in history, TRIPS is the first multilateral IP treaty that refers to it.

TRIPS places much emphasis on enforcement. With respect to the general enforcement obligations, procedures must be available that 'permit effective action against any act of infringement of intellectual property rights'. They must be fair, equitable and not unnecessarily complicated, costly or time-consuming. Members are not required to put in place a judicial system for enforcing IP rights separate from that for the enforcement of law in general. Moreover, TRIPS creates no obligation to shift resources away from the enforcement of law in general towards the enforcement of IP rights. Nonetheless, poor countries may face a difficult dilemma when determining how to allocate the scarce resources they have for enforcement. The judicial authorities must be granted the power to require infringers to pay damages adequate to compensate the right holder for the injury suffered as a result of the infringement. Members are required to provide for criminal procedures and penalties 'at least in cases of wilful trademark counterfeiting or copyright piracy on a commercial scale'. Remedies may include imprisonment and/or monetary fines. Such remedies may also be applied in other cases of IP infringement if done 'wilfully and on a commercial scale'.

The developing countries and the former centrally planned socialist states were allowed a period of five years from the date of entry into force of the WTO Agreement to apply the full provisions of TRIPS: 1 January 2000. But developing country members that are required to extend patent protection to areas of technology not hitherto covered in their laws were permitted to delay such extension until 1 January 2005. The least-developed countries were allowed until 1 January 2006 to apply TRIPS in full. However, all countries had to apply the national treatment and most-favoured nation principles by 1996. Countries that have joined the WTO since then are required also to comply with these deadlines.

The most relevant section of TRIPS for this book is the one dealing with patents. According to the first paragraph of Article 27 (Patentable Subject Matter), 'patents shall be available for any inventions, whether products or processes, in all fields of technology, provided that they are new, involve an inventive step and are capable of industrial application'. Paragraph 27.1 also requires that patents be available and patent rights enjoyable 'without discrimination as to the place of invention, the field of technology and whether products are imported or locally produced'. The reference to place of invention required the USA to change its patent system. At the time it was discriminatory against foreign inventions in the sense that US courts at the time did not accept foreign evidence of dates of invention. But the rest of the paragraph is generally very favourable for all high-technology corporations, since they dislike the idea that technological fields can be excluded from patentability and fear the imposition of requirements that patent-protected goods be manufactured in every country they hold patents in.

Certain defined exclusions are allowable, the most significant being in Paragraphs 2 and 3. Paragraph 2 states:

Members may exclude from patentability inventions, the prevention within their territory of the commercial exploitation of which is necessary to protect ordre public or morality, including to protect human, animal or plant life or health or to avoid serious prejudice to the environment, provided that such exclusion is not made merely because the exploitation is prohibited by their law.

The terms 'ordre public' and 'morality' are not defined in TRIPS, although references to human, animal or plant life or health and the environment provide some context. The language of Article 27.2 follows very closely that of the EPC, yet, even in Europe, the true meaning and potential extent of the ordre public/morality exclusions remain unresolved. In French civil law, 'ordre public' has a wider meaning than 'public order' and is more akin to 'public policy'. According to one interpretation, 'although the expression includes "public order" in so far as this relates to, for example, rioting, the expression primarily covers such matters as good government, the administration of justice, public services, national economic policy and the proper conduct of affairs in the general interest of the state and society' (UK Board of Trade, 1970: 68). Accepting this rather broad interpretation of the term appears to give WTO members quite a lot of freedom to exclude inventions they consider to be undesirable. But legal experts tend to assume that TRIPS compatibility requires governments to apply the ordre public and morality exclusions narrowly on a case-by-case basis rather than to broad classes of patents such as life forms in their broadest sense (Moufang, 1998). Otherwise, such patents would have been outlawed by TRIPS or, at the very least, the option to outlaw them would have been explicitly indicated.

Article 27 Paragraph 3 states that members may also exclude from patentability

(a) diagnostic, therapeutic and surgical methods for the treatment of humans or animals;
(b) plants and animals other than micro-organisms, and essentially biological processes for the production of plants or animals other than non-biological and microbiological processes. However, Members shall provide for the protection of plant varieties either by patents or by an effective sui generis system or by any combination thereof.

This means that with respect to *products* plants and animals may be excluded from patentability. As regards *processes* essentially biological processes for the production of plants or animals may also be excluded. But patents *must* be available for microorganisms as *products* and for non-biological and microbiological *processes* for producing plants or animals. Patent protection need not be available for plant varieties but an effective IP system is still obligatory. This may be an UPOV-type plant variety right system, an alternative system yet to be devised, or some combination of systems (see Table 3.1).

Much of the language is difficult and open to conflicting interpretations. For example, it is possible to argue that an application relating to a genetically engineered plant is bound to include plant varieties within its scope whether or not the word 'variety' even appears in the specification. This is important because, in

Table 3.1 Article 27.3(b): a summary of its provisions

WTO members may exclude from patent protection:	WTO members must provide IP protection for:
Plants	Microorganisms (by patents)
Animals	Non-biological processes (by patents)
Essentially biological processes for the production of plants or animals	Microbiological processes (by patents)
Plant varieties	Plant varieties (by an IP system which may be patents, a sui generis alternative, or a combination)

some jurisdictions, plants can be patented but plant varieties cannot. In others, neither can, but there may be a separate IP system exclusively for plant varieties. Even terms like 'microorganism' can be interpreted differently from one legal jurisdiction to another. According to the EPO, for example, 'microorganism' 'includes not only bacteria and yeasts, but also fungi, algae, protozoa and human, animal and plant cells, i.e. all generally unicellular organisms with dimensions beneath the limits of vision which can be propagated and manipulated in a laboratory. Plasmids and viruses are also considered to fall under this definition'. Similarly, the Japan Patent Office interprets 'microorganism' to include 'yeasts, moulds, mushrooms, bacteria, actinomycetes, unicellular algae, viruses, protozoa, etc.' and also 'undifferentiated animal or plant cells as well as animal or plant tissue cultures' (JPO, 2000: 17). These definitions seem rather overexpansive from a strictly scientific point of view. It is not at all obvious that a single cell from a multicellular organism is itself an organism even if it has been cultured in a laboratory. In view of the economic stakes involved, one can expect some creative interpretations of legal texts like TRIPS from lawyers representing or favouring business interests. For example, according to Josef Straus of the Max-Planck Institute for Foreign and International Patent, Copyright and Competition Law and AIPPI (1998:109), 'if micro-organisms are mandatorily declared subject matter eligible for patent protection, naturally occurring biochemical substances, such as sequences of nucleotides (DNA), per argumentum a maiore ad minus are also to be regarded as subject matter, for which WTO Members have to offer product patent protection'. He therefore links the stated obligation to protect microorganisms to an unstated requirement to extend protection to DNA sequences, as if the latter falls within the scope of the former. This link does not seem very logical or, for that matter, scientific.

Patent Regulation: a Moving Target

Before looking more closely into the dynamics of patent evolution, which we will do in the next few chapters, a few points are worth making. First, over the last 120 years patent rights have gradually been strengthened and have come to embrace new kinds of subject matter. These trends became especially marked from the 1960s. Second, governments and businesses must surely have shifted their positions on IP rights quite radically for such changes to have taken place. As we saw, the initial position of Geigy was that patents are for parasites. Certainly, no successful European chemical or pharmaceutical firm would hold this view today. After all, Novartis, a descendant corporation of Geigy, is an active promoter of strong IP rights throughout the world. Third, patents are juridical and regulatory artefacts that originated in the West, and, as patent law evolved, the European and North American countries pioneered virtually all the reforms that were then adopted internationally. Fourth, developing countries initially preferred to continue with relatively weak patent regimes providing low levels of protection and enforcement, but, in the 1990s, most of them reluctantly agreed to match the high standards of the developed countries. This reluctance and their minimal influence in shaping the evolution of patent standards make it reasonable to doubt that many of these new standards are appropriate for them.

Notes

1   Cited in Machlup and Penrose (1950: 1).
2   As with the United States today.
3   Although this was from grant rather than the date of filing the application.
4   These dates should be treated with caution. Historians disagree about the starting dates, ending dates and duration of the British industrial revolution.
5   Other European countries which experienced early industrialization characterized by technological advancement in the eighteenth century include Holland (textile finishing and shipbuilding), Germany, Switzerland and Spain (calico printing) and Italy (silk throwing) (Berg and Bruland, 1998: 12).
6   See Charles Dickens' 'Poor Man's Tale of a Patent'. The unfortunate protagonist cites a friend of his whose time-consuming and expensive efforts to acquire a patent led him to conclude despairingly 'that the whole gang of Hanapers and Chaffwaxes must be done away with, and that England has been chaffed and waxed sufficient'.
7   The two best known advocates of 'infant industry' protectionism during this time were the American Alexander Hamilton and the German Friedrich List. Hamilton, the first US Treasury Secretary, was the more influential in that he was directly engaged in policy making, whereas List probably did not greatly affect government economic policy anywhere, with the possible exception of Russia (von Tunzelmann, 1995: 171). On the other hand, he may have been one of the main inspirations for the German system of technical education which became highly advanced in the nineteenth century and remains so today (Freeman and Soete, 1997: 297). Hamilton's firm belief in the need for

protective tariffs, subsidies and import substitution industrialization was to some extent implemented in the USA in the early years of the republic, especially from 1828 to 1833. List died 25 years before the formation of the German Empire. Even so, the new Empire's economic and political nationalism influenced its trade policies in ways that were fairly consistent with List's ideas.

8   From 1848 a number of attempts to enact patent legislation were rejected on the basis that patents would interfere with free trade and thus be unconstitutional (Haber, 1958: 203). Geigy supported the 1888 patent law since it excluded chemical substances and processes.

9   This statement contrasts sharply with that of John Duessing, a more recent representative of the company, who in 1989 stated that 'it is Ciba-Geigy's position that legal protection of intellectual property serves the public interest by stimulating continuing investment in technological innovation' (Duessing, 1989: 22).

10 Though, as we have seen, patent laws were most commonly regarded by legislatures and judiciaries as public policy instruments.

11 This view did not, apparently, extend to copyright over foreign works. In 1837, 'Henry Clay, a senator from Kentucky, presented a petition by 56 British authors arguing for recognition of their literary property rights. The petition, which alleged that authors had "suffered from injury in their reputation and property", was met by stern defence of America's utilitarian approach to copyright.' Claims that the widespread copying of foreign works 'furthered dissemination of the Enlightenment often appeared alongside less principled arguments that the American publishing industry, which employed an estimated 200,000 people, would lose a significant amount of business if foreign books were granted copyright protection' (Burkitt, 2001: 156–7).

12 'Germany received its first genuine recognition as an industrial nation at the Paris exhibition of 1867' (Wegner, 1993: 17).

13 Romania, Holland, Italy, Sweden, Prussia, Greece, Switzerland, Brazil, the USA, Wurtemburg and Britain were officially represented (Coulter, 1991: 175).

14 Ecuador, El Salvador and Guatemala left the Union in 1886, 1887 and 1895, respectively.

15 Having made this point, though, Germany still did not feel secure enough to join the Union until it had become a serious rival to Britain as an industrial power.

16 On the other hand, a few developing countries acted in the reverse direction. For example, in the late 1960s and early 1970s, Brazil and India passed laws to exclude pharmaceuticals as such from patentability (as well as processes to manufacture them, in Brazil's case).

17 On China, see Alford (1993).

18 For example, according to Stephen Ladas (at one time a chairman of the International Chamber of Commerce's Commission on International Protection of Industrial Property), at the fourth revision conference in London in 1934, 'as usual the International Bureau, in cooperation with the British government, prepared the work of the Conference on the basis of resolutions adopted by non-governmental organizations, such as particularly the International Association for the Protection of Industrial Property and the International Chamber of Commerce' (Ladas, 1975: 83).

19 The ICC was founded in 1921 and immediately established a permanent Commission for the International Protection of Industrial Property.

20 However, they had one major success in the field of copyright law, securing the adoption of the 1967 Stockholm Protocol to the Berne Convention (Braithwaite and Drahos, 2000: 61).

21   The resolution ('patentability of chemical products') stated that

the Conference,

Considering that in order to promote technical progress, inventions much be protected to the greatest possible extent,

Recommends that the member countries of the Union study the possibility of providing, in their national legislations, for the protection by patents of new chemical products, independently of their manufacturing process, with such limitations and conditions as may seem advisable. (Quoted in BIRPI, 1958: 313)

22   The adoption of the European Patent Convention diminished the relevance of this Convention, which only gathered enough state parties to enter into force in 1980, by which time it was redundant.

23   As Chapter 6 shows, this actually happened.

24   Of course, harmonization would result as well. This is because national patent systems would have to be consistent with the substantive provisions and principles of the Convention.

25   The other organ set up by the convention is the Administrative Council, which consists of representatives of all contracting parties (usually the heads of the national patent offices).

26   This provision has become highly controversial. Developing countries and indigenous groups claim that it supports the misappropriation of traditional knowledge, which they refer to as 'biopiracy' (see Chapter 9). The concern is that a patent claiming such undocumented foreign knowledge could not be challenged for lack of novelty. The only means left to those seeking to overturn the patent would be to prove that the owner was not the actual inventor of the subject matter claimed by the patent holder.

Chapter 4

Organic Chemistry and the Synthetic Dyestuff Industry

The first men to bring their expertise in the manufacture of synthetic dyes to Basel were French. They carried their knowledge into neighbouring countries. They soon arrived in large numbers, fleeing the unusual situation in France. Their contemporaries compared this to the Revocation of the Edict of Nantes as if they were fleeing religious persecution, escaping the orthodox religion ordered by the government. The knowledge those Huguenots imported proved to be of economic advantage to the adjacent countries; this time, however, the refugees were fleeing the dictates of the French patent law. (Christian Simon, 1998)[1]

From Aniline to Indigo

From the 1820s onwards, impressive advances were made in Europe in the discovery, isolation and elucidation of organic compounds. One of the effects of the rapid accumulation and dissemination of this knowledge was that, while 'in the 1850s manufacture had been empirical – by the end of the next decade it was becoming scientific' (Haber, 1958: 81). These advances spawned a new industry, that of synthetic dyestuffs, which evolved rapidly from the 1860s onwards. Behind this rapid evolution were advances, trends and new research priorities in pure chemistry, fashion and medicine, and the need to dispose of coal tar, an industrial waste product that was produced in high volumes during this age (Stolz and Schwaiberger, 1987). While the scientific advances of the time made this new industry possible, its initial attractiveness as a potentially profitable business was due to the high demand for new colours, especially in French high society. But its beginnings were to some extent serendipitous.

According to most accounts,[2] the industry dates back to 1856, when William Perkin, a young British student, accidentally created one of the first coal tar dyes, aniline purple, while attempting but failing to synthesize quinine. Soon after, Perkin patented his discovery in Britain and formed a company to commercialize it.

The aniline dyes, which were derived from benzene, were the first generation of the coal tar dyes. The most commercially important aniline dye was aniline red, otherwise known as fuchsine or magenta, invented by Françoise Verguin. The French firm Renard Frères patented fuchsine in 1859 in both France and Britain.

Apart from being a lucrative product in itself – it is still on the market – fuchsine is an intermediate for making many other dyes. During the 1850s and early 1860s, other companies in Britain and France developed a growing number of new products and processes. At the same time, significant breakthroughs in elucidating the chemical structures of the coal tar derivatives were being made in industry and academia, not just in these two countries, but also in Germany.

The second generation of synthetic dyes were the azos. The first ones, Manchester Yellow and Manchester Brown, were discovered in 1864 by two German chemists, working at the time for British firms, Heinrich Caro and Carl Martius. Within 40 years, more than 50 per cent of the commercial dye products were azos (Haber, 1958: 83).

The third generation of synthetic dyes appeared in 1869 with the synthesis of the natural dye, alizarin. A year previously, two German academic scientists, Carl Graebe and Carl Liebermann, developed a formula to synthesize alizarin. After they patented their discovery a race began to find a way to produce it on a commercial scale. Caro, who had moved to the new German firm Badische Anilin- & Soda-Fabrik AG (BASF), developed a promising process and filed a patent jointly with Graebe and Liebermann in Britain just one day before Perkin, who had come up with a very similar process. The alizarin phase was very important for a number of reasons. In the context of this book, perhaps the most important is that, unlike the anilines and azos, the commercialization of synthetic alizarin actually substituted for a natural product, madder.

The fourth stage in the evolution of the synthetic dyestuff industry arrived with the manufacture and successful commercialization of synthetic indigo. This achievement was especially important. It required an unprecedented commitment to in-house research and development, which turned out to be one of the defining features of the second industrial revolution. More specifically, it stimulated the development of the twentieth-century fine chemical and pharmaceutical industries. It also ensured the dominance of German firms in various chemical product markets.

The French dyestuff industry dominated the aniline phase, while the early part of the azo phase marked the leadership of the British firms (Bensaude-Vincent and Stengers, 1996: 183). So by the mid-1860s Britain was pre-eminent, with France in second place. There did not appear to be any serious rivals at the time, but from the beginning of the alizarin phase, the German industry rapidly achieved almost absolute dominance. The following sections will seek explanations, among other factors, in the patent laws of the various European countries. In turn, they will analyse these patent laws through the new institutionalist approach. The intention is to see how far interest group activism explains the introduction of provisions that were beneficial for the dyestuff industry and the persistence, removal or modification of those which were not.

The Rise of Germany and Switzerland

Germany

In 1862, August Hofmann, the London-based German scientist who had trained Perkin, expressed firm confidence that Britain would be the leading synthetic dyestuff producer for many years to come because of its coal reserves, its huge production of coal tar and its enormous market for textiles (Murmann and Landau, 1998: 30). He was wrong. By 1913, German companies had captured 85 per cent of the global market for dyestuffs. Switzerland, the only other major exporter was in second place albeit with a mere 10 per cent. Germany was equally dominant in the pharmaceutical sector.

The rise of Germany from the 1870s as a major industrial power with its dominant chemical and pharmaceutical industries can be attributed to at least three main factors. These are government investment in education and training, in-house research and development and company/academic collaborations, and government industrial and trade policy.

The Prussian government provided a great deal of support for scientific and technical education and training throughout the nineteenth century (Freeman and Soete, 1997: 297; Murmann and Landau, 1998: 36–7). As well as introducing mass primary education from the late eighteenth century, Germany established the world's foremost higher education system. Its research universities educated large numbers of organic chemistry students. During the middle of the century some highly talented graduates moved to Britain and carried out research that was of enormous benefit to the British chemical industry. When chemists like Hofmann, Caro, Martius and Witt returned to Germany during the 1860s[3] they helped to turn the new firms from imitators into the most innovative chemical companies in the world in less than two decades.

Concerning the second factor, new German firms like Bayer, Hoechst (both founded in 1863), BASF (1865) and AGFA (1867) were established to copy French and German dyes, and were able to do so because there was no single patent law covering all the pre-unification German states. For foreign firms, the only alternative was to file patents in each of the different states that had patent laws at the time. Since this was troublesome, they often did not bother to file in any state.

Nonetheless, the main German dyestuff firms decided early on both to invest in research and development and to collaborate with university researchers. Thus the role of the inventor–entrepreneur was superseded by the advent of professional research and development departments (Freeman and Soete, 1997: 106; Homburg, 1992; Meyer-Thurow, 1982) in which teams of scientists collaborated to solve technical problems. 'It was the German dyestuff industry which first realized that it could be profitable to put the business of research for new products and development of new chemical processes on a more regular, systematic and professional basis' (Freeman and Soete, 1997: 299).

The huge profits from products like alizarin based on highly advanced new processes helped companies to expand and to invest in even more expensive research and development such as the synthesis of indigo and the early twentieth-century development of a process for producing ammonia from atmospheric nitrogen (the Haber–Bosch process). Academic researchers were often invited to collaborate with company chemists or hired as consultants (Johnson, 1992).

Turning to government industrial and trade policy, despite the political dominance of the Prussian Junkers (the land-owning elite) during the early years, the new German state identified the national interest with the success of its emerging industrial sector and decided actively to support it. Consequently, while 'the British industrial revolution was more or less carried out by the hands of private individuals ... Germany's entry into the industrial era was orchestrated by government bureaucracies' (Murmann and Landau, 1998: 40). Not only did the government actively seek to create a healthy climate for companies to flourish, such as by protecting them from foreign competition, it took a permissive if not supportive stance towards cooperative inter-firm alliances to fix prices and rationalize sales networks (ibid.: 32). Such industrial cooperation also spurred the formation of trade associations by companies to further their common interests. For example, the chemical industry set up such an association to promote the intellectual property interests of its members (ibid.: 40). The eminent business historian, Alfred Chandler, has appropriately referred to this system as 'cooperative managerial capitalism' (1990).

Switzerland

Switzerland, like Germany, experienced rapid growth in its chemicals sector during this period. Many of the first synthetic dye chemists in Switzerland were actually French chemists and entrepreneurs who had relocated to Basle, a city with long-established textile and dye-making industries (Simon, 1998: 17–18). Like Germany, academy–industry collaborations encouraged by government were crucial to the enhancement of scientific and technological capabilities (ibid.: 13), while close relationships between companies and financial institutions allowed businesses to secure credit necessary to expand their research and development capabilities. The Swiss firms began by manufacturing such bulk dye products as fuchsine and alizarin but soon found themselves unable to compete with the German firms, which were the main suppliers of their intermediates and base products (Haber, 1958: 119–20). In response, firms like Ciba, Geigy and Sandoz shifted their production to high-quality dyes and pharmaceuticals mostly for export. This strategy was so successful that, by the 1890s, Switzerland was already the world's second biggest dyestuff producer.

Patents, Dyestuffs and the European Chemical Industries

If we accept that the advance of globally competitive domestic high-technology firms is likely to be beneficial for a country,[4] as the decline of such firms is probably disadvantageous, we have to conclude that Germany and Switzerland gained from the success of their chemical firms at the expense of France and Britain. If it is true that their respective patent systems helped determine whether countries were 'winners' or 'losers', they clearly had implications – positive or negative – for the public interest. In fact, there is little doubt that the patent systems of each country, including the fact that they were so different, played a major role in determining the outcome of the race for supremacy in the global dyestuffs market and later in the pharmaceuticals sectors as well.

Germany

The development of German patent law in the late nineteenth century was very much driven by interest groups. Although German industrialists had limited involvement in party politics, they 'were represented in politics through extraparliamentary lobbying channels. An elaborate system of well-organized and well-financed employers' associations acted as very effective mouthpieces for their interests' (Horstmeyer, 1998: 245).

The German Chemical Association (Deutsche Chemische Gessellschaft) was founded in 1867 under the presidency of Hofmann, and consisted of academic scientists and private sector chemists and businessmen. Its aim was to stimulate academic–industrial collaboration (Johnson, 1992: 173). The Association strongly favoured a patent law and sought to convince Bismarck of the need for such legislation. Without a countrywide patent system barriers to entry were low, enabling many new chemical firms to spring up in the early 1870s. But, with the economic recession that began in 1873, many small firms went bankrupt and the chemical industry consolidated so that the market became dominated by a few large firms. Many of these surviving businesses saw a need for a patent law to protect their innovations (ibid.: 175). So in 1874 a group of high-technology firms jointly set up a pressure group called the Deutsche Patentschutz-Verein (German Society for Patent Protection) to lobby for a patent law that would benefit German industry. Werner Siemens was the president. Martius represented the interests of the synthetic dyestuff industry on the organization's board, which also included Hofmann.

Within German industry as a whole there were a number of conflicting views. While the Society of German Engineers lobbied in favour of a patent law, there were still differences about the kind of patent law needed. Siemens, who was one of the most powerful industrialists of the time, was gravely concerned that rival British and American firms would take out many patents for inventions that they would not work in Germany, and which would severely restrict the research and commercial opportunities of German companies (Kronstein and Till, 1947: 773–4).

The chemical industry was also divided. Some firms (for example, BASF) favoured a patent law which protected processes but not products, and were thus unhappy that the first draft of the patent law would have provided protection of chemical products as such. They argued that this created no incentive to improve production processes (Johnson, 1992: 175). On the other hand, the co-founder of Hoechst,[5] Adolf Brüning, wanted the chemical industry to be completely excluded from the patent system (Kronstein and Till, 1947: 774). His view was that the French and British chemical industries had been harmed because the laws there had allowed excessively strong monopoly protection for intermediate products, whereas – as he saw it – the lack of a German patent law had allowed the chemical industry to expand. Although the synthetic dyestuff firms had not completely reached a consensus, the board of the Chemical Association submitted a petition to the Reichstag which argued in favour of patents for methods of manufacturing chemical products but not the products themselves. The stated grounds were that 'a chemical product can be obtained by various methods and from different starting materials; the grant of a patent for the product itself would prevent better processes discovered subsequently from being brought into effect in the interest of the public and of the inventors' (Bercovitz-Rodriguez, 1990: 6). In the event, the Chemical Association's position was heeded and adopted by virtue of Section 1 of the 1877 Patent Law, according to which

> Patents are granted for new inventions which permit of an industrial realization. The exceptions are: ... 2. Inventions of articles of food, drinks and medicine as well as of substances manufactured by a chemical process in so far as the inventions do not relate to a certain process for manufacturing such articles.

The language is somewhat vague but implies that, while processes alone could be patented, chemical products could only be protected if manufactured by a specific process and by no other. Since the interpretation of the courts (until 1888) was that sale of a chemical made through a patented process did not constitute infringement (Grubb, 1999: 23), chemical products were effectively excluded. While this provision encouraged chemists to be creative and devise original processes, it also encouraged anti-competitive 'blocking patents' intended to close off broad areas of research from competitors (Haber, 1958: 203). Another noteworthy provision, which also appears to have reflected the interests of many German firms, was Section 11, according to which a patent could be withdrawn after three years, either

> if the patentee neglects to work his invention in the Country to an adequate extent or to do all that was requisite for securing the said working; [or] when it appears conducive to the public interest that permission to use the invention be granted to others and the patentee refuses to grant such permission for a suitable compensation and on good security.

A third provision of great importance to the chemical industry was the publication of patent applications and awarded patents, ensuring the rapid dissemination of state-of-the-art knowledge. It had already become evident that keeping chemical processes secret provided no more than a few months' protection (Hornix, 1992: 90), so the industry as a whole probably saw publication as being advantageous. In fact, dissemination of technical information has from as far back as the late eighteenth century been considered to be one of its most important functions (see Merges, 1997: 657), and for Germany it was a key objective. Similarly, the Japanese patent system has over the years treated dissemination as being at least as important as rewarding invention, on the basis that the circulation of knowledge accelerates the rate of further invention.

A fourth feature of the law that served the interests of the larger research-based companies (for reasons we will soon come to) was the exclusion of all mention of 'inventors'. The right holders were 'applicants'. This was justified by the argument propounded by these firms that modern inventions were collectively achieved and depended primarily on capital investment in laboratories, equipment and skilled employees (Gispen, 1989: 265).[6]

Most historians of the European synthetic dyestuff industries with a view on the matter (for example, Homburg, 1992: 110; Johnson, 1992: 176) agree that the 1877 patent law had a positive effect overall, encouraging the establishment of research and development departments in all the major firms. The availability of protection for chemical processes but not products reflected the prevalent commercial and research strategies of the German firms at that time. They soon realized that chemical dyes were not only products, but were also likely to be intermediates for other products. Therefore patenting dyes directly could have inhibited the kinds of innovation that allowed German firms to compete with their British counterparts. Process innovation was all-important for them because, whereas British firms with the advantage of a huge market for textiles were mostly interested in creating as many new products as possible, the concern of German firms was to develop processes enabling them to improve efficiency and cut costs while also meeting the requirements of the dyers for the widest possible range of colours for all fabrics. But they soon found they could achieve cost efficiencies best by putting on the market a massive range of colours for all fabrics, using the same production equipment to create them. Emphasizing process innovation as a research strategy and product diversity as a marketing strategy resulted in the cost-effective generation of an extraordinarily large range of new and relatively inexpensive products. On the eve of the First World War, Bayer had 2000 different dyestuffs (Wengenroth, 1997: 143) while Hoechst made as many as 10 000 (Murmann and Landau, 1998: 31). The development of such huge product portfolios was not demand-driven, but with them the big three German firms 'had a firm grip on every conceivable composition of hydrocarbons, *firmly shielded by a wall of patents and tacit knowledge*' (Wengenroth, 1997: 144; emphasis added).

Allegedly, this grip was strengthened by submitting patent specifications that not only failed to disclose sufficient information to repeat the invention, but also included deliberate mistakes.[7] According to William Pope, a Cambridge University chemistry professor writing in 1917,

> The Bayer Company, like the other German fine chemical firms, holds many thousands of carefully drawn patents ... it must be understood that many of these patents are bogus, that is to say, contain deliberate misstatements for the purpose of misleading inquiring minds as to the manner in which important products are manufactured by the firm. In fact, some German patents are drawn for the purpose of discouraging investigation by more practical methods; thus, any one who attempted to repeat the method of manufacturing a dye stuff protected by Salzmann and Krüger in the German Patent No. 12096 would be pretty certain to kill himself during the operation. (Pope, 1917: 18)

On the other hand, the development of the azo dyes rendered inadequate, from the position of industry, the German patent law's provisions concerning chemical processes, and is a useful case study illustrating how extending patent law to chemicals entails some unavoidable complexities. It is useful to look at this situation and see how the regulatory system responded to it in the context of three reasons why innovation in the field of industrial chemistry, particularly during its early stages, challenged the patent system in hitherto unforeseen ways.

The first reason has do with the danger that broad patent protection can stifle innovation in new industries where the learning curve is particularly steep. The dyestuff industry was a case in point. During its infancy, some of the most innovative activity centred on *existing* chemical substances. This was, first, because compounds may have many uses that would have been inconceivable to the original discoverer or manufacturer of the compound. For example, research on some of the dyestuffs revealed that they also had pharmaceutical properties. Second, it was likely that ways would soon be found to manufacture the substance in a more efficient and cost-effective way than its original inventor had managed to do. Third, the substance might have turned out to be an intermediate for the manufacture of a large number of other useful substances which individually could have required minimal additional effort, expense or inventiveness to discover. For these three reasons, allowing chemical substances to be patented may have fatally discouraged innovation by allowing excessively strong monopolies. This explains why the German chemical industry lobbied against product patents on chemicals in the 1870s. That this situation has changed in more recent times explains why the trend in Europe since the Second World War has been to allow patents for chemical products.

The second major difficulty, and this is particularly relevant to the azo dyes, is that a whole family of compounds may share the same useful characteristic. Thus the application of a chemical process may generate large numbers of related substances producing the same effect. How broadly should patent applicants be allowed to extend their claims? Should it be allowable only to patent a process for one and only one substance? Or should it be possible to go to the other extreme, casting the net as widely as possible to claim as many classes of related substances as is theoretically conceivable 'besides the substances actually used in the "invented" process' (van den Belt and Rip, 1989: 152)? The dilemma is that protection could be so inadequate as to be worthless, or so strong as to inhibit innovation. Striking the right balance between rewarding inventors adequately without hindering follow-on innovators is never easy. But patent offices, courts and legislators had no prior experience and had to wait until problems arose and then figure out how to deal with them. For example, in 1887, the German Patent Office decided it had to respond to the proliferation of chemical patent applications claiming not just the actual substances used in the process that was the subject of the application, but also various classes of analogue, homologue and isomer.[8] It did so by introducing a new regulation requiring chemical patent applicants to provide samples of all substances claimed in the application (van den Belt and Rip, 1989: 152). But the court case described in the next paragraph provided a more definitive solution that was also preferred by the industry.

The third problem is that the patent doctrines of the period had been formulated with mechanical inventions in mind, and not chemical processes.[9] Therefore difficulties were bound to appear. In the case of azo dyes, an important issue that soon arose was that of whether or to what extent it should be considered inventive to apply a known process to manufacture a new dye. The problem was not resolved until an 1889 Supreme Court case relating to the Congo Red dye. Caro acted as an expert witness, but it was the intervention of Carl Duisberg, later to oversee the development of Bayer's massive research and development structure, that proved to be especially decisive. The outcome was the formulation by the court of a doctrine called 'the new technical effect', which allowed priority in certain cases to be given to industrial applicability over true inventiveness. According to Duisberg, adoption by the courts of this new principle saved the azo dye industry. But the court's decision was much more important even than this. First, it enabled the bigger firms to amass large patent holdings for inventions based on their organized large-scale research programmes. In consequence it became economically more feasible for chemical firms to invest in organized large-scale in-house research and development. Second, it was a key stage in a gradual change in perception shared by industry, the patent office and the courts from one that treated inventorship as an individual activity inspired – so it was often said – by flashes of genius, to one that considered it as a collective and routinized corporate endeavour.

For industry there were two advantages. First, companies sought to accumulate massive patent holdings in order to block research by rival companies and dominate markets. Having to demonstrate a genuine flash of genius – that is to say, a significant inventive step – would have made this strategy more difficult. Second, companies preferred to hire inventors and make them assign their inventions to their employers rather than to have to compete with them or at least to have to pay them financial compensation (Meyer-Thurow, 1982: 378–9). Treating inventorship as a collective activity placed each scientist in a more subordinate position than would have been the case otherwise. Thus it was not necessarily advantageous for corporations in Germany or elsewhere to extol the genius of the 'inventor-heroes' when promoting their IP interests.[10] Similarly, if we briefly change century and continent, Charles Kettering of General Motors commented in 1941 – it must be said erroneously and perhaps dishonestly – that 'a one-man invention isn't very possible these days', and argued that it would be unfair to reward individuals for what were basically collective endeavours (quoted in Owens, 1991: 1081). Kettering's comment may well have been inspired by a controversial US Supreme Court judgment that same year,[11] which denied the patentability of a mechanical device on the grounds that the inventor's skill had not 'reached the level of inventive genius which the Constitution authorizes Congress to award'.[12]

In 1877, another chemical industry lobby group, the Verein zur Wahrung der Interessen der chemischen Industrie Deutschlands (Society for Safeguarding the Interests of the German Chemical Industry), was founded to influence the government, including its trade policy and patent regulation (Johnson, 1992: 177). In the event, German law was reformed in 1891 to incorporate the new technical effect doctrine and statutorily recognize another Supreme Court decision in 1888 that sale of a chemical made through a patented process infringed the patent. The latter change benefited the German chemical industry by preventing Swiss firms from exporting such chemicals to Germany. The prohibition on the patenting of chemical substances as such remained. This was in accordance with the demands of the Society, which held that 'such comprehensive protection has ... always been considered by the German chemical industry as an obstacle prejudicial to the discovery of new and improved processes' (in Bercovitz-Rodriguez, 1990: 6). All of this makes evident, to borrow the words of two recent commentators, that 'the interface between the German chemical industry and the government was well-developed in the last quarter of the nineteenth century, allowing such important collective policy initiatives as the passage of a patent law to be especially tailored to the needs of the chemical industry' (Murmann and Landau, 1998: 66).

Finally, it is worth mentioning here that the German companies' attempts to use patents to exclude competitors in foreign markets were assisted greatly if they could acquire protection of chemical substances, and not just of processes. So their control was particularly strong in Britain and the USA, where both kinds of protection were available. A 1912 United States Tariff Board study found that as many as '98 per cent of applications for patents in the chemical field had been assigned to German firms and were never worked in the United States' (quoted in Noble, 1977: 16). Complaints about this situation prompted the drafting of several patent reform bills in the early twentieth century to abolish product protection, and to require the working of patents. These were opposed by other interest groups representing more successful – and influential – American industries, patent lawyers and prominent entrepreneurs like Thomas Edison and Leo Baekeland, the inventor of Bakelite (ibid.: 105–8).

Switzerland

The Swiss chemical industry was at least to some extent a child of the French patent law. While such dramatic statements as the one used to begin this chapter may be exaggerated (Farrar, 1974), the combination of the French patent law and the absence of a domestic one undoubtedly provided a huge impetus to the incipient Swiss dyestuff industry from which the country's chemical and pharmaceutical sectors have benefited to this day.

The Swiss chemical industry first opposed the patent system, but when it became inevitable that there would be one[13] it demanded to be kept outside the system (Penrose, 1951: 17). The companies justified this position with the argument that patent law cannot accommodate the complexities of innovation in the field of chemistry and is therefore inappropriate. But they were mainly concerned that they would be left vulnerable to their German competitors. While the second concern was understandable, the first was somewhat hypocritical, given that some Swiss chemical firms were becoming very active users of other countries' patent systems. In consequence of such opposition, the 1888 patent law required inventions to be demonstrated by a model, thus effectively excluding chemical substances and processes from patentability. It also provided compulsory working and licensing (ibid.: 123). This prohibition on chemical process patents continued until 1907, when Switzerland finally bowed to German pressure. Such pressure was effective owing to the dependence of natural resource-poor Switzerland's chemical industry on the German market (which was its biggest) and on German chemical firms for supplies of coal tar distillates and other chemicals needed to produce the dyes (Haber, 1958: 119). The ban on product protection continued for several more decades, though.

Britain

Unlike the case of Germany and Switzerland, the British dyestuff industry inherited an ancient patent system which, in spite of some reforms during the nineteenth century, failed to meet its requirements. The 1852 Patent Law Amendment Act had been passed four years prior to Perkin's great discovery, but apparently without any consideration of chemical inventions. It took several years for the courts to establish rules for interpreting claims in chemicals and in the meantime litigation was a frequent and very serious distraction for many companies (Travis, 1993: 43). Compared to their German counterparts, the dyestuff firms were slow to form an industry-wide interest group to pursue their interests (Murmann and Landau, 1998: 40) and it took a long time for the government to take account of their needs. With its huge textile industry, Britain was the world's biggest market for dyes, and German companies had filed many patents there even before their country had its own unified patent law.

In later years, the British firms had to contend with ever-increasing numbers of patents by German companies that were adept at strategic patenting. In doing so, they effectively blocked many potentially lucrative research and development possibilities (Haber, 1958: 200; Wengenroth, 1997: 144), thereby using the law to stifle innovation in Britain at the same time as they were helping to develop an innovation-friendly patent law in their own country. Concerns about this situation were raised in the House of Commons in April 1883,[14] and again at various times in the early part of the following century. The Act passed that same year allayed them by providing for compulsory licensing in certain cases including failure to work the patent in the UK. Unfortunately, this provision was difficult to put into practice and failed to make the British firms any more competitive.

At the turn of the century, the government established a committee chaired by Sir Edward Fry to investigate the working of the patent system. Patent agents, inventors and businessmen were among those giving evidence. The dyestuff industry was represented by Ivan Levinstein, a German-born industrialist from Manchester, and a passionate and dedicated activist for patent reform. Invited to be as radical as he wished by the Master of the Rolls, Lord Alverstone, he proposed that, 'if the department [that is, the Board of Trade] is anxious to bring back an important industry which we have almost lost in this country, principally through our patent laws, then we ought to follow the example of France and Germany and say that a patentee must manufacture the patented article in the country within a certain time, otherwise the patent may be revoked' (UK Board of Trade, 1901). In response to the Committee's Report, the patent law was amended in 1902 in a way which allowed for the possibility of revocation in the case of non-working.

In part it was the threat to the Indian indigo trade posed by imports of BASF and Hoechst's patent-protected synthetic indigo, a matter that Levinstein had been wise enough to stress, that convinced the government of the need to reform the patent system. This is hardly surprising given that 'the indigo trade was important to the Empire, unlike azo dyes that had little or no impact on natives, planters, traders, the stock market and other vested interests' (Reed, 1992: 117). The other big issue, mentioned above, was the way that German chemical firms were said to be flooding the country with unworked blocking patents. Their British rivals complained about this situation, as did their parliamentary allies. Undoubtedly, the German firms were patenting on a huge scale compared to their British counterparts and a large proportion of these patents were never worked (see Table 4.1).

But the amendment act was a very watered down version of what Levinstein had proposed and made little if any difference. By this time the German dyestuff producers had achieved such economies of scale that they could reduce prices to undercut their domestic competitors and still make a profit. However, Levinstein was persistent and managed to impress David Lloyd George, President of the Board of Trade (and future Prime Minister), with his views (ibid.: 118). In 1907, Lloyd George introduced new legislation with strengthened revocation provisions intended to put stronger pressure on the German synthetic dyestuff makers to work their patents in Britain. The 'Act to consolidate the enactments relating to Patents for Inventions and the Registration of Designs and certain enactments relating to Trade Marks', which was partly modelled on its counterpart German legislation, successfully induced the main German dyestuff companies to set up factories in Britain to manufacture their patented dyes as well as drugs like Salvarsan and Novocain. Even so, it was not until after the First World War that the government took a strategic approach towards the development and regulation of its key high-technology industries such as organic chemicals and pharmaceuticals (see Chapter 5).

Table 4.1   Comparison of the number of completed English patents for coal tar products taken during 1886–1900, by six largest English and six largest German firms

German firms		English firms	
Badische Aniline Works (BASF)	179	Brooke, Simpson & Spiller	7
Meister, Lucius & Brüning (Hoechst)	231	Clayton Aniline Co.	21
Farbfabriken Bayer & Co.	306	Levinstein	19
Berlin Aniline Co.	119	Read Holliday & Co.	28
L. Cassella & Co.	75	Claus & Rèe	9
Farbwerk Mühlheim, Leonhardt & Co.	38	W. G. Thompson	2
Total	948	Total	86

Source: Green (1950 [1901]).

France

As mentioned before, the French patent system allowed patent scope to be construed very broadly so that process patents included the resulting product and a patented product would embrace all possible methods of manufacturing it. In addition, the law required patented inventions to be worked. Both features turned out to have perverse consequences.

Soon after Renard Frères patented fuchsine in 1859, the company asserted its monopoly position by taking alleged infringers to court. In 1863, Renard Frères successfully sued a rival firm, Monnet et Dury, which was making fuchsine by a different process (Haber, 1958: 112). With such a strong monopoly position over what was not only a product but a key intermediate for other dyes, the firm transformed itself into a much larger company, the Société la Fuchsine. Instead of diversifying its product range and improving its manufacturing processes it concentrated on asserting its monopoly position by charging high prices and suing infringers (Aftalion, 1991: 39). The result was that many dye chemists and even some dyestuff firms relocated abroad, some of those that remained reverted to production of natural dyes, and smuggling of dyes from Germany and Switzerland increased (van den Belt, 1992: 62). The Société, which evidently had no incentive to be innovative, declined and went bankrupt in 1868.

The French patent law cannot be blamed for the demise of the French dyestuff industry, which did not completely disappear anyway. But the patent law did not reflect the fact that rapid innovation during these early stages in the development of the industry meant that enabling strong monopoly protection did not only discourage innovation, at least within the country; such monopolies could never be secure for any length of time anyway if neighbouring countries did not have patent laws (ibid.: 63). 'Verguin and Renard's patent on magenta ... did not prevent the Gerbers of Mulhouse from developing a cheaper process ... they simply emigrated to Basel in order to be able to exploit it freely' (Bensaude-Vincent and Stengers, 1996: 184). Moreover, the rule that merely importing a patented product would lead to revocation of the patent did not necessarily serve the interests of the domestic firms. Indeed, the French chemical firms were apparently well aware that compulsory working rendered them even more vulnerable to the capture of domestic markets by German and Swiss firms setting up branch factories in France (Penrose, 1951: 155). Most likely the domestic chemical industry had never achieved sufficient economic importance for its concerns to be taken seriously enough by policy makers or the politicians.

Patents and Industrial Development: Lessons from the Dyestuff Industry

Evidently, patents were not a prerequisite for economic and technological advancement in all countries, and may not have been in any. But, since we cannot turn the clock back and rerun past centuries without a patent system, there is much that we will never be sure of. On the other hand, it is very likely that patents did in at least some cases stimulate the development and diffusion of new technologies that were the foundation for rapid industrial development.[15] It is also probably true that inappropriate systems hindered such progress. Unlike the French and British governments, Germany had a patent strategy in the nineteenth century. The 1877 law was intended to benefit German industry and the economic well-being of the new nation. The involvement of industry in drawing up the legislation was therefore only to be expected. Indeed, it was a sensible course of action. The patent law appears to have been successful given Germany's subsequent rapid industrial development, and its emergence as an economic rival to Britain. In Switzerland, the delay in introducing a patent system was largely due to the country's unique constitutional complexities. Nonetheless, as with Germany, the Swiss chemical industry from its earliest days strongly influenced the development of national patent law.

If we accept that the development of world class industrial sectors is likely to benefit the national economy, we can conclude that allowing such a policy-making role for industry was probably a good thing in Germany's and Switzerland's cases.

But the lesson is not that private industry should dictate to governments how national patent systems ought to be designed because we all benefit by allowing them to do so; even less that firms and industrial associations should be able to dictate to foreign governments in countries where they have – or intend to have – commercial interests. Rather, countries should have the freedom to design patent systems for strategic purposes. As major stakeholders, companies and others who benefit economically from patent systems, such as patent agents and attorneys, may reasonably advise governments on patent policy, but they should certainly not monopolize this role.

This chapter should lead us to another important conclusion, which is that, just because some past patent systems probably did stimulate economic development, this does not mean that today's developing countries ought to implement strong patent rights as they are being pressured to do by the developed countries. Not even the most successful of these historical patent systems came close to TRIPS compatibility. For one thing, the rights given to holders were generally quite weak by modern standards; for another, they tended often to be discriminatory in favour of the interests of domestic inventors and technology importers. This is something that TRIPS expressly forbids.

Notes

1 Simon (1998: 17).
2 See Travis (1993) for the most comprehensive account of the synthetic dyestuff industry.
3 Where they were able to exploit the relevant British patents (some of which were for their own inventions). See Bensaude-Vincent and Stengers (1996: 185).
4 In terms, for example, of foreign exchange receipts, increased income per capita, job creation and availability of useful new products. However, it should not be taken as a given that the financial success of domestic companies necessarily indicates enhanced net social and/or economic welfare of the citizenry; even more so in the case of the citizenry of foreign countries where these firms invest and/or to which they export.
5 Then known as Meister, Lucius & Brüning.
6 Interestingly, from 1936, Nazi-ruled Germany rejected the long-established 'applicant principle' (Anmelderprinzip) in favour of the 'inventor principle' (Erfinderprinzip) (Beier, 1986: 322; Nicolai, 1972: 109). The drafters of the law evidently considered it important to protect the interests of the individual while at the same time subordinating them to the interests of the state on behalf of the community (see Klauer, 1936).
7 Complaints about such practices were common and were made up to and during the First World War (for example, Perkin, 1915: 421).
8 Isomers are variants of a compound that contain the same atoms arranged differently. In other words, their ingredients are identical but their structures are different. The actual difference may be extremely trivial.
9 Similarly, inventions in the biotechnology field have tended to be treated by patent offices and the courts as if they were chemical inventions even though they differ in some fundamental ways (see Chapter 6).

10 Lobbyists tend to adopt the rhetoric most likely to impress policy makers. As Chapter 7 shows, the inventor–hero rhetoric was deployed in the campaign that resulted in the 1930 US Plant Patent Act.

11 In *Cuno Engineering Corporation* v. *Automatic Devices Corporation* (1941) 314 US 84.

12 This was a common view in the courts during the 1940s. Indeed, during the Second World War period, the courts were hardly favourable to patent holders: 89 per cent of the patents involved in the cases brought before them were declared invalid (Vaughan, 1951: 782). Killing the flash of genius concept in the USA was thus much longer in coming than in Germany, probably because of the individualist ideology which pervades American society.

13 Owing in large part to lobbying by the timepiece industry.

14 At the second reading of the Patents for Inventions Bill, as reported in *Hansard* (1883), 16 April: 360, 363.

15 For well-researched and convincing evidence to support this view in the UK context, see Dutton (1984).

Chapter 5

The Pharmaceutical Industry

The manufacture of synthetic medicinal agents, artificial perfumes, sweetening materials, antitoxines, nutritives, and photographic developers are all outgrowths of the coal-tar industry, and in great part still remain attached to the colour works where they originated. Of these subsidiary industries the most important is the manufacture of synthetic medicinal preparations, which has already attained to large proportions, and bids fair to revolutionise medical science. (Arthur G. Green, F.I.C., F.C.S., 1901)[1]

The Scientific Foundations of the Modern Pharmaceutical Industry

The nineteenth century experienced some major pharmacological breakthroughs, especially in the extraction and purification of the active principles of plant-based drugs. Pharmacists and doctors were able to sell and administer powerful alkaloid substances such as morphine, codeine, quinine and cocaine whose purity, strength and dosage could at last be regulated (Porter, 1997: 333–4). There is little doubt that such advances made the use of traditional natural product remedies appear unscientific, unless they were exploited as sources of active compounds rather than as drugs themselves. Consequently, 'since the late 1800s, when specific agents were isolated and characterized, the need for standardization and synthesis of natural substances favoured the development of the drug industry' (Duffin, 1999: 107).

Modern pharmaceutical science is inherently multidisciplinary. Apart from synthetic organic chemistry, it is based on pharmacology, physiology, immunology, bacteriology and fermentation science, among other life science disciplines. While scientists and institutions from various countries contributed to the development of these new fields of enquiry, the modern pharmaceutical industry was invented in late nineteenth-century Germany. Bayer and Hoechst were the most prominent pioneering firms. In hindsight, there are very good reasons why the industry emerged in Germany and is, to some extent at least, an offshoot of dyestuff research and development.

The application of synthetic chemistry to drug discovery began to bear fruit from the late nineteenth century, and the dyestuff firms were at the forefront, along with a small number of longer-established pharmacy firms. Arguably, Bayer became the world's first pharmaceutical company when, in 1888, it placed on the market an anti-pyretic drug that it sold as Phenactin. 'For the first time, a drug had been conceived, developed, tested, and marketed, all by a private company. It marked the creation of the modern drug industry, the marriage of science and business that has transformed this century, making huge profits even as it saves lives' (Mann and Plummer, 1991: 23).

By the outbreak of the First World War, Bayer and other German firms had developed a range of pharmaceutical products based on advanced research carried out in-house and in universities and hospitals. To give an early example, in 1874 at St Mary's Hospital in London, a therapeutic compound developed by a team led by Frederick Pierce turned out to be 'one of the first drugs ever produced by modifying a natural molecule' (Stone and Darlington, 2000: 93). Two decades later, Bayer adopted this new chemical and subsequently marketed it under the brand name 'Heroin'. But, without doubt, the most famous (as opposed to notorious) drug produced in these early years of the pharmaceutical industry was Bayer's Aspirin.

Another hugely significant advance around the turn of the century was Salvarsan. This arsenical compound, synthesized by Paul Ehrlich, was discovered by him and his colleagues to be effective against syphilis, and patented in 1909 by Hoechst. In fact, most of the early chemotherapeutic drugs came out of the laboratories of the German dyestuff companies or of academic chemists who had connections with these firms.

Advances in bacteriology and immunology associated with Pasteur, Koch and Ehrlich also catalysed the emergence of the modern pharmaceutical industry. Pasteur and Koch showed that many illnesses were caused by invasive bacteria, identified the microbes causing several of the major diseases, and produced a number of highly effective vaccines. Discovering the role of white blood cells in destroying disease-causing bacteria inspired the idea of using biological agents to fight disease. This, and the realization made in 1888 by two of Pasteur's students that it was not necessarily the bacterial cells but the toxins they produced which caused disease, led eventually to the discovery and industrial production of penicillin and the antibiotics (Bynum, 1994: 160). These are substances produced by fungi or bacteria which inhibit or destroy other bacteria yet cause no harm to humans. This huge advance for pharmaceutical science and, as it turned out, for the pharmaceutical industry, was nonetheless somewhat slow in coming, not taking place until the 1940s.

The insight that blood serum also contained anti-bacterial agents inspired another scientific approach to pharmaceutical research and development. The bacteriologist Paul Ehrlich, impressed by the specificity of coal tar dye staining applied to human and animal tissue, investigated the chemical structures of various dyes (Porter, 1997: 450). His aim was to discover synthetic versions of natural antibodies. Eventually, this strategy led to the twentieth-century chemotherapeutic revolution whose origins by many accounts lie in the sulphonamide drugs, first discovered in 1935.

Patent law may originally have had something to do with this orientation towards synthetic chemistry. In Germany, among the court decisions from 1888 to 1890 which expanded the scope of patentability in chemistry was one which to some extent circumvented the pharmaceutical exception in applying these changes to medicines as long as they were chemically synthesized substances (Wimmer, 1998: 287–8). These changes probably encouraged German and Swiss dyestuff firms (which were dependent on the German market) to move into pharmaceuticals and to manufacture synthetic rather than natural products.

From the 1940s to the 1960s, though, many of the most important new drugs were based on the discovery of substances found in nature, such as microorganisms and hormones. This situation favoured companies whose expertise lay in natural product research and fermentation science. Since many of these companies were American or British, these two countries became relatively more innovative than the German, Swiss and French firms whose scientific and technological traditions were more on the side of synthetic chemistry. By the mid-1960s, it was becoming apparent that the balance of industrial power was shifting from the chemical–pharmaceutical giants like Bayer, Hoechst, DuPont and ICI to those firms whose background was related more closely to the biological sciences (Thomas, 1994: 478). As the next chapter will show, the new biotechnologies are pushing pharmaceutical research and development ever closer to biology and away from chemistry (though chemistry continues to be the source of much of the scientific and legal discourse).

Patent law turned out not to be an insurmountable obstacle to the protection and exclusive commercialization of such products. In most legal jurisdictions the mere discovery of a compound found in nature does not constitute a patentable invention. But, in time, the courts in several countries determined that isolated and purified natural substances could be patented, as could partially and completely synthetic versions.[2]

Nowadays, the situation is somewhat confusing. To many in the pharmaceutical industry, natural product research is quite unappealing, being slow and expensive (ten Kate and Laird, 1999: 56), especially when the therapeutic effect involves the interaction of a complex of chemicals acting together. Drug discovery is generally considered to be a laboratory-based activity carried out by skilled technicians employing advanced methods such as combinatorial chemistry allowing for the generation of huge numbers of new compounds. Rather than seek new chemicals existing in nature, companies often prefer to build up and screen huge 'libraries of synthetic compounds from basic inorganic and petroleum-based chemicals' (ibid.: 50).

One can only be impressed at the ability of chemists to construct completely novel molecules, that they have created 10 million since the birth of synthetic chemistry, and that pharmaceutical companies can now synthesize 25 000 varieties of a single molecule (Bensaude-Vincent and Stengers, 1996: 254–5). It is plausible that combinatorial chemistry and the new biotechnologies will herald a new era in which rational drug design is *the* method of discovering new therapeutic compounds and old-fashioned serendipity is no longer necessary.

Even so, the pharmaceutical industry is still surprisingly dependent on natural products and even on the traditional knowledge of rural communities, including those inhabiting isolated parts of the globe such as the Amazon (Plotkin, 2000). University of Illinois pharmacologist Norman Farnsworth found that 119 plant-based compounds were used in medicine worldwide in 1988, of which 74 per cent had the same or related uses as the medicinal plants from which they were derived (Farnsworth, 1988). In the same paper, he also indicated that 25 per cent of the total sales value of drugs sold in OECD countries as a whole was constituted by products containing at least one plant-derived ingredient. Using these findings, an economic study estimated that the total market value of plant-based medicines sold in OECD countries in 1990 was US$61 billion (Principe, 1998: 44–5). A more up-to-date estimate for the United States is that, from 1989 to 1995, 60 per cent of new anti-cancer and anti-infective drugs were of 'natural origin', meaning that they were either 'original natural products, products derived semisynthetically from natural products, or synthetic products based on natural product models' (Cragg *et al.*, 1997: 52).

Moreover, it continues to be difficult for therapeutic molecules to be designed and manufactured from scratch without using existing chemical structures as initial leads. Even the new combinatorial chemistry techniques need to work on existing lead structures to generate their compound libraries, and some of these will originate from natural sources (ten Kate and Laird, 1999: 50, 57). This difficulty in developing completely new substances explains why the first biopharmaceuticals were not novel proteins but naturally occurring ones like insulin and human growth hormone that were produced in transgenic microorganisms (see the next chapter).

Drug Discovery in the Twentieth Century: a Brief Survey

Considering the tremendous advances in organic chemistry during the nineteenth and early twentieth centuries, and the establishment of microbiology as a scientific discipline, it may seem strange that the therapeutic revolution was so long in coming. Until the Second World War, the number of new chemical entities was small, the research-based pharmaceutical industry hardly existed, especially outside Germany, and most of the drugs available would be considered primitive to today's doctors, pharmacists and patients. According to the medical journalist James Le Fanu (1999: 206),

> The newly qualified doctor setting up practice in the 1930s had a dozen or so proven remedies with which to treat the multiplicity of different diseases he encountered every day: aspirin for rheumatic fever, digoxin for heart failure, the hormones thyroxine and insulin for an underactive thyroid and diabetes respectively, salvarsan for syphilis, bromides for those who needed a sedative, barbiturates for epilepsy, and morphine for pain. Thirty years later, when the same doctor would have been approaching retirement, those dozen remedies had grown to over 2,000.

This lack of early success probably had much to do with the basic lack of understanding about cell function. This meant that discovering compounds affecting the functioning of target cells was of necessity heavily dependent on serendipity (Le Fanu, 1999: 209). Once cell function was better understood, researchers became less dependent on good fortune. Be that as it may, good luck continues often to be an essential condition for success.

Our intention is not to provide an exhaustive account of drug discovery over the course of the twentieth century. Rather, we focus on what are generally considered to be among the most significant breakthroughs. The three therapeutic revolutions are chosen for a number of reasons and not just because they resulted in the saving of millions of lives and the improvement of the lives of many others suffering from non-fatal chronic illnesses. Each of them involved the development of not just one but many successful and profitable drugs. They also played a major role in fostering the growth and transformation of the pharmaceutical industry. Not only did the industry begin to generate huge profits, but success and the likelihood of further success encouraged drug companies to invest increasingly large sums of money in the discovery and development of more drugs. In short, these three revolutions provided the conditions for the emergence of today's research-based pharmaceutical industry.

The sulphonamide revolution was founded on the working hypothesis first formulated by Paul Ehrlich, that the ability of dye chemicals to stain microbes and tissues selectively might enable them to affect the metabolism of disease-causing microbes without damaging or killing friendly ones and tissues. The story begins in the late 1920s, when Gerhard Domagk, a senior researcher at I.G. Farbenindustrie, which was formed in 1925 by the merger of the main German chemical firms, decided to follow Ehrlich's example by testing his company's dyes for therapeutic effects. In 1932, he discovered that an azo dye given the name of Prontosil Red inhibited streptococcal infections in mice, and in 1935 he published the results of his experiments. The dye turned out to produce a bacteriostatic effect, which is to say that it did not kill bacteria outright, but prevented them from reproducing. Domagk's company subsequently played a major role in the sulphonamide revolution, and his achievement was recognized with a Nobel Prize.

The first country after Germany where commercial and scientific activity in this area took place was France. Roussel Laboratories in that country had the advantage of being able to copy I.G. Farben's French patent on Prontosil Red. This was because French patent law at the time allowed it to be protected as a dye but not as a medicine (Sneader, 1985: 287). Subsequent research at the Pasteur Institute in Paris led to the discovery of a more effective substance, called sulphanilamide. This chemical was actually the active part of the prontosil compound, released into the body as the dye was metabolized. It worked by inhibiting the multiplication of bacteria, thereby helping the immune system to eradicate them (Weatherall, 1990: 150). Since sulphanilamide had been synthesized three decades earlier and described in a publication, it was unpatentable.

Soon after, a British company called May and Baker developed a related drug called M&B 693 that was more effective against streptococci as well as other organisms including pneumococci, and was also less toxic (Sneader, 1985: 288). Other similar substances were subsequently synthesized and found also to have therapeutic effects against a range of infectious diseases, including leprosy. These became known collectively as the sulphonamides, or sulpha drugs (Weatherall, 1990: 152). Basil Achilladelis notes that 'the companies that rushed to ride the [sulphonamide] bandwagon, and did so successfully, were predominantly *chemical companies with strong R&D expertise in dyestuffs*: Ciba, Geigy, Sandoz, Hoffman LaRoche, as well as ICI, American Cyanamid, Rhône-Poulenc/May and Baker' (Achilladelis, 1993: 285). Merck and Sharp and Dohme (which merged in 1953), which were also involved, were among the few exceptions to this rule (ibid.: 286).

The sulpha drugs were undoubtedly a tremendous boon for the many patients who might otherwise have lost their lives. They also contributed to future drug discovery. Research into the mode of action of sulphanilamide led to the formulation of a new working hypothesis that guided scientists in their design of new drugs for specific microbial targets, competitive antagonism. The idea is that certain chemicals play a vital role in metabolic processes that are specific to particular species of microbe. The possibility arises that structurally related chemicals can be designed which 'trick' the target microbe into taking them up and using them in place of the real substance. But since they do not perform the same role, the process cannot take place, and the microbe is weakened or destroyed (Weatherall, 1990: 152–4). Adoption of this principle led to the development of several important drugs. These include para-amino salicylic acid (PAS), a treatment for tuberculosis discovered in 1946 by the Danish doctor Jorgen Lehmann; azathioprine, an immuno-suppressive drug developed in a US lab of Burroughs Wellcome by George Hitchings and Gertrude Elion; and the beta-blockers such as propronalol, that were pioneered in the 1960s by James Black, then at ICI. A decade later, Black was responsible for another triumph of rational drug design, the anti-ulcerant cimetidine. Under the brand name of Tagamet, this drug generated massive revenues for Smith, Kline and French, where he was employed at the time.

Unfortunately, there was at least one tragic incident. In 1937, 76 people in the USA lost their lives after taking the highly toxic Elixir of Sulphanilamide. The government responded by introducing regulations requiring that drugs be tested for safety before they could be sold to the public (Mann, 1999: 35). These measures were subsequently adopted elsewhere. Allowing drugs to be sold without safety testing is of course unthinkable now.

The discovery of penicillin is often, though not perhaps correctly (since earlier claims exist), traced to 1928, when Alexander Fleming found a mould displaying antibacterial properties in his laboratory at St Mary's Hospital in London. Little progress was made for a decade. This changed when Howard Florey and Ernst Chain at Oxford University decided to study penicillin and, with the help of Norman Heatley and the financial assistance of the Rockefeller Foundation, produced enough for a very small-scale clinical trial that proved its effectiveness. With the Second World War under way, the urgent need to scale up production was manifest, but companies like ICI, Burroughs Wellcome and Boots, while interested, were unable or unwilling to invest in the development of new technologies to mass-produce penicillin. This may have been because the Medical Research Council, which had also funded the Oxford team's research, believed it would be unethical to file patents. Without the possibility of market exclusivity, the companies might have been less willing to invest large sums of money in research (ibid.: 51). But this is unlikely to be the whole story. A recent history of Glaxo reveals that the company made efforts to contact Florey expressing interest in penicillin, but he did not reply to the two letters sent to him. To the author of this history, 'these events contrasted with Florey's later assertion that he had contacted several British pharmaceutical manufacturers without success' (Jones, 2001: 64) In fact, at least three British companies – ICI, Glaxo and Kemball-Bishop – produced increasing quantities of penicillin from the early 1940s using surface fermentation. But neither the existing technologies nor minor improvements to them were sufficient for mass production on anything like the scale achieved soon after in the USA.

Whatever the exact truth, Florey felt he had no alternative but to go to the USA if he wanted production levels to meet the high wartime demand. Heatley, who accompanied Florey to the USA, and scientists at the US Department of Agriculture (USDA) discovered that corn-steep liquor was an excellent medium for culturing penicillin and managed to increase production considerably. Subsequently, four US pharmaceutical companies – Merck, Pfizer, Lederle and Squibb – became involved in penicillin research. Pfizer's patented deep fermentation technology turned out to be especially productive and generated tremendous profits for the company. By 1944, 19 US companies were producing penicillin, with five of them producing 88 per cent of the total (Temin, 1979: 435). In time the market became less concentrated as more companies entered it and the price fell.

Penicillin was no one-off. Various types of penicillin and semi-synthetic analogues came on the market during the following decades, including those effective against resistant strains of disease-causing microbes like staphylococcus. And while its discovery was accidental, penicillin inspired scientists to search for other microorganisms producing substances that are toxic for other microbes but harmless to humans. The result was the discovery and development of such antibiotics as streptomycin (1943), cephalosporin (1945) and tetracycline (1953). Many of the antibiotics came from the soil, but there were a range of sources including a chicken's throat (streptomycin), a sewage outlet (cephalosporin) and monkey dung (fusidic acid) (Le Fanu, 1999: 13). It was largely out of the investment of profits from the antibiotics revolution into research and development that today's research-based pharmaceutical industry emerged, especially in the USA and Britain.

While not usually considered to be as significant in the commercial sense as the antibiotics, the development of the anti-inflammatory steroid drugs was hugely important for the pharmaceutical industry. Like the antibiotics, the cortico-steroids are naturally-occurring substances whose seemingly miraculous therapeutic effects could not have been predicted by pharmaceutical chemists. Nonetheless, their discovery was not purely accidental either. In 1948, Philip Hensch at the Mayo Clinic in Rochester, Minnesota decided to experiment by treating a rheumatoid arthritis sufferer with a synthetic version of a secretion from the adrenal gland that had been sent to the hospital by the Merck company. This compound, later known as cortisone, resulted in rapid improvements to the condition of the patient and to several others during the following months.

Why did Hensch decide to try this particular compound? First, he had already observed that the condition of rheumatoid arthritis sufferers improved when they were pregnant or had jaundice. In fact, other afflictions such as hay fever and asthma also went into remission under these conditions. This led him to speculate that a hormone might be responsible. Second, he was fortunate enough to work at the same establishment as Edward Kendall, who had been studying the adrenal hormones. Kendall had isolated some of the adrenal hormones, including one named Compound E. With the war under way and rumours that the Germans had found a way to enable their pilots to fly at extraordinarily high altitudes through injections of an adrenal hormone, the US Air Force began a research programme and encouraged firms and laboratories already involved in this area to intensify their work. But it was not until 1948 that Merck managed to produce enough Compound E to test on a patient. This was no mean achievement. At that time 'it took the slaughter of forty head of cattle to treat one patient for one day by a process with forty-two chemical steps' (Werth, 1994: 202).

Although cortisone turned out to have some unpleasant side-effects, the drug and the derivatives subsequently developed (collectively known as the steroids) had a major impact since they successfully treated a tremendous range of hitherto untreatable diseases that were not obviously related and whose causes were hardly understood. Among others, these include Hodgkin's disease, cerebral oedema, glandular fever, septic shock and male infertility (Le Fanu, 1999: 25).

Other important breakthroughs, such as the beta-blockers, took place during the post-Second World War period. But from the 1970s the number of new drugs placed on the market began to decline. According to one study, between 1969 and 1989 the number of new chemical entities launched per year on the world market fell from over 90 to under 40 (CIPA, 1998). And increasingly the 'new' chemical entities are so-called 'me-too' drugs, which are not significant improvements upon existing treatments (Le Fanu, 1999: 246). This was recognized early on by the pharmaceutical industry. In a study published in 1973, the authors were told by several industry representatives 'that the end of the first chemotherapeutic revolution is almost in sight' (Taylor and Silberston, 1973: 365). The situation has reached the stage where 65 per cent of 'new' drugs approved by the Food and Drug Administration for sale in the USA from 1989 to 2000 contained active ingredients found in existing products. Of these newly-approved drugs, 54 per cent 'differed from the marketed product in dosage form, route of administration, or were combined with another active ingredient', while 11 per cent 'were identical to products already available on the US market' (Hunt, 2002: 3).

There are two possible explanations for this situation. First, the pharmaceutical industry had to deal with increasingly stringent safety regulations. Partly in response to the thalidomide tragedy, drugs had to be rigorously tested for safety and effectiveness before they could be sold. These regulations were introduced at about the same time as the number of new drugs declined, which suggests the possibility of a connection. This is plausible considering that compliance substantially raised the cost of research and development. In the United Kingdom, for example, 'by 1978 the "development time" for each new drug had increased to around ten years, while the "development costs" had escalated from £5 million in the 1960s to £25 million in the mid-1970s to a staggering £150 million by the 1990s' (Le Fanu, 1999: 247). Moreover, while such testing was undoubtedly a good thing, it is possible that several drugs that could have provided substantial benefits for patients in spite of their side-effects were weeded out that ought not to have been. Walter Sneader, a medical historian, has suggested that if current safety standards had been applied to aspirin and paracetamol, they might well not have been approved (1985: 87).[3]

Second, it is possible to argue that, as long as disease processes are not well understood and researchers must depend to a large extent on serendipity, even the prepared mind must eventually contend with the law of diminishing returns (Le Fanu, 1999: 237). And, while rational drug design has had some major successes (such as the beta-blockers), its promise is far from being realized as yet. It almost goes without saying that the pharmaceutical industry is keen to accentuate the first of the two explanations.

While important drugs, including treatments for HIV/AIDS, continue to be developed and manufactured, it is a fact of economic life that the most profitable medicines are not necessarily the ones that save the most people's lives or even that save any lives at all. This was recognized even by the industry from at least as far back as the 1950s. Henry Gadsden, a head of Merck shortly after it had merged with Sharp and Dohme, told his researchers in a meeting that 'there are more well people than sick people. We should make products for people who are well' (quoted in Werth, 1994: 131). Examples of such products he mentioned – to the disgust of the scientists present – included a quick-tanning formula and a treatment for straightening hair. Since that time, vast sums of money have been spent on a range of 'lifestyle drugs' which may admittedly improve the quality of peoples' lives but are not exactly lifesavers.

The Growth of the Research-based Pharmaceutical Industries in the Twentieth Century

Nowadays, the pharmaceutical industry is usually considered to consist of the research-based companies, which are responsible for the development and sale of new prescription drugs, and the generic drug companies, which sell drugs that are not patent-protected, usually because the patents protecting the product have expired. This distinction is not universally accepted. For one thing, some research-based companies have generic subsidiaries, and, for another, it is just as plausible to divide the industry into producers of brand-name (that is, trade mark-protected) drugs and producers of generics. This alternative classification of drug companies has some merit given the importance of brand names, and also that governments often fund a great deal of basic pharmaceutical research, especially that of the USA, which benefits the industry as a whole. In other words, the state often pays government agencies and universities to carry out much of the research that the 'research-based' sector would otherwise have to do itself or perhaps even never would. Some companies are reluctant to admit this and even claim the credit for research they benefited from but did not themselves undertake. For example, Bristol-Myers Squibb played down the significant role of the US government in discovering and developing Taxol, and in bearing nearly all of the costs of doing so (Goodman and Walsh, 2001). It is also true that companies claiming to be research and development-based often market under-licence products developed by other companies. During 2001, for example, GlaxoSmithKline in-licensed ten products discovered and developed elsewhere. The managing director of one of the larger Indian drug companies explained to the author that in his view most of the conceptual breakthroughs that form the basis for the development of innovative medicines are achieved by university- and public sector-based scientists and not in corporate research and development labs. He also considers that many research-based companies nowadays produce mostly 'me-too' drugs, which do not achieve significant therapeutic advances. We will see more about this in the next section. But suffice to say, at this point, that, while such criticisms may go too far, they are not without merit.

What we can say is that, over the last 120 years, new therapeutic chemical substances have been discovered and developed in the laboratories of universities, government research institutions and companies in several countries. However, when investigating the origins of the most significant pharmaceutical products, and bearing in mind this book's emphasis on industry as opposed to the public sector, it becomes apparent that firms from four countries have made an especially large contribution. German companies played a pioneering role, and their example was followed in very quick time by their Swiss counterparts, which interestingly also tended to be dyestuff manufacturers. The US industry was also quite an early developer, while the British drug companies took a long time to commit themselves to pharmaceutical research and development but ultimately became highly successful.

For these reasons the present account focuses on the pharmaceutical industries of these four countries, tracing some of the major commercial and business developments that have taken place in each of them over the last century. It finishes by describing the state of the pharmaceutical industry at the beginning of the twenty-first century.

Germany: early Dominance, continued Success

The first-ever pharmaceutical products were developed in-house or by chemists based in German universities and licensed to companies, most of which were primarily dyestuff firms. Several reasons may be given to explain why these companies decided to move into drug development and were successful in doing so. First, there was good reason to believe that the research strategies they had adopted and the mass production capabilities they had acquired could be harnessed to drug discovery. Second, the same equipment they used for dyestuff production could also be used for drug production. Third, they soon realized that pharmaceutical compounds could be developed from analogous or even identical raw materials (Stolz and Schwaiberger, 1987: 195). Investigating Paul Ehrlich's hypothesis that some dyestuffs have properties allowing them to treat infective agents but without harming human tissue, it seemed feasible to carry out research aimed at discovering dual-use substances to dye clothes and heal the sick (Bynum, 1994: 167; Porter, 1997: 450). Fourth, as their dyes became increasingly profitable, large funds became available to plough back into research and development. In short, since pharmaceutical research and development could be carried out with the same research strategies, technologies and equipment (Wengenroth, 1997: 144), drug development was a commercially attractive and feasible proposition.

Even before the turn of the twentieth century, Hoechst, Bayer, AGFA and the main Swiss dyestuff firms were producing pharmaceuticals. And until well into the century virtually all the important new chemotherapeutic drugs were developed by German firms. This was despite the fact that most were still primarily dyestuff producers that treated drugs as no more than a promising sideline. These included Hoechst's Antipyrin (1883), Pyramidon (1896), Novocain (1905) and Salvarsan (1909), Bayer's Phenactin (1888), Sulfonal and Aspirin (both 1889), and Kalle's Antifebrin (1886). Antifebrin is interesting because it was probably the first drug to be marketed under its brand name in competition with generic versions. This business strategy was adopted because processes to manufacture the substance were well-known and therefore unpatentable. It succeeded because so many physicians accepted the brand name rather than the chemical term of acetanilid even though Kalle charged a higher price than its competitors (Mann and Plummer, 1991: 22–3). Another important drug, E. Merck's Veronal (1903), was an exception because its producer was not a dyestuff firm but had begun as a pharmacist shop and subsequently became a bulk producer of alkaloids. In common with another former pharmacy business, Schering, E. Merck's US branch separated and eventually became a major research-based pharmaceutical corporation that outgrew its parent by some considerable distance. In Merck's case the separation took place after the First World War. The Schering split followed the Second World War.

As mentioned earlier, the main German chemical companies merged in 1925 to form I.G. Farbenindustrie, which immediately became a dominant player in various types of chemical product, including pharmaceuticals. At the end of the Second

World War, I.G. Farben was broken up and Hoechst and Bayer were revived as separate companies. For much of the second half of the century, both were among the world's biggest pharmaceutical companies. However, in 1999, Hoechst merged with Rhône-Poulenc to form a new company, Aventis.

Switzerland: a Successful Follower[4]

The Swiss pharmaceutical industry, like its German counterpart, benefited from early advances in synthetic chemistry. Three of the four most successful companies during the twentieth century – Sandoz, Ciba and Geigy – began as dyestuff manufacturers. In 1895, Sandoz was the first of these companies to graduate to pharmaceuticals when it began producing Antipyrin, originally developed by Hoechst. In 1917, the company established a pharmaceutical research laboratory. Five years after Sandoz, Ciba moved into pharmaceuticals, developing two products, Vioform (an antiseptic) and Salen (for rheumatism). Geigy set up its pharmaceutical research department in 1938, and 11 years later marketed its first major drug, an anti-rheumatic called Butazolidin. Other important drugs that came out of the Geigy labs after the Second World War included Tofranil (a psychotropic drug), Hygrotone (for high blood pressure) and Tegretol (for epilepsy). In 1970, Ciba and Geigy merged to form Ciba-Geigy, although the 'Geigy' part of the name was dropped 22 years later. Finally, 'Ciba' and 'Sandoz' effectively disappeared when the two companies merged in 1996 to form Novartis.

The other Swiss pharmaceutical giant of the twentieth century, Hoffman LaRoche, is different in that it was founded in 1896 specifically to produce pharmaceuticals. Before the First World War, Roche produced several successful products, including Aidin (a thyroid preparation), Airol (an antiseptic) and Sirolin (a cough syrup) and Digalen (a purified digitalis preparation), both of which were marketed for six decades. During the inter-war period, Roche distinguished itself by its development of synthetic vitamin products and analgesics. After the Second World War, Roche became one of the world's biggest drug companies, largely on the strength of its successful development of a series of tranquillizers of the benzodiazepine class of chemicals, most notably Librium, Mogadon and Valium.

The United States: towards Global Leadership

While the German and Swiss drug discovery approaches were based on synthetic organic chemistry, the North American and British strategy was initially geared towards extraction and purification of natural products (Achilladelis, 1993: 283). The German and Swiss firms were the most successful up to the mid-1930s, but, from the Second World War onwards, the US industry began to dominate. And, from the 1970s, several British pharmaceutical firms also joined the ranks of the world's most innovative and commercially successful.

The impetus for early growth of the US pharmaceutical industry came from such factors as the growing population, the availability of chemists and medical scientists trained in American and German universities, and the close links between university scientists and companies (Liebenau, 1984: 339). In addition, drug regulation introduced in 1902, which required a government laboratory to monitor the production of new drugs for safety, increased competition and encouraged innovation and growth. 'The Act made possible a new means of competition: competition based upon the quality of laboratory facilities that the company could provide and the stringency of the standards which they could meet. It also implied that the leading producers could benefit by extremely tough standards which would be difficult for smaller companies to equal' (ibid.: 341). Company laboratories no longer 'used simply to standardise basic products or to fiddle with new combinations of drugs, but rather they were now in the business of setting standards, meeting the requirements of the regulators, and producing as many novel products as they were capable of doing which would distinguish their product lines from those of their competitors' (ibid.).

After the USA joined the First World War in 1917, the government decided the country needed to become self-sufficient in the production of drugs. At the time, many important drugs (as well as dyes and other chemicals) in high demand were made only by German companies. When the war ended in November 1918, the Alien Property Custodian was established under the Trading with the Enemy Act to confiscate and sell off the German-owned patents. The 4767 chemical patents, which included drugs such as Novocain and Salvarsan, were sold to the Chemical Foundation, which represented the US chemicals sector, for only US$266 400 and then licensed to companies (Greenberg, 1926: 23; Roe, 1943: 702). Even though it turned out that many of these patents did not fully disclose the inventions claimed (see below), the US industry benefited to some extent, albeit less than was hoped for. For example, Sterling Drug was transformed by its acquisition of Bayer's US properties, including aspirin. At least as important as the transfer of these patents, the war resulted in the loss by some German companies of their US branches (such as Merck). Perhaps the most important outcome of the crisis created by the war was that the US government (as did the British government) finally decided to follow Germany in adopting industry policies specifically geared to promoting the development of their domestic chemical (including pharmaceutical) industries (Steen, 1995).

Even before the antibiotics and cortico-steroids eras, American companies began to achieve some good results from their research. A few pioneering firms such as Abbott Laboratories, Parke Davis and Co., and E.R. Squibb began from the 1920s to invest profitably in research in such areas as vitamins and hormones (Chandler, 1990: 164). Eli Lilly became the first commercial producer of insulin, which had been discovered by University of Toronto scientists (see below).

However, it was not until the Second World War that the US pharmaceutical industry became committed to any great extent to in-house research and development (Mowery and Rosenberg, 1998: 96; Noble, 1977: 118). The stimulus for this was the desperate need for anti-infectives to treat injured combatants. But it would be incorrect to suggest that research and development was purely in-house. On the contrary, then and up to the present time, the US industry benefited tremendously from collaborations with universities where biomedical research programmes were reaching very high standards, and also from the tremendous expansion in government spending on such research which continues to be substantial. Between 1950 and 1965, the biomedical research budget of the National Institutes of Health (NIH) 'grew by no less than 18 per cent per year in real terms, and by 1965, the federal government accounted for almost two-thirds of all spending on biomedical research' (Mowery and Rosenberg, 1998: 96). Although the federal government share of biomedical research and development declined thereafter, it still made up a substantial 39 per cent of the ($30 billion) total in 1993, compared to 50 per cent for industry-funded research and development (ibid.: 97).

The US pharmaceutical industry did not advance rapidly because the firms had outstanding expertise in synthetic chemistry, as did their German rivals, but because their expertise in natural product research and also in chemical engineering enabled them to scale up production of fermentation-based products to unprecedented levels (ibid.: 95–6). So while the sulphonamide revolution was a European one, the antibiotics revolution was largely American (even though the initial breakthroughs took place in Britain), as indeed was the biotechnology revolution which, as we will find later, 'represented a fundamental discontinuity in the nature of pharmaceutical research, a transition from the realm of chemistry to that of biology' (ibid.: 99).

The discovery of the antibiotics created opportunities for the pharmaceutical industry, but also presented difficulties. The problem was that product life cycles were likely to be quite short, owing to the fact that anti-infectives such as antibiotics were bound to induce resistance after a certain period. But while this situation placed a lot of competitive pressure on firms, the potential for attaining high rewards from successful research and development was very great.

It has been estimated that, from 1942 to 1986, 31 natural and semi-synthetic antibacterials were developed that could be classed as radical innovations in the sense of being 'innovations based on different scientific principles, technology or materials which have replaced or competed successfully with existing products and processes, and gave rise to a swarm of incremental innovations' (Achilladelis, 1993: 281–2). Of these (mostly antibiotic) products, 26 were developed or co-developed by US firms. Seven were developed or co-developed by British firms, two each by German and Swiss firms, and one each by Danish and Japanese companies.

The United Kingdom: a Slow Starter that Caught up

The British pharmaceutical industry developed into a successful research and development-based one much later than that of the USA. The country's early advances in synthetic chemistry did not, unlike the German case, lead to the development of new drugs. It cannot at all have helped that companies during the early twentieth century generally employed very few chemists. And, given the positive influence of drug safety regulations in the USA, the fact that they were virtually non-existent in Britain until as late as 1922, when the Dangerous Drugs Act was passed, to be followed in 1933 by the Pharmacy and Poisons Act (Slinn, 1995: 172), was likely also to have hindered the development of a world-class pharmaceuticals sector.

In the main, the British pharmaceutical industry in the pre-First World War era consisted of rather conservative small and medium-sized family firms. Most of these companies extracted drug ingredients from imported plants and minerals for wholesalers, pharmacists and physicians (ibid.: 169–70). Some of them also prepared their own proprietary remedies from these ingredients. Often these companies were originally retailers that had later on moved into manufacturing. Examples include Boots and Allen and Hanburys.[5] Other firms, like May and Baker, began as manufacturing chemists before becoming retailers.

Burroughs Wellcome, formed in 1880 by two American pharmacists who had emigrated to Britain, was an exception to the rule that the industry had little interest in research and development. Sir Henry Wellcome's 'introduction of a research and development laboratory was a direct effort to adopt methods which his American colleagues had originally brought across the Atlantic from Germany' (Liebenau, 1984: 336). The Wellcome Chemical Research Laboratories, set up in 1896, played an important role 'as providers of qualified and experienced research scientists to other companies, including Boots, Glaxo, and May and Baker' (Slinn, 1995: 174). This firm also introduced the tablet form of drug manufacture and delivery which had been pioneered in both Germany and the United States (ibid.: 184).

In spite of its relative backwardness in pharmaceuticals, Britain enjoyed a trade surplus on the eve of the First World War. In 1913, drug imports were worth £2 million, whereas exports were valued as £2·4 million (Ibid.: 174–5). Even so, the outbreak of the war made plain to the government how dependent the country had become on German dyestuffs and drugs, and how the patent system seemed to reinforce such dependence.

The drug whose unavailability caused most concern was Salvarsan. Unfortunately, it was extremely difficult to manufacture in a form safe enough to administer to patients. The Board of Trade authorized Burroughs Wellcome, Poulenc Frères and May and Baker to manufacture the drug which, once produced, needed to be tested for impurities. This was carried out by the recently-founded Medical Research Committee (later renamed the Medical Research Council). Another important drug whose supply was interrupted was Bayer's aspirin, which was protected by several patents covering the substance itself, its intermediates and the design of the manufacturing plant, and also by the company's trade mark (Fairley, 1978: 139). As with Salvarsan, these patents did not provide all the information needed to mass-produce the product. Realizing this, the government offered a prize of £20 000 to the first person in Britain or the Commonwealth to develop a feasible manufacturing process. The winner was George Nicholas, a chemist from Melbourne, Australia, who called his product 'Aspro'.

The lessons of the war were not lost on the government or industry. For one thing, the government took a more mercantilist approach to strategic industries. The 1921 Safeguarding of Industries Act imposed import tariffs on certain goods, including fine chemicals (Abraham, 2002: 233; Owen, 1999: 363). And, for another, the industry began to make efforts to improve its research and development capabilities. Two companies that increased their involvement in pharmaceutical research during the inter-war period and became highly successful decades later were Beecham and Glaxo. Beecham's Powders, a proprietary aspirin-based cold remedy launched in 1926, was a popular product for decades. Glaxo began life as a department of a company called Joseph Nathan that manufactured a dried milk product named 'Glaxo'. In 1924, the company negotiated a licence to extract vitamin D from fish oil using (and improving upon) a process patented by Columbia University. Glaxo Department subsequently produced a range of vitamin products and other dietary supplements, and was turned into a private limited company in 1935.

Nevertheless, the British pharmaceutical industry continued to consist during the inter-war period of small and medium-sized firms that were solely producers of drugs. In contrast, the chemical industry of the time in the UK and Germany was undergoing a radical consolidation phase that resulted in the creation of two very large firms, Imperial Chemical Industries (ICI) and I.G. Farben. The former, formed in 1926, initially had little interest in drugs, while I.G. Farben, created in 1925 out of Bayer, BASF, Hoechst and five other companies, was from the start a major developer and exporter of drugs.

Not surprisingly, then, the industry's progress was steady but unspectacular. But in the late 1930s, May and Baker, by that time owned by the French firm Rhône-Poulenc, became one of the first British pharmaceutical companies to develop an internationally important new product, M&B 693, and from the end of the Second World War the British pharmaceutical industry began to take off. Nonetheless, in the early 1960s, the major British firms like Glaxo, Beecham, ICI (which had only set up its pharmaceuticals division in 1942) and Wellcome were still minor players globally. In fact, some of the UK-based subsidiaries of US firms had higher sales in the UK market (Jones, 2001: 163). A decade later, the 10 largest pharmaceutical companies were exclusively American, Swiss and German, with the three biggest companies being Roche, Merck and Hoechst. Glaxo, the biggest British company was only sixteenth. While the USA was the largest producer of pharmaceuticals, West Germany was the biggest exporter (ibid.: 174).

When the antibiotics revolution first got under way, British companies seeking to produce these new kinds of drug had little choice but to license the patented deep fermentation processes developed by US companies like Merck and Squibb. Despite the resentment this situation aroused, it did not appear to hold back the British licensee firms, especially Glaxo. In fact, they went on to discover and manufacture a wave of profitable natural and semi-synthetic penicillins and antibiotics. These not only generated large returns, but also financed, and justified, increased investment in research and development. The most financially successful and innovative British companies during the antibiotics revolution were Glaxo and Beecham. From the 1950s, Glaxo increased its focus on prescription drugs, and not just penicillins and antibiotics, but also the cortico-steroids. By increasing its product portfolio through in-house research and development, mergers and acquisitions,[6] and its decision to market its products in North America and Europe, Glaxo gradually became a major transnational research-based pharmaceutical company.

From 1959, Beecham became very successful at developing semi-synthetic penicillins, starting that year with phenethicillin (marketed under the name Broxil), and following up, most notably, with ampicillin (Penbritin) and amoxycillin (Amoxil). Thanks to these and other successes, the company's pharmaceutical sales increased nearly 16-fold between 1960 and 1970.

From the early 1970s, the international competitiveness of the British pharmaceutical industry began to increase, and by the 1980s this was becoming very apparent. In 1982, Glaxo, the largest British firm (based on its turnover of prescription drugs), was still at only number 20 in the world league table, way behind the big three, which were then Hoechst, Bayer and Merck (ibid.: 163). But by the late 1980s, the British pharmaceutical sector's share of the world market was second only to that of the USA, with Glaxo also reaching second place in sales (Thomas, 1994: 454).

The 1990s saw continued success for the British pharmaceutical industry, but also some major changes. Concerned that the patent protection of its most successful product, Zantac, was nearing the end of its life, Glaxo took over Wellcome in 1995. In January 2000, Glaxo merged with SmithKline Beecham – itself the result of a 1989 merger between Beecham and SmithKline Beckman – to form what would become the world's largest pharmaceutical company, GlaxoSmithKline, with a 7 per cent share of the global prescription drug market and a research and development budget of £2·4 billion (Jones, 2001: 442). In 1993, a new pharmaceutical company, Zeneca, was created that comprised the pharmaceutical activities of ICI. In 1999, Zeneca merged with the Swedish company, Astra, to form AstraZeneca, which then also became one of the world's largest pharmaceutical corporations thanks to the world's best-selling prescription drug, the anti-ulcerant Losec.[7]

The Present-day Global Pharmaceutical Industry

While the science and technology of pharmaceutical research and development has been transformed over the last hundred years, there are marked continuities in terms of the identities of the major producer countries and of the businesses involved. Today's pharmaceutical industry is dominated by transnational corporations almost entirely from the USA and western Europe, especially the UK, Switzerland and Germany. Neither Japan nor the newly-industrializing economies have any large 'top 10' transnational drug firms. Table 5.1 shows the top 20 corporations by sales and global market share in 2000. Only one is not from the USA or western Europe.

The dominance of the US pharmaceutical industry, which, as we have seen, was an early developer (albeit after Germany) has been long-standing, though its peak period of dominance was the middle of the twentieth century. From 1941 to 1963, 60 per cent of new drugs were discovered in the USA, about 8 per cent originated in Switzerland, 6 per cent in Germany and 5 per cent in Britain (Slinn, 1995: 181). From 1975 to 1994, US firms were still the most innovative but relatively less so. The British industry had become the second most innovative in terms of the numbers of new drugs being placed on the market. Clearly, those countries that were among the first to establish pharmaceutical industries continue to be among those with the biggest and most scientifically advanced firms. And most of these firms were established during the early years of the industry in the nineteenth or early twentieth centuries.

However, this picture of continuity may be deceptive. The last decade of the twentieth century saw a tremendous change in the industry, with several mergers and acquisitions involving most of the biggest companies, and resulting in some very large corporations indeed whose nationalities are not always so obvious as they were before (see Table 5.2). This situation is a consequence of a decline in the quantity – and allegedly also the quality – of new chemical entities reaching the market. Many of those that do closely resemble existing ones in terms of their chemical structures and therapeutic effects, and are disparagingly referred to by some commentators as 'me-too drugs'. Consequently, the global market for pharmaceuticals has become extremely competitive albeit also highly concentrated at the level of therapeutic groups. The most vulnerable companies are those which have become excessively dependent on one or two highly profitable drugs nearing the end of their patent lives, but lack the security of having a large portfolio of potential best-sellers in the pipeline. As the twentieth century came to an end, famous names like Wellcome, Beechams, Ciba, Geigy, Hoechst and Rhône-Poulenc disappeared from the list of big names in the pharmaceutical industry.

Pharmaceutical Patent Law in the Twentieth Century: Evolution and Business Strategy

The Importance of Patents

Pharmaceutical companies need to make increasingly large research and development investments not only to discover new products but especially to secure government authorization to sell them. According to the Tufts Center for the Study of Drug Development (2001), the average cost to develop a new drug in the United States rose from US$54 million in 1979 (at 1976 dollars), to $231 million in 1991 (at 1987 dollars), and as much as $802 million in 2001. While such statistics are

Table 5.1   The top 20 pharmaceutical companies by global market share and sales, 2000

Company	Country	Sales (£bn)	Global market share (%)
1. Pfizer	USA	15 266	7.3
2. GlaxoSmithKline	UK	14 533	6.9
3. Merck	USA	10 875	5.2
4. AstraZeneca	UK	9 423	4.5
5. Bristol-Myers Squibb	USA	8 758	4.2
6. Novartis	SWI	8 187	3.9
7. Johnson and Johnson	USA	8 152	3.9
8. Aventis	FRA	7 457	3.6
9. Pharmacia	USA	6 758	3.2
10. American Home Products	USA	6 310	3.0
Leading 10		**95 721**	**45.7**
11. Lilly	USA	6 149	2.9
12. Hoffman LaRoche	SWI	6 103	2.9
13. Abbott	USA	5 153	2.5
14. Schering-Plough	USA	5 104	2.4
15. Bayer	GER	4 059	1.9
16. Takeda	JAP	3 691	1.8
17. Boehringer Ingelheim	GER	2 906	1.4
18. Sanofi-Synthélabo	FRA	2 403	1.1
19. Amgen	USA	2 028	1.0
20. Schering AG	GER	1 941	0.9
Leading 20		**135 258**	**64.6**

Source: IMS, published on website of Association of the British Pharmaceutical Industry (*http://www.abpi.org.uk/statistics/section.asp?sect=1*).

welcomed by the industry for their propaganda value, the methodologies used to produce these estimates are problematical to those who believe the figures are unrealistically high.[8] For example, a civil society organization called Public Citizen (2001) has calculated that the total for 1991 should be only about $110 million. PhRMA took this alternative study seriously enough to commission the accountancy firm Ernst and Young to produce a response.

Wherever the truth lies, there is no doubt that many (though by no means all) of the new drugs entering the market cost a great deal of money to develop. Owing to past tragedies, especially thalidomide, new drugs in the industrialized countries must now undergo extensive clinical trials to demonstrate safety. These are hugely

Table 5.2 Mergers and acquisitions in pharmaceuticals, 1989–2000

Year	Companies involved (nationality)
1989	Dow (US)/Marion (US)
	Bristol-Myers (US)/Squibb (US)
	SmithKline (US)/Beecham (UK)
1990	Rhône-Poulenc (France)/Rorer (US)
	Roche (Swiss)/Genentech (US)
1994	SmithKline Beecham (US/UK)/Sterling Health (US)
	BASF (Germany)/Boots (UK)
	American Home Products (US)/American Cyanamid (US)
	Elf Sanofi (France)/Sterling Drug (US)
	Roche (Swiss)/Syntex (US)
1995	Glaxo (UK)/Wellcome (UK)
	Hoechst (German)/Marion Merrell Dow (US)
	Pharmacia (Swedish)/Upjohn (US)
	Rhône-Poulenc (French)/Fisons (UK)
1996	Ciba-Geigy (Swiss)/Sandoz (Swiss) = Novartis
1997	Roche (Swiss)/Boehringer Mannheim (Germany)
1999	Hoechst (Germany)/Rhône-Poulenc (France) = Aventis
	Astra (Swedish)/Zeneca (UK)
2000	Glaxo Wellcome (UK)/SmithKline Beecham (UK/US)
	Pfizer (US)/Warner-Lambert (US)

Source: Owen (1999: 382).

expensive in both time and money. Since patents have to be filed at the drug discovery phase prior to the development period, by the time the product reaches the market the patent may well have less than half of its 20-year term left to run. Consequently, 'new drugs must be sold worldwide, since no company can fully exploit a patented product, recouping its research and development costs solely in its own home market, even in the two largest national markets, the USA and Japan' (Slinn, 1995: 168).

Patents are extremely important for pharmaceutical companies. Monopoly protection of a commercially successful drug provides huge returns that more than make up for the required investment in discovery and development. Several surveys (for example, Levin *et al.*, 1987; Mansfield, 1986; Taylor and Silberston, 1973) indicate that pharmaceuticals are one of the few industrial sectors in which patents are effective means to capture returns from research and development. This effectiveness is enhanced by the ways – sometimes highly questionable – in which these companies use the patent system. It is important in this context to understand that drugs are not usually protected by single patents whose expiry allows anybody to produce the drug. As Carlos Correa of the University of Buenos Aires explains (2001a:11),

> Only a few (several dozen) 'new chemical entities' ... are developed and patented each year. Nonetheless, thousands of patents are granted annually in this sector. This paradox can be explained by the enormous capacity that the sector's major firms have built up not only for developing authentic inventions, but also for taking out patents on secondary, occasionally trivial developments, in order to extend their monopoly over a product or process, beyond that allowed by the original patent.

Thus pharmaceutical companies use patents (and also trade marks) strategically in order to restrict competition, in some cases for several years beyond the 20-year patent duration. 'Evergreening' or 'line extensions' are terms used to refer to the use of IP rights in order to extend the monopoly or at least the market dominance of a drug beyond the life of the original patent protecting it. We can get an idea of how much is at stake when we consider that 'drugs with annual sales of some $45 billion are set to go off patent between 2001 and 2005' (Reuters, 2001a). It should not be surprising, then, that drug companies will try to stretch out their exclusive rights over blockbuster drugs for as long as possible, especially when they are heavily dependent on a small number of such highly profitable products (or even just one). For example, firms might seek to obtain patents on new delivery methods for the drug, on reduced dosage regimens, or on new versions of the active compound or combinations that are more effective or that produce fewer side-effects than the original substance. Another tactic that may be possible, in the case of those drugs that, when metabolized by the body, are transformed into another substance which directly causes the therapeutic effect, is to patent also this latter chemical.[9, 10] Doubtless, companies other than the owner of the patent protecting the original substance will also seek to acquire such patents. But in many cases these firms will prefer to license their patents to the first company, since the latter already enjoys the monopoly position and is therefore better placed to make commercial use of them. In addition, pharmaceutical companies, like those in other industries, use patents for a range of strategic purposes such as creating broad zones of exclusion around their inventions, preventing other companies from exploiting their own patents, and enhancing bargaining positions in cross-licensing deals (Granstrand, 1999: 218–22; Rivette and Klein, 2000).[11]

Generally, such practices are legal. But other practices may not be, such as setting up price-fixing cartels with other patent-holding firms. They may also collude with generic producers, for example by paying them to drop their legal challenges to vulnerable patents or to agree to delay selling their own versions of drugs after the product patent has expired. For example, Bayer came to an agreement in 1997 with a generic company called Barr Pharmaceuticals. By this deal, Barr agreed to drop its legal challenge to Bayer's patent on its commercially successful antibiotic, Cipro (ciprofloxacin). In exchange, Bayer agreed to pay Barr around US$28 million a year until 2003, when the patent on Cipro is due to expire. Two other companies are also alleged to have been paid by Bayer not to challenge its patent (Reuters, 2001b; USA Today, 2001). In 2001, Abbott Laboratories was accused of paying generic firms to delay the commercialization of generic versions of Hytrin, a commercially successful treatment for hypertension and enlarged prostate (Austin, 2001).

Companies also use trade mark law to extend their market power beyond the patented drug's expiry date.[12] Patented drugs are usually marketed under their brand name rather than the generic name. Since generic producers cannot use this name, it is often very difficult for them to promote their alternative product effectively. Therefore physicians may continue to prescribe the branded product even if it is more expensive than the generic version. In fact, in many countries, physicians may not even know that alternatives exist. In the case of known compounds whose therapeutic properties were discovered several years after their discovery, this form of protection may, in the absence of product patent protection, be the most effective one available.[13]

A good example is an anti-cancer substance derived from the Pacific Yew (Taxus brevifolia). The compound in question was first isolated in 1966 by Monroe Wall, who was working at the Research Triangle Institute in North Carolina. The following year he gave it the name 'taxol'. In 1971, Wall and his colleague Mansukh Wani published the results of their work, including their elucidation of taxol's chemical structure (Goodman and Walsh, 2001: 56–7). In 1991, the US National Cancer Institute signed a research and development agreement with Bristol-Myers Squibb. According to the contract, Bristol-Myers Squibb was given access to the NCI's clinical trial data, and authorized to develop taxol as a commercial product, subject to the approval of the government's Food and Drug Administration (FDA). As it turned out, since much of the research and development had already been carried out by the NCI, this approval was granted as early as December of the following year (just four months after the application was submitted). Inexplicably, despite the existence of more than 600 published articles using the name 'taxol' to refer to the compound, the US Patent and Trademark Office accepted the company's application to register 'taxol' as a trade mark. 'Thereafter, all references to taxol would be required to carry the registered sign, hence taxol became Taxol®' (ibid.: 169–70). Subsequently, the company succeeded in registering the name in over 50 countries, and actively defended its newly-acquired rights to a word it had had nothing to do with coining or applying to the substance in question. This action by the company, which essentially privatized a word that had been coined over 25 years earlier and had become common currency among scientists, was condemned by *Nature*, the prestigious science magazine, which was then warned by the company's lawyers that it must use the word only in association with the product sold by Bristol-Myers Squibb (see *Nature*, 1995: 370). By 2000, taxol was generating over US$1·5 billion in annual sales (B-MS, 2001).

In addition, trade mark law in certain countries can be used to protect the colour and form of the capsules. And to make the legal minefield even more treacherous for generic firms, the original producer of a drug may try to assert copyright over the printed information accompanying the product. According to Frederick Abbott of Florida State University, 'despite the apparent overreaching in arguing that "take two tablets every four hours" is the subject of copyright protection, the pharmaceutical manufacturers do not hesitate to delay the introduction of generic drugs with litigation over this question' (2002: 41).

In restricting price competition, the benefits of such tactics for the original producers can be substantial. There again, the recent wave of mergers and acquisitions, a phenomenon linked to the loss of revenues faced by some companies owing to the expiry of patents protecting particularly lucrative products, shows that 'evergreening' has its limits as a business strategy. It may be a panacea for a weak product pipeline, but it is certainly not a cure. In response to this situation, pharmaceutical firms and business associations actively seek to influence government intellectual property and health regulation. In doing so, they often find themselves competing over the relevant regulatory spaces with health and consumer lobby groups that can compensate for their lack of economic strength by effective organization and the moral force of their arguments.

One approach frequently used by the corporate sector is propagandizing. This may take such forms as advice, gentle persuasion, veiled or overt threats, and the publication (for example on their websites or in newspaper advertisements) of statistics that are selected and interpreted in order to back up whatever their demands are. In addition to producing their own propaganda literature, pharmaceutical business associations sometimes fund research in order to provide 'objective' evidence demonstrating the legitimacy of their claims.[14] When it suits their interests they portray their business as a dynamic and innovative one that provides, not just advanced healthcare, but jobs and a huge positive contribution to the trade balance. But they may also try to convey the impression that they are suffering from unfriendly regulations and being unfairly victimized by uninformed activists with a hostile agenda. Pharmaceutical corporations and business associations often find it expedient to instil in governments and policy makers certain impressions about the position of the national industry in the global market 'league table' to back their demands for a regulatory environment most conducive to the pursuit of profit. They may seek to show how strong this position is or they may argue that it is declining. Whichever the case, the regulatory environment is sure to be one of the main causes.

According to PhRMA (1998), of the 152 major new drugs launched between 1975 and 1994, 45 per cent came from the USA, 14 per cent originated in Britain, and 9 per cent in Switzerland. The figure for the USA is lower than the immediate post-Second World War period, but there is no suggestion of any decline in either of PhRMA's 1998 or 1999 reports. Instead, PhRMA (1999: 10) praises the government for its relatively laissez-faire regulatory framework:

It is no accident that the US leads the world in pharmaceutical research and development and that US companies have developed the lion's share of the important drugs of the past few decades. That's because, in contrast to the rest of the world, the US has a relatively free market for pharmaceuticals – one that rewards risk with at least the possibility of commensurate profit.

The European Federation of Pharmaceutical Industries and Associations is less positive about Europe's prospects. Taking the total of new chemical and biological entities (NCEs and NBEs) placed on the market between 1975 and 1994 (numbering about a thousand), EFPIA's figures show that the share provided by US and Japanese firms has increased, while Europe's share, which has been higher than the others throughout this period, has declined steadily, from 65 per cent of the total between 1960 and 1965, to 60 per cent from 1975 to 1979, falling to only 36 per cent between 1990 and 1994. EFPIA seeks to demonstrate how important the pharmaceutical industry is to the European economy (which is undoubtedly true) while arguing that it is suffering from competition from the USA and Japan, where the regulatory environment is, apparently, more innovation-friendly. On the other hand, without explicitly mentioning the US government's continuing substantial financial commitment to biomedical research and development, EFPIA pointedly contrasts the USA with Europe where 'pharmaceutical R&D is funded almost entirely out of pharmaceutical companies' own earnings' (EFPIA, 1998: 22).

While both PhRMA and EFPIA claim to be opposed to state intervention in the market,[15] they fully support it when it comes to intellectual property regulation, since they do not consider this to be state intervention at all – which is bad – but the best way to support innovation, which of course makes it good. These organizations also link their patent-related demands to the interests of patients. According to EFPIA (1999), 'without the limited period of exclusivity conferred by a patent on a product most new cures would not be created'. EFPIA also warns that failure to remove the TRIPS provision on exhaustion of IP rights will, among other things, 'create potential health risks'. And PhRMA (1998: 79) claims that, 'without patent protection, it is highly unlikely that a company would be rewarded for its invention – or, more importantly, that patients would receive many new medicines'.

So is such persuasion anything new? And if it is not – as our new institutionalist approach would lead us to suspect – to what extent has it been behind the development of patent law over the years? The rest of this chapter should provide some answers.

The United States

Knowing more about the development of the American pharmaceutical industry, one can readily understand that the companies' picture of an ideal patent regime would look very different over time. So in the early days when the industry was relatively backward compared to foreign competitors and producing few if any original products, its interests lay in a patent system offering fairly weak protection and containing public interest provisions such as working requirements and compulsory licensing. As it became more innovative, it preferred a system allowing the new types of product to be protected while opposing public interest or antitrust measures to weaken protection. Once the cost of doing research increased and the number of new products began to decline, one would expect the industry to seek privileges such as extended protection terms and to become more adept and aggressive in using IP systems strategically. Finally, as the industry became an important producer for international markets, one could predict that it would favour strong levels of patent protection around the world.

Those are our expectations. But were these assumed preferences ones that the companies actually held? And how successful was the US pharmaceutical industry in influencing patent law and policy anyway? This part of the chapter should provide some answers.

It is important first to be aware that the patent system has not always been popular. During the 1920s and 1930s, there was a strong mood of distrust towards big business. The antitrust movement was especially powerful during the Roosevelt administration, which took power in 1933. The patent system did not escape the critical scrutiny of the 'trust-busters', and Congress heard numerous condemnations of patents and calls for the rights to be rolled back such as through compulsory licensing, especially during the 1938–41 hearings to the Temporary National Economic Committee, which the administration and Congress had jointly convened (Owens, 1991). But this movement went into decline when the USA entered the war in 1941. Recognition by the politicians that big business commitment to technological innovation was so important not only for the country's economic advancement but also for winning the war probably had much to do with this. So the Committee's recommendation for compulsory licensing was rejected in 1945 by the President Roosevelt-appointed National Patent Planning Commission. Given the Commission's inclusion of representatives of large corporations like General Electric and General Motors, this outcome was probably inevitable anyway. Nonetheless, these businesses did not always get their way in the courts, where anti-patent sentiments were very common during the 1950s and beyond. Yet despite the hostility directed at patents from time to time, the US patent system has at almost all times been more supportive of the interests of owners than have those of Europe. The USA has never required patents to be domestically worked, and compulsory licensing has been kept outside the patent system itself but left to competition and antitrust regulators to impose whenever this is deemed necessary.

Consequently, whenever a given industrial sector prefers weak protection levels (by the standards of the time), it has to campaign for a lowering of the standards rather than for a maintenance of the status quo. This is of course likely to encounter the opposition of more successful and economically important sectors. In fact, the US pharmaceutical industry did favour weakening protection in the early twentieth century. They justified this on the grounds that they were victims of unfair competition from abroad. In 1919, the American Pharmaceutical Association, an organization founded in 1852 to represent pharmacists, publicly denounced the 'unfair monopolies on medicinal chemicals and dyes' held by German companies that they accused of abusing the US patent and trade mark systems. The Association alleged that they were doing this in two ways (APA, 1919: 77–9).

The first was to deliberately miss out important information when disclosing their inventions to the Patent Office. Consequently, they could not be copied by others even after the patent (or patents) protecting the chemical product or process had expired. Given that British companies were making similar complaints at this time, the Association's concerns were probably legitimate. One of the more extreme cases was the famous Haber–Bosch nitrogen fixation process, which was protected by several US patents owned by BASF. It took many years of effort and millions of dollars in research expenditure for scientists to replicate it even after the patents had been expropriated by the government during the First World War. According to one account, 'the Badische Company had effectively bulwarked this discovery with strong, broad patents which detailed meticulously the apparatus, temperatures, and pressures, but cleverly avoided particulars as to the catalysts employed or their preparation. This last information was the core of the process so far as its practical operation was concerned'.[16]

The second way, which is common today and is not usually considered any more to be wrong, was to secure indefinite control over trade marks covering the names of drugs. This was very beneficial to companies seeking to maintain as far as possible their monopoly control over drugs after the patents protecting them had expired. Such control of the name, in the rather bitter words of F.C. Stewart, Director of the Scientific Department of H.K. Mulford Company and Chairman of the Committee on Patents and Trademarks of the American Pharmaceutical Association, 'practically enable[d] the commercial introducer to convert the entire educational machinery of the medical and pharmaceutical professions into a great advertising bureau for exploiting the sick room' (Stewart, 1919: 75).

The Association advocated changes to the law allowing only chemical processes to be patented. If product protection continued to be permitted, the law should provide for compulsory licensing. With respect to trade marks on drug names, protection should expire at the same time as the patent. This is certainly not a position that the US pharmaceutical industry would hold today! It is interesting to note that the Association took a strictly utilitarian line on IP rights:

> It should be understood that the patent and trademark laws, like all other laws, are primarily designed to benefit the public at large and only secondarily to benefit the individual ... There are some who assume that the object of the Patent Law is to protect inventors in their so-called natural right to the exclusive manufacture and sale of their inventions and the object of the Trademark Law is to protect and foster monopolies. Nothing is further from the truth. The objects of the Patent and Trademark Laws are altruistic and not egoistic.

It may be worth mentioning that such a view is quite common among generic producers and firms in today's developing countries that fear competition from wealthier and more technologically advanced foreign companies better able to take advantage of IP protection.

The Association failed to achieve reforms to the patent and trade mark laws. It cannot have helped their cause that the changes they proposed conflicted with the interests of businesses in other sectors that had benefited greatly from the existing standards of protection and whose desire for reform was limited to improving their efficiency. It is interesting to speculate whether the changes they wanted to see would have been made if the USA had not decided to take part in the war and then to expropriate the 4500 German-owned US chemical patents. As we will see, the British patent law *was* changed at this time to prohibit the patenting of chemical substances.

As the US pharmaceutical industry began to develop its own products, its interests did become rather different. Since its first products were not, as in Germany and Switzerland, synthetic chemicals but were of natural origin, the question arose of whether these could be protected. The product of nature doctrine, which was formulated in the previous century, set certain limits on the extent to which natural substances and life forms could be protected. Nevertheless, as the US pharmaceutical industry increased its ability to develop new products, the Patent Office was often quite flexible in its application of the doctrine to the extent of allowing purified or isolated natural products to be protected. In addition, the courts sometimes interpreted the law in ways that favoured owners in cases where the bounds of patentability relating to new kinds of product were unclear and needed to be demarcated.

A good example is a 1911 case relating to two patents issued in 1903 and 1904 for a glandular extractive product in the form of a purified form of adrenaline, and for this compound in a solution with salt and a preservative. Parke Davis and Co., which was accused by the H.K. Mulford Co. of infringing its patents, defended itself on a number of grounds, one of which was that the inventions were mere products of nature and that this made the patents invalid. The judge, ruling in favour of Mulford, held that

Takamine [the inventor] was the first to make it available for any use by removing it from the other gland-tissue in which it was found, and, while it is of course possible logically to call this a purification of the principle, it became for every practical purpose a new thing commercially and therapeutically.[17, 18]

Robert Merges and Richard Nelson have used this case to argue, with justification, that the practice of claiming, not just a method of producing a purified natural substance but the end-product as well, can result in patents that are unnecessarily broad:

The adrenaline patent would be infringed by the use of a radically different, and better, process for making the same natural product unless the characteristics of the product were judged substantially different. Yet the argument is not convincing that what the original inventor invented was the product, in addition to her particular process for making it. (Merges and Nelson, 1990: 67)

However, court decisions sometimes frustrated the interests of those seeking to expand protection to cover new subject matters. In 1939, the Court of Customs and Patent Appeals upheld a US Patent Office rejection of claims relating to vitamin C isolated from lemon juice.[19] The main basis for the ruling was that, while the two inventors had been first to isolate vitamin C crystals from lemon juice, they had not been first to isolate vitamin C from *any* source. There again, this was not exactly a subject matter issue, since it did not preclude the patenting of vitamins that had not previously been isolated.

Proof of this came a decade later. In December 1947, scientists at Merck isolated a cobalt-containing substance called cyanocobalamin from a microorganism called Streptomyces griseus, the source also of the antibiotic streptomycin (see below).[20] This substance, which was useful in treating pernicious anaemia, was christened vitamin B_{12} by the scientists who had isolated it, and was patented by the company. The substance was protected by two US patents: 2 563 794 ('Vitamin B-12'), which was issued in 1951, and 2 703 302 ('Vitamin B-12 active composition and process of preparing same'), which was issued in 1955. Although the product claims of the latter patent were invalidated by a district court in 1957, they were reinstated on appeal. Both patents were the subject of another court case in 1967. The court upheld the first patent entirely, stating:

> The patentees of the '794 patent have given to the world, for the first time, a medicine that can be used successfully in treating all patients suffering with pernicious anemia, a medicine that is subject to accurate standardization, and avoids the unfavorable reactions of the earlier liver extracts. It did not exist in nature in the form in which the patentees produced it, and nothing in the prior art either suggested or anticipated it.[21]

Although five of the 12 claims in the second patent were invalidated, the principle that a 'composition of matter' consisting of a purified form of a natural product could be patented subject to passing the tests of non-obviousness and utility was not called into question.

Two early pharmaceutical breakthroughs that also turned out to be patentable despite their being new types of subject were insulin and the antibiotic streptomycin. These are interesting cases, not least because the companies involved were heavily dependent on their collaborations with universities where the initial discoveries had been made, and in consequence found it expedient not to jeopardize their reputation by asserting their rights in the aggressive way that subsequently became the norm in the industry.

In 1923[22] and 1924,[23] two US patents for isolated and purified insulin and the extractive process were granted and assigned to the University of Toronto. The inventors of the earlier invention were Frederick Banting (who became a Nobel laureate that year) and three colleagues from the university, while the inventor named in the second patent was a scientist employed by the Eli Lilly company. The reason for the assignment of the latter patent to Toronto was that the two had come up with an agreement whereby Eli Lilly would enjoy temporary monopoly rights in the US market for insulin. In exchange, they would collaborate to further develop insulin and scale up production, and pool patent rights from any follow-up inventions. Although the patent pooling deal only applied to non-US patents, Toronto persuaded Eli Lilly to assign the patent to the university. One reason the company agreed to this was that Washington University had come up with a similar invention which made the patent's validity questionable (Bliss, 1982: 139, 180–81). This suggests a hard-nosed commercial motivation that one does not normally associate with universities, at least not of that era.[24] But while the university's dealings with Eli Lilly were undoubtedly very shrewd, its motivation was public-spirited. Toronto's intention was to prevent any company from holding a secure and long-term monopoly position in the USA. As for Canada, the university granted production rights to Connaught Medical Research Laboratories, which it had established in 1914 to carry out medical research and the not-for-profit production and distribution of health products to the Canadian public.[25] Banting and his colleagues gave up the rights to their British and Canadian patents to the university in exchange for a nominal sum of one dollar each with no royalties (Fishbein, 1937: 899). From 1922, Connaught worked closely with scientists at Eli Lilly to purify insulin and increase production. Thanks to its control of the insulin patents, the university was able to force companies licensed to manufacture insulin to send their batches to the university's Insulin Committee for assessment of quality and approval for sale. The patents also enabled it to fulfil its public service role by ploughing back revenue from the patents into further research, including support for a paediatric research foundation.[26]

In 1948, Merck was granted a patent for crystalline salts of the antibiotic, streptomycin, and for a process for preparing them. Streptomycin, the second antibiotic to come onto the market after penicillin and the first drug to be effective against tuberculosis, was discovered by Selman Waksman of Rutgers University, who had received financial support for his research from Merck. In exchange for royalties to the university, Waksman agreed to assign to the company any patents arising from his research. At that stage there was no certainty that his discoveries would turn out to be patentable anyway. In the event, they were. Although streptomycin was a natural product that could hardly have been invented by the Merck scientist named in the patent, it was claimed to the satisfaction of the examiner that, 'for the first time, streptomycin is available in a form which not only has valuable therapeutic properties but also can be produced, distributed, and administered in a practicable way'.[27] Subsequently, Waksman managed to persuade

Merck, concerned perhaps not to be seen to be exploiting what had recently become a state university, to transfer ownership of all patents to the Rutgers Research and Endowment Foundation so that production could be licensed to as many manufacturers as possible. Not surprisingly, while the university earned millions of dollars, the price of streptomycin fell during the following decade as competition increased and production methods improved (Sneader, 1985: 325; Temin, 1979: 436). From 1946 to 1950 alone, it dropped 70-fold (Weatherall, 1990: 181).

Subsequently, the regulatory environment changed in ways that made the drug firms more determined to keep price levels high by preventing competitors from entering the market for their drugs. Most of the reforms were introduced after the war and had to do with safety and efficacy testing, but an important early change came in with the 1938 Food, Drug and Cosmetic Act, which divided drugs into over-the-counter drugs and prescription (or 'ethical') drugs. The latter could only be sold with a doctor's prescription. While prescription drug sales promotion was aimed at the doctors, the actual buyers were wholesalers, pharmacies and hospitals. Doctors generally had no particular reason to treat price as a factor in determining which drugs to prescribe. Therefore, the demand for drugs was more price-inelastic than it would have been if the buyers and the prescribers were the same people (Steele, 1962: 139–43; Temin, 1979: 434–5). The streptomycin patent was in itself an important new regulatory development since it clarified to the industry that the new antibiotics were patentable despite being 'products of nature' (Steel, 1962: 136; Temin, 1979: 436).

In spite of all this, as companies began to discover and market increasing numbers of effective but very similar antibiotics, there was a very real threat of price-reducing competition. This actually happened in the case of both penicillin and streptomycin. In the USA, the price per dose of penicillin fell from $20 during the Second World War (when the government purchased all penicillin produced) to $1 in 1946, and to 10 cents in 1949. Between 1948 and 1955, the price of streptomycin plunged from $20 per gram to only 15 cents (Achilladelis, 1993: 287).

The companies responded in three ways (ibid.: 288). First, they adopted strategic IP policies. For example, they protected their drugs by a combination of patents and trade marks, and asserted their rights aggressively in the courts. Ironically, the German companies who pioneered this tactic earlier in the century had been condemned for doing so by the American firms of the time. Second, those companies that developed new drugs but did not market their own products (such as Merck and Pfizer) set up large sales teams or acquired or merged with companies that already had them. Third, they sought to keep competitors out and prices high for as long as their patents remained in force. Three options were available to them that could under certain circumstances be adopted simultaneously. One way was to restrict patent licensing.[28] Among the first companies to adopt this tactic in a collective way were the five that cornered the market in broad spectrum antibiotics. The synthetic steroid producers followed their example from the late 1950s (Temin, 1979: 442). Companies that continued to license their patents to all-comers often found it unprofitable to do so. This was the experience of Ciba, with its plant-derived drug reserpine (Serpasil),[29] and with isoniazid, a tuberculosis treatment that had been developed independently by Hoffman LaRoche and Squibb (Frost, 1963: 97). The second option was to license patents using highly restrictive provisions that, for example, prevented licensees from supplying foreign markets and required them to purchase the intermediate chemicals from the licensors, or that retained the rights of licensors to follow-on innovations by licensees. The third option was to cooperate in certain ways with competitors selling similar products, for example by sharing patents and fixing prices.

One of the most controversial instances of the use of patents to support anti-competitive behaviour by the industry took place during the 1950s when five companies formed an international antibiotics cartel. The story begins with the introduction of the broad spectrum antibiotics, whose chemical structures were unknown when they first came to market, but turned out often to be extremely similar to each other. The earliest of these products were Lederle's Aureomycin (introduced in 1948), Parke Davis' Chloromycetin (1949),[30] and Pfizer's Terramycin (1950). The similarity of these products stimulated intense competition which was reflected not just in increased marketing and advertising expenditures but also in a determination to elucidate the chemical structures of these drugs and to develop portfolios of related compounds. Pfizer's research proved the close affinity of Aureomycin and Terramycin and resulted in a very similar but more effective new substance, which was the first ever semi-synthetic antibiotic. This was patented and given the name 'tetracycline'. Lederle also discovered tetracycline by the same method and filed patent applications. Subsequently, Bristol and Hayden Chemical Corporation came up with tetracycline by another method and also applied for patents. Pfizer's and Bristol's patents were granted in 1955 after being initially rejected (Sneader, 1985: 327).

The other companies' patent applications failed. However, it was extremely doubtful that either patent should really have been awarded and the companies themselves were apparently fully aware that they were vulnerable to legal challenge (Braithwaite, 1984: 184–5). But by agreeing to recognize Pfizer's patent and to limit competition, a group of five companies – Pfizer, Cyanamid (Lederle's parent company), Bristol, Squibb and Upjohn – cornered the tetracycline market and managed to ensure that the price of their closely related products remained high and almost equal for about a decade. According to John Braithwaite, the situation suggested that the patent was providing 'a cover for conspiratorial behaviour to partition a market which in the absence of the patent would have been clearly illegal' (ibid.: 184). The prices began to decline from the early 1960s during the US Senate's investigation of anti-competitive behaviour by the pharmaceutical industry, and afterwards when a generic drug producer, McKesson and Robbins, entered the market and stayed there by convincing Pfizer that it was willing to face a patent infringement suit with confidence that the court would find in its favour. Although the government failed – despite its determined efforts – to prove that the companies had violated antitrust law or had defrauded the Patent Office, they had to pay hundreds of millions of dollars in legal settlements. Nonetheless, the profits the five companies made not just in the USA but worldwide through their control of tetracycline were enormous, and helped turn them into major pharmaceutical corporations (ibid.: 176; Temin, 1979: 441). One can only speculate about how many people's lives might have been saved if prices had been allowed to fall earlier.

Unsurprisingly, such behaviour provoked a backlash. Politicians responded by subjecting the industry to very close scrutiny. From 1959 to 1962, the Senate Subcommittee on Antitrust and Monopoly, under the chairmanship of Senator Estes Kefauver, carried out an inquiry into the pharmaceutical industry. After three years of hearings, the subcommittee concluded that the drug companies were charging too much for their drugs and making excessive profits. Through patenting and branding, Kefauver and the subcommittee believed, they were free to charge as much as they liked, and were using this freedom to excess. Yet many of these companies were spending more money on sales promotion than on research. Moreover, many seemed more interested in developing modified versions of existing drugs than in trying to achieve genuine therapeutic advances. The subcommittee believed that the patent system encouraged such 'inventing-around' owing to the fact that chemical substances were protectable, and not just processes (Kefauver, 1966: 29–99).

Some of the subcommittee's findings were subsequently discredited, such as the claim that countries without patents produced a higher quantity of therapeutically advanced drugs than those with patents. In fact, the breakdown of important drugs (as listed by the subcommittee) that were discovered by countries allowing product patents, only process patents, and no patents at all for drugs, was 94:82:0, respectively (Cooper, 1966: 160). Nonetheless, the subcommittee made a strong case that many companies had indeed been indulging in profiteering and anti-competitive behaviour with the help of the patent system, and that the public was ill-served by such practices. Even so, attempts to introduce legislation to drastically weaken patent rights failed, and the industry managed to get away with its profits intact, albeit with a tarnished reputation.

Two decades later, the pharmaceutical industry became the focus of further legislative activity, this time successful, in the form of the 1984 Drug Price Competition and Patent Term Restoration Act (usually referred to as 'the Hatch–Waxman Act'). Powerful as the research-based sector was, and experienced as it was in lobbying members of Congress, it finally had an effective competitor on Capitol Hill in the form of the generic manufacturers. These latter firms' IP-related interests were of course quite different and they had become sufficiently well-organized to ensure that any legislation affecting them would not stunt their growth.

For the research-based firms, the Act allowed patent term extensions of up to five years to compensate for the restriction on the effective protection term because of the time needed to acquire the FDA's marketing approval. There was of course some justification for this. It was taking increasingly long periods of time for the FDA to approve new chemical entities for sale, and this was reducing the effective period of market exclusivity. But the fact that the agrochemical industry, whose products also took a great deal of time and expense to get approved for sale, was unable to acquire a similar privilege is a testament to the political influence of the pharmaceutical companies.

As for the generic firms, the Act meant that they would only need to file a so-called Abbreviated New Drug Application (ANDA) with the FDA, rather than go through extensive clinical trials to demonstrate the safety and efficacy of their version of the soon to go off patent drug. This meant that approval could take as little as three months. Second, the legislation incorporated the so-called 'Bolar exemption', which meant that certain acts performed before the expiry date of the patent that would normally infringe it were allowed as long as they were related to seeking FDA approval and did not constitute commercial use. The Bolar exemption was named after a court case involving Hoffman LaRoche and a generic producer called Bolar, and has been incorporated into the patent laws of several countries.[31]

Alfred Engelberg, formerly of the Generic Pharmaceutical Industrial Association (GPIA), describes the legislative process which led to the Act as 'a congressionally supervised negotiation between the generic and brand-name pharmaceutical industries in which the parties were compelled to reach a compromise by the legislature' (1999: 390). In this negotiation the respective sections of the industry were represented by the Pharmaceutical Manufacturers Association (PMA, now PhRMA) and the GPIA. According to Engelberg, the Act did not advance the interests of either side of the pharmaceutical industry, or of the public (ibid.: 392): 'patent-term extensions and the Bolar exemption are self-cancelling provisions, which, taken together, have no effect on the length of the exclusive marketing period of most drugs. The patent certification procedures are being abused by both sides and produce no public benefit that would not otherwise occur'. When we consider that as many as 19 per cent of prescription drugs sold in the USA that year were generics, it was no surprise that the generics sector had become more influential and that the research-based firms in consequence had to compromise. Since then, the competition facing companies whose drugs have just gone off patent has increased considerably despite their increasingly creative evergreening strategies. By 1996, thanks in large part to the Hatch–Waxman Act, the generics sector of the industry had increased its share to 43 per cent (Engelberg, 1999).

Significantly, the effective patent life of drugs seems again to be lengthening. The Tufts Center for the Study of Drug Development reported in 2000 that average clinical development times had shortened from over seven years in the early 1990s to less than five years, while average FDA approval times had shortened from around three years to about one (Kaitin, 2000). Moreover, the same decade saw a marked increase in the number of new drug applications subsequently approved for sale by the FDA. According to Jennifer Washburn, writing in *The American Prospect* (2001), 'whereas in the early 1990s the FDA approved 60 per cent of the industry's applications for new products, by the end of the decade 80 per cent were getting approved'. If such trends continue, the extension provided by the

Hatch–Waxman Act may soon no longer be necessary. In this case, though, we can expect determined efforts from the industry to block its removal.

Despite the assertiveness of the generics sector and their rather different interests, the self-styled research-based firms are as influential as ever in the corridors of power. Their interests are represented by an army of Washington-based lobbyists, and they are generous donors to the electoral campaigns of parties and politicians. However, there is a growing number of pressure groups that seek to counter this influence. In spite of their relative lack of financial muscle, some of these groups carry out very impressive research and include some sophisticated and effective activists, such as Consumer Project on Technology and Public Citizen.

The United Kingdom

Like the US system, the British patent system at the start of the twentieth century provided owners with strong rights by the standards of the day. But, as will soon become clear, the historical development of the two systems took quite divergent courses, so that for much of the century they varied quite widely, and offered quite different levels of protection for pharmaceutical inventions. Interest group politics provides at least part of the explanation.

As was explained earlier, the British pharmaceutical industry was a slow developer, and its economic importance prior to the First World War was thus quite small. Neither was it particularly innovative, so it had little use for the patent system. When it came to patent reform, while elements within the much larger chemical industry were very vocal and gained the ears of policy makers and politicians, the drug manufacturers had very little to say. Probably the most vocal and effective of these elements was Ivan Levinstein, who was mentioned in Chapter 4.

The first legislative development in patent law that had a direct bearing on the interests of the pharmaceutical industry took place in 1919 with the passage of an amendment to the 1907 Patents and Designs Act. As a consequence of wartime shortages of important products, the political establishment was ready to adopt a more mercantilist and defensive attitude towards strategic industries. The legislation reflected this attitude very strongly.

The 1919 'Act to amend the Patents and Designs Acts' brought British patent law further into line with the law in most of Europe in that, while it extended the duration of patents from 14 to 16 years for the benefit of inventors who had been prevented from working their patents by the war, it singled out chemicals, foods and medicines for weakened protection. Patent protection was available only for those chemical substances produced by the particular process or processes claimed in the application. According to the Act,

> in the case of inventions relating to substances prepared or produced by chemical processes or intended for food and medicine, the specification shall not include claims for

the substance itself, except when prepared or produced by the special methods or processes of manufacture described and claimed or by their obvious chemical equivalents.

In effect, then, the achievement of secure product protection required applicants to anticipate all possible ways of manufacturing the chemical. The main purpose of these measures was to make it easier for British firms to circumvent the patent monopolies of the German dyestuff firms while acquiring their own (process) patents into the bargain. But the law did not make it too easy for them either. In infringement cases concerning new chemicals protected by a patented process, the burden of proof was on the party whose manufacture of the chemical was alleged to infringe the patent.

Another measure affecting holders of patents for inventions 'intended for or capable of being used for the preparation or production of food or medicine', was that applicants for a licence could acquire one from the comptroller general (the head of the Patent Office). In settling the terms of the licence including royalty payments, the comptroller was required to take into account 'the desirability of making the food or medicine available to the public at the lowest possible price consistent with giving to the inventor due reward for the research leading to the invention'.

Clearly, the dyestuff industry was not the sole concern. The wartime shortage of drugs was obviously another factor in the wording of this section of the legislation. However, the government's interest was not primarily to increase the international competitiveness of the British pharmaceutical industry but to ensure greater self-sufficiency and create a level playing field for the country, bearing in mind that neither Germany, France nor Switzerland allowed chemical products to be protected except through the patenting of manufacturing processes.

It must be said that the pharmaceutical industry was not very influential in government or Parliament at that time. In fact, the industry did not even have a trade association to represent its interests until as late as 1929, when the Wholesale Druggists Trade Association (renamed the Association of the British Pharmaceutical Industry in 1948) was founded 'to advance the interests of its members through improved organisation especially regarding departmental or parliamentary legislation affecting the drug trade' (Abraham, 2002: 232). Evidently, the government did not need to be persuaded by the industry that the measures it introduced were necessary for the country.

In 1930, the Board of Trade set up a committee under the chairmanship of Sir Charles Sargant to advise the government on possible reforms to the patents and designs law and on practices of the Patent Office (UK Board of Trade, 1931). In all, 53 individuals gave evidence, including five from the Chartered Institute of Patent Agents, three from the British Medical Association, two from the Medical Research Council and two from Joseph Nathan and Co. Nonetheless, the interests of the chemical industry were still given far more attention than those of the much smaller pharmaceutical industry. This may not have concerned the drug companies too much, though, as both sectors were primarily concerned to prevent foreign companies from using the patent system to dominate the domestic market. As it was, no substantial changes were made to the patent system during the inter-war era, which was a period of consolidation and gradual progress for the pharmaceutical industry.

The lessons learned from the Second World War were quite different from those of the First World War. In 1918, the British pharmaceutical industry barely existed. In 1945, this was hardly the case. And in the years that followed, exports of various types of product including pharmaceuticals played an important role in Britain's postwar economic recovery (Abraham, 2002: 238). Moreover, the new Labour government was extremely concerned about public health, including the availability of drugs, and was willing to take radical measures. In 1946, the National Health Service Act was passed, leading two years later to the establishment of the NHS.

The NHS formed a key plank in the construction of the welfare state, extending free medical care – including prescription drugs – to the whole population. This had two effects, of which one was favourable to the industry and the other much less so (though on balance the creation of the NHS was beneficial for the drug manufacturers). First, it vastly expanded the market for drugs. Second, the government essentially because a monopsonist, that is to say a sole buyer. In addition to its obvious interest in controlling expenditure, it thus had a very strong bargaining position vis-à-vis the industry.

The 1949 Patents Act took on board the recommendations of the Swan Committee, whose report was published two years earlier. Regarding the bar on the patenting of substances 'produced by chemical processes or intended for food or medicine', the committee's report had the following to say:

> It has been strongly urged that this limitation on the claiming of new substances should be removed as not being in accordance with modern technical developments. It has been argued that the real invention lies in the discovery of a new substance, with new and useful properties, and that the process of manufacture often involves little novelty in itself. Many valuable new substances are produced by synthesising a large number of possible compounds by known methods and then determining which of the new substances have useful properties. It has also been pointed out that the limitation imposed by this sub-section has little practical value, and that it merely encourages the drafting of a specification to cover all conceivable methods of manufacture, so that, in effect, it is the substance itself and not the process of manufacture which is protected by the patent. (UK Board of Trade, 1947)

Impressed with these arguments for removing the bar on complete product protection[32] in respect of chemicals, the committee faced a choice. The first was to allow such protection for chemicals whether or not they were intended for food or medicine. The second, which it preferred, was to maintain the bar on protection of substances intended for food or medicine except by a specified process but to allow full protection of other chemicals. For the sake of legal certainty, the committee recommended the first course of action, and this was implemented by the government in the 1949 Act. But it recommended retaining the 1919 provision on acquiring licences from the comptroller in the case of foods and medicines. This measure was maintained under Section 41 of the new legislation.

The new legislation contained two other interesting provisions. The first, another committee recommendation, was that any application may be refused that 'claims as an invention a substance capable of being used as food or medicine which is a mixture of known ingredients possessing only the aggregate of the known properties of the ingredients, or that it claims as an invention a process producing such a substance by mere admixture'. In other words, mere recipes and mixtures lacking synergistic effects creating unforeseen new properties were unpatentable (Satchell, 1970: 187–8). The second was that claims to a new substance were to be 'construed as not extending to that substance when found in nature'. A patent examiner writing in 1970 had the following to say about this provision:

> This raises the question whether the person who first discloses the chemical constitution of a substance which is known in nature, for example, an alkaloid or an enzyme, and prepares it by a synthetic method, should be allowed to claim the synthetic product, notwithstanding that it is indistinguishable from the natural product. So far we have not been called upon to decide this question. Where an applicant has discovered for the first time the chemical constitution of such a compound and has disclosed at least one method by which it may be synthesized, a claim to the compound defined by its chemical constitution might be allowed under British law. (Ibid.: 180)

Universal healthcare provision is of course expensive, which is why successive governments were concerned to keep drug prices at reasonable levels. Yet these same governments generally accepted the desirability of allowing drug companies to patent their inventions and of respecting patent rights unless there were very good reasons not to. As things turned out, it was not always easy to meet the needs of patients and deal with budgetary constraints without intruding on patent monopolies.

In 1961, the government decided to confront the broad spectrum antibiotics cartel by authorizing the NHS Hospital Services to purchase imported (mostly Italian) generic versions of several of these drugs whose patents were still in force. This action saved the NHS £4 million. Generic producers were encouraged by this and began to apply for compulsory licences. Consequently, 50 Section 41 applications were submitted to the comptroller during the 1960s. Before 1960, no applications at all had been submitted. However, of the 50 applications only four were allowed, most of the rest being withdrawn. This situation was due to the difficult legal procedures that applicants needed to comply with. Even so, the very possibility of compulsory licences probably encouraged the patent-holding firms to be more cooperative about prices than they would otherwise have been.

Pfizer was not at all happy with this situation and decided to make a stand by taking the Ministry (now Department) of Health to court for infringing its patent on tetracycline. In 1965, the House of Lords decided that the ministry was acting within the provisions of the 1949 Act that permitted use – but not sale – of inventions by 'services of the Crown' subject to payment of royalties to the patentee. Although the decision did not allow the General Medical and Pharmaceutical Services, through which 80 per cent of NHS-provided drugs were consumed, to do the same thing, 'the pharmaceutical companies were aghast at what they felt to be abrogation by the State of the fundamental principle of patent rights. Prophecies were made that the British industry would wind up its drug research and become totally dependent on foreign developments' (Taylor and Silberston, 1973: 237).

As it turned out, such prophecies were unjustified. This was so despite the fact that worse was to follow for the industry. In 1967, the Sainsbury Committee, set up to investigate the relationship between the pharmaceutical industry and the NHS, published a report which recommended that the General Medical and Pharmaceutical Services also be treated as a service of the Crown with authority to acquire generic versions of patent-protected drugs (UK Ministry of Health, 1967). The government was initially reluctant to implement this, owing no doubt to pressure from the industry. But the provision was incorporated through an opposition amendment into the 1968 Health Services and Public Health Act (Hancher, 1990: 321).

On the other hand, Section 41 compulsory licences were abolished as recommended by another committee established by the Board of Trade to examine the patent system and the patent law ('the Banks Committee'), whose report was presented to Parliament in 1970 (UK Board of Trade, 1970). The government of the time was reluctant to act upon the recommendation, but in 1977 another government did so through legislation incorporating the European Patent Convention into UK law. Its decision to do so was part of a negotiation with the industry in which the latter agreed to cooperate on the introduction of advertising regulations (Hancher, 1990: 323).

Nowadays, the government identifies the economic health of the nation with that of the pharmaceutical industry. This is understandable given that it is one of the country's most innovative and successful in terms of export performance. But the government continues to have an interest in ensuring that the drugs it purchases on behalf of the public provide value for money. Thanks to the NHS, the prices of drugs and their relationship with the patent system is not a highly charged political issue as it is in the USA and many developing countries. The final report of the Pharmaceutical Industry Competitiveness Task Force, which consisted of representatives from government and industry in equal number, and was published in 2001, had little if anything to say about the UK patent system (UK Dept of Health, 2001). In contrast, the industry was very eager to ensure that the government took heed of its IP interests at the international and European Union levels. It seems clear from the report that the government was extremely sympathetic to these interests.

Continental Europe

The patent laws of France, Germany, Switzerland and other western European countries have evolved along somewhat different paths. Even so, one can make two fairly reliable generalizations. First, most of these countries did not allow pharmaceutical substances to be patented as such for most of the twentieth century. Only the processes for manufacturing them could be. Second, this situation started to change from around 1960, so that by the early 1990s virtually all of them provided product protection for pharmaceuticals.

One might suppose that pharmaceutical industry lobbying was behind the changed situation. In fact, this was not always the case. For example, the change to the German patent system allowing full product protection of pharmaceutical substances was introduced in January 1968 with the entry into force of an Interim Law that removed the following text from the German patent law: 'excluded from patentability are: ... (2) inventions relating to foods, luxury provisions, and drugs, as well as substances produced by chemical processes to the extent that they do not relate to a particular process for the production of these articles'. The main purpose of the measure was to facilitate the work of the German Patent Office and the Federal Patent Court. Companies had effectively overcome the bar on patenting chemical substances by acquiring multiple patents covering all conceivable manufacturing processes. Partly in consequence of this, the Patent Office had a massive backlog of unexamined patent applications that it was anxious to clear (Nastelski, 1972: 268). Another reason to enact the change was to harmonize German law with the emerging new European standards being established by the 1963 Convention on the Unification of Certain Points of Substantive Law on Patents for Invention. In addition, policy makers no longer saw any particular need to maintain the bar on product protection for chemicals. Long gone were the days when such a bar was deemed necessary to protect the industry from foreign competition.

On the other hand, the 1978 overturning of the bar on patents for pharmaceuticals in Italy was a direct result of corporate activism. More than 10 companies acting together challenged the constitutionality of the bar in the Constitutional Court. The court concurred with the companies, on two grounds. The first was that the bar unfairly discriminated against pharmaceutical entrepreneurs and inventors employed in the sector, since they had no legal entitlement to compensation for their inventions. The second was that the Italian Republic had a constitutional obligation to protect and encourage scientific research.

Nonetheless, the 1963 convention and the European Patent Convention were crucial forces for harmonization of European patent law in the area, among others, of pharmaceutical inventions. Once the texts of these treaties had been agreed, countries had little alternative but to fall into line.

But why did it take so long for many European countries to allow product patents for pharmaceuticals? It is important first to be aware that many countries have for public policy reasons excluded or restricted pharmaceutical products from patentability, and that even in western Europe (though never in the USA) this situation persisted in many countries for most of the twentieth century. The main scientific explanation for the removal of the exclusion in western European countries during the mid- to late-twentieth century lies in the changing research strategies pursued by the modern pharmaceutical industry from the post-Second World War period owing largely to the difficulty in coming up with new substances – in marked contrast to the enormous ranges of dyestuffs rapidly developed by Hoechst and Bayer. Moreover, the research and development costs per product rose considerably. It is frequently claimed that an average of 10 000 substances will need to be tested to come up with a new therapeutic product, and a drug will not go on the market until it has been subjected to pharmacological and toxicological tests and extensive clinical trials. Given the increasing scarcity of new chemical entities (NCEs) entering the market, companies have more to lose from failing to prevent competitors from copying them or inventing around them to develop similar me-too products. This situation is likely to affect both the research strategies of firms and their IP interests. The commercial promise of product innovation increases, while process innovation becomes less interesting. And when it comes to IP, strong and broad patent protection becomes more important than ever.

The industry's demands for stronger and broader protection bore fruit in 1992, when the European Council adopted a Regulation requiring European Union countries to provide monopoly rights for medicinal products beyond the life of the basic patents protecting them, to make up for the time taken to secure marketing authorization (Bently and Sherman, 2001: 551).[33] These rights are known as supplementary protection certificates (SPCs). Applications by a patent holder for an SPC must be made to the national patent offices within six months of receiving marketing authorization for the drug in question in that country. EFPIA and the major European drug companies lobbied hard for these rights on the grounds that such privileges were available to their American and Japanese competitors in their domestic markets. But the industry did not completely get its own way. As a result of campaigning by patient and consumer groups and generic producers, the maximum possible extension period was just five years (Cornish, 1999: 159; NCC, 1991: 47). This was somewhat shorter than EFPIA's original demand for an effective patent life of 20 years.

The Pharmaceutical Industry, the Evolution of Patent Law and the Public Interest

Like other types of business, the pharmaceutical industry seeks to maximize its profits. As a major user of the patent system, the industry in the developed world understandably seeks to influence intellectual property policy making. This chapter has shown that this is nothing new. But while, in the past, the outcome of their efforts was a weakening of rights, nowadays the research-based or branded companies among them consistently lobby for ever-stronger rights. Given the economic importance of the industry in countries like the USA, the UK, Germany and Switzerland, and the support they get from the patent community in persuading policy makers that stronger rights are good for the country, it is hardly surprising that they are so often successful. Consequently, if we compare today's patent systems of North America and Europe with those of a hundred years ago and follow the trends during the intervening years, we find that the legal rights available to pharmaceutical inventors have never been stronger or more secure in all of these countries than they are today.

On the basis of what we have learned so far, let us try to answer four very important questions. First, how did pharmaceutical corporations use patent law and other IP rights to maximize returns from their research and development investments through the market-place? Second, what did corporations do when they found patent systems to be inadequate in furthering their interests? Third, how successful were their attempts to change patent systems? Fourth, can it be concluded that patent law stimulated scientific and technological advancement and thereby resulted in more cures than there would have been without patents?

Taking the first question, pharmaceutical companies used patents and other IP rights, especially trade marks, in various ways and for different purposes. Using IP rights strategically to exclude competitors from markets in particular drugs, or classes of drugs, was pioneered by German businesses and has become increasingly sophisticated over the years. The evergreening tactics described in this chapter provide some good examples. While the overall goal of such behaviour has always been to maximize profits, the specific aims of using IP rights include those of recouping and profiting from huge and growing research and development investments, differentiating one company's products from similar ones produced by a rival, and of maintaining high price levels for as long as possible by preventing generic producers from entering the market. The use of IP rights and licences to cartelize the supply of broad spectrum antibiotics is a good example of how a number of objectives were achieved, though profit maximization was of course the primary one.

Pharmaceutical businesses are never completely satisfied with the levels of protection available, at least not for long. Companies tending to favour increased levels of protection are those which are innovative or that invest large sums of money in the attempt to be so, and those that may have little to show for their present research expenditures but at least have some products developed earlier that continue to generate large revenues. Companies that are not in the business of being innovative, such as generic producers, are happier with weaker IP systems. In countries where a firm's innovation level is typical of the industry as a whole, it is likely to collaborate politically with other companies, perhaps through a business association, to persuade the government to reform IP rights so that they better meet their needs. This may result in increased or decreased levels of protection. But, as levels of innovation increase across the industries, preferences for stronger levels of protection arise and may well prove to be irresistible. The history of the European and North American pharmaceutical industries as recounted in this chapter bears this out.

One should not go too far and assume that IP reform is necessarily imposed by a particular group of powerful firms – in this case brand-name or research-based pharmaceuticals. For one thing, legislation is sometimes based in part on negotiations between different business groupings, as with the 1984 Hatch–Waxman Act in the USA. In other cases, regulators act on their own initiative, as when the bar on pharmaceutical product patents was lifted in Germany in 1968. Also attempts by the industry to reform patent systems do not always succeed. For example, they may fail to convince policy makers that the economic stakes are high enough for the national economy to justify the cost of reform. Or perhaps the proposed changes would hurt wealthier or more influential industries. This is what happened to the US pharmaceutical industry just after the First World War, when it sought unsuccessfully to weaken the patent system.

The most difficult question to answer is the last one. As was said at the end of Chapter 4, we cannot turn the clock back and rerun past centuries without a patent system and then compare the number of life-saving and enhancing remedies, not to speak of the number of jobs and the various other economic benefits of profitable industries, that have arisen with those that a patent-free world would have created (although Chapter 10 attempts to make such a comparison, albeit speculatively). But there is circumstantial evidence that, on balance, patents were probably a positive force for pharmaceutical innovation even with their obvious drawbacks, such as their tactical deployment to build excessively broad and long-lasting monopolies.

But all of this rather misses the point. The key issue facing policy makers today is not whether or not to have a patent system, but how to design a patent system that meets certain objectives, among which are to improve the health of the population while establishing or maintaining an innovative and wealth-generating pharmaceutical industry.[34] Patents definitely have a role to play. But how to design an optimal patent system that meets both of these objectives effectively is extremely difficult. Does history help? To a certain extent it does. It cautions against a one-size-fits-all approach of the kind that the TRIPS Agreement arguably represents. It also demonstrates how important it is for policy makers to base their patent reform decisions on an understanding of developments in science and technology and their implications for intellectual property regulation, *and* on the need to listen to the views of as many different interests as possible.

Notes

1   Green (1915 [1901]: 190).
2   In 1884, the Commissioner of the United States Patent Office (see *Cochrane* v. *Badische Anilin & Soda Fabrik* (1884), 111 US 293 Commissioner's Decisions 230) denied a patent for synthetic alizarin because it was a copy of what existed in nature and therefore

lacked novelty. But, over time, patent offices and courts began to allow such patents as long as the claims did not extend to the chemical in its natural state.

3 Carl Djerassi, the renowned steroid chemist, points out (2001: 282–3) that aspirin causes birth defects in various animals but only rarely in humans. Because new drugs must now be tested on animals, if aspirin had been discovered more recently than it was, it is unlikely that it would ever have reached the market.

4 This section is based largely on information on the history of these companies available on the websites of Novartis (*http://www.novartis.com*) and Hoffman LaRoche (*http://www.roche.com*).

5 This company was acquired by Glaxo in 1958.

6 Involving such companies as Allen and Hanburys (1958), Evans (1960) and British Drug Houses (1968).

7 Named Prilosec in the United States.

8 For example, see the critiques of the Center's studies by Public Citizen (*http://www.citizen.org*).

9 In one early case (in 1964), Colgate-Palmolive successfully appealed against the rejection of a patent on a metabolite with antidepressant properties. The metabolite was formed in the bodies of people treated with a therapeutic substance that had already been patented (see Rollins, 1983). But such strategies can fail (or at least only partially succeed). For example, Merrell Dow sought to extend its monopoly on an antihistamine drug called terfenadine by arguing that, since the patented metabolite could not be produced without taking the drug, the monopoly should expire only upon expiry of the metabolite patent. Courts in the USA and Germany both upheld Merrell Dow's metabolite patents in those countries but held that supplying terfenadine would not be an infringing act. In Britain, Merrell Dow's infringement claims were also dismissed on the grounds that the metabolite was not new. On appeal, the House of Lord not only upheld the lower court's decision but essentially invalidated the patent. See *Merrell Dow v. HN Norton* (1996), *Intellectual Property Reports*, 33: 1–14; Grubb (1999: 212–13).

10 Correa (2001a: 11–12) provides a list of patenting targets chosen by companies to extend their monopolies on drugs. These include polymorphs (crystalline forms of the active compound); pharmaceutical forms (that is, new ways of administering the active compound); selective inventions (elements selected from a group that were not specifically named in earlier patents claiming the group); analogy processes; combinations of known products; optical isomers; active metabolites; prodrugs (inactive compounds that produce active metabolites when introduced into the body); new salts of known substances; variants of existing manufacturing processes; and new uses for old products.

11 Some apparently anti-competitive practices are described approvingly (and even enthusiastically) in a Harvard Business School publication (Rivette and Kline, 2000: 58). According to the authors, 'clustering' means 'building a patent wall around a product', preferably consisting of a large quantity of interlocking patents. 'Bracketing' means surrounding a competitor's key patent with so many of one's own that it cannot be commercialized. Ove Granstrand of Chalmers University of Technology in Sweden describes six different patent strategies: (i) ad hoc blocking and 'inventing around', (ii) strategic patent searching, (iii) 'blanketing' and 'flooding', (iv) 'fencing', (v) 'surrounding', and (vi) combination into patent networks (1999: 219–22).

12 As the American Pharmaceutical Association mentioned in its 1919 report, this is not a new practice.

13   Although the manufacturer may have patents on, for example, production processes and formulations, and these may still provide quite substantial protection.
14   Examples of this include Rapp and Rozek (1990), and Attaran and Gillespie-White (2001).
15   Especially price controls to limit national health care budgets. Both EFPIA and PhRMA claim that pharmaceuticals contribute a relatively small percentage of total expenditure, so that lower prices cannot compensate for the reduced incentive to innovate. Even if this is true, the overwhelming majority of people in the world cannot rely on state support but must pay their own medical bills.
16   Haynes (1945), quoted in Mowery and Rosenberg (1998: 74).
17   *Parke Davis and Co.* v. *H.K. Mulford and Co.*, 189 Fed. 95 (S.D.N.Y. 1911), affirmed, 196 Fed. 496 (2nd Cir. 1912).
18   Controversially, Parke Davis registered 'adrenaline' as a trade mark in the United States. Consequently, the natural substance is referred to as epinephrine in that country.
19   *In re King and Waugh* (1939), *United States Patent Quarterly*, 43: 400–402.
20   In doing so, Merck beat Glaxo by five months.
21   *Merck and Co., Inc.* v. *Chase Chemical Company et al.* (1967), *United States Patent Quarterly*, 155: 152.
22   US patent number 1 469 994 ('Extract obtainable from the mammalian pancreas or from the related glands in fishes, useful in the treatment of diabetes mellitus, and a method of preparing it'). The inventors named in the patent were Frederick Banting, Charles Best and James Collip.
23   US patent number 1 520 673 ('Purified antidiabetic product and method of making it'). The named inventor was George Walden.
24   Nonetheless, the IP and commercialization policies of some universities attracted controversy even in those days. Perhaps most controversially, the University of Wisconsin gained considerable royalties from the 1920s onwards thanks to the assertiveness of the Wisconsin Alumni Research Foundation, which was set up to maximize the university's income from its patents (some of which were health-related). The university and the foundation encountered heavy criticism over several decades from those who felt that universities should not be associated with such behaviour (see Weiner, 1989: 95–9).
25   The university sold Connaught in 1972. In 1999, it became the Connaught Campus of Pasteur Aventis, the vaccines division of Aventis.
26   See C.J. Rutty (2000), 'Dr Robert Davies Defries (1889–1975): "Canada's Mr Public Health"' (*http://www.healthheritageresearch.com/Defries-biopaper.html*); 'Discovery of Insulin' website (*http://www.discoveryofinsulin.com/Experiments.htm*); also Fishbein (1937: 893).
27   See US patent number 2 446 102 ('Complex salts of streptomycin and process for preparing the same').
28   Licensing nonetheless had its uses, as it does today. For example, it may have been useful to patent-holding companies unable to meet a large international demand for a product. In addition, licensee companies may be better equipped than the patent holders to market the product. And small companies discovering a new chemical entity but lacking the funds to cover the research, development and marketing may have had no alternative. Such is the case for many present-day dedicated biotechnology firms.
29   It is possible that Ciba's decision to license reserpine came about because it was

uncertain about the validity of its patent, since the compound was the isolated active principle of an Indian medicinal plant used for centuries in traditional medicine (Steele, 1962: 159).

30   Chloromycetin, or chloramphenicol (by its generic name), turned out to have harmful side-effects. The resultant decline in sales was a factor in Parke Davis' decline and 1959 merger with Warner Lambert (Achilladelis, 1993: 288). However, sales of the drug enjoyed a revival in the 1960s because the company's sales representatives were able to reassure physicians that, with care, the drug could be used safely (Kefauver, 1966: 88).

31   These include Canada, Australia, Israel, Argentina and Thailand (Correa, 2001b: 36).

32   Complete protection in the sense that it included all possible methods of manufacture.

33   A similar regulation was passed in 1996 for plant protection products.

34   In many poor countries, it is hardly realistic to expect a pharmaceutical industry to spring up because of patents. Therefore their interest in pharmaceutical patenting is likely to be restricted to that of ensuring that the health of the population is improved, or is at least not worsened.

Chapter 6

Biotechnology, Genomics and the New Life Science Corporations

We wish to suggest a structure for the salt of deoxyribose nucleic acid (D.N.A.). This structure has novel features which are of considerable biological interest ... It has not escaped our notice that the specific pairing we have postulated immediately suggests a possible copying mechanism for the genetic material. (James Watson and Francis Crick, 1953)

The fact that microorganisms, as distinguished from chemical compounds, are alive is a distinction without legal significance. (Judge Rich, United States Court of Customs and Patent Appeals, 1977)

Food – Health – Hope (Monsanto, 1998)

Life as Chemistry: the Scientific Foundations of Biotechnology

What is Biotechnology?

Biotechnology sounds like a neologism (like so many other words with the 'bio' prefix), but was actually coined early in the twentieth century by a Hungarian agricultural engineer called Karl Ereky, who included within its meaning 'all such work by which products are produced from raw materials with the aid of living organisms' (quoted in Bud, 1993: 27). Over time it has acquired a confusing variety of definitions. It may be defined quite broadly or much more narrowly. Typical of a broad definition is that of the (now defunct) United States Office of Technology Assessment: 'biotechnology, broadly defined, includes any technique that uses living organisms (or parts of organisms) to make or modify products, to improve plants or animals, or to develop micro-organisms for specific uses' (OTA, 1989).

Alternatively, *biotechnologies* may be divided by generation (for example, see Acharya, 1999). Thus the first generation includes traditional technologies like beer brewing and bread making. These go back at least to the Sumerians of ancient Mesopotamia. The second begins with the microbiological applications developed by Pasteur and continues with the mass production by fermentation of the antibiotics. Tissue culture and modern plant and animal breeding also fall within this generation. The third generation includes techniques like recombinant DNA, monoclonal antibodies, polymerase chain reaction (PCR) and cloning, whose emergence was triggered by post-Second World War advances in molecular biology and the even newer science of genomics. Most innovation in these new fields takes place in the United States, western Europe and Japan. Nowadays, biotechnology is often treated as being synonymous with the third generation of biotechnologies. This is how the word is used in this chapter.

The uniqueness of modern biotechnology lies, in the words of anthropologist Paul Rabinow (1996: 20), 'in its potential to get away from nature, to construct artificial conditions in which specific variables can be known in such a way that they can be manipulated. This knowledge then forms the basis for remaking nature according to our norms'.

The Science and Technology of Biotechnology

Biotechnology is an interdisciplinary enterprise, a scientific melting-pot whose language of communication and expression is that of chemistry (Kornberg, 1995: 3). It draws, not only upon a wide range of life sciences, but also on other less obviously related sciences like computer science and chemical engineering. Biotechnology also brings together a diversity of industrial sectors that benefit from using it.

For Arthur Kornberg, a Nobel laureate for his pioneering research on DNA synthesis, 'the most rational understanding of life' is 'its reduction to the molecular details of chemistry' (1995: 4). This conceptualization of life as essentially chemical, embodied in – and promoted through – the discourse of biotechnology, is undoubtedly appealing to those who esteem modern science for its progressiveness and rationality. As will be explained below, using this way of imagining life to base arguments for extending protectable subject matter to microorganisms, plants and animals played a significant role in the evolution of patent law in various countries from the 1980s, and ultimately in the global regime too.

Genes, proteins and the engineering of life While modern biotechnology is very much a late twentieth-century phenomenon, it is the result of scientific advances that go back well over a century. What was the state of the relevant science at the start of the twentieth century? The basic rules of heredity had been worked out in the 1860s by Gregor Mendel, whose findings were rediscovered in 1900. Chromosomes had been discovered, also in the 1860s, and were found to behave in a systematic manner during cell division. Why they did this and for what purpose were barely understood. Nucleic acid had also been identified in cells but was not considered to play any role in heredity. In short, the relevant science at this time was still rudimentary, consisting as it did of some basic, albeit important, rules and bits of information that were yet to constitute a coherent discipline.

Such a discipline, that of molecular biology, emerged in the following decades.[1] The term was actually coined by a scientist working at the Rockefeller Foundation, an important source of research funding and scientific guidance in this area between the 1930s and the late 1950s (Kay, 1993: 4–6). According to a historical account by French scientist Michel Morange (1998: 1–2), 'molecular biology is a result of the encounter between genetics and biochemistry, two branches of biology that developed at the beginning of the twentieth century... Strictly speaking, molecular biology is not a new discipline, but rather a new way of looking at organisms as reservoirs and transmitters of information'.

One of the most important early advances took place in 1944, when three researchers at the Rockefeller Institute in New York – Oswald Avery, Colin McLeod and Maclyn McCarty – discovered that DNA carries genetic information. Soon after, it became apparent to scientists that DNA, and not proteins as many of them had thought, provides the chemical language of instruction for the transmission of genetic traits.

In consequence of this discovery, groups of researchers undertook to elucidate the structure of the DNA macromolecule. The 'competitors' included Linus Pauling, the renowned American biochemist, working at the California Institute of Technology, Maurice Wilkins and Rosalind Franklin at King's College, London, and James Watson and Francis Crick at Cambridge University. As is now well known, Watson and Crick were first to come up with the double helix model, which they announced in May 1953 in a short article in *Nature*.

Crucial as this breakthrough was, it was more of a beginning than an end. At least as important was the discovery in the following decade of how DNA instructs cells to assemble amino acids, which form the building blocks of proteins. In brief, each gene contains the instructions for the synthesis of one or more proteins. Just as proteins consist of chains of amino acids, each gene may be subdivided into units called codons that comprise three nucleotide base pairs and code for (by way of a closely related chemical called ribonucleic acid (RNA)) the preparation of a particular amino acid. These amino acids are then combined in a specified way to form the required protein (that is, the one 'expressed' by the gene).

The fact that DNA rather than proteins were now known to carry the genetic information did not make the study of proteins less important or new discoveries about them any less revolutionary. In the early 1950s, Linus Pauling successfully worked out the basic rules determining the structures of proteins. This is important because the specificity of different types of protein and the processes by which they form cannot be inferred from their chemical composition alone, but requires one also to understand the three-dimensional form that they assume. This achievement was hugely significant:

> Pauling's discovery, like Watson and Crick's ... inverted the hierarchy of science. For seventy-five years, researchers had been baffled about whether proteins conformed to discrete shapes and whether those shapes determined their activity. Pauling not only answered with a resounding yes, but detailed all the major motifs by which they were formed ... In structure lay function, and what a molecule did determined its importance. Synthetic chemistry, which didn't explain molecular behavior but only reproduced it, fell in stature. (Werth, 1994: 204)

Important as these discoveries were, no commercial applications were identified. This all changed after the 1973 development of the recombinant DNA technique (often shortened to 'rDNA') by Stanley Cohen at Stanford University and Herbert Boyer at University of California at San Francisco (UCSF). The technique, which enabled foreign genes to be inserted into microorganisms and passed on to others through cell division, was patented by Stanford and licensed widely, earning over $200 million in royalties between 1975 and 1997, when the patent expired (McKelvey, 1996: xix).[2] These were shared between the two universities and the inventors. A few years later, in large part thanks to this invention, the era of commercial biotechnology got under way.

After recombinant DNA, the next major scientific breakthrough with commercial implications was the 1975 development of hybridoma technology by Georges Köhler and Cesar Milstein, working in Cambridge at the Medical Research Council's Laboratory of Molecular Biology, the same institution where Watson and Crick made their famous discovery. Hybridoma cells result from the fusion of a type of cancer cell known as a myeloma with another antibody-producing cell. Hybridomas produce multiple antibodies of a highly specific type, which are called monoclonal antibodies. The MRC chose not to patent the technology, a decision that provoked heavy criticism, including that from Margaret Thatcher when she was British Prime Minister. There were high hopes that the technology would prove to be extremely valuable for both diagnostics and therapeutics. As it turned out, while several diagnostic tests were commercialized in the following years, it took two decades for monoclonal antibody (MAb) drugs to reach the market. However, the first to do so, Centocor's ReoPro (abciximab), which was approved in 1995, has been a great commercial success. And IDEC Pharmaceuticals' Rituxan (approved in 1997), being the first MAb cancer treatment (for non-Hodgkin's lymphoma), already seems certain to become a lucrative product. In fact, it generated sales of $152 million in its first year alone (Robbins-Roth, 2000: 56). In 2000, it was reported that 'about a quarter of all biotech drugs in development are MAb, and around 30 products are in use or being investigated' (Breedveld, 2000: 735).

Unlike rDNA and hybridomas, the polymerase chain reaction (PCR) technology came out of a corporate laboratory. Kary Mullis, a scientist working for the California-based Cetus Corporation (like so many of the early DBFs), was credited with the invention, which is usually dated to 1985. PCR technology provides a means rapidly to replicate potentially vast quantities of a selected DNA section in a test tube. The technology works by using taq polymerase, an enzyme from a thermophilic (heat-resistant) bacterium that was discovered in a hot spring in Yellowstone National Park. PCR is an extremely valuable research tool with many applications, including genome sequencing and diagnostics. In recognition of its scientific importance, Mullis was awarded the Nobel Prize in 1993, the first DBF-based scientist to receive this accolade.

During the 1980s and 1990s, genetic engineering became increasingly sophisticated, with genes being transferred not just to microorganisms but also to plants and animals. For example, genes have been inserted into crops that make them resistant to insect pests or to herbicides (not coincidentally, these are normally those marketed by the same company) and to increase the shelf-life of agricultural produce. And a cancer-causing gene was inserted into a mouse, resulting in the controversial Harvard oncomouse that was patented in 1988.

Another new technique developed during this period was animal cloning based on nuclear transfer; that is to say, the insertion of a cell nucleus into an egg cell that has had its nucleus removed. In 1996, the now world famous sheep called Dolly was cloned by Ian Wilmut and Keith Campbell at Roslin Institute in Scotland from a cell taken from a mature sheep's udder. It was not the first cloned animal but the first to be cloned from an adult mammal (see Wilmut *et al.*, 2000).

Genomics and the human genome project Not even a history of the science and technology of biotechnology as brief as this one is complete without a description of genomics, which refers to the mapping, sequencing and analysis of the full set of genes (that is, the genome) of different organisms or species. As one might expect, the human genome has always been the most interesting for governments and foundations, as well as for companies seeking to identify commercial applications from genomics.

The Human Genome Project was launched in 1990 as an international public consortium with the objective of sequencing every one of the three billion nucleotides within the 23 chromosome pairs found in human cells,[3] and publicly disclosing the data for the benefit of science. Given that genes take up only about 3–5 per cent of the genome, this was a much more ambitious task than just decoding the then estimated 100 000 or so genes, which in itself would have been a huge undertaking. The organizers expected the work to be completed by 2005.

Initially, two techniques were adopted for the mapping part of the work: physical mapping and gene mapping. Physical mapping involves breaking DNA into multiple fragments using bacterial enzymes called restriction enzymes, inserting them into bacteria or yeast cells, and then matching the overlapping pieces.

Gene mapping dates back to the early twentieth century, but had become much more sophisticated in the early 1980s. Around that time, David Botstein at MIT and Ronald Davis at Stanford University, among others, proposed the idea of locating genes along the chromosomes by first randomly seeking out DNA sections which commonly vary between different individuals. These sections are known as markers, and the more of them that can be found the better. By studying families whose members frequently share distinctive traits such as faulty gene-related diseases, scientists can compare incidences of the markers with incidences of the traits. If the two tend to coincide, the responsible gene is likely to be nearby (though still not necessarily all that easy to find). The method considerably aided the search for several gene variants (or alleles) causing, or increasing susceptibility to, dangerous diseases such as Huntington's chorea, cystic fibrosis and breast cancer. Robert Cook-Deegan, formerly of the NIH, describes Botstein and Davis' technique as 'the conceptual engine that drove human genetics from the era of the horse-drawn carriage into the age of the automobile' (1994: 29–30).

The actual sequencing was based on a method pioneered by Frederick Sanger at Cambridge, who used it to sequence a virus in 1977. Over time, the process was rapidly accelerated thanks mainly to the introduction of increasingly fast sequencing machines.

In spite of being an international project, the USA has made an extremely large contribution in terms of funding and the actual sequencing work. The United Kingdom has made the second biggest overall contribution, ahead of France, Japan, Germany and China, which all participated. The Wellcome Trust, a UK medical foundation, was one of the biggest single funders of the Project (though well behind the US government), providing £210 million by February 2001, and the Sanger Centre near Cambridge sequenced a total of eight chromosomes (Cookson, 2001). In fact, the Sanger Centre was the only non-American among the five institutions responsible for 85 per cent of the sequencing achieved by October 2000 (Regalado, 2001).[4]

From the start, scientists debated priorities, concerned as they were to complete their work as quickly and cheaply as possible. Some felt it would be better to focus first on finding the genes and leave the whole genome sequencing for later. Others disagreed. Although many scientists went on to seek out, map and sequence genes, the whole genome strategy carried the day. As for methods, the first controversy took place in 1991. A scientist at the National Institute of Health called Craig Venter, eager to sequence and map protein-coding regions of the genome, adopted a short-cut method of identifying genes using so-called 'expressed sequence tags' (ESTs). The EST method takes advantage of the established principle that messenger RNA can be converted back to DNA using an enzyme called reverse transcriptase. Messenger RNA ('mRNA' for short) is the chemical that relays the genetic code from the nucleus to the site in the cell (the ribosome) where it is translated for the assembly of the protein-forming amino acids. The result of applying reverse transcriptase is a substance called complementary DNA (often shortened to 'cDNA'). Essentially, cDNA has the same sequence as the gene but without the non-coding nucleotides sometimes referred to as 'junk DNA' but more formally as 'introns'. By sequencing the ends of these pieces of cDNA, one obtains partially encoded gene fragments called ESTs. When stretches of RNA are extracted from specialized cells, such as brain cells, the ESTs derived from them can help to identify genes that are useful in the functioning of that particular cell or the organ of which it forms a part. Of course, the EST short-cut strategy does not provide the full gene sequence. Neither can an EST in itself provide enough information to indicate the function of the related gene. For these reasons, the strategy immediately attracted criticism from some quarters.

But what was even more controversial than the method itself was that, in 1991 and 1992, the NIH filed patent applications claiming rights over thousands of ESTs. This move was condemned not only by other agencies involved in the Project but also by the Human Genome Organization, which had been set up by scientists to coordinate the project internationally. Even representatives of the biotechnology sector condemned the move. James Watson famously described NIH's actions as 'sheer lunacy' and resigned from his position at the NIH, where he was head of the Office of Human Genome Research and in this position the de facto leader of the international Project. The Medical Research Council decided in its wisdom to respond by also filing similar patent applications. In 1994, the NIH withdrew its appeal against the Patent and Trademark Office (PTO)'s initial rejection of its applications and agreed, as did the MRC, no longer to patent gene fragments having no known function (Coghlan, 1994).

By 1998, the Human Genome Project had made considerable progress, although only 3–5 per cent of the genome had actually been sequenced. This does not sound impressive, but the expectation from the start was that sequencing would accelerate quite rapidly in the final years. In May of that year a rival was to appear in the form of a new company called Celera Genomics that was headed by Craig Venter, who had since left the NIH. Celera was set up by a company called Perkin-Elmer (now called Applera Corporation), which also owned Applied Biosystems, the leading producer of automated DNA sequencing machines. Armed with an initial investment of $75 million from Perkin-Elmer and an array of these machines, Celera got to work. The approach adopted was the so-called 'whole-genome shotgun strategy', which would entail breaking the human genome into tens of millions of fragments, sequencing the pieces about 10 times over (a plan that was subsequently scaled down by nearly half) and then reassembling them.

On 26 June 2000, at the White House in the presence of President Clinton, Craig Venter and Francis Collins, director of the NIH's National Human Genome Research Institute, and coordinator of the public project, temporarily put aside their differences to announce jointly that they had ordered most of the full genome sequence. This was really just a public relations stunt, since the public project had only sequenced 90 per cent of the genome and was just a 'rough draft'. And as Celera's 'first assembly' was only available to subscribers, Venter's claim to have a more complete version was not easily verifiable.

In February 2001, the International Human Genome Sequencing Consortium that was implementing the public project and Celera both announced they had compiled almost complete human genetic sequences by publishing detailed reports of their work in *Nature* and in *Science* (see International Human Genome Sequencing Consortium, 2001; Venter *et al.*, 2001). The two reports came up with considerably reduced estimates of the total number of human genes as compared with the commonly cited figure of around 100 000. The Consortium's estimated number was 30 000–40 000. Celera's was 26 000–38 000. An important implication of the reduced figure is that, since there are many more proteins than there are genes and not all genes code for proteins, many of those that do must be able somehow to generate (or help to generate) more than one protein.

Apart from being a huge feat in itself, the mapping and sequencing of the human genome is certain to be a tremendously useful source of information for biomedical scientists for years to come, and of course for industry. Data provided by the public consortium has already helped in the identification of about 30 diseases linked to faulty genes (International Human Genome Sequencing Consortium, 2001: 911). And knowing more about human genes and proteins should substantially increase the number of drug targets for drug discovery research.

It is important to observe that, while the consortium had updated its data on a daily basis without attaching any strings (and continues to do so), Venter *et al.*, embedded the following notice on data availability in the final endnote of their *Science* article:

> The genome sequence and additional supporting information are available to academic scientists at the Web site (www.celera.com). Instructions for obtaining a DVD of the genome sequence can be obtained through the Web site. For commercial scientists wishing to verify the results presented here, the genome data are available upon signing a Material Transfer Agreement, which can also be found on the Web site.

Academic scientists expecting unconditional access to Celera's data would have been disappointed. They are required to sign and submit a document known as the 'Celera Free Public Access Agreement for Celera Whole Genome Sequence', which provides a royalty-free, non-exclusive and non-transferable licence to access the genomic data but forbids their distribution to other academic scientists. Somewhat disturbingly, also, the Agreement states that 'the Celera Data, both the primary sequence assembly and the representation thereof, is a copyrighted work of PE Corporation (NY)'. Aside from the point that treating the genetic code as a literary work is an absurdity, claiming legal ownership over such raw information hardly encourages the open exchanges of raw data and research results that scientific progress depends on.

Table 6.1 presents most of the truly significant scientific breakthroughs in biotechnology to date. It is worthwhile to point out here that dates should not necessarily be treated as definitive. Discovery dates can plausibly be based on initial conceptualization, the first publication announcing it, or on proof of the discovered phenomenon or that the invented technique actually works. For example, it was only in 1973 that DNA was proved beyond doubt to have a double helical structure (Davies, 2001: 25). So was the discovery of this phenomenon achieved in 1953 or two decades later? Similarly, Kary Mullis' discovery of a technique for making PCR was based on his conceptualization of the invention, which apparently came to him in April 1983 while driving to his weekend retreat. So was PCR invented then or in 1985? In fact, the situation may be even more complicated than this. In 1991, Du Pont challenged the PCR patent on the basis that it had been conceptualized by earlier scientists and was therefore not a true invention. The fact that the challenge failed, though, would tend to support the view that Mullis deserves the benefit of the doubt.

To take another example, Marie-Claire King of University of California, Berkeley showed in 1990 both that breast and ovarian cancer could run in families,

Table 6.1 Scientific breakthroughs in biotechnology

1951	George Gey and colleagues establish first 'immortal' human cell line
1953	James Watson and Francis Crick discover the double helix structure of DNA
1961–6	Marshall Nirenberg, Heinrich Matthaei, Severo Ochoa, Gobind Khorana and others decipher the genetic code for the 20 amino acids involved in producing proteins
1973	Stanley Cohen and Herbert Boyer demonstrate gene splicing (recombinant DNA) technique
1975	Georges Köhler and Cesar Millstein produce monoclonal antibodies using hybridoma technology
1977	Genome of NX174 virus sequenced by Frederick Sanger using his dideoxy sequencing method
	Genentech clones human gene, causing a human protein (somatostatin) to be expressed in bacteria
1978	Genentech clones human insulin
1981	Leroy Hood and colleagues at California Institute of Technology invent automated gene sequencing machine
1983	First plant gene to be inserted in a plant of a different species
1985	Invention of polymerase chain reaction (PCR)
1995	Genome of first free-living organism (H. influenzae) sequenced by Craig Venter and Hamilton Smith at The Institute of Genome Research using 'whole-genome shotgun sequencing' technique
1996	Dolly, the first mammal cloned from an adult cell, is born/created
1998	Genome of first animal (C. elegans) sequenced by Robert Waterston, John Sulston and colleagues of Washington University and the Sanger Centre
2001	Human genome sequenced in draft form by the Human Genome Project and Celera Genomics

Source: Acharya (1999), with modifications.

and that a variant of a gene located somewhere on chromosome 17 given the name BRCA1 substantially increased a woman's susceptibility to both cancers. But Myriad Genetics was first to sequence (and subsequently patent) the gene.[5] To Kevin Davies, founding editor of *Nature Genetics*, 'in a way, she [that is, King] *had* discovered the breast cancer gene, even though she narrowly lost the race to determine its sequence'. Subsequently, another variant gene linked to breast cancer incidence dubbed BRCA2 was also patented by Myriad even though the 'invention' drew heavily on publicly available sequence data and a considerable amount of public sector research. It is more accurate to say that BRCA2 was discovered by a team led by Mike Stratton at the Institute of Cancer Research in Surrey, UK, which had determined that the gene was located somewhere on chromosome 13. What happened was that, in November 1995, the Sanger Centre and Washington University's Genome Sequencing Center jointly released onto the Internet a sequence of 900 000 nucleotide bases containing the gene. Their intention was to accelerate the identification of the gene's precise location but without favouring any of the research groups involved in the race. The Institute of Cancer Research, Myriad's main competitor, filed a UK patent in the same month as a means of preventing Myriad from controlling both genes. The application claimed a 1000 base pair stretch of cDNA but not the whole sequence of the gene. Myriad, drawing on automated sequencing technological capacity that the ICR could not match, quickly sequenced the whole gene, and filed a US patent application the month after (Aldhous, 1996: 8).

The BRCA patent controversies raise serious questions about the appropriateness of patenting DNA sequences. More will be said about this later, but at this point it is important to realize that conceiving the incidence of a disease (or of resistance to a disease) as being related to a specific allele and then discovering this allele to the point of localizing it to part of a chromosome are substantial intellectual achievements. They require a considerable amount of painstaking and time-consuming research. Sequencing the already discovered allele, on the other hand, is relatively routine with the rapid sequencing machines now available. So it seems rather perverse that the performers of the latter task should be able to receive a patent while the performers of the conception and discovery can receive limited, if any, legal protection unless they keep it secret, which of course would prevent others from being able to sequence the gene and develop the diagnostic test, which is where the money is made. A one-time Cetus Corporation scientist called Norman Arnheim observed that 'conception, development and application are all scientific issues – invention is a question for patent lawyers' (quoted in Rabinow, 1998: 8). In fact, they are not just for scientists to debate. The winner-take-all nature of patents converts them also into political issues.

The Business of Biotechnology

The USA pioneered commercial biotechnology and continues to be the world leader by some considerable distance. Why is this? There is no single explanation, but the private sector has undoubtedly benefited enormously from basic research by universities, hospitals and the government, which has been a massive investor in biomedical research over several decades. And, since the early 1990s, the US government has adopted a more competitive attitude towards research it sponsors. Increasingly, government biomedical research funding there is aimed at strengthening the competitive positions of the national pharmaceutical and health biotechnology sectors, reducing healthcare costs, and at securing higher returns on public research investment (Kornberg, 1995: 11–13). From 1994 to 1998, the Federal government was spending at least $20 billion a year on biotechnology research, about double the expenditure in all the European Union member countries combined. In both the US and EU cases, about half is allocated to biopharmaceutical-related research (Senker and van Zwanenberg, 2001: 54).

Private finance is also much easier to secure in the USA than elsewhere. Academics and businessmen wishing to found DBFs can tap into venture capital funds that exist on a scale unmatched in any other country. And thanks to an early wave of optimism that new products would soon reach the market, many DBFs secured extraordinarily large cash injections through initial public offerings (IPOs), enabling them to invest heavily in research. So, although there are more DBFs in Europe than in the USA, they tend to be smaller, employ fewer scientists, and their market capitalization is far lower (ibid.).

As it turned out, much of the initial optimism was misplaced. During the 1980s only 10 biopharmaceuticals were approved for sale by the FDA, of which just three were developed and marketed by DBFs. The others were licensed to established pharmaceutical companies (Powell, 1999: 50). From the late 1980s, it became more difficult for many of these DBFs to attract further investments, and few of them succeeded in generating enough new products to join the ranks of the large science-based transnational corporations.

In consequence, several DBFs were taken over by their larger rivals. Others have found ways to avoid this fate. Patenting has undoubtedly helped some small firms to maintain their independence. According to one commentator, 'outright acquisitions of the new biotechnology firms were effectively blocked by the extensive cross-licensing agreements among different partners' (Harrison, 1997: 67). On the other hand, the ownership of a key patent or a large portfolio of patents may serve as a signal to a larger company that the DBF would make a good purchase. To some DBFs (or at least their investors), being bought by a bigger company is a mark of success rather than failure.

DBFs have also kept their independence by entering into strategic alliances with other DBFs and the bigger longer-established firms, and by forming extensive research, development and marketing networks containing DBFs, large firms and (albeit to a decreasing extent) government and university research institutions.[6] Such alliances and networks hold the promise of happily marrying the basic research expertise of the DBFs and universities with the drug development experience and marketing strength of the pharmaceutical and chemical companies and of course their much deeper pockets. To give one example of the success (and perhaps the sheer necessity) of such collaborating, the aforementioned anti-cancer MAb drug Rituxan involved a worldwide partnership of companies including IDEC, Genentech, Hoffman LaRoche and Zenyaku Kogyo Co.[7]

Innovation in commercial biotechnology outside the USA has taken place almost exclusively in Japan, and in Europe where the most successful countries so far are the UK, Germany and France. As with the US case, industry in these countries has enjoyed the benefit of ground-breaking research carried out in universities and public sector research agencies.

Most government funding and commercial activity has been in the area of health biotechnology. In fact, at least 60 per cent of the biotechnology firms (that is, DBFs and other firms that do biotechnology) in the USA and Europe are engaged in human and animal health. The types of product being developed include so-called 'biopharmaceuticals' such as genetically engineered therapeutic proteins and vaccines. Other common types of product are diagnostic kits for diseases linked to genetic defects. Health biotechnology is used not only to develop new types of drug but also to enhance the efficiency of the drug discovery process. In fact, this has become the main objective of health biotechnology research. According to one commentator,

> Partly ... due to the high costs of production, using genetic engineering to make human proteins is currently seen to be a minor use in pharmaceuticals. The major use of genetic engineering is to improve the efficiency of the drug discovery process, in combination with a better understanding of the workings of the body. Combining that knowledge implies that pharmaceuticals can be more directly designed to do certain things. (McKelvey, 1996: xxi)

Agricultural biotechnology is the second most important biotechnology field in the USA and Europe. Much of this research is geared towards the development of new seed products with introduced traits providing mainly agronomic benefits such as disease resistance, pest resistance, herbicide tolerance and also extended shelf-life of harvested produce. Little of the research has been directed so far at improving output quality for the benefit of consumers, although this situation is beginning to change. This is one important reason why genetically modified (GM) crops are so controversial in Europe. The perception among many people is that consumers are expected to accept the unknown risks of consuming GM products and bear the consequences should something go wrong. Yet, unlike genetically engineered pharmaceuticals, these products provide no obvious additional benefits for the public, as they would if they were cheaper or more nutritious. Unlike the healthcare case, there are few agricultural DBFs, even in the USA.

Of the two fields, healthcare products tend to be more commercially attractive. This is because they have potentially much higher returns, and because demand tends to be far less cyclical. Most of the remaining biotechnology companies provide industrial or environmental products and services such as industrial enzymes and pollution diagnostics. Because of its commercial importance and future potential, this chapter focuses mainly on the healthcare sector.

The biotechnology and genomics revolutions have created completely new commercial opportunities, and spawned four types of business. These are (i) the technology providers who manufacture the DNA sequencing machines and other equipment (for example, Applied Biosystems and Amersham Biosciences); (ii) the information providers (such as Incyte and Celera) that collect and organize sequencing information; (iii) the research firms, consisting mainly of the DBFs that generally do the upstream research but lack the resources or the ambition to do the downstream product development and marketing; and (iv) the health, agricultural and industrial biotechnology firms. These include the larger vertically integrated DBFs (for example, Amgen and Genentech) and much longer established businesses, which are mostly pharmaceutical, chemical and life science corporations. These business types are not necessarily discrete. For example, while Incyte and Celera are essentially information providers, Millennium Pharmaceuticals and Human Genome Sciences are also involved in drug discovery and development.

Table 6.2 lists and dates some of the major commercial breakthroughs in biotechnology to date.

Table 6.2 Commercial breakthroughs in biotechnology

1976	Herbert Boyer and Robert Swanson found Genentech
1980	First biotechnology IPO, raising $35 million for Genentech
1981	First monoclonal antibody diagnostic kits approved in the USA
1982	First rDNA animal vaccine approved in Europe
	First rDNA pharmaceutical product (human insulin) approved in USA and UK
	Applied Biosystems markets protein sequencer
1985	First rDNA pharmaceutical product (human growth hormone) marketed by a DBF
1990	US FDA approves first bioengineered food additive (rennin used to produce cheese)
1995	FDA approves first MAb drug, Centocor/Eli Lilly's ReoPro

Source: Acharya (1999), with modifications.

Commercial biotechnology is far from being the preserve of small research-intensive biotech 'boutiques'. This is not only because pharmaceutical companies increasingly do biotechnological research and development themselves, but because of the recent emergence of a type of integrated business enterprise called the 'life science corporation'. Such corporations, which include Monsanto (now part of Pharmacia), Du Pont, Novartis, AstraZeneca and Aventis, among others, are so large that they hold dominant global positions in two or more industrial fields that were previously considered to be completely separate (see Table 6.3).

How did the life science corporations develop? Essentially, they emerged out of a wave of mergers, acquisitions, joint ventures and strategic partnerships involving companies in a wide range of fields such as chemicals, seeds, processed foods, dietary supplements and pharmaceuticals. Although the initial consolidation process began in the early 1970s, it was really from the 1980s that biology and more specifically biotechnology provided a strong enough glue to bond these rather different fields together with the promise of boundless profits.

Why biotechnology? The chemical firms were seeking an escape from the stagnation they were suffering from as they found themselves turning into low-margin commodity businesses. Pharmaceutical companies feared that lucrative product pipelines would come to an end with no new drugs to replace them. It was widely believed that, just as organic chemistry in an earlier age was applied to the search for new dyes and resulted in the discovery of medicines, perfumes and photographic chemicals as well, biotechnological research was likewise bound to have synergistic effects. Moreover, it was felt that products could be designed specifically to be sold with an existing product as a package so that customers would need to buy them both together. The power of such visions convinced many chemical and pharmaceutical executives, who then convinced their investors, that the future was biological. The result was the construction of conglomerates with interests integrating agrochemicals, seeds, genetically modified plants, animal and human diagnostic products, and biopharmaceuticals.

The life science corporations appeared in North America and Europe in ways that were quite similar. During the 1970s, US chemical giants like Dow, American Cyanamid, Du Pont and Monsanto encountered decreased profits, higher costs (especially after the oil price crises) and public criticism stemming from concern about industrial pollution. They responded by moving into or increasing their involvement in fine chemicals sectors like agrochemicals and pharmaceuticals. These offered much higher profit margins, especially with the availability of effective monopoly protection through the patent system.

Table 6.3 Major life science corporations, 1998

Company	1998 turnover (bn US$)
Bayer (Germany)	29.0
BASF (Germany)	28.8
Du Pont (USA)	24.7
Hoechst (Germany)	23.3
Novartis (Switzerland)	20.6
AstraZeneca (Sweden/UK)	16.0
American Home Products (USA)	13.5
Rhône-Poulenc (France)	13.7
Monsanto (USA)	8.6

Source: Bijman (1999).

By the early 1980s, Monsanto had overcome its early scepticism and gone biological in a pioneering fashion by buying into DBFs and establishing its own research facilities, most successfully in plant biotechnology. This was partly because it could afford to. It made huge profits from two agrochemicals called Roundup and Lasso, and agrobiotechnology seemed like a promising area to invest in: in theory, the number of possible biotech applications in agribusiness is almost endless. But it also felt it needed to do so, because the patents on these products would eventually expire and new products needed to be developed to replace them or alternatively to help maintain high demand beyond the life of the patents protecting them. Having decided to commit itself heavily to agricultural biotechnology, Monsanto's attentions were bound to turn to the seed companies. As Martin Kenney (writing in 1986) correctly predicted, 'the seed will become the proprietary nexus for plant genetic engineering. The seed is a vehicle for conveying the fruits of molecular biological research to the farmer, and thereby realizing a profit on the incorporated research' (223). This was well understood by Monsanto, which proceeded to buy up numerous seed companies, as did other agrochemical, petrochemical and pharmaceutical companies, including Sandoz, Ciba-Geigy and Shell.

But the move into biotechnology was not the only reason for this latter trend. The 1970 United States Plant Variety Protection Act increased expectations of seed industry profits and thereby helped to stimulate an upsurge in mergers and acquisitions by chemical firms with 'larger fertilizer, herbicide, insecticide, and fungicide product lines that generally are far more important in terms of total revenue and profit than are seeds' (Buttel and Belsky, 1987). Nonetheless, biotechnology has had an effect, given that 'a substantial amount of plant research in private firms has been aimed at developing various types of seed-chemical packages that reinforce rather than threaten sales of agricultural chemicals' (ibid.). For example, Monsanto developed and patented transgenic soybeans, canola, cotton and corn containing a gene providing resistance to its Roundup (glyphosate) herbicides. Monsanto's patents protect the gene for Roundup resistance and all plants containing it, and these have several more years to run. As farmers who buy these 'Roundup Ready' seeds are contractually obliged to purchase Monsanto's patented herbicides, sales of the seeds are good for sales of the herbicides and vice versa. It is unclear, however, that this strategy will work in the long term. Roundup Ultra went off patent in 2000 and farmers may well turn to cheaper versions sold by competitors.

As in North America, the life science concept in Europe was held up as the way of the future, albeit a little more cautiously. This was due perhaps to a more realistic assessment of the situation, at least compared to Monsanto's. While the attractions of biotechnology were just as great, companies were not merging out of strength. After all, no long-established company like Hoechst or Rhône-Poulenc would voluntarily sacrifice its independence and its name (as they did in 1999, when they merged to form Aventis) just to save money by closing some offices and laying off a few hundred scientists unless it was in trouble. In fact, a major factor driving the consolidation trend of recent years is the significant number of patent expiries relating to very profitable drugs, coupled with the lack of new drugs coming on the market to replace them. And even before the creation of Aventis, the life science business concept was beginning to look non-viable. Agribusiness is cyclic and was going through an unprofitable period. For what were principally pharmaceutical firms, this sector began to look like a heavy burden instead of an asset, and the desire to offload the seed and agrochemical business became irresistible in some cases. For example, Novartis and AstraZeneca spun off their agribusiness divisions in 2000 and combined them to form Syngenta.

To make matter worse, anti-biotech activists, especially in Europe, effectively exposed the reality behind Monsanto's incongruous 'touchy-feely' rhetoric. To a European public that rightly or wrongly believes its capitalism to be just a little less ruthless and slightly more honest, Monsanto's 'food, health, hope' slogan almost demanded a cynical response. So a company with a reputation for spying on farmers and humiliating those suspected of replanting their seed, and for aggressively promoting GM food in the wake of the BSE crisis, was so seduced by its own propaganda that the hostility it encountered was quite unexpected. Monsanto's European competitors were more than a little irritated by its failure to comprehend that the public, especially in the UK, was sceptical if not fearful about biotechnology and needed gentle reassurance, especially when the benefits for consumers were non-existent.

Monsanto paid a heavy price. Although its financial problems were mainly the result of heavy debt accrued through acquisitions of seed companies like DeKalb, Asgrow, Cargill International and Plant Breeding International, the anti-Monsanto campaigns in Europe and elsewhere were damaging. In 2000, it merged with Pharmacia-Upjohn to form a new company called Pharmacia. Monsanto is the pesticide and seed subsidiary of this larger company.

Commercial Biotechnology in the United States

The first company set up to exploit the new biotechnological applications coming out of the universities was Genentech, founded in 1976 by a venture capitalist called Robert Swanson, with Herbert Boyer, co-inventor of the rDNA technology, acting as an independent consultant. Genentech, whose name is short for 'genetic engineering technology', and is now owned by Hoffman LaRoche, raised considerable funds with its first public offering in 1980. Its successful launch encouraged other university researchers to move into this emerging sector or to launch new firms themselves. During the early and mid-1980s, there was a wave of successful initial public offerings by biotechnology start-up companies following in Genentech's footsteps, the biggest being that of Cetus which raised $107 million (Robins-Roth, 2000: 21). The founders of many of these companies hoped eventually to turn them into integrated pharmaceutical corporations. Only in a few cases have such ambitions been realized.

In 1982, genetically engineered human insulin became the first biopharmaceutical product to reach the market. The product was developed by Genentech but marketed by

Eli Lilly, an established pharmaceutical company which, as we saw earlier, has long had an interest in this product. At that time, the insulin on the market was extracted from ground-up pig and cow pancreases and could cause allergic reactions in some diabetes sufferers. Claims that human insulin is better for diabetes sufferers despite its higher price have been widely accepted. But James Le Fanu is far more sceptical, pointing out that human insulin also produces harmful side-effects. Recent reports do suggest that it may be lethal for some users (Picard, 2002). He also notes that its production is unnecessary because animal insulin is just as effective and was being produced in adequate quantities until 'Eli Lilly decided to "phase out" its production of animal-based insulin so it was less readily available' (Le Fanu, 1999: 289).

Table 6.4 'Patenting life': milestones in biotechnology patent protection

1873	Pasteur receives US patent no. 141,072 which claims a yeast as an 'article of manufacture'
1969	German Federal Supreme Court accepts principle that animal breeding methods are patentable
1975	German Federal Supreme Court declares that microorganisms are patentable
1980	*Diamond* v. *Chakrabarty* affirms that microorganisms are patentable in the USA
1985	US PTO appeals board decides that plants, seeds and plant tissue cultures are patentable
1987	US PTO announces that multicellular organisms are patentable
1988	EPO grants first patent on plant US PTO issues 'oncomouse patent'
1995	EPO declares that DNA is 'not "life", but a chemical substance which carries genetic information', and therefore constitutes patentable subject matter
1998	First patent covering ESTs awarded to Incyte Pharmaceuticals
2001	Oxford GlycoSciences files patent applications on 4000 human proteins and the genes that code for them

Later in that decade, Genentech managed not only to develop but also to market two genetically engineered human proteins as pharmaceutical products. These were human growth hormone, which was approved in 1985 and marketed as Protropin, and tissue plasminogen activator (tPA), a 'clot-buster' drug for heart attack patients approved in 1987 and sold as Activase. Amgen followed in Genentech's footsteps two years later with Epogen (erythropoietin), a hormone used to treat anaemia caused by kidney failure.

By the end of the decade, biotechnology had succeeded in developing over 75 FDA-approved drugs, vaccines and diagnostic tests, with hundreds more undergoing clinical trials. Nonetheless, these are very early days and the potential is far from being realized. Amgen and Genentech are among the few DBFs that have become integrated pharmaceutical corporations, although in Genentech's case this came at the cost of sacrificing its independence. The USA is likely to continue to be the source of most new biopharmaceuticals, whether or not the laboratories where the new drugs are being discovered and developed are owned by domestic firms or those European firms like Hoffman LaRoche that have been buying US DBFs such as Genentech.

Commercial Biotechnology in Europe and Japan

While the US system has been relatively effective at turning new discoveries made by public sector and university researchers into commercial products, Europe and Japan have been less successful in putting together the downstream linkages from fundraising for basic research all the way to commercialization. The most successful countries in commercial biotechnology are the UK, Germany and France. The first two countries have a significant number of DBFs, many of which are university spin-offs,[8] but in France and the rest of continental Europe the existing large science-based pharmaceutical and chemical firms have from the start been responsible for virtually all the private sector biotechnology research and development. Like their US counterparts, they tended to be quite cautious about biotechnology and were thus rather slow to set up in-house biotech research and development programmes. In Japan, investment in biotechnology has come from a wide range of industries and not just pharmaceutical and chemical firms. These include manufacturers of beer, foods and even watches (Bud, 1993: 198).

Since the 1980s the European Community countries and Japan have been preoccupied with catching up with the USA. Both the European Commission and the national governments have sought to stimulate biotechnology research and development through industrial policy and more business-friendly product and IP regulation (Senker, 1998). The Japanese government has likewise acted to encourage commercial biotechnology and enhance international competitiveness (see Fransman and Tanaka, 1999: 202–55; Howells and Neary, 1995: 212–20). It remains to be seen whether Europe or Japan can catch up with the USA, whose lead is considerable.

Biotechnology and the Patent System

The Importance of Patents

The growth and consolidation of the US biotechnology sector is closely linked to the expansion of patent law into the protection of life forms and their structural and functional components (see Table 6.4). What led to these regulatory changes taking place and why did other countries, such as the European Community member states and Japan, feel the need to follow suit?

The underlying reason is the huge importance of patent protection in the biotechnology field. Biotechnology was and continues to be a high-risk and extremely research-intensive activity, and for DBFs especially[9] it has always been crucial to be able to secure large amounts of investment capital just to stay in business. Patent portfolios are the main magnet for outside investors – which also include larger science-based firms – and the larger the portfolio (usually measured by the quantity of patents rather than their quality), the greater the interest from investors. In common with other industries, patents also become a form of currency in inter-firm transactions:

> Few products can be developed, tested, approved by regulatory agencies, and on the markets in time to generate enough cash to save most biotechnology companies. For many companies, the patent becomes the product – the product that can be dangled before the investment community for more funds, or the product that can literally be sold to other companies. (Fowler, 1994: 173)

Research decisions in many companies can depend as much, if not more, on the advice of patent lawyers as on the opinions of the scientists. Naturally, companies have a strong interest in securing patents that encompass the broadest possible scope and whose claims are drawn in ways that seek to anticipate future scientific developments. For example,

> the biotech firm Genetics Institute decides which version of a drug to develop partly based on which iteration shows the best results in clinical trials but also according to which version can command the strongest patent protection. Genetics Institute's patent counsel says the strength of the potential patent position is 'a leading factor' in deciding which research to pursue. (Rivette and Klein, 2000: 58; see also Macdonald, 2001: 14)

No doubt, also, the strength of competitors' patent positions helps companies to decide which research *not* to pursue. The extent of biotechnology patenting has increased tremendously in the last two decades. If we consider just DNA sequences, Giles Stokes of Derwent Information, a company that provides patent and scientific information, explains that they 'first began appearing in patents in 1980, just 16 sequences all year. By 1990 that figure had risen to over 6,000 sequences. Throughout the 1990s the growth in the patenting of sequences expanded exponentially, and this looks set to continue. In 2000 over 355,000 sequences were published in patents, a 5000 per cent increase over 1990' (Stokes, 2001).

And it is not just companies that are doing the patenting. A survey commissioned by the *Guardian* newspaper in 2000 revealed that the US Department of Health and Human Services was one of the biggest applicants for patents claiming human gene sequences. The only companies that had claimed more genes were Genset, Ribozyme, Genetics Institute, Genzyme, Hyseq and Human Genome Sciences (see

Guardian, 2000). Universities, especially in the USA, are also actively patenting biotechnology inventions. Nonetheless, the overwhelming majority of bio-technology patents are held by companies. In the agrobiotechnology field, for example, six companies are responsible for three-quarters of all US patents granted to the top 30 patent-holding firms. These are Monsanto, Du Pont, Syngenta, Dow, Aventis and Grupo Pulsar (ETC Group, 2001: 7; Graff, 2002).

Biotechnology Patenting in the United States

It is surely not coincidental that the USA pioneered both the commercialization of biotechnology applications and products and the development of patent law to protect them. Before the 1980s, the patent situation with respect to biotechnology processes and products was highly uncertain. While clearly non-biological process technologies such as recombinant DNA could be patented in the USA, the product of nature doctrine was assumed by the Patent and Trademark Office – and by most scientists – entirely to preclude the patenting of life forms and their structural and functional components. The meaning of the product of nature doctrine is that organisms or substances as they occur in nature cannot be considered as inventions and are not therefore patentable. And, at this time, the new DBFs were yet to organize themselves into a single trade association to further their collective legal and regulatory interests.[10]

This situation began to change in 1980 with the US Supreme Court decision in *Diamond* v. *Chakrabarty* to allow the patenting of a new man-made oil-eating bacterium. This outcome – highly successful for industry – was a case of forum shifting achieved not by a DBF or even a pharmaceutical company, but by a firm traditionally involved in quite unrelated research activities, General Electric.[11]

Scepticism about the patentability of living organisms was to be expected. At around the time that General Electric filed its patent in 1972, of the four million US patents issued since 1790, only 70 had protected 'mixtures or compounds that included microorganisms in unmodified form' (Kevles, 1994: 111). Only Pasteur's yeast culture product patent exclusively covered living organisms. The product of nature doctrine had since the 1880s apparently precluded the patenting of any further life forms. At least that was the view of the PTO when it rejected the application's claims directed to the microorganism itself. Within the emergent biotechnology sector it was likewise generally assumed that microorganisms could not be patented.

General Electric's patent lawyers had a different attitude, working as they did for a long-established industrial corporation whose use of the patent system dates back to its formation in the 1890s. So while the scientist involved, Anand Chakrabarty, doubted that his microorganism could be patented, the company lawyer assigned to the case, Leo MaLossi, saw no logical reason why it could not. 'To MaLossi, aware that by now scientists understood living matter, including bacteria to be chemicals, Chakrabarty's bugs were manufactures, new compositions of matter – and, hence, patentable' (ibid.: 117).

The patent was initially rejected by the Patent and Trademark Office. But this decision was overturned by the Court of Customs and Patent Appeals. In hindsight this was the most likely outcome. A few months earlier, Judge Rich of the court had made the following statement when delivering the majority opinion at the conclusion of a similar case:[12] 'we think the fact that microorganisms, as distinguished from chemical compounds, are alive is a distinction without legal significance' (quoted in ibid.: 120). He also opined that microorganisms 'are much more akin to inanimate chemical compositions such as reactants, reagents, and catalysts than they are to horses and honeybees or raspberries and roses' (quoted in van Overwalle, 1999: 178).

When the same court ruled again a year later on the patentability of the Chakrabarty and Bergy microorganisms, Rich argued that there is 'no legally significant difference between active chemicals which are classified as "dead" and organisms used for their chemical reactions which take place because they are "alive"' (quoted in Kevles, 1994: 126). There is no question that this life as chemistry conceptualization inherent to MaLossi and Rich's arguments is a powerful one. Indeed, it is now recognized by other patent offices, including the EPO.

In 1980, the PTO's Supreme Court appeal against the ruling of the Court of Customs and Patent Appeals was rejected by a five to four majority. In making this decision, the court was not of course taking the view that all parts of the microorganism had been made by Chakrabarty. Rather, it was treating the microorganism as a natural compound that had been structurally modified and thus transformed into a new 'article of manufacture' or 'composition of matter' that was no longer natural. By treating the microorganism as a natural chemical substance into which a useful new characteristic had been introduced and thereby rendered unnatural, the court found that it was patentable in accordance with long-established practice with respect to chemical products that allowed a natural chemical to be the basis for an invention as long as it was modified by adding something to it (such as a gene), subtracting something from it (that is, purifying it), mixing it with something else to create a new or synergistic effect, or structurally modifying it so that it differs in an identifiable manner from what it was before (see Bozicevic, 1987: 422–3).

The decision in *Diamond* v. *Chakrabarty* was the first success in a campaign by industry to clarify (and later to change) patent rules in the biotechnology field in ways that suited their interests. General Electric did not pursue this affair because the invention in question had commercial promise but because the company was seeking to ensure that the barrier to the patenting of microorganisms would henceforth be lifted. Not surprisingly, Generic Electric attracted support from pro-patent interests with several amicus briefs filed by companies and organizations such as Genentech, the Pharmaceutical Manufacturers Association and the American Patent Law Association. (In fact, most of the 10 amicus briefs supported GE's position.) Among the arguments made to the court by Genentech and the PMA were that patents as compared to trade secrecy allowed for greater public accountability, and that allowing patents would encourage innovation and enhance the country's competitiveness in an emerging high-technology field (Kevles, 1994: 129–30). In other words, according to these groups, permitting the patenting of microorganisms is in the national and public interest. In propounding such a justification, they were claiming patent rights on public interest grounds rather than on the basis of desert. This was clearly a prudent strategy, but should be contrasted with the way some of these same interests sought to frame similar claims at the international level later in that decade (see Chapter 8).

Interestingly, the PMA in its amicus brief was keen to assert that, if a line should be drawn, it should not be placed between the living and the non-living but between unicellular and multicellular life forms. It referred to the British Patent Act of 1977 and the European Patent Convention, both of which explicitly exclude plant varieties and animals but not microorganisms. This was of course strategic. The PMA would have preferred no subject matter restrictions, but the battle to further extend patent protection could wait for another day.

In hindsight it is difficult to imagine any other outcome, given the collective economic power of the interests which stood to gain and the forum in which the legal breakthrough was achieved. According to Fowler (1994: 150),

> The GE–Chakrabarty case was a major tactical victory for the industry. Not only did it secure the protection it had long sought, but it did so through a new arena, the court system. The courts were neither fast nor cheap, but they were faster and cheaper than the political process. They were also foreign territory to most advocacy groups.

However, forum shifting can have unintended consequences. The Supreme Court is a very high-profile venue to discuss an issue with such clear moral ramifications. So, while the awarding of the equivalent UK patent attracted little if any interest outside the patent community (Cornish, 1999: 217; Grubb, 1999: 227), taking this case to the Supreme Court galvanized opposition from individuals[13] and civil society organizations that continue to oppose patenting life in the USA and elsewhere.

Five years later, the PTO's Board of Patent Appeals and Interferences in *ex parte Hibberd* reversed the PTO's earlier rejection of a patent claiming corn plants and seeds as well as plant tissue cultures. The plants were produced through conventional cross-breeding, but relied on new techniques such as cell culture and genetic analysis (but not rDNA). The applicant was a DBF called Molecular Genetics Research and Development. This case opened the way for the patenting of plants. By 1988, 42 patents on crop plants had been issued (OTA, 1989: 76). To date there are more than 1800 patents with claims to plants, seeds, or plant parts or tissues.

In 1987, the PTO Board produced another groundbreaking ruling (in *ex parte Allen*) concerning a patent application on polyploid oysters. Although the patent was rejected, the ruling established that multicellular organisms were patentable. Soon after, Donald Quigg, the Commissioner of Patents and Trademarks, publicly announced that the PTO would examine 'claims directed to multicellular living organisms, including animals' as long as they do not include human beings within their scope. He also clarified that 'an article of manufacture or composition of matter occurring in nature will not be considered patentable unless given a new form, quality, properties or combination not present in the original article existing in nature in accordance with existing law' (Quigg, 1987: 328). The following year, the first-ever animal patent was granted for 'a transgenic nonhuman mammal all of whose germ cells and somatic cells contain a recombinant activated oncogene sequence'.The patent is commonly referred to as the oncomouse patent, since it describes a mouse into which a gene has been inserted which induces increased susceptibility to cancer.

Nonetheless, Quigg's announcement was not in itself sufficient to settle the question of whether or not plants and animals are patentable. In December 2001, the Supreme Court finally confirmed the legality of patents on plants. The opportunity to do so arose because lawyers representing a company called J.E.M. Ag Supply, that was being sued by Pioneer Hi-Bred for patent infringement, requested the court to determine whether plant-related patents are invalid because of the existence of two IP laws designed specifically to protect plants: the 1930 Townsend–Purnell Plant Patent Act[14] and the 1970 Plant Variety Protection Act (see Chapter 7). The situation provoked enough concern for the US government and the Biotechnology Industry Organization to submit amicus briefs to the court. In the event, the court rejected J.E.M.'s position. As for animals, because no alternative IP system was created specifically for them, such an argument cannot be tried anyway. And since no other convincing arguments have been forthcoming to persuade courts or legislators that non-human animals are a special case, the situation for animal-related patents seems to be quite secure for the present time.

Two other developments in intellectual property regulation during the 1980s were very important, even though they were not directly concerned with biotechnology. The first of these was the 1980 passage by Congress of the Amendments to the Patent and Trademark Act, commonly known as the Bayh–Dole Act. The Act was intended to encourage universities and public research agencies to file patents on inventions arising from government-funded research as a means of facilitating technology transfer to the private sector. Given that 'the number of new university patents has increased from about 280 a year before 1980 to more than 2,600 a year in 1997' (Long, 1999: 268), the Act almost certainly increased the propensity of such institutions to do so. The second was the 1982 establishment by Congress of the Court of Appeals for the Federal Circuit (CAFC) to hear all patent appeal cases. The CAFC is widely acknowledged to have a strong tendency to uphold patents. This should not be surprising given that 'a very large group of large high technology firms and trade associations in the telecommunications, computer and pharmaceutical industries was essentially responsible for the creation of the CAFC. The group believed that a court devoted to patent cases would better represent its interests' (Silverman, 1990, quoted in Macdonald, 2001: 11). In addition to these developments, as Chapter 8 will show, the US government was also one of the main actors in strengthening IP protection worldwide in support of its science-based corporations (and copyright and trade mark industries).

Continued attempts by organizations such as Jeremy Rifkin's Foundation on Economic Trends to roll back the tide had to face the organized opposition of industry and even universities that saw the licensing of biotech patenting as a potentially huge earner for them. Daniel Kevles, a historian of science at Yale University, explains that, in congressional hearings during the early 1990s, 'patent attorneys, biotech representatives, and several congressmen warned that restrictions or a moratorium on the patenting of life or its parts would put the US at a competitive disadvantage internationally and impede research on cures and therapies for disease' (2001: 31). These alleged negative consequences were clearly very persuasive.

In 1993, the patent interests of the domestic biotechnology sector were further strengthened – one might say even privileged – with the passage of the Biotechnology Patent Act. The law was intended to prevent a situation in which foreign companies could import into the USA a product manufactured through known processes that, being so, could not be claimed in a domestic firm's patent covering elements of the product. The legislation was inspired by a 1991 court decision involving Amgen and a Japanese company called Chugai, relating to the production and importation of recombinant erythropoietin (EPO). The court determined that Amgen could not assert its patent to prevent Chugai from importing EPO produced in Japan through the recombinant DNA technology. This was because previous court decisions had determined that the scope of Amgen's patent covered only the cDNA coding for EPO and host cells transformed by the EPO-expressing gene. It did not cover the recombinant EPO itself, or the process which had of course been invented earlier by Cohen and Boyer. Chugai was in the advantageous position of having licensed a patent owned by Genetics Institute that covered the rEPO itself (see Barton, 1991: 44, 46). This allowed it to produce the EPO using the cDNA patented by Amgen and the same technique *as long as* its production was carried out abroad, with the EPO then exported to the USA.

For lawmakers, this experience pointed to the need to change the law to protect an emerging industrial sector considered vital to the future of the US economy. The legislation essentially dispensed with the normal patentability requirements in respect of processes as long as they were being employed to manufacture something new. In part, the Act stated that 'a claimed process of making or using a medicine, manufacture, or composition of matter is not obvious under this section if – (1) the machine, manufacture, or composition of matter is novel .. and nonobvious ... (2) the claimed process is a biotechnological process' (Borson, 1995: 485–6). Such are the industry's persuasive powers that they can even make basic patentability requirements disappear from the law!

So far we have had little to say about DNA. Since the rejection of the NIH's patent applications on ESTs, the PTO has sought to deal with the tricky issue of separating the patentable from the unpatentable. In 1996, facing patent applications claiming thousands of sequences from companies like Incyte and Human Genome Sciences, it decided to allow up to 10 sequences to be claimed in each application. The year after, the PTO clarified that applicants could claim, not only an EST, but also 'a purified and isolated composition comprising (the EST sequence)' (quoted in Grubb, 1999: 248). In other words, it was possible to claim the whole gene of which the EST sequence was a part. In 1998, Incyte became the first company to be granted a patent covering ESTs.

Europe and Japan: Racing to the Top – or the Bottom?

The USA certainly pioneered the patenting of animals, but not of microorganisms or plants.[15] Nonetheless, it was the first country routinely to grant patents on these types of organism. There is little doubt that the patenting of biotechnological inventions is much more controversial in Europe, and has encountered far more organized opposition. But, at the same time, European governments and the European Commission are concerned not to be left behind in the biotechnology revolution by the USA and Japan. Several governments and the Commission have been persuaded by industry that the lack of strong patent rights is highly disadvantageous for the European biotech sector.

How has the European Union responded to these conflicting pressures? In 1989, the European Commission, concerned about the legal uncertainties which, it was felt, could be prejudicial to the future of biotechnology in Europe, and fearing that some European countries might respond to mounting controversy by banning patents on living organisms and genes, drafted a Directive on the Legal Protection of Biotechnological Inventions. The aim was to harmonize patent law relating to biotechnology around high minimum standards, while preventing member states from 'backsliding' (Grubb, 1999: 253–4). However, it took nine years for the Directive to be approved by the European Parliament and to enter into force. Opposition throughout was stiff, from within the Parliament (especially from the Greens), which rejected an earlier text in 1995, and outside from several environmental, development, religious and anti-genetic engineering civil society organizations, and even a group representing indigenous peoples of the Amazon. Some European governments were unhappy with the Directive even after its approval. The Dutch government brought an action against the European Parliament and the Council of the European Union before the Court of Justice of the European Communities in October 1998 to have the Directive nullified, and subsequently gained the support of Italy and Norway. The grounds for the action included allegations that the Directive has an incorrect legal basis, breaches obligations under international law (including the Convention on Biological Diversity) and violates human rights. In October 2001, the court dismissed the action. Nonetheless, opposition remains and some governments are still unenthusiastic about the Directive. By the end of 2001, only four countries – the UK, Ireland, Finland and

Denmark – had fully incorporated the Directive into their national law one year after the deadline by which all EU members were supposed to have done so.

According to Article 3(2) of the Directive, 'Biological material which is isolated from its natural environment or produced by means of a technical process may be the subject of an invention even if it previously occurred in nature.' Also, by virtue of Article 5(2), 'An element isolated from the human body or otherwise produced by means of a technical process, including the sequence or partial sequence of a gene, may constitute a patentable invention, even if the structure of that element is identical to that of a natural element.' These provisions are very similar to the EPO Guidelines for Examination, which is of course intentional. The Guidelines clarify:

> If a substance found in nature has first to be isolated from its surrounding and a process for obtaining it is developed, that process is patentable. Moreover, if the substance can be properly characterised either by its structure, by the process by which is it obtained or by other parameters ... and it is 'new' in the absolute sense of having no previously recognised existence, then the substance per se may be patentable.

A sequence or partial sequence of a gene may also be patented as long as an industrial application is disclosed. This is consistent with EPO practice. In a 1995 case (Howard Florey/Relaxin), the Opposition Division of the EPO declared DNA to be 'not "life", but a chemical substance which carries genetic information', and therefore patentable just as any other chemicals are.

Explicit exclusions include animal and plant varieties and essentially biological processes for the production of plants and animals. Article 2.2 clarifies that 'a process for the production of plants or animals is essentially biological if it consists entirely of natural phenomena such as crossing or selection'. This definition has been adopted also by the EPO. Also excluded on the grounds that commercial exploitation of them would be contrary to ordre public or morality are

> (a) processes for cloning human beings; (b) processes for modifying the germ line genetic identity of human beings; (c) uses of human embryos for industrial or commercial purposes; [and] (d) processes for modifying the genetic identity of animals which are likely to cause them suffering without any substantial medical benefit to man or animal, and also animals resulting from such processes.

There have also been setbacks for the life science industries. In 1995, the EPO Technical Board of Appeal in *Greenpeace* v. *Plant Genetic Systems NV* ruled on an appeal against the upholding of a plant-related patent. The Board determined that a claim for plant cells contained in a plant is unpatentable since it does not exclude plant varieties from its scope (see Llewelyn, 1995). This implied that transgenic plants per se were unpatentable because of the plant variety exclusion. Consequently, for the next four years, the EPO stopped accepting claims on plants per se. Similarly, the oncomouse patent was initially rejected on the grounds of being for an animal variety.

This situation, a victory for Greenpeace, was of course highly unsatisfactory in the view of the life science corporations. But things changed in a more favourable direction in December 1999 when the EPO Enlarged Board of Appeal decided that, while genetically modified plant varieties are unpatentable, 'a claim wherein specific plant varieties are not individually claimed is not excluded from patentability under Article 53(b), EPC even though it may embrace plant varieties'.[16]

Opponents of biotechnological patenting, such as Greenpeace, have sought to make use of the morality and ordre public exclusions in Article 53(*a*) of the EPC and try to expand their application. But they have not been very successful. In the famous oncomouse case, the EPO's Examining Division was initially reluctant to apply any kind of morality criterion but was instructed to do so by the Technical Board of Appeal (TBA). In 1991, the Examining Division responded by formulating a balancing test for this particular case that would take into account the following: (i) the interest of mankind in providing remedies for dangerous diseases; (ii) protection against uncontrolled dissemination of unwanted genes; and (iii) prevention of cruelty to animals. On this basis, the Examination Division determined that, since the potential benefits of the invention outweighed the negative factors, the patent should be granted, and the EPO consequently did so. However, this patent has remained controversial among environmental and animal welfare groups, and opposition proceedings have continued ever since.

In the above-mentioned *Greenpeace* v. *Plant Genetic Systems* case, Greenpeace succeeded in having six of the 44 claims deleted from the patent. But perhaps the most interesting aspect of the case for our purposes is that the TBA was challenged to apply the morality and ordre public exclusions. The TBA concluded that an invention is 'immoral' if the general public would consider it so abhorrent that patenting would be inconceivable. But it provided no clarification on how 'abhorrent' should be interpreted, nor how opponents of a patent should demonstrate that the general public regards the invention as immoral. The TBA rejected the evidence of surveys and opinion polls provided by Greenpeace as inadmissible, arguing that 'surveys and opinion polls do not necessarily reflect ... moral norms that are deeply rooted in European culture' (quoted in Warren-Jones, 2001: 165). With respect to ordre public, the TBA placed the burden of proof on the patent's opponents by requiring convincing evidence that exploitation of the patent would be seriously prejudicial to the environment. The TBA's rather narrow interpretations of the exceptions led them to reject their application to this particular case.

Evidently, legal uncertainties continue for the time being. Nonetheless, the general trend in European national and regional patent regulation is for a loosening of the eligibility requirements in favour of industrial interests such that discoveries seem no longer to be distinguishable from inventions. Despite this apparent race to the bottom, one saving grace is that patent examination standards are much higher at the EPO than at the USPTO.

Japan has tended to follow – and in some cases to precede – the USA in encouraging biotechnology patenting by opening up its patent law to the protection of life forms. Legislation passed in 1959 had excluded the following five categories of subject matter from patentability: (i) foods and additives; (ii) drugs and methods to combine two or more drugs; (iii) substances produced chemically; (iv) substances produced by a method of transforming atomic nuclei; and (v) products which are likely to disturb public order or good morals or to be injurious to public health. In 1976, the law was revised to remove the first three categories, and in 1994, the fourth one was also deleted, leaving just (v) as the remaining exception.

Subsequently, Japan has become quite permissive in terms of patentable subject matter. In 1979, the Japan Patent Office issued standards for the patenting of biotechnological inventions under the following categories: (i) microorganisms, (ii) processes for producing microorganisms, (iii) processes using microorganisms, (iv) products obtained from microbiological sources, and (v) DNA and RNA molecules or sub-cellular units (Howells and Neary, 1995: 159). From proteins in 1976 and microorganisms in 1979, plants became patentable in 1985 and animals in 1993. While a change in the law allowed proteins to be patented, the lifting of the bar on microorganisms, plant and animals came through changes to the examiners' guidelines. During these years, and ever since, the patenting of biotechnological inventions has aroused little of the controversy that Europe has experienced, and is now very common.

Are Patents Inappropriate for Biotechnological Inventions?

Biotechnology patenting raises a number of important policy questions. Should the application of patent systems be modified to accommodate new areas of research that are risky and expensive even if the resulting discoveries appear to lack genuine novelty or inventiveness, as traditionally defined under patent law? Conversely, to what extent should the design and application of rules that allow the patenting of basic research tools take into account the possible damaging effects of such patenting on downstream innovation?

But concerns about biotechnology patenting are not just about good public policy making. Those who doubt the appropriateness of patenting biotechnological inventions are likely to argue that the very notion of scientists inventing a life form, seed, cell line, protein or DNA sequence is fundamentally incorrect or even sacrilegious. It is important to examine all these objections closely. After all, supporters of biotechnology patenting would like us to think that extending patents to such things does not give rise to any special problems that existing rules and doctrines (such as those relating to chemicals) cannot resolve. And if they are right about this, perhaps we should not care too much about biotechnology patenting.

Fundamental issues When it comes to fundamental objections, these patents clearly do challenge some quite fundamental tenets of patent law and jurisprudence. One of the most frequently expressed opinions is that patents on life forms render the invention/discovery distinction meaningless and thereby allow pure discoveries to be patented. In dealing with this issue, we will discuss first DNA and then life forms.

In the case of DNA, it is worth noting that, despite the extent of patenting going on, some DBFs and pharmaceutical companies disagree with the patenting of both naturally occurring DNA sequences and cDNA. But others take the view that, if DNA is just a chemical, then complementary DNA (cDNA) sequences at least should be patentable provided that they fulfil the criteria of novelty, inventive step and industrial applicability. In a 1998 article in *Science*, John Doll, director of biotechnology examination at the US PTO, clarified that DNA sequences such as ESTs and SNPs (single nucleotide polymorphisms) can be patented if the applicant discloses specific utilities such as that the sequence is useful for chromosome mapping or identification, gene mapping, tagging genes with known function such as including increasing predisposition to a disease, and forensic identification (Doll, 1998).

But one should be very sceptical about this in spite of a recent rule change by the PTO making the utility requirement more demanding. This is because techniques for isolating and purifying DNA sequences are well-known and no longer require a great deal of skill to use. Even if nobody knew about the naturally occurring equivalent, such a claim should still arguably fail for the lack of an inventive step on the basis of the techniques employed being routine. Nonetheless, as we have seen, several countries do allow isolated and purified DNA sequences to be patented as long as a credible use is disclosed.

But the problem goes further even than this. It is now understood better than before that Francis Crick's Central Dogma, that DNA makes RNA makes protein, is not reliable in every case. All genes have a function but not all of them are involved in protein-making processes. To make matters even more complicated, different genes may occupy the same strand of DNA to the extent that it may be extremely difficult to determine where one begins and another ends. Further, the whole protein-making process is complex and still to some extent a mystery. What is becoming apparent, though, is that successful protein manufacture requires the involvement of more than one gene. This is because the various processes which need to take place simultaneously are themselves regulated by other proteins which in turn are coded for by other genes. So granting patents on a gene on the basis that it performs a single function such as coding for a particular protein or that it is associated with a disease is problematic. This is because it simplistically assumes that genes have independent functions. In fact, because genomes should more accurately be seen as consisting largely of multiple intersecting mini-ecosystems rather than as a single collection of separately functioning 'Lego bricks', this is conceptually wrong. Therefore treating genes as patentable inventions on the basis of a single function is a reflection more of ignorance than of insight, and is essentially anti-innovation, since it potentially hinders opportunities for follow-on researchers to carry out further investigations on genes that a company or university had previously patented on the basis that its scientists had discovered one out of possibly numerous functions. Increasingly, company representatives express frustration that so much basic genetic information is being privatized by other companies through the patent system. Typically, the complainers are from the pharmaceutical and life science firms, while those being criticized are DBFs.

As for life forms, it is frequently argued that the patenting of genetically modified organisms should be banned on the basis that a living thing is not a human invention but a discovery or a creation of God. For example, according to a statement by the Church of Scotland's Society, Religion and Technology Project,

> An animal, plant or micro-organism owes its creation ultimately to God, not human endeavour. It cannot be interpreted as an invention or a process, in the normal sense of either word. It has a life of its own, which inanimate matter does not. In genetic engineering, moreover, only a tiny fraction of the makeup of the organism can be said to be a product of the scientists. The organism is still essentially a living entity, not an invention. A genetically modified mouse is in a completely different category from a mouse trap. (SRT Project, 1997)

Religious objections on principle to the patenting of life forms certainly deserve to be respected, but one should not assume that inventions must be completely human-made to be classed legitimately as inventions. In Europe and North America, which have the most experience in the patenting of apparently natural substances, there has never been any kind of blanket exclusion of certain types of invention on the basis that because they were not 100 per cent human-made they cannot be patented. This seems perfectly reasonable, though admittedly it is very difficult to consider an animal as a human invention. An organism should probably not be treated by the law as a single chemical, and a more convincing case needs to be made that inserting or breeding a piece of DNA into an organism should entitle one to property rights not only over the whole organism but over all of its progeny too (Funder, 1999: 568).[17] This is not because it is less than 100 per cent human-made but because, as the Church of Scotland rightly argues, the functioning and behaviour of the life form are mostly out of the control of the 'inventor'. It is the difficulty of making such a convincing case that tends to lead to the common fall-back argument that the research and development that makes these kinds of 'invention' possible is so expensive and risky that only a patent can provide the necessary inducement. In other words, we should bend the rules for industry because this research would not take place otherwise. There is some merit to this argument, though it seems likely that at least some of the research would carry on regardless.

Another comment one can make on the Church of Scotland statement is that patents are not just for invented machines and chemicals but may include new processes to create things that may or may not already exist, and even new uses of existing things. It is the act of invention not just the thing invented that a patent is awarded for. So while one may agree (as I do) that an oncomouse is not an invention, the bringing into being of such a mouse did result from human endeavour involving activity that probably deserves to be considered as inventive. It seems fair to reward such inventive work in some way. It may after all be far more beneficial to human welfare in its application to cancer research than yet another mousetrap. But how? One argument is that we should allow the procedure for creating it to be patented, but not the mouse itself. Another argument that is just as logical, is that the oncomouse could be patented as long as it is produced by the technique described in the patent. In other words, we should allow a product-by-process patent but not a product-by-any process patent. Alternatively, we might come up with another legal protection system in place of patents.

It is absolutely true, though, that the invention/discovery distinction has been blurred to the point of becoming almost meaningless. There are those within the patent community who agree with the critics about this but claim that it is nothing to be concerned about. Discovering something does not mean that no novelty or inventive step is involved, some of them would argue. History may even be on their side. Erich Kaufer pointed out that, 'during the Middle Ages, the term "invention" had a meaning much closer to what we would now call "discovery" … than the meaning accepted under modern patent law' (Kaufer, 1980: 2). Yet it is important to make the distinction. If we do not, we simply legitimize the lowering of patentability standards and allow things to be patented that simply should not be.

In short, while there may be a case for applying patent law to DNA, proteins, cells and living organisms, at least to some degree, doing so is fundamentally problematic, is bound to lead to problems (as the next section will make even clearer) and is on balance probably best avoided. All of these are more than 'just chemicals'. That the law treats them as such is testament to the creativity of pro-industry lawyers and the high economic stakes involved.

Policy-related issues As we have seen, most developed countries have adopted various measures to support commercial biotechnology. To allow companies to appropriate commercially valuable knowledge, industry and the patent community have persuaded governments and courts to be permissive in terms of applying (or not applying) certain customary requirements and to expand the availability of intellectual property protection. Sometimes this has been done by relaxing the rules obliging applicants to fully disclose the invention and demonstrate its novelty, industrial applicability or utility, and inventive step, and by making new rules providing greater legal certainty. On balance, many if not most of these regulatory changes may have served a useful purpose in fostering biotechnological innovation. But there have been some negative consequences. We deal first with issues of interpretation that have arisen because of the specificities of patenting in the biotechnology fields, and then look at some of these consequences.

One of the ways in which inventors in this field have benefited from liberal policy making relates to the concept of exhaustion of rights. Once a patent-protected product is sold by the owner or the licensee, his or her rights over that product are usually exhausted unless there is a contract of sale imposing conditions on buyers. When it comes to living things, the rights are not exhausted when the 'product' is sold but extend to the progeny whether or not the progeny is 'manufactured' by the 'inventors'. In this sense we are making a concession to the biotechnology patent owner in order to make the patent monopoly meaningful.[18] After all, a strict application of the exhaustion doctrine would make the right so weak as to be almost useless.

In addition, inventions described in a patent are normally meant to be repeatable in the sense that technicians 'skilled in the art' (to use the common patent terminology) reading the specification should be able to repeat the invention, that is, come to the same result. But natural processes, even human directed ones, are to some extent random, and such techniques as animal cloning and genetic engineering are still not exact sciences despite the claims of many proponents. For every successful outcome there are likely to be hundreds of failures. But again, patent offices and policy makers tend to give the applicants the benefit of the doubt.

Also disclosing the invention should be detailed and provide instruction so that the state of the art progresses. But living things cannot be described in the way that mechanical inventions can. In the last few decades, policy makers have come up with a solution, which is to require applicants to deposit specimens. To be fair, this is a very good solution, since it makes the invention more accessible than could any description, no matter how comprehensive.

So what we have done is to bend the rules for biotechnology inventors to meet their demands if not necessarily their genuine needs. This need not be a problem if negative consequences do not arise. But they do. Now when we consider the issue of perverse consequences, we need to bear in mind first that, in longer-established industries and technological fields, legislators and patent offices may be experienced and impartial enough to ensure that the extent of the rights available and which are granted are optimal as far as the public interest is concerned. Even then, this is difficult to achieve. The challenge is much greater still with new technologies such as biotechnology, especially if governments are pressured by powerful economic interests, and if patent offices lack the resources to conduct adequate prior art searches and examinations.

In consequence of recent developments in the field of biotechnology patenting, three situations have arisen that should be of major concern to policy makers.[19] First, a disproportionately large quantity of patents is being granted in relation to the number of commercial products based upon them. This is because of the enormous quantity of patents on genes and gene fragments, whose existence raises the cost of doing research owing to the need to license related parts of the genome that are 'owned' by different institutions. Second, the scope of a patent can sometimes be drawn so broadly as to allow monopoly protection to cover a range of possible products including many unforeseen by the applicant. Both situations can create perverse incentives which may reduce the rate of innovation. Third, there is a consolidation of patent ownership and global market shares in the hands of a small number of corporate life science giants. This situation can be attributed to a combination of possible factors, some of which may operate synergistically, including privatization of industry and of research, stricter environmental and/or safety regulation, trade liberalization, mergers and acquisitions, and also intellectual property rights. Let us look at these situations more closely.

In a now well-known article in *Science*, Michael Heller and Rebecca Eisenberg warned of an emerging IP problem in the USA in the field of biomedical research which they call the 'tragedy of the anticommons' (1998). What they refer to is a situation in which the increased patenting of pre-market, or 'upstream' research 'may be stifling life-saving innovations further downstream in the course of research and product development'. One way this can happen is based on the fact that developing future commercial products such as therapeutic proteins or genetic diagnostic tests often requires the use of multiple gene fragments, an increasing number of which are being patented. The cost of research and development will be affected by the existence of so many of these patents because a company intending to develop such products will need to acquire licences from other patent holders, and thus will incur large (and possibly prohibitive) transaction costs. Since the first patent covering ESTs was controversially awarded to Incyte Pharmaceuticals in 1998, this problem could become more serious.

Potential for such anti-commons situations also appears to exist in agrobiotechnology. Technology transfers in this sector can consist of highly complex and expensive bundles of transactions. A good example is GoldenRice, which is so called because it is genetically modified to produce beta-carotene. Its proponents believe that, once developed, it could be enormously beneficial to people in countries where vitamin A deficiency is a serious problem and where rice is a staple food.[20] The product and the technologies for making it are the subject of numerous patents of which at least 40 are held in the USA and in most European countries. According to a study by a technology transfer organization called International Service for the Acquisition of Agri-biotech Applications (which also owns the 'GoldenRice' trade mark), 'depending on the country of use, between zero and 40 licenses of IP rights would be required, from a dozen or so entities' (Kryder *et al.*, 2000: vii).

There is little that patent offices can do themselves about such 'tragedies' except leave it to the patent holders involved either to accept the high transaction costs entailed by their need to acquire or license other firms' patents or to collaborate with their rivals by setting up private collective rights organizations (CROs) to pool their patents. The advantage for members of setting up such a CRO would be to reduce the transaction costs that would otherwise be incurred by the need both to negotiate multiple licensing arrangements among them and to distribute royalties from non-member technology licensees (see Merges, 1996). Although CROs would presumably reduce transaction costs for non-member licensees as well, there is also a danger that CROs can become too dominant in the market, leading to reduction of competition and the stifling of innovation.

According to Arti Rai of the University of Pennsylvania (1999: 840–41), the history of patent pools does not give cause for optimism in this regard. First, some of the best known pools were set up only after protracted litigation. Second, past patent pools were sometimes deemed anti-competitive and therefore illegal under antitrust law. Third, in the biotechnology case, the partners would include a diversity of organizations such as universities, government research agencies, small firms and transnationals. Past experience suggests, in her view, that patent pools have most often come about among homogeneous partners that have previous experience of collaborating. This third reason may be overstated, though, since as we have seen such types of collaboration involving different types of organization do take place in biotechnology. But logically the best outcome is probably a change in the rules so that such basic research tools as DNA sequences cannot be patented at all.

The second problem has been with modern biotechnology from the start. Cohen and Boyer's recombinant DNA patent described a method of inserting genes only into E. coli, yet it covered applications of the technology for a much wider range of microorganisms. This did not prove to be a big problem because it was so widely licensed. But because it is a platform technology, refusing to license it would certainly have slowed down innovation. Similarly, the Harvard oncomouse patent disclosed a mouse containing a certain oncogene, but its scope embraced all non-human mammals into which the gene may be introduced, plus their progeny.[21] A more recent example is US patent 5 159 135 awarded in 1992 to Agracetus for *all* transgenic cotton. The patent claims covered any variety of cotton produced by means of any gene transfer technology. The patenting of genes is bound to raise the issue of excessive breadth (in addition of course to the other problems with gene patenting). Since many and perhaps all genes perform several roles, granting a patent on the gene itself to the first person to discover any role is based on bad science and mistaken on public policy grounds because it is likely to discourage others from investigating other roles that may even be more significant. At the same time, with the product protection acquired and a product in the pipeline, the owners may not see any particular need to discover other functions.

This can be a life or death issue. Patents on genes linked to particular diseases tend to claim a range of applications including diagnostic tests, and owners can be quite determined in enforcing their rights even though the validity of such patents is often considered to be extremely questionable. Even non-commercial entities like public sector hospitals may be the target of companies demanding royalties. It was recently reported, for example, that, 'after the gene for the iron overload condition haemochromatosis was patented, 30 per cent of labs surveyed stopped testing for the disease-causing gene variant, or developing such tests' (Kleiner, 2002: 6). David Porteous, Head of Medical Genetics at Edinburgh University, has complained of patent-related legal problems affecting the freedom of scientists in Scotland to conduct gene-based diagnostic tests for breast cancer. This is despite the fact that geneticists do not even need to read Myriad's patent specifications since all the knowledge required to conduct the test is already in the public domain.[22]

It is fair to say that in individual cases solutions can sometimes be found. The law usually allows opponents to file oppositions or re-examination requests with the patent office. Over-broad patents can also be challenged in the courts if opponents have enough money. In 1994, the above Agracetus-owned patent was cancelled by the US PTO 'on the basis that other researchers already knew what was disclosed in the patent application as being novel and new' (NBIAP/ISB, 1995). The cancellation followed complaints about the patent's excessive breadth from other companies, the USDA, civil society organizations and a re-examination request made on behalf of an anonymous party. Also Calgene's attempt to acquire a patent covering all transgenic plants of the Brassica genus failed when the PTO 'denied the broadest claims and awarded the company rights only to Brassica cells transformed using Calgene's method' (NBIAP/ISB, 1994).

The problem could also be dealt with through more careful examinations, but this raises another worrying issue. Nowadays, patent offices are required to become more service oriented and financially self-sufficient. They are expected to demonstrate their efficiency by examining patents speedily and avoiding backlogs. The danger is that the proportion both of excessively broad scope patents and of issued patents lacking genuine novelty and inventive step will increase. In fact, this is known to be a serious problem in the USA, where patent examiners are not given sufficient time to do their work properly. While the non-patent-owning public is obviously not a customer of the patent system as such, it is still meant to benefit from the system. However, public interest organizations opposed to such trends and also to specific patents are likely to find that mounting legal challenges to improperly granted patents requires financial commitments well beyond their means.

The court systems can also become too friendly towards the position of existing patent holders. The CAFC, whose origins were briefly explained earlier and which reversed the tendency of many appeals courts in the USA to be sceptical about the validity of patents, has been criticized for bias in favour of patent holders and for being too accepting of arguments put forward by patent-holding legal representatives. For example, two commentators have argued – specifically in the context of DNA-based patents – that, while the obviousness test is supposed to provide the means to establish an appropriate breadth, patent examiners are now finding it difficult to apply the test properly because of the 'ill-fitting and inapplicable traditional chemical patent law doctrines' that lawyers representing the biotechnology firms have persuaded the CAFC to accept (Varma and Abraham, 1996: 85). The consequence is that too many patents are being granted and upheld that should not be.

However, these problems are to some extent technical, and adjustments may be made in the courts to correct the situation. Moreover, there are signs that the court may be moving in the opposite direction. One such sign is the 1997 decision in *Regents of the University of California* v. *Eli Lilly and Co.* to invalidate claims on the basis that 'the disclosure of a single species of genetic material does not provide an adequate written description necessary to support patent claims to a broad genus of written material' (Sung and Pelto, 1998: 892). This suggests that the situation may improve as the CAFC becomes more accustomed to dealing with biotechnology patents.

Another example evidencing a possible new trend is the November 2000 decision in *Festo* v. *Shoketsu* to severely constrain the application of the so-called 'doctrine of equivalents'. The doctrine, which has been adopted in a number of legal jurisdictions (such as the USA and Germany), is meant to ensure that the inventor is able to secure a fair remuneration for unforeseen embodiments that would be obvious to somebody skilled in the art (see Grubb, 1999: 381–4; Lederer, 1999). In essence, it extends the scope of a patent beyond the actual language of the claims to prevent others from reading the patent and inventing around it without doing anything that would not be obvious to a trained technician. Although the case was unrelated to biotechnology, it may well limit patent coverage in this field as in others.

Another sign of a change in direction, this time at the USPTO, is the new rule announced in January 2001 for DNA-related patent examinations. Patent applications disclosing DNA sequences must now provide convincing evidence that their utility is specific, substantial and credible (see USPTO, 2001). However, many more far-reaching proposals were rejected, and it seems to the author at least that DNA sequences should not be patentable at all, at least until scientists have found a way to develop useful proteins that do not exist in nature. We are still some time away from being able to do this.

With respect to the third problem, biotech-related patent ownership is becoming concentrated in the hands of a small number of very large companies. Taking the situation in agricultural biotechnology, the Nuffield Council on Bioethics (1999: 46) reported recently that consolidation 'continues to shorten the list of owners of the important "enabling" intellectual property for plant genetic modification and plant molecular genetics'. Moreover, 'there are now six major industrial groups who between them control most of the technology which gives freedom to undertake commercial R&D in the area of GM crops'. These are (i) Agrevo and Plant Genetic Systems (PGS); (ii) Du Pont and Pioneer; (iii) ELM, DNAP, Asgrow and Seminis; (iv) Monsanto, Calgene, DeKalb, Agracetus, PBI, Hybritech and Delta and Pine Land Co.; (v) Novartis; and (vi) Zeneca, Mogen and Avanta.

The question is, does patent ownership merely reflect such concentration, or does it also reinforce it? The answer is not entirely clear. For one thing, as we have seen, DBFs need patents to survive. Therefore, without such patents, a lot of small companies could not exist. On the other hand, large companies are unlikely to be interested in taking over smaller companies that have no patents. In this sense, patents with high potential value are a signal that the owning DBF is doing good research and owns rights that have the potential to generate large future profits. Conversely, a DBF with no valuable patents is unlikely to attract a bigger company. In this sense, then, patents encourage consolidation.

Biotechnology Patenting and New Institutionalism

This rather lengthy discussion on the problems of patenting shows that patents are probably inappropriate in the biotechnology field, at least for products if not for processes, and that some alternative legal system of protection may be worth considering. So how can we explain the increasingly generous protection that has been extended in the past two decades to this new area of scientific and commercial activity (and the slight rebalancing that may be taking place in the USA)?

Given that the main interest in biotechnological patenting came from small firms, and that these constituted a very small industrial sector in the 1980s, new institutionalism would suggest that the persuasive powers of the patent community must have played a major role. Our account does indeed suggest that the patent community did perform an extremely important role. In particular, the life as chemistry perspective lent itself, as was of course intended, to the view that extending protection to biotechnological inventions including life forms was nothing new or radical but a matter of simple logic. Patent lawyers made this case very well and persuasively enough to convince the courts. Once the PTO found itself isolated, it had little alternative but to fall into line. In any case, PTO commissioners are not apolitical career civil servants but political appointees that cannot be expected to take positions that conflict with government policy, which became extremely pro-patent (or at least pro-patent owner) at this time.

As for the companies, they were also more influential than their small size would otherwise suggest. This may be explained by the fact that, once the public felt assured that biotechnology was safe, the companies immediately acquired a very positive image (assisted by a lot of hype) that inclined policy makers and politicians to support them on the basis much more of future promise than of early achievements, which were actually few in number. Furthermore, the USA had a head start on the rest of the world and friendly patent regulation was considered necessary to maintain this lead. It is very fortunate for the industry that the emergence of biotechnology coincided with the beginning of a new pro-patent era in the USA that was made evident by the Bayh-Dole Act, the creation of the CAFC, and the increasingly laisser-faire attitude towards corporate concentration and the use of patents to reinforce such concentration. For politicians concerned about the competitiveness of American industry in the world and eager to encourage the development of a promising new industrial sector, it is difficult to imagine why they would have taken more notice of Jeremy Rifkin than of Genentech. On the other hand, the slight rebalancing of the past few years is certainly linked to concerns from the longer-established companies that patenting may have gone too far and that the tragedy of the anti-commons is now a real problem.

As for Europe, such explanations are no doubt also relevant to some extent. But perhaps the most important one was that industry and the patent community worked determinedly to persuade the European Commission that, for Europe to catch up with the USA and also to prevent companies from moving across the Atlantic, it would have to adopt similar patent policies.

Notes

1   Among the most comprehensive historical accounts of the rise of molecular biology and the achievements of its practitioners are Kay (1993, 2000), Judson (1996) and Morange (1998).
2   The initial patent application was filed in 1974, but was overridden by subsequent applications. The definitive patent (number 4 237 224) was filed in 1979 and awarded in 1980. The title of the patent was 'Process for producing biologically functional molecular chimeras'.
3   Males have 24 different chromosomes while females have 23. This is because, in addition to the 22 pairs we all inherit, males also have an X and a Y chromosome while females have two Ys but no Xs.
4   The 'big five' were (in descending order): the MIT/Whitehead Institute Center for Genome Research; the Sanger Centre; Washington University Genome Sequencing Center; the US Department of Energy Joint Genome Institute; and Baylor College of Medicine Human Genome Sequencing Center.
5   Patents on BRCA1 were granted to Myriad at the USPTO in 1999 and the EPO in 2001.
6   Such networks exist also in Europe and Japan, though the role of DBFs tends to be less important (Joly, 1999: 4). It is worth noting that such networks are not necessarily confined within national boundaries. Japanese and European firms often look to collaborate with US firms (Barbanti *et al.*, 1999: 25; Kenney, 1986: 243).
7   Drug and Market Development (1998: 264).
8   'A spin-off is a company that is formed by individuals who were former employees of the parent organisation (a research centre or a foreign firm) and a core technology that is transferred from the parent organisation' (WTO WGTTT, 2002: 35).
9   DBFs typically invest the equivalent of over 50 per cent of sales revenues in research and development.
10   The Biotechnology Industry Organization was not founded until 1993, when two smaller organizations agreed to merge.
11   Although the PTO was responsible for the shift in forum, GE was aware that the Supreme Court was an ideal arena to achieve its aim.
12   *In re Bergy – Application of Malcolm E. Bergy* (1977), *United States Patent Quarterly*, 195: 344, 346.
13   Most prominently, Jeremy Rifkin and Pat Mooney.
14   So called after the names of its two congressional sponsors.
15   Although it was not until 1988 that the EPO awarded the first patent on a plant (to the US biotechnology company Agrigenetics), several European countries allowed plant patents from the mid-twentieth century (see Chapter 7).
16   EPO Decision G 01/98 (*http://www.european-patent-office.org/dg3/biblio/g980001ex1.htm*).
17   Interestingly, the EPO Examining Division initially rejected claims to the progeny of transgenic non-human mammals included in the oncomouse patent application, on the basis that the applicant was illegitimately seeking to circumvent the essentially

biological process exception. But as Amanda Warren-Jones of Liverpool University explains (2001: 123), 'the Technical Board pointed out that, since the claim was fundamentally a product, the issue did not arise. The Board also indicated that, while not an issue for consideration in the case, claims to progeny could not be assumed to be the result of "biological processes"'. To this author the second argument seems rather far-fetched.

18   This point also applies to PBRs.

19   Though it must be said that related situations arise outside the biotechnology field too.

20   It is fair to say that some scientists and anti-biotechnology activists doubt that GoldenRice will do much if anything for people affected by vitamin A deficiency and dismiss its promotion as nothing more than corporate public relations. It falls beyond the scope of this book to evaluate the claims and counter-claims.

21   In the European patent, the exact phrase is 'a transgenic eucaryotic animal ..., said animal preferably being a rodent'.

22   He made this point at an April 2001 conference hosted by Edinburgh University that the author attended.

Chapter 7

Plant Breeding, the Seed Industry and Plant Breeders' Rights

In years to come, much of the food consumed, many of the clothes worn and even the houses occupied by man may be radically changed by the mass attack of plant breeders so that the future generations may speak of a horticultural revolution rivaling, if not surpassing, the great industrial revolution. (Joseph Rossman, US Patent Officer, 1931)[1]

Nothing that Congress could do to help farming would be of greater value and permanence than to give the plant breeder the same status as the mechanical and chemical inventors now have through the patent law. (Thomas Edison, 1930)[2]

A new plant produced by artificial cross-fertilization is not to be considered as a natural product ... for the production thereof is effected by the controlling action of man. The fact that natural forces also cooperate in no way alters this decision. Natural forces also cooperate even in the course of chemical processes, but it is man who initially provides the special conditions under which the natural forces will then act. (Franz and Freda Wuesthoff, 1952)

The Science of Plant Breeding

When it comes to protecting the products of new technological fields (or for that matter products of old technological fields that have hitherto been unprotected), the options available to policy makers are to fit such products into existing IP categories or to create new IP rights. In the words of the eminent IP scholar William Cornish (1993: 54–5),

Intellectual property may be extended to new subject matter either by accretion or by emulation. Accretion involves re-defining an existing right so as to encompass the novel material; emulation requires the creation of a new and distinct right by analogy drawn more or less eclectically from the types already known.

This book has shown that the first option was taken when it came to organic chemistry, pharmaceutical science and biotechnology. In each case, the patent system was stretched in ways that the industries concerned generally found to be satisfactory (albeit with some disagreement about how far and at what speed the stretching should be done). Similarly, copyright (and then patent) law was extended

175

to protect computer programs. But when it came to developing legal means to enable private plant breeders to appropriate the outputs of their research, the interest groups concerned, especially those based in Europe, favoured the emulation option in the form of the UPOV Convention. To understand this preference for emulation over accretion, it is important first to know something about the nature of plant breeding and why it differs in important respects from the kinds of invention for which patents are considered more suitable (or at least less unsuitable), and the specific obstacles to appropriation that the businesses concerned needed to overcome.

Very soon after the 1900 rediscovery of Mendel's insights into the rules of heredity, scientists, especially in Britain, sought to apply them to crop improvement. Another valuable innovation during the early part of the century was the development of 'pure lines' of self-pollinating crops. Pure lines breed true to type and contain consistent and identifiable traits that can be transferred to other plants. According to two experts on the politics of modern agriculture, Robin Pistorius and Jeroen van Wijk (1999: 36), 'while Mendelian breeding allowed for a controlled mixing of genetic characteristics, pure line breeding offered a practical method to "fix" them in succeeding generations'.

Breeding new plant varieties is actually a very laborious and time-consuming process.[3] It takes about seven to 10 years to get from the first cross to the marketable variety (Bliss, 1989: 70). The first task is to determine the objectives of the breeding programme. One obvious goal is to produce varieties with higher yields, but there are many other possible objectives such as the development of varieties with added or improved characteristics such as pest resistance, disease resistance or drought tolerance. Breeders must also respond to varying farming conditions and to the ever-changing demands of food-processing companies, supermarket chains and of course the consumers. Nowadays, some companies have started breeding programmes directed at organic farmers.

The basic conventional technique is known as 'crossing and selecting', which involves crossing two or more parent lines or varieties with desirable traits to produce multiple offspring. Of these, the best plants are selected and allowed to breed again. Again, the best ones are selected for breeding and the process is repeated a number of times. After about 12 generations, an improved variety is produced that breeds true and is ready to be planted by farmers.

But breeding is rarely this simple. For one thing, a new variety may derive from 50 or more parental lines. For another, a variety used in the breeding programme may be the source of only one desirable trait and many undesirable ones. So how does the breeder incorporate this single trait into his or her new variety while excluding the others? To explain in the simplest terms, let us call plants from the parent line or new variety into which the single trait is to be introduced 'Group A'. We shall then call members of the 'donor' plants (which could well be a wild or semi-domesticated relative) 'Group B'. These Group B plants, then, are the source of just one desirable trait out of many unwanted ones, for which as little as one allele may be responsible. For the breeder to transfer this allele without the undesirable ones, he must first cross Group A and Group B plants and then 'back-cross' those offspring containing the trait with plants from Group A. This is repeated through the generations, selecting plants that retain the trait and back-crossing them with Group A plants. In time, the proportion of genes from Group B plants contained in the offspring goes down from 50–50 in the first generation to a negligible figure.

These approaches generally work well with crops like wheat, rice and sorghum that self-pollinate. These tend to be genetically stable and consequently breed true. But, as with humans and animals, inbreeding can be deleterious for cross-pollinators such as maize, millet and many of the pulses. This is not such a problem for plants that can reproduce asexually, such as vines, apple trees and potatoes. But for cereals and pulses, which cannot, the breeder must find another approach.

Corn breeders in the early twentieth century came up with a solution by applying the rediscovered principles of Mendelian genetics. George Shull, a breeder working at a US government research centre, managed to induce the characteristic of (what he called) 'heterosis' in the corn plants resulting from his cross-breeding of inbred pure lines. This phenomenon, commonly referred to as 'hybrid vigour', is manifested in heightened yields. But, because they are hybrids, the offspring cannot breed true and the yield enhancements thus last only for a single generation. So, while farmers stand to benefit from seeds providing this hybrid vigour, they need to buy seeds at the beginning of every planting season to enjoy equally productive future harvests. This necessity was and continues to be a boon for the seed companies.

The hybrid route to the breeding of better seeds is generally assumed to be a very good thing for farmers and for the development of the seed industry, but sceptics argue that the massive investments in the development of hybrid varieties that were made in the 1920s and 1930s could have been allocated to breeding based on more conventional techniques that would have achieved similar yield increases but without preventing farmers from being able to replant their harvested seeds.

Jean-Pierre Berlan and Richard Lewontin (1998) are particularly negative, arguing that hybridization is a kind of 'deterioration technique' that not only enables seed companies to eradicate on-farm saving and exchange but actually eliminates all opportunities to improve crops through selective breeding. Farmers may gain in the short term, but widespread adoption of hybrid varieties may not necessarily best favour their long term interests. As they put it,

> In reality, what distinguishes this varietal type from all the others is the reduction in yield in the next generation – that is, in plain terms, sterility ... But varietal progress can only come from improving populations by selection, the very thing that this quest for hybrids prevents. Apparently unaware of what they are doing, the agricultural geneticists have dialectically overturned reality: they state they are using a biological phenomenon, heterosis, to increase yield, while actually using inbreeding to create sterility. But if they were politically successful in sterilising maize, they had to focus attention on the illusion created by selection – improvement – to mask their real objective.

It is likely to be true that in the early days hybrid productivity was not much greater than their conventionally bred counterparts (Bugos and Kevles, 1992: 88), but, from the middle of the century, increased private investment was considerably improving the yields of hybrid corn. Unfortunately for breeders (and presumably for farmers), hybridization does not work for some of the most economically important crops, such as wheat. This of course presents problems for breeders. Plants are self-reproducing. With no law to prevent it, there is nothing to stop farmers from replanting harvesting seed, or even multiplying seed for the purpose of selling it in competition with the breeder (assuming this would be more profitable for them than selling harvested produce).

Apart from these techniques, second generation biotechnologies like tissue and cell culture development have been used for several decades. These enable scientists to regenerate large numbers of plants that are genetically identical and free from disease. These techniques do not replace conventional breeding but can improve its efficiency. More recently, genetic engineering techniques are being used by DBFs and life science corporations to move foreign genes into plants coming, not just from other plant species, but from completely different forms of life. For example, scientists have succeeded in inducing insect resistance in crops like corn and cotton by inserting genes from a soil microbe called Bacillus thuringiensis that is toxic for certain insects. These techniques include cell fusion, and direct gene transfer into tissue cultures using bacteria or viruses as carriers of the foreign DNA, and such devices as high-velocity 'gene guns' which shoot DNA-containing 'bullets' into cell nuclei. Genomics is also useful in identifying useful genes and the plants which contain them.

The increased use of such methods has led some to wonder if conventional plant breeding is on the way to becoming obsolete, and with it – one might add – those IP systems that have been designed specifically to protect plant varieties produced in the traditional way.[4] We will address this matter below. It is sufficient at this point to say that there is no sign of any decline in conventional breeding, and the number of PBR titles being granted worldwide is not falling either.[5]

The Emergence of the Modern Seed Industry

From Neolithic times, farmers have set aside some of their harvested seeds for replanting. They selected such seeds on the basis that the plants producing them possessed desirable traits such as drought or disease resistance or frost tolerance. Over the generations, this practice resulted in ever-increasing quantities of locally adapted varieties known as 'landraces' or (less formally and more politically correctly) 'folk varieties'. Until the advent of professional breeding, all crop improvement was carried out on-farm by the farmers. This situation changed in North America and Europe from the late nineteenth century as the profession of farming became a separate one from crop improvement, and breeding became not just empirical and experimental but also scientific. In many other parts of the world this separation has barely taken place.

During the nineteenth-century westward expansion of the United States, the government sought to encourage settlement. One way to do this was to entrust the farmers themselves with the selection, breeding and multiplication of seed. To this effect, the Patent Office, first, and then the United States Department of Agriculture, provided farmers with free seed packets for them to experiment on. At the time the seed industry was small and insignificant. Farmers used these seeds and those introduced by the immigrants arriving in the USA to breed varieties adapted to suit their own needs and the local ecological conditions. The number of such varieties increased enormously. Later, these farmer-bred and selected crop varieties formed the basis of the public and private sector breeding programmes (Fowler, 1994: 19–20, 45).

Cary Fowler argues that the separation of farming from breeding, the undermining of the customary practice of seed saving in the case of hybridized crops, and the commodification of the seed cannot be explained by advances in plant breeding science and technology alone (ibid.: 32). When scientifically bred seeds came onto the market, subsistence agriculture had largely been replaced by commercial farming anyway. Mechanized harvesting and the consolidation of land-holdings had made seed selection non-viable compared to the greater convenience of purchasing mechanically cleaned seed from dealers. And, since most farmers were no longer improving seeds themselves, the attraction of selecting and replanting was declining even before scientifically bred varieties were becoming widely available.

In 1890, 596 firms were involved in commercial seed production (ibid.: 38). Having formed a business association called the American Seed Trade Association (ASTA) a few years earlier, they were becoming active in defending their interests. One of ASTA's early campaigns was to stop the government from providing farmers with seeds. This failed for lack of support from the public and Congress, many of whose members sent seed packets to constituents.[6] However, during the first two decades of the twentieth century, the government increasingly sent seeds only of the most common varieties to farmers, while passing on the more exotic germplasm to the government experiment stations and colleges. A later campaign from the First World War onwards was to oppose the saving of seed by the farmers.

Shortly after the First World War, the Secretary of Agriculture, Henry C. Wallace, father of one of the main private sector advocates of hybrid crop breeding,[7] decided that the USDA would henceforth support research aimed at the development of hybrids and ending farmer participation in breeding programmes. The implications of the emergence of corn hybrids for private sector breeding cannot be underestimated. Several of the world's major twentieth-century seed companies first came to prominence through their successful breeding of hybrid corn varieties. These include Pioneer Hi-Bred, DeKalb, Pfister and Funk. Hybrids continue to be commercially very important. 'Of the US$15 billion market in commercial seed at present, hybrids account for approximately 40% of sales, and most of the profit' (Sehgal, 1996: 18). According to Jack Kloppenburg of the University of Wisconsin (1988: 93), 'hybridization is ... a mechanism for circumventing the biological barrier that the seed had presented to the penetration of plant breeding and seed production by private enterprise'. This was well understood by some of the pioneering scientists involved in the development of hybrid corn, who realized that the absence of genetic stability in the harvested seed gave them a kind of virtual IP protection which they could back up by using trade secrecy law. Indeed, the determination of companies to prevent unauthorized access to their inbred parent lines could be very intense. Unfortunately, several of the other major food crops, such as wheat, do not so easily lend themselves to hybridization. For these, breeders needed to find other means to control the use and production of their varieties. This is where lack of IP protection became an issue.

Contrary to the US situation, virtually all the cultivable land in nineteenth-century Europe had been farmed on for a very long time. Most of those major crops whose origins were exotic, like wheat, rye, maize, potatoes and tomatoes, had become well-established and integrated into local farming systems for centuries or even millennia. Although some such crops were vulnerable to devastating diseases due to widespread genetic uniformity (most notoriously potatoes), European farmers developed a huge range of varieties over the centuries to suit local conditions (Vellvé, 1992: 28). European governments generally did not find it necessary to encourage farmers to breed new varieties themselves, as in the US case.

Agricultural intensification took place under different circumstances and with different aims. In Europe, land was in short supply but labour was plentiful, rather than the other way round. Farms tended to be smaller and did not lend themselves so easily to mechanization. Attempts to increase productivity came through other techniques to grow more food on existing land (Pistorius and van Wijk, 1999: 30).

Introducing new species and formal experimental breeding were carried out first by wealthy landowners, and from the early twentieth century by the small family seed firms. These firms descended from farmers that made it their main business to provide seed for other farmers and who then started breeding programmes to meet better the requirements of their customers (Heitz, 1987: 62). As in the USA, public research institutions and universities were also carrying out breeding work which benefited the emerging private plant breeding sector. By the time of the Second World War, Germany, the USA, Sweden and the Soviet Union were the leading plant-breeding nations (Thornström and Hossfeld, 2002: 39). In countries like Britain and France, government-supported research during the first half of the century was often directed to tropical agriculture rather than temperate-zone crops. This was to develop and improve the production of certain crops in the colonies. Both countries reoriented their breeding efforts as these colonies became independent, and France subsequently developed the world's second largest private seed sector. Britain, though, had few seed firms until the 1960s, and most breeding, especially of major crops like wheat, was left to the public sector. This situation has changed, but the seed sector is still much smaller than that of France.

From the late nineteenth century, a number of European governments became alarmed about the unregulated nature of the trade and the extent of fraudulent sales. This situation was problematic for farmers, legitimate breeders and governments that had become concerned at the need to increase productivity to meet the demands of the urban populations that were growing rapidly during this era of industrialization. In the early decades of the twentieth century, many governments responded first by establishing seed testing stations, and then by certifying seed (Pistorius and van Wijk, 1999: 32). The latter also provided to a certain limited extent a kind of IP protection for breeders (ibid.: 79).

IP Rights and Plants before the UPOV Convention

The idea of a separate IP system for plant varieties goes back to the early nineteenth century. An 1833 Papal States edict provided IP protection for plants, but was apparently not implemented (Heitz, 1987). A few European countries introduced trade mark-type protection for new seeds during the 1920s, but the most important legal development in the first half of the century was the 1930 US Townsend–Purnell Plant Patent Act, and it is with this country that we begin.

The story of how the Plant Patent Act became law supports the contention that the evolution of IP rights cannot be explained purely by new needs arising from developments in science and technology. This is because the Act protected a class of plants that hitherto had received relatively little attention from scientific breeders – asexually reproduced plants – while excluding sexually reproduced plants, which had become the target of most of the scientific breeding programmes of the period (Fowler, 1994: 74). In fact, the existence of the Plant Patent Act can be attributed almost entirely to the political activities of organized interests and very little to the advancement of scientific plant breeding.

Why was the nursery industry able to succeed in achieving an IP system specifically to protect its interests 40 years before the seed industry? First, it is important to understand why the nursery industry had so much to gain from securing IP protection. As Fowler explains (ibid.: 91), while the creation of new varieties of fruit tree and woody ornamental species was normally left to chance mutation and pollen-bearing insects, the technique of grafting allowed the reproduction of thousands of genetically uniform, identifiable and stable plant varieties. So while new varieties were often little more than discoveries, the possibility of mass-producing identical plants as well as the very real threat of forgery by rival firms made the idea of acquiring IP protection in some form very desirable.

Several seed and nursery trade associations were established in the USA from the late nineteenth century, including ASTA (founded in 1883) and the American

Association of Nurserymen (AAN, founded in 1875). While ASTA prioritized non-IP issues of concern to its members such as the abolition of the government's free seed programme, several important nursery companies became politically active in promoting IP legislation from as early as 1906 (ibid.: 80–81). In 1923, the AAN set up a National Committee on Plant Patents that was subsequently chaired by Paul Stark of Stark Brothers Nurseries, the country's biggest nursery company. The Committee not only persuaded the USDA and other trade associations like ASTA that an IP system for plants was needed, but was also involved in drafting the legislation that Congress passed in 1930. The actual text of the law was written by Stark and a Washington attorney called Harry C. Robb, Sr.

To achieve success, two important strategic decisions were made. First, ASTA was persuaded by Stark to accept the exclusion of sexually reproducing plants for the time being. Ostensibly, this was because of doubts that such plants would maintain their essential characteristics through the generations. Second, tuber-propagated crops were excluded, officially on the grounds that the part of the plant used for propagation was also the edible part of the plant. Effectively, the exception covered two species, Irish potatoes and Jerusalem artichokes. In the first case, the underlying motive was to prevent opposition in Congress from those concerned about monopolies on staple food crops (Heitz, 1987: 63). In the second, it was felt that, since enforcing patents on tuber-propagated crops would be impossible anyway, including them in the system would reflect badly on the legislation and erode its support (Bugos and Kevles, 1992: 83). The bill met with little in the way of informed or organized opposition within Congress or from outside.

Another key to success was the coordinated and determined effort of Stark and the AAN Committee to frame their demand for an IP system as an issue of equality and fairness: if industrial inventors and authors could acquire legal protection, why should plant breeders be denied equivalent protection? Both in government and in Congress this somewhat dishonest approach proved highly effective. To help the cause, the plight of Luther Burbank, a highly productive breeder who failed to get rich was often referred to. Over the years, Stark had licensed many of Burbank's cultivars. And when Burbank died in 1926, he stipulated in his will that his farm become the Stark-Burbank Research Laboratories and Experimental Grounds. In this way, Stark inherited a great many more of Burbank's varieties free of charge (ibid.: 81). According to one account (ibid.: 82), 'with sentimental nods to Luther Burbank, who was said to have made no money from his plants, the bill's enthusiasts promised that it would rescue plant breeders from vulnerability to piracy and the fate of an impoverished death'.

It is far from ironic that Plant Patent number 1 went, not to a plant breeder at all, but to a landscape gardener for a climbing rose he had not even bred himself. The rose was a variety that had been developed by a well-known breeder of the time called Dr Van Fleet and that the 'inventor' Henry Bosenberg had purchased. Discovering among the roses he bought a flower that bloomed for a longer period than the others, he propagated the plant, named it 'New Dawn', and applied for a patent (Cook, 1932: 398). Neither was it coincidental that six of the first 18 and nine of the first 84 patents were granted to Burbank's estate and assigned by his widow to Stark Nurseries (Bugos and Kevles, 1992: 84; Fowler, 1994: 87). It could hardly have been more obvious that Stark had a vested interest in the legislation he had co-written.

One can understand how successful the propagandizing was from the words of a report on the bill produced by the House Committee on Patents, which found that 'a plant discovery resulting from cultivation is unique, isolated, and is not repeated by nature, nor can it be reproduced by nature unaided by man'. Interestingly, the report also denied any apparent distinction 'between the part played by the plant originator in the development of new plants, and the part played by the chemist in the development of new compositions of matter' (quoted in Krosin, 1985: 226).

The Plant Patent Act, which remains in force today with some revisions, gave rights to whoever 'has invented or discovered and asexually reproduced any distinct and new variety of plant, other than a tuber propagated plant'. Using the word 'invented' served a useful strategic purpose, while the word 'discovered' allowed for the protection of varieties that were not the result of scientific breeding, that is to say, most varieties for which the nursery companies sought protection. Although allowing 'discoveries' seems to conflict with the product of nature doctrine, supporters of the Act could justify it on the basis that protection was limited to discoveries made in fields and orchards rather than uncultivated places where human agency would be impossible to prove (Bugos and Kevles, 1992: 82).[8]

It is hardly controversial to point out that the Plant Patent Act has not been an overwhelming success. By 1950, only 911 plant patents had been issued, which is a tiny number compared with the many thousands of other patents granted during that 20-year period (ibid.: 86).[9] This disparity had nothing to do with any extra difficulty in acquiring a plant patent. After all, the only formal requirements were novelty and distinctiveness (and these were applied in an extremely permissive manner), and that the plant be reproduced asexually. But it was largely because it was so easy to get such patents that the system was of little value. It was not long after the Act came into effect that concerns were raised that plant patents were being granted that should not have been (Allyn, 1933b). Robert Cook, editor of the *Journal of Heredity*, writing in 1936, estimated that 79–90 per cent of the patents issued would be declared invalid by the courts if they were given the chance to decide on the validity of all the plant patents that had been issued up to that time (republished in Cook, 1937). The main reason why plant patents were not as useful as conventional patents is the lax distinctiveness requirement. In fact, a brief description and illustrations were sufficient. Since the difference between a protected plant and others in existence could be so slight, it was extremely difficult to prove that another trader selling a plant with very similar phenotypical characteristics was infringing the patent.

Apart from some revisions to the Plant Patent Act, there was no further legislative activity in this area for four decades, during which sexually reproducing plants remained unprotected. Glenn Bugos and Daniel Kevles, in their history of plant-related IP protection in the USA believe the likeliest explanation is that, during the 1940s and 1950s, the US agricultural system prospered through massive increases in food exports and also 'because the lure of hybridization joined with the system of contracts, bonds, certifications, and trademarks to make additional intellectual property protection seem unnecessary' (1992: 88).

The protection of sexually reproducing varieties finally came in 1970, through the passage of the Plant Variety Protection Act. The ASTA was very much behind this legislation, which was partly modelled on the Plant Patent Act and the UPOV Convention.[10] The initial draft was written by John Sutherland of ASTA and a lawyer hired by ASTA called Louis Robertson (Fowler, 1994: 108–9). The bill encountered surprising last-minute opposition from two food producers, Campbell Soup Company and Heinz. In his testimony to a subcommittee of the House Committee on Agriculture that was discussing it, Eldrow Reeve of Campbell's claimed (quoted in ibid.: 112) that the Plant Variety Protection Act would 'severely impede progress in the development of new varieties of plants' on the grounds that it would discourage exchanges of germplasm between breeders and thereby slow down the development of new varieties. Representatives from Campbell's and Heinz indicated that they would only support the bill if six crops were expressly excluded from protection. These crops were okra, celery, peppers, tomatoes, carrots and cucumbers. The basic reason for taking this position was that the food-processing firms wanted to avoid paying high seed prices and royalty payments. For Campbell's, another major concern was to ensure that its own breeding programmes continued to enjoy free access to tomato germplasm. Rather than take a stand, the seed industry chose not to jeopardize the passage of the bill and accepted the food industry's demands.

As for Europe, the general rule prior to the Second World War was that plants could not be protected under IP law in any country. But the situation was not entirely clear, and patents were occasionally granted. In 1936, for example, the German Appeal Board accepted an application for a patent that claimed

> 1. Seed material of a race of lupinus mutabilis and lupinus Cruikshanksii which race is increased in fat content above 14 per cent and is made completely or almost completely free of alkaloid; 2. The use of the grain harvest from seed material in accordance with claim 1 for producing oils, fats, press-cakes, rubble and the like. (Quoted in Benjamin, 1936: 462)

Countries adopted a range of approaches during the 1940s and early 1950s, from denying all protection (for example, Britain and Denmark), to allowing patents (Italy from 1948, France from 1949, Belgium from 1950) and creating specific IP systems for plant varieties. Examples of such systems included the Dutch Breeding and Material Seed Ordinance of 1941, the Austrian Plant Cultivation Law of 1946, and the German Law on the Protection of Varieties and the Seeds of Cultivated

Plants of 1953, on which the UPOV Convention was partly modelled.[11] Further afield, South Africa followed the US example in modifying its patent law in 1952.

Despite these initially divergent approaches, the relatively uniform climatic and agronomic conditions throughout much of Europe, and the postwar moves to enhance the integration of the west European economies, provided good reasons to harmonize intellectual property legislation as soon as the appropriate form of protection could be agreed upon.

The UPOV Convention

From the start, the question of how best to protect plant varieties in Europe has been answered differently by lawyers, breeders, farmers and agriculture ministries. Gerd Winter of the University of Bremen made the following interesting comment on the interest group politics of German plant-related IP regulation during the pre-UPOV era, in which he describes a conflict of regulatory approaches and interests that explains much about the establishment of the UPOV Convention:

> As to the debate about the traditional breeding of plants which randomly also concerned micro-organisms and animals, it seems that the promotional impetus towards patenting was … mainly based on the professional interests of the patent lawyers. The breeders who could have been expected to nourish the flame were content with the minor protection provided by plant variety legislation. This seems to be due to the fact that in Germany commercial breeding has traditionally been practised by small co-operative societies of farmers. Therefore the breeders could not form an interest independent from or even opposed to the farmers' interest. (Winter, 1992: 175–6).

The existence of the UPOV Convention can be attributed largely to two organizations, the AIPPI and ASSINSEL, which shared the strategic view that the complex and uncertain situation in Europe needed to be dealt with at the international level.

At the 1952 AIPPI Congress, the delegates, partly at the urging of ASSINSEL, discussed the issue of plant varieties. There was general agreement that plant varieties should be protected in some way. The most concrete ideas came from the German AIPPI group, which submitted a detailed technical report arguing that both patents and an alternative system should be available to breeders. As the authors, Franz and Freda Wuesthoff, explained (1952), it is a normal requirement of patentability that other people skilled in the art should be able to reproduce the invention described in the specification. That is to say, following the instructions provided in the specification should result in the invention as claimed. But, as they explained, when it comes to plant breeding, being able reliably to reproduce the new variety from the beginning is difficult because it depends on natural processes over which breeders do not have total control, and which are to some extent random. But repeating the whole breeding process is not necessarily important or even necessary. What really matters is that the new plant that has been brought into existence can be directly propagated. For sexually reproducing plants, this means that they must breed true so that the offspring are identical to their parents.

As the two authors saw it, the solutions were to change the patent system by taking a permissive view of the reproducibility requirement and to extend the range of patentable subject matter in those countries where plants were not considered to constitute inventions, and to develop a new or modified IP system for the more incremental innovations. They considered that patents in their present form would accommodate a certain amount of innovation in plant breeding and should be made available to breeders. But, for many new varieties, workable IP protection would require a relaxation of the novelty and inventive step requirements so that varieties reflecting incremental improvements on existing ones and that were already known about could nonetheless be protected.

The Congress could not reach a consensus on the means of protection, as AIPPI failed also to do at its 1954 Congress. One of the main reasons was that some of the patent lawyer members of AIPPI opposed the patenting of plant varieties on the grounds that doing so would stretch basic patent law concepts like inventiveness to the point of undermining the credibility of the patent system (Bugos and Kevles, 1992: 90). This failure to agree had important consequences. According to one study,

> The 1952 proposal by the German Group for an alternative form of protection for inventions in the area of plant breeding, coupled with AIPPI's inaction and the ready availability of more restricted forms of plant variety protection in several foreign countries, proved a welcome invitation for establishing an entirely new and exclusive form of plant variety protection, contrary to the German Group's plea for concurrent forms of protection for inventions involving plant breeding. (Bent *et al.*, 1987: 51)

In the event, ASSINSEL's members decided at their own Congress in 1956 to abandon the patent route and to call for an international conference to consider the possibility of developing a new international instrument for protecting plant varieties. ASSINSEL requested the French government to organize what became the International Conference for the Protection of New Varieties of Plants (Heitz, 1987: 82). The Conference, which convened in May 1957 in Paris, established the basic principles of plant breeders' rights that were later incorporated into the UPOV Convention. The governments of West Germany, Austria, Italy, Belgium, Spain and Holland were invited and attended, as did observers representing Denmark, Norway and Switzerland. It is worth noting that governments were requested to send at least one representative from their agriculture ministries. These generally favoured increased private sector involvement in plant breeding but were opposed to the creation of patent monopolies (Pistorius and van Wijk, 1999: 79). The Bureaux Internationaux Réunis de la Protection de la Propriété

Intellectuelle (BIRPI) and the Food and Agriculture Organization of the UN also sent observers.

Eight members of this rather select group of countries agreed to set up a Committee of Experts, which it charged with the following tasks: (a) studying the legal problems arising out of the protection of the breeder's right as defined by the Conference; (b) giving as precise formulations as might be appropriate of the basic technical and economic principles laid down by the Conference; and (c) preparing the first draft of an international convention for submission to a later session of the Conference itself. All the governments plus the United Kingdom appointed individuals to the Committee, which met twice before appointing a Drafting Group to develop a legal text. One of the important issues the Committee had to decide upon was whether the PBR system should be incorporated into the general framework of the Paris Convention, or whether a separate convention was necessary.[12] It decided in favour of the latter but recommended that the new office administering the convention should work closely with the BIRPI.

The second meeting of the International Conference for the Protection of New Varieties of Plants took place in November 1961, with 12 European countries being invited, as were BIRPI, the FAO, the European Economic Community, the Organization of Economic Cooperation and Development (OECD), ASSINSEL, AIPPI, the Communauté Internationale des Obtenteurs de Plantes Ornementales de Reproduction Asexuée (CIOPORA), and the Fédération Internationale du Commerce des Semences (FIS).

The International Convention for the Protection of New Varieties of Plants (the UPOV Convention) was adopted in Paris in 1961 and entered into force in 1968 once it had been ratified by three countries.[13] The delay can be explained by the fact that so few countries had PBR systems at this time. It was revised in 1972, 1978 and 1991. The 1978 Act entered into force in 1981, and the 1991 Act in 1998. The Convention established the International Union for the Protection of New Varieties of Plants, which is based in Geneva and has a close association with WIPO to the extent that the latter organization's director-general is also secretary-general of UPOV.

Table 7.1 lists the PBR laws introduced in various UPOV member countries and the years in which they became law. Some of these were initially incompatible with UPOV and have since been revised. UPOV membership requires that legislation be reviewed by the organization and amended if deemed to be in conflict with the Convention, and in so doing harmonizes national PBR law. In Europe, this harmonization process has reached the stage of having a Community Plant Variety Rights Office. The Office, which was established through Regulation 2100/94 which came into force in 1995, provides a unitary right covering the whole European Union.

Table 7.1 Legislation introducing plant breeders' rights in selected countries

Country	Law	Year
UK	Plant Varieties and Seeds Act	1964
Netherlands	Seeds Act	1967
West Germany	Plant Variety Protection Law	1968
USA	Plant Variety Protection Act	1970
France	Decree No. 71-454 of the Intellectual Property Code	1971
Argentina	Law on Seeds and Phytogenetic Creations	1973
Israel	Plant Breeders' Rights Law	1973
New Zealand	Plant Varieties Act	1973
Switzerland	Federal Law on New Plant Varieties	1975
South Africa	Plant Breeders' Rights Act	1976
Japan	Seeds and Seedlings Act	1978
Norway	Plant Breeders' Rights Act	1993
South Korea	Seed Industry Law	1995

Note: Many of these laws have been amended subsequently. Those listed introduced UPOV-
type PBRs for the first time.

Compared to the Paris Convention, the UPOV Convention's provisions are
extremely detailed and specific. To be eligible for protection, plant varieties must be
novel, distinct, stable and uniform (in UPOV 1991) or homogeneous (in UPOV
1978). To be novel, the variety must not have been offered for sale or marketed, with
the agreement of the breeder or his successor in title, in the source country, or for
longer than a limited number of years in any other country. To be distinct, the variety
must be distinguishable by one or more characteristics from any other variety whose
existence is a matter of common knowledge. To be considered as stable, the variety
must remain true to its description after repeated reproduction or propagation.
Neither uniformity or homogeneity are defined in any explicit manner. Unlike
patents there is no disclosure requirement. Instead, applicants are required to submit
the plant material for which protection is sought to the responsible governmental
authority for testing to ensure that the above eligibility requirements have been met.
This material may then be used by a government institution to establish whether the
eligibility criteria are adequately met through propagation trials.

UPOV 1978 defines the scope of protection as the breeder's right to authorize the
following acts: 'the production for purposes of commercial marketing; the offering
for sale; and the marketing of the reproductive or vegetative propagating material,
as such, of the variety'. The 1991 version extends the scope of the breeders' rights
in two ways. First, it increases the number of acts for which prior authorization of
the breeder is required. These include 'production or reproduction; conditioning for
the purpose of propagation; offering for sale; selling or other marketing; exporting;

importing; stocking for the above purposes'. Second, such acts are not just in respect of the reproductive or vegetative propagating material, but also encompass harvested material obtained through the use of propagating material, and so-called 'essentially derived' varieties.

However, the right of breeders both to use protected varieties as an initial source of variation for the creation of new varieties and to market these varieties without authorization from the original breeder (the 'breeders' exemption') is upheld in both versions. One difference is that that UPOV 1991 extends rights to varieties which are essentially derived from the protected variety.

There is no reference in the 1978 version to the right of farmers to re-sow seed harvested from protected varieties for their own use (often referred to as 'farmers' privilege'). The Convention establishes minimum standards such that the breeder's prior authorization is required for at least the three acts mentioned above. Thus countries that are members of the 1978 Convention are free to uphold farmers' privilege or eliminate it. Most of them uphold it, either explicitly or by default.

The 1991 version is more specific about this. Whereas the scope of the breeder's right includes production or reproduction and conditioning for the purpose of propagation (Article 14), governments can use their discretion in deciding whether to uphold the farmers' privilege. According to Article 15, the breeder's right in relation to a variety may be restricted 'in order to permit farmers to use for propagating purposes, on their own holdings, the product of the harvest which they have obtained by planting ... the protected variety'. There is therefore a strong possibility that some governments will act upon Articles 14 and 15 by further restricting or eliminating farmers' privilege, but this remains to be seen. At present the strength of the farmer's privilege varies quite widely. France has no farmers' privilege at all, while the USA until the 1990s allowed farmers even to sell protected seed as long as their 'primary farming occupation is the growing of crops for sale for other than reproductive purposes'. The ASTA lobbied to narrow farmers' privilege, and succeeded in 1994 when the Plant Variety Protection Act was amended to prevent the unauthorized sale of seed of varieties whose protection certificate was issued from 4 April of that year (Rories, 2001: 742–3).

UPOV 1991 extends protection from at least 15 years to a minimum of 20 years. This later version is silent on the matter of double (that is, both patent and PBR) protection whereas the earlier version stated that members 'may recognise the right of the breeder provided for in this Convention by the grant either of a special title of protection or of a patent'. Removing the bar on double protection was intended to ensure that the USA remained compliant with UPOV.

Is the 1991 revision a move towards patent-like protection, as some argue it is? According to Peter Lange of ASSINSEL, PBRs and patents differ in quite fundamental ways, in terms not just of criteria for protection, but also of how the rights and obligations of producers and users are balanced. Table 7.2 provides a comparison of UPOV 1978, 1991 and patents, and bears this out. Lange argues that 'breeding (including genetic engineering) is always based on what already

Table 7.2 Comparison of main provisions of UPOV 1978/1991 and patent law[a]

Provisions	UPOV 1978	UPOV 1991	Patent law under TRIPS
Protection coverage	Plant varieties of nationally defined species	Plant varieties of all genera and species	Inventions
Requirements	Novelty Distinctness Homogeneity Stability Variety denomination	Novelty Distinctness Uniformity Stability Variety denomination	Novelty Inventive step (or non-obviousness) Industrial application Enabling disclosure
Protection term	Min. 15 years from issue (Min. 18 years for vines and trees)	Min. 20 years from issue (Min. 25 years for vines and trees)	Min. 20 years from filing
Protection scope	*Minimum scope:* producing for purposes of commercial marketing, offering for sale and marketing of propagating material of the variety	*Minimum scope:* producing, conditioning, offering for sale, selling or other marketing, exporting, importing, stocking for above purposes of propagating material of the variety Also some acts in relation to harvested material if obtained through an unauthorized use of propagating material and if the breeder has had no reasonable opportunity to exercise his right in relation to the propagating material	*In respect of the product:* making, using, offering for sale, selling, or importing *In respect of a process:* using the process; doing any of the above-mentioned acts in respect of a product obtained directly by means of the process

Breeders' exemption	Yes	Yes Also, *essentially derived* varieties cannot be exploited in certain circumstances without permission of holder of rights in the protected initial variety	Up to national laws, but likely to be limited to scientific and/or experimental use
Farmers' privilege	In practice, yes	Up to national laws	Up to national laws[b]
Prohibition of double protection	Any species eligible for PBR cannot be patented	No	Up to national laws

Notes:
[a] Based upon van Wijk *et al.* (1993), with modifications.
[b] Article II of the EU biotechnology inventions directive provides for farmers' privilege.

exists, requires a broad range of variability and demands the free use of material' (1997). Moreover,

> Since the purpose of plant variety protection is not to protect an invention, for instance a specific property in plant material, but the creation (including the discovery) of a new plant variety (that is to say a unique new 'shuffled' genotype with a corresponding phenotypical expression) ... there must be the continuing possibility of using the protected material of competitors to develop new varieties with a new and unique genotype (for example, by crossing – that is to say a new 'reshuffle'), without there being dependency [on the authorization of PBR holders].

The overwhelming majority of the 50 UPOV members (as of 7 January 2002) are in Europe, North America, Latin America, the Far East and Australasia. This seems to reflect the fact that in many developing countries, especially in Africa, private sector involvement in plant breeding and seed supply is quite limited. Moreover, in many of these countries small-scale farming communities are responsible for much of the plant breeding and seed distribution, as they have been for centuries. Consequently, until recently there would have been few domestic beneficiaries of a PBR system, especially if state involvement in breeding was also quite limited.

However, the interest of developing countries in joining UPOV is increasing. In many if not most cases, this is not because of any strong domestic demand for PBRs, but because of their obligations under Article 27.3(*b*) of TRIPS. The UPOV system is the only sui generis system for plant varieties that exists in international law. This is not to say that other models have not been developed, but that these have not yet been implemented by any country and remain to be tested.[14] Moreover, the UPOV system is being actively promoted worldwide by the organization itself as well as by the USA and the EU.

Are Plant Breeders' Rights Obsolete?

The UPOV system has found itself under attack from a number of quarters. Legal experts and practitioners schooled in patent law are sometimes unsympathetic towards the Convention and its basic principles. Some of them find it difficult to understand why it should be possible for protected varieties to be used as source material by breeders, and have called for limiting the research exemption. In 1988, for example, AIPPI (1988: 222) recommended in a resolution on biotechnology that Article 5(3) of UPOV 1978, 'which permits the free utilisation of a protected variety as an initial source for breeding new varieties should be amended to provide, at least, for a royalty in the case of commercial exploitation of that new variety'. Joseph Straus of the Max Planck Institute and AIPPI actually referred to the research exemption as 'highly controversial' (1987: 730) as if breeders felt the same way. Implicit in some of these criticisms seems to be a perception that advances in biotechnology will tend to diminish the need for traditional plant breeding and the freedom of access to germplasm which most breeders feel strongly about maintaining. Nonetheless, members of the patent community are not so hostile to PBRs as to call for their replacement with patents but tend rather to argue that the EPC's exclusion of plant varieties and the TRIPS Agreement's option to exclude them from patentability should be removed (for example, see Straus, 1987).[15]

Plant breeders tend to be defensive about UPOV, as do the organization's own officials. Often breeders are quite suspicious about patenting and worry about the possible impacts of other companies' patents on their breeding programmes. Unlike patent lawyers, plant breeders and other supporters of UPOV continue to stress the importance of access to genetic material, including that which is IPR protected. Barry Greengrass, former vice secretary-general of UPOV, pointedly mentioned (at an AIPPI congress as it happens) this 'perennial complaint' about the research exemption as one that was 'primarily ... on the part of patent specialists rather than plant breeders' (Greengrass, 1989: 631). To be fair, breeders were also concerned that the exemption could be abused by those engaging in cosmetic breeding. But by introducing the concept of essentially derived varieties, UPOV 1991 responded in a way that did not significantly weaken the exemption. So there is little sign that PBRs will become indistinguishable from patent rights in terms of the level of exclusivity provided. The research exemption is just too important for breeders and is likely to remain so even as biotechnological methods are increasingly adopted in crop development.

It is tempting to assume that a system that is dear to the hearts of many plant breeders but not to those of corporate patent lawyers or to the businesses they all work for is doomed to wither away and be replaced by patents, which provide stronger and broader protection. After all, so many seed companies have been taken over by the life science and other corporations that now dominate this industrial sector. Why should the views of breeders and the no longer independent seed companies carry any weight within the corporations they are now part of when they contribute such a small share of the profits of these giants? In fact, the evidence suggests that PBRs are not about to disappear. PBR applications show no signs of decreasing in North America or western Europe. Moreover, the UPOV system attracts less criticism from the patent community than it did in the late 1980s when there was probably a greater expectation that plant breeding would be superseded by biotechnology. This suggests that the advantages of the system are better understood by the patent lawyers and the life science corporations. Alternatively, these corporations are happy to let their seed subsidiaries do what they think is right with respect to IP protection without interfering. But, wherever the truth lies, it seems that, as long as an IP system has corporate users who believe they benefit from its existence, its future is secure. After all, as this chapter shows, it was these users that created it in the first place.

Notes

1   Rossman (1931: 21).
2   Quoted in Rossman (1931: 8).
3   The following section on plant breeding draws heavily on Tudge (2000: 218–26).
4   Some members of the patent community seem to believe this even if they do not express it explicitly.
5   UPOV statistics show that 8621 applications were submitted worldwide in 1993, and this number rose to 9178 in 2000. Between the same years, the number of PBR titles issued rose from 5731 to 7020.
6   The free seed programme was finally discontinued during the inter-war period.
7   The son, Henry A. Wallace, who was also a Secretary of Agriculture, founded the world's biggest hybrid seed corn company, Pioneer Hi-Bred.
8   An earlier version of the bill was even more permissive. It stated that 'the words, "invented" and "discovered" as used in this section, in regard to asexually reproduced plants, shall be interpreted to include invention and discovery in the sense of finding a thing already existing and reproducing the same as well as in the sense of creating' (quoted in Allyn, 1933a: 965).
9   Admittedly, this is not really a fair comparison, since patents protect inventions in a wide range of technological fields, while the Plant Patent Act protects those of only one field. Nonetheless, the numbers are small enough to justify doubts that it has succeeded in fostering genuine innovation in plant breeding on any significant scale.
10   See Fowler (1994: 108–18) for a detailed legislative history of the PVPA.
11   For brief descriptions of this law, see Heitz (1987: 75–6) and Wuesthoff (1957: 27).

12 Interestingly, the 1958 revision conference of the Paris Convention failed to address the question of plant variety protection despite the best efforts of AIPPI and the ICC. This may well reflect continued scepticism among patent office representatives taking part in the conference about the applicability of patenting.

13 These countries were West Germany, Holland and the UK.

14 Such models include the Organization of African Unity's 'African model legislation for the protection of the rights of local communities, farmers and breeders, and for the regulation of access to biological resources', and the 'Convention of Farmers and Breeders' which was produced by an Indian advocacy group called Gene Campaign. Both were drafted in the late 1990s. India's recently passed PBR legislation is unusual in that it diverges from the UPOV standards and may provide a suitable model for other developing countries.

15 On the other hand, Margaret Llewelyn of the University of Sheffield has suggested that, rather than remove the EPC exclusion, it might be preferable to extend PBRs to cover not just varieties but other plant material (Llewelyn, 2000).

Chapter 8

Towards a Global IP Regime:
Trade and Diplomacy

Industry has identified a major problem for international trade. It crafted a solution, reduced it to a concrete proposal and sold it to our own and other governments. (James Enyart, Director, International Affairs, Monsanto Agricultural Company, 1990)

The companies have ... played simultaneously the role of the patients, the diagnosticians, and the prescribing physicians. (Surendra J. Patel, former Director, Technology Division, UNCTAD, 1989)

Trade and the Increasing Value of Intangible Assets

As was explained in Chapter 1, the role of IP rights in international trade, the global economy and international relations has grown considerably, especially since the 1970s. This is linked to the recent tremendous advances in information and communications technology and the life sciences, including biotechnology. US corporations have been responsible for many of these advances. They have also been among the main beneficiaries. For example, the United States is the home of creative industries (such as film production companies and TV networks) whose content can be more easily and inexpensively disseminated throughout the world than ever before. The country's continued economic pre-eminence is generally perceived to be largely a consequence of this situation and also to be dependent upon maintaining such technological and market dominance.

But all those national economies in which high technology corporations are concentrated have experienced a transformation in the composition of their export trade in manufactures. OECD figures show that, since 1970 for most developed countries, the contribution of advanced technologies to economic performance in terms of manufacturing value added and exports has increased substantially (OECD, 1996).

As for technology ownership, a similar story of developed country (especially US) interest in high levels of IP protection can be inferred from the relevant statistics. It is not only IP-protected products, technologies and services that are major exports of developed countries like the USA; it is also the rights themselves in the form of licences to use patented processes, techniques and designs, copyrights, trade marks and franchises. According to Michael Ryan of the Brookings Institution (1998: 2),

US multinational manufacturing enterprises increasingly transfer intellectual property internationally through the industrial processes that they sell abroad. Exports, as measured by royalties and licensing fees, amounted to about US$27 billion in 1995, while imports amounted to only US$6·3 billion. At least US$20 billion of the exports are transactions between US firms and their foreign affiliates.[1]

This balance of payments surplus is far higher than for any other country. Interestingly, most of the major industrialized countries do not have a balance of payments surplus for royalties and licence fees. According to International Monetary Fund figures (in Maskus, 1998), the United Kingdom is one of the few which also enjoyed a surplus. But it was far smaller than that of the USA (US$1·71 bn compared with US$20·66 bn). Countries with sizeable deficits included not only large developing countries like India (–US$68 mn [1992 figure]) and Brazil (–US$497 mn), but major economic and technological powers like Japan (–US$3·35 bn) and Germany (–US$2·66 bn). This is bound to puzzle many non-economists, especially considering the heavy corporate research and development commitments which are well-known features of the private sectors of the latter two countries. But there is a simple explanation. This is that 'German and Japanese firms exploit their technological advantage mainly through exports, whilst US and UK firms rely much more on direct foreign investment, which results in a higher volume of measured royalty income' (Patel and Pavitt, 1995: 24). So Germany and Japan have just as much reason as the USA and UK to favour strong and enforceable IP protection in overseas markets, if not for exactly the same reasons.

Domestic Interest Groups, IP Rights, and US Trade Policy

In September 1986, contracting parties to the General Agreement on Tariffs and Trade (GATT) meeting at Punta del Este, Uruguay, agreed to include 'trade-related aspects of intellectual property rights, including trade in counterfeit goods' as a subject for negotiations in the forthcoming trade round, which became known as 'the Uruguay Round'. Eight years later, the outcome of these negotiations was a substantial and far-reaching document known as the Agreement on Trade-related Aspects of Intellectual Property Rights (TRIPS).

Why did developing countries, many of which are as dubious today as they were in 1986 about the relationship between trade liberalization and IP rights, agree to negotiate a comprehensive agreement setting such high minimum standards of protection and enforcement? There are two plausible ways to interpret the behaviour of developing countries. Both of these emphasize the important role of pro-IP business associations and lobby groups as well as the power of certain developed countries to threaten and punish developing countries for being uncooperative on intellectual property rule making and enforcement. The first is that they were willing to accept the whole WTO package of agreements out of a conviction that the benefits of the other Uruguay Round agreements would outweigh the economic and social costs of TRIPS. In short, TRIPS was a loss but the WTO package was a net gain. Alternatively, developing countries might have considered TRIPS and the WTO agreements as a whole to be unsatisfactory, but had little choice but to accept it since the carrot of improved access to developed-country markets was irresistible, and the stick of strengthened trade barriers and even unilateral sanctions expected to result from a refusal to raise IP standards was to be avoided at all costs. Accordingly, the establishment of the WTO was welcomed because they expected (overoptimistically as it turned out) that it would insulate them from the aggressive unilateralism being adopted by some developed countries.

What we can say at this stage is that the internationalization of developed country-level IP standards through TRIPS was not an inevitable consequence of the technological changes described in earlier chapters, the impacts of these changes on international trade or the free-riding opportunities that exist when valuable products are sold in countries where legal protection is lacking. While these were of course important factors, the insertion of 'trade-related' intellectual property rights into the Uruguay Round agenda and the subsequent adoption of an agreed text for an IP agreement required the effective lobbying activities in the USA of legal and policy entrepreneurs and corporations, and a government and political establishment that, during the 1980s, was especially receptive to the diagnoses and prescriptions propounded by these individuals, firms and business associations. While organizations like the International Intellectual Property Alliance and the Business Software Alliance, and companies like IBM and Pfizer played a decisive role in this highly successful movement, the vital importance of these 'entrepreneurs of ideas' should not be overlooked (Braithwaite and Drahos, 2000: 571).[2]

Our account starts by describing the process by which groups favouring strong international IP protection came to define the problem as being trade-related and saw the GATT negotiations as the key to a solution. Second, we consider why the US government was predisposed to identifying the interests of these groups with the national interest. Third, we clarify the specific institutional framework that enabled interest groups to capture – or at least to develop a close partnership with – the executive branches of the US government dealing with trade-related issues.

The first attempt to frame intellectual property rights as a trade-related issue was made by the Levi Strauss Corporation, which, together with a number of other trade mark-holding firms, organized as the Anti-Counterfeiting Coalition, lobbied for the inclusion of an anti-counterfeiting code in the 1973–9 GATT Tokyo Round. They belatedly secured the support of the US government, but the initiative was too little, too late and failed. However, following the lead set by the trade mark industries, the copyright, patent and semiconductor industries followed suit during the early 1980s in framing the relative (and sometimes absolute) lack of effective IP protection in overseas markets as a trade-related issue *and* a problem for the US economy that the government ought to respond to. So, by the time the contracting parties of the GATT met in Punta del Este to launch another trade round, US transnational corporations had forged a broad cross-sectoral alliance and developed a coordinated strategy.

Braithwaite and Drahos (2000: 75) consider the IP community operating at the international level to be an epistemic community, the dominant core of which 'is comprised of transnational elites with important intellectual property portfolios to protect – and their lawyers. Lawyers, by virtue of their technical knowledge, are a driving force in this epistemic community'. It was these lawyers, and also lobbyists, consultants and certain company heads, that defined the problems and solutions in new ways and sold these diagnoses and cures to other members of the IP community, Congress, the US government, and then to governments and business associations in Europe and Japan. The 'solution' was effectively to impose on the world their interpretation of fair competition in high-technology and creative industrial sectors by means of the global standardization of national IP regulation as far as possible equivalent to the standards existing in the US. Paradoxically, the forum in which these regulations were to be agreed upon was an organization whose role was to prescribe the *de*regulation of international trade.

Braithwaite and Drahos (ibid.: 204) identify certain individuals who played a decisive part in mobilizing support for the inclusion of 'trade-related' IP rights as a major Uruguay Round agenda item with the aim of formulating a legal instrument that would bind all members of what would become the World Trade Organization. While these included chief executive officers of major corporations (such as Edmund Pratt of Pfizer and John Opel of IBM), others had only their ideas to contribute. These latter individuals included two lawyers (Eric Smith and Jon Baumgarten) and a private consultant (Jacques Gorlin), all of whom were instrumental in conceptualizing intellectual property as a trade-related issue and then developing the political strategy that would ultimately result in TRIPS. The advantages of pursuing the objective of setting high standards of IP protection and enforcement throughout the world by way of the GATT were fourfold.

First, if successful, the strategy would globalize these standards much more rapidly than could be achieved through the WIPO-administered conventions. This is, first, because it allowed for the possibility of including all the main IP rights in a single agreement (which could also incorporate by reference provisions of the major WIPO conventions) and, second, because once it was agreed that the Uruguay Round agreements had to be accepted as a package (that is, a 'single undertaking'), countries could not opt out of any one of them and be members of the WTO. 'The United States saw that tying obligations to protect intellectual property rights to other trade commitments under GATT would provide the desired vehicle for pressuring recalcitrant trading partners' (McGrath, 1996: 399).

Second, the broad agenda of the Uruguay Round provided opportunities for linkage-bargain diplomacy that WIPO, with its exclusive focus on IP rights, did not allow. Hard bargaining by the USA, Europe and Japan on IP rights could thus be linked to concessions in such areas as textiles and agriculture, where exporting countries in the developing world were eager to achieve favourable agreements (Ryan, 1998; Sell, 1998).

Third, GATT was a highly developed world-friendly agency as compared with the United Nations Conference on Trade and Development (UNCTAD), which was the UN forum most experienced in analyzing trade and IP rights. Without a doubt, UNCTAD would have been a far better place for developing countries to negotiate new global IP norms. UNCTAD had since the 1970s produced a series of technical reports that were critical of the developmental aspects of the prevailing international IP system (for example, UNCTAD 1974, 1975). The organization served as a rallying place for developing-country governments interested in the possibility of lowering regulatory standards that would enable them to introduce more appropriate IP systems for their level of development. UNCTAD was seen as an unsuitable organization in spite of – or quite possibly because of – its technical competence in this field because its governance structure made it hard for developed countries to reverse its pro-developing country orientation. The institution found itself deliberately marginalized in the 1980s and the victim (as was WIPO) of a successful forum-shifting strategy led by the USA.

Fourth, the GATT had a well-established dispute settlement mechanism, albeit flawed (Jackson, 1997: 112–17). WIPO has no enforcement or dispute settlement mechanisms except through the treaties that it administers, and these treaties do not provide much recourse for countries concerned about the non-compliance of other parties.

The reason why the US government was predisposed to identifying the interests of these groups with those of the country is closely linked to a mood of pessimism that infected the political elites during the 1980s. There was widespread concern that the US economy was weakening and had become uncompetitive, and there was a danger of sinking into terminal decline. In large part this was due to increasing competition in various high-technology sectors from other countries, especially Japan, that the USA had hitherto dominated, and manufacturing generally from low-wage newly industrializing economies (NIEs) like South Korea, Taiwan and (though not strictly an NIE) China. This was generally felt to be attributable to unfair trade, investment and industrial policies, including intellectual property and technology licensing regulations. These allegedly reserved domestic markets for local firms, while helping these countries to export their goods in massive quantities to the USA and consequently to enjoy sizeable trade surpluses. A related complaint was that these countries were condoning what was seen as blatant and widespread intellectual property piracy.

Having shown why the US government and Congress were likely to be susceptible from the 1980s onwards to interpretive custody of organized pro-IP producer interests, it is important to understand how these interests were able to mediate their influence in order to get their way. In fact, the interest groups succeeded in influencing the development of trade law and policy by incorporating their demands in the relevant legislation[3] and, if not actually capturing, in at least working in close partnership with, the key government agencies engaged in trade policy.

In general, it is much easier for producer interests to influence trade law and policy through Congress than by seeking to influence the president directly. One of the main reasons is that the executive is likely to be concerned with a broad range of short- and long-term issues of which trade is just one, albeit important, topic. It is also worth bearing in mind that the relationship between Congress and the presidency is in varying degrees both cooperative and competitive. Those government agencies which Congress has some control over are more promising regulatory spaces for producer interests to occupy than those which are closer to the executive, such as the State Department. The main agencies dealing with trade are the Office of the USTR – considered the most important – the Department of Commerce and the United States International Trade Commission (ITC).

According to Paul Mundo of Drew University in the USA (1999: 53–4), the USTR was 'a creature of Congress' that became 'a conduit of congressional and interest-group pressure on the executive, beginning a process of drawing trade policy authority away from the State Department, which was considered by many legislators as making trade issues too easily a distant second to broader foreign policy objectives'. However, although 'Congress placed the agency in the Executive Office of the President to coordinate trade policy and to provide a congressional outpost near the president ... the USTR has become an instrument of the president' (ibid.: 96). In reality, the USTR has been captured by producer interest groups and has been persuaded consistently and faithfully to incorporate their demands in the country's international trade diplomacy.

Likewise, the Commerce Department has for long been considered among the most pro-business of the government departments. Mundo (1999) notes that 'to create a more accommodating environment for injured industries, Congress shifted considerable authority to the business-friendly Commerce Department, much of which had been the Treasury Department's responsibility'.

The ITC's official mandate is to provide objective trade expertise to both the legislative and executive branches of government, determine the impact of imports on US industries and direct actions against certain 'unfair trade practices', such as intellectual property piracy. Like the USTR, the ITC was given increased decision-making powers by the 1974 Trade Act 'with the goal of limiting presidential discretion in mind' (ibid.: 115). Of the three, the ITC is generally considered to be more independent not only from Congress and the president but also from interest groups.

Close to, but outside, the government is another very important institution, the Advisory Committee on Trade Policy and Negotiations (ACTPN). This body was established by the 1974 Trade Act to enable the private sector to advise the government on trade policy and multilateral negotiations. The ACTPN consists mainly of representatives of major patent-holding firms. Under the leadership of Pfizer's CEO, backed up by his IBM counterpart, the ACTPN successfully recruited groups such as the Pharmaceutical Manufacturers Association and the Chemical Manufacturers of America, and actively sought to educate congressmen and the USTR officials in the arcane subject of IP rights and its importance for the USA, as well as the need for a multilateral solution with GATT as the best available forum.

It is erroneous to assume that interest groups are monolithic even when the corporations they constitute are major transnationals. Interest groups may be well-organized and coordinated or disorganized and uncoordinated, and within interest group coalitions there may be a diversity of attitudes towards liberalization and protectionism, and considerable disagreements about strategy. Where there is a strong consensus they may advocate radical positions. If this is not possible the result may be bland positions that do little to further the interests of any coalition members. During the years leading to the Punta del Este Ministerial Conference the patent and copyright industries agreed on the need for strong and enforceable IP protection throughout the world, but differed in their favoured approaches. The patent industries preferred a multilateral approach with the goal of globalizing US standards of IP protection. The copyright industries were concerned less with the standards of protection in foreign copyright laws than with their levels of enforcement. They tended to the view that bilateralism or coercive unilateralism supported by specific provisions in trade law and justified by their own estimates of losses due to piracy in overseas markets would be the best tactic to engage the US government in supporting their interests. It was not until shortly before the conference that both sides accepted that the two strategies were complementary (Ryan, 1998: 11).

Establishing the Global Regime: Coercion, Persuasion, Learning and Alliance Building

Understanding the process by which the US government became an aggressive promoter of high-level IP regulatory standards on behalf of these domestic interest groups does not tell us why so many countries agreed to sign an agreement which did not appear to be in their interests and about which the European countries and Japan were initially sceptical.

Technological determinism cannot explain TRIPS. Power is central to any plausible explanation. Ideas were also important. Indeed, TRIPS was achieved against the odds. 'It was an implausible accomplishment to persuade a trade liberalization regime to incorporate a major new form of trade regulation, to persuade a body concerned to increase competition in the world economy to extend the life of patent monopolies and other intellectual property monopoly rights. More, it was a remarkable accomplishment to persuade 100 countries who were net importers of intellectual property rights to sign an Agreement to dramatically increase the cost of intellectual property imports' (Braithwaite and Drahos, 2000: 203–4).

Once the USTR had been persuaded that it was in the interests of the country to pursue the IP demands coming from the ACTPN at the GATT, the next task was to form an international alliance including the businesses and governments of western Europe and Japan while neutralizing resistance from opposing countries.

The support of European and Japanese business was considered necessary for any proposal on IP rights at Punta del Este to succeed. The Intellectual Property Committee (IPC) was established in March 1986 with this objective in mind. The IPC was set up at the initiative of Pratt and Opel (working closely with Gorlin) and consisted of these individuals plus the CEOs of 12 other US corporations, including Monsanto and Merck. The IPC very quickly built a close relationship in the USA with the USTR, Department of Commerce and Congress, and internationally with two European and Japanese peak business associations, the Union of Industrial and Employers' Confederations of Europe (UNICE) and Keidanren.

Even with the support of the US, Japanese and Swiss governments and the European Community, there was no certainty that the IPC would get its way. The Group of Ten developing countries within the GATT – India, Brazil, Argentina, Cuba, Egypt, Nicaragua, Nigeria, Peru, Tanzania and Yugoslavia – took a determined stand against the use of GATT as a forum for negotiating global IP standards (Ryan, 1998: 108). Even after the Punta del Este conference, the IPC still had a battle on its hands. Here threats and coercion came to play an important role.

From 1985 and especially 1989 onwards, the USA used its own trade rules to publicly criticize, threaten and punish individual countries whose IP standards were lower than its own and therefore 'inadequate' (Blakeney, 1996: 4). Section 301 (Actions by United States Trade Representative) of the United States Trade Act was amended in 1984 'at the urging of' the copyright industries' (Ryan, 1998: 70). The amended Section 301 specifically included failure to protect intellectual property as one of the 'unfair trade practices' that could result in a USTR investigation and possible sanctions, and authorized the USTR to initiate its own cases so as to protect US firms from retaliatory action by foreign governments (Sell, 1998: 133). On patents, the first targets of the USTR under its new powers were (i) Korea, which allowed only process patents on foods, chemicals and drugs and offered protection periods of only 12 years from publication,[4] and (ii) Brazil, which (since 1969) entirely excluded pharmaceutical products and process from patentability. Both countries eventually responded to threats of sanctions and removal of trade benefits provided under the Generalized System of Preferences[5] – in the Korean case – and actual sanctions (Brazil).[6] As Ryan explains (1998: 108), the singling out of Korea and Brazil was a deliberate attempt 'to bully the developing countries to the GATT negotiating table. The action was intended to signal that negotiations could go on one-by-one under threat of bilateral trade sanctions or they could take place within the GATT round, but negotiations would take place'.

The 1988 Omnibus Trade and Competitiveness Act in its Special 301 provision (a new, strengthened version of the Section 301 of the earlier legislation) further strengthened the authority of the USTR in order to insulate decision making on trade retaliation from foreign policy or national security considerations, and required the USTR annually to 'identify those foreign countries that deny adequate and effective protection of intellectual property rights, or deny fair and equitable market access to United States persons that rely upon intellectual property protection'. According to Ryan (ibid.: 80), 'the Special 301 announcement is the result of a business–government process initiated in February each year when the USTR calls for public comment.... The USTR, a lean agency with a small staff, relies extensively on the information provided by these [business] groups to arrive at its agenda'.

It is largely due to the mandate of the USTR actively to pursue the complaints of US firms and business associations that the developing countries eventually succumbed to TRIPS. Active use of the 301 process 'proved so successful that disputes over intellectual property issues during the Uruguay Round became disputes between the intellectual property triumvirate, the USA, Europe and Japan. By the final stages of the negotiations, developing countries had long given up resisting the TRIPS proposal' (Braithwaite and Drahos, 2000).

It was not just arrogance on the part of James Enyart, director of international affairs at Monsanto Agricultural Company, which led him to boast that 'industry [that is, the IPC] has identified a major problem for international trade. It crafted a solution, reduced it to a concrete proposal and sold it to our own and other governments' (1990: 56). It was also the truth.

Even so, it is not only developing-country governments that are dissatisfied with TRIPS. Many firms, including the pharmaceutical transnationals, were unhappy about the compromises and concessions achieved by developing countries, such as the transition periods, which Harvey Bale, then vice-president of the Pharmaceutical Manufacturers Association,[7] called 'an unacceptable proposition' when they appeared in the December 1991 consolidated text prepared by Negotiating Group Chairman Ambassador Lars Anell and the GATT Secretariat, which became (with some modifications) the final text of TRIPS (see Watkins, 1992). Neither were the life science businesses happy with the compromises between the USA and Europe which resulted in language that among other things permitted exclusions on the patenting of plants and animals. It is not surprising, then, that the US Congress has not renounced Special 301, and reserves the USTR's right to initiate bilateral negotiations with countries whose IP standards may be TRIPS-compatible but still lower than those of the USA (see Drahos, 2001). Mark Ritchie, an activist working for the Institute for Agriculture and Trade Policy, perceptively anticipated the continuation of unilateralism as early as February 1992. Noting that 'most US transnational corporations feel betrayed by GATT', he concluded that 'they now believe their interests will be better served by recourse to unilateral trade threats and sanctions than by a multilateral accord' (quoted in Watkins, 1992).

One is led to the conclusion, then, that of the three strategies available to the developed countries of coercion, propaganda and forum shifting, the first and third were the most important and were very successful, while the second was used the least since its potential effectiveness was fairly limited. Indeed, developed-country governments and business associations did not even try to convince developing countries that what is good for Pfizer or IBM is good for the world. According to Bhagwati (1998: 79–80), those governments and firms supporting TRIPS had little faith that arguments founded on utilitarian logic could prevail, and implicitly held to the following 'rights-based argument: we invented the stuff, so it's ours, and anybody who doesn't agree to our terms and conditions for using it is engaging in piracy and theft'. On the other hand, without the determined efforts of US business interests, the strategic acumen of the Washington-based policy entrepreneurs and the unique organizational structure of the US government that allowed these groups and individuals to influence national trade policy to such an extent, only persuasion could have succeeded. And considering how difficult it would be to convince over 100 governments that serving the IP interests of Pfizer and IBM would be good for their countries, it seems implausible that TRIPS could ever have been achieved without the strategic exercise of power by those with the capacity to wield it.

However, coercion of the South by the North is not the complete explanation. Indeed, framing the TRIPS negotiations as a North versus South conflict and their outcome as a total defeat for the latter is justifiable but fails to do complete justice to the complex nature of the negotiations and the wide diversity of interests being pursued. For one thing, it was becoming ever more apparent that the developing world is extremely heterogeneous in terms of countries' levels of industrialization and social and political development. Some African countries were still virtually devoid of manufacturing sectors and were becoming poorer and more indebted. Latin American countries were relatively industrialized but several had experienced little significant economic progress for some time and were generally heavily indebted too. Others, especially in Asia, had extremely dynamic export-oriented industrial economies, with firms beginning to develop their own IP-protectable products and technologies. Therefore the IP interests of different developing countries in international trade negotiations varied. For another, the IP interests of different industrial sectors within these countries could vary quite widely. For example, one sector may be a highly competitive producer of high-technology goods or services, and/or may be heavily dependent on proprietary technologies from overseas. Other sectors, such as agriculture, may use simpler technologies and produce mostly for local and domestic markets. Therefore, just as there were bound to be disagreements between developing countries over the appropriate stance that should be taken in trade negotiations, countries were likely to be divided internally as well. There were individuals and firms in developing countries who came round to the view that TRIPS was good for them as well as for Pfizer, and also those (most probably the vast majority) that remained unpersuaded.

Notes

1 The United Nations Development Programme notes (1999: 68) that 70 per cent of total royalty and licence fee payments worldwide are between TNCs and their overseas affiliates.

2 For an authoritative account of the negotiators by an insider (India's negotiator from 1989–90), see Watal (2001: 11–47). See also Gervais (1998) for a detailed negotiating history.

3 Specifically, the 1974 US Trade Act and the 1988 Omnibus Trade and Competitiveness Act.

4 The European Community took similar measures against Korea in 1987 for alleged IP-related 'offences', withdrawing Generalized System of Preferences (GSP) benefits for certain Korean goods imported into Europe (Žigić, 2000: 28).

5 The option of withdrawing GSP benefits from countries with inadequate IP protection was incorporated in the 1984 Act at the urging of the copyright industry umbrella association, the International Intellectual Property Alliance (Sell, 1998: 135).

6 In Brazil's case, this action was in response to a complaint about the country from the Pharmaceutical Manufacturers Association.

7 And currently director-general of the International Federation of Pharmaceutical Manufacturers Associations.

Chapter 9

Forums of Resistance?

The extension of intellectual property rights through the legislative and judicial process (without improvement in efforts to conserve genetic diversity) was a sign to nongovernment organizations that a new arena was needed. In order to continue there also needed to be a redefining and repackaging of the arguments and the goals ... the challenge ... was to develop a new strategy and set it to work in a new but potentially friendlier arena.... The strategy was developed to protect the 'property rights' of the Third World through challenging industrialized countries' access to genetic diversity. (Cary Fowler, former political activist, 1994)[1]

This book's historical approach has made several important things clear which might not be apparent from a purely present-day analysis. First, support for private rights over inventions – whether mousetraps, microorganisms or methods of manufacturing them – and new plant varieties has trade implications whether or not we regard such IP rights as being supportive of liberalization or protectionism. As a consequence there will be both winners and losers. Whether or not the winners will gain enough for the losers to be compensated is impossible to know for certain, but we can be sure that, however big the gains, the losers will not get much out of the bargain, at least in the short term.

Second, classifying the award of patents and plant variety certificates to companies financing invention and the breeding of new plant varieties as meretricious granting of private rights and/or as the bestowal of monopoly privileges needs to be justified rather than accepted as given. The fact that the latter term is used increasingly rarely can be explained by the ascendancy in governments of views consistent with, or even identical to, those of corporations and other members of the patent community.

Third, in spite of the mainly instrumentalist reasons for creating national patent systems, the history of patents and PBRs seriously undermines the public interest approach to economic regulation in the IP context. As Chapter 2 predicted, these systems ostensibly exist to perform a public policy function, but in practice this function tends to be usurped by interest groups. One of the main implications is that, if a patent or PBR system is failing to fulfil its public policy function, the causes are as much political in nature as they are technical.

Fourth, understanding how the patent and PBR systems evolved requires more than a single explanation. Power is central to most of the changes, but power has to be deployed strategically to carry the day and compromises must sometimes be made. Moreover, court decisions are not necessarily popular with the corporate giants. Power was a factor in the extension of patentable subject matter to include drugs, microorganisms, plants, animals and genes, the gradual reduction of exceptions, the existence of the UPOV Convention and its particular features, and in the 'successful' conclusion of the TRIPS negotiations and the specific form the agreement took. But none of these were inevitable consequences of the demanders having more money and political influence than their opponents. After all, courts do not necessarily side with the rich and powerful. And not every IPR-related policy decision is a response to pressure from interest groups. Also powerful groups with common interests sometimes fail to agree and may allow weaker groups to exploit their lack of unity.

Fifth, while the international IP regime as currently contoured reflects the hegemony of the United States, the west European countries and Japan, and the economic dominance and political influence of high-technology transnational corporations, this does not make it the best IP regime that these countries and businesses could imagine. Even for the most powerful interest groups, creating a new regulatory system is likely to be beyond their means. This means they have to do their best with the system that exists and try to shape it so that it furthers their interests to the maximum extent. If no IP system had ever been created it is unlikely that a decision by these countries or big business to design one would result in something closely resembling the present one.

Driving the general tendencies towards stronger and more expansive rights is an active network of interest groups whose influence derives from their interpretive custody of the patent system. Consequently, legislatures, government ministries and international trade negotiators – at least those of the industrialized countries – tend to assume that improving the system means strengthening the rights it affords and, if deemed necessary, creating new rights.

At a more philosophical level, what appears to be going on is that judiciaries and legislatures in many legal jurisdictions have this century tended to move along the instrumentalism–proprietarianism continuum in the direction of the latter (see Drahos, 1996). So, for example, the notion that patent rights should sometimes be limited for the purpose of keeping prices of essential foods and medicines at a level that the poor can afford is increasingly being dispensed with by legislatures and trade ministries. This trend has not been unidirectional. There has in fact always been a tension between the two resulting in a degree of unpredictability such that legislators, policy makers and the courts sometimes revert to instrumentalism. This situation is in large part due to the fact that IP law relates to and is shaped by other areas of law and policy which it may complement or conflict with, or of which it may even be a component. Examples include such areas as competition and international trade.

Nowadays, improving the system tends to imply strengthening the rights available. Increasingly, strong patent rights are regarded by governments as an essential component of national innovation policy for achieving the 'knowledge-based economy'. So to take this line is to be pro-innovation and to oppose it is to be reactionary, neo-Luddite and even anti-capitalist. For example, Bruce Lehman, formerly (US) Commissioner of Patents and Trademarks and previously a lobbyist for the software industry,[2] was quoted in 1996 as saying: 'everybody has their own parochial interests … there are people who would just as soon not have an intellectual property system. That's the information-should-be-free crowd. Well, how do they suppose [we'll] have capitalism if there's no property? What do they want to go to, socialism? Communism?'[3, 4] And there is no question that developed country trade negotiators frequently echo the proposals of their domestic corporations that advocate stronger rights.

It is possible to consider this situation as one part of a larger trend taking place during the historical period covered in this chapter. According to Eggertsson (1990: 143),

> It is generally agreed that in the past 100 years or so, Western governments have increasingly restricted the property rights of owners of inputs, particularly nonlabour inputs, and increased the role of the state in economic activity. In many cases the rights of labour and consumers have been enhanced, and in other cases the structure of rights has been changed to benefit one occupation or industry at the expense of another.

The life science industries appear to be cases in point. It has been convenient to treat genetic resources as free inputs belonging to nobody while states have gradually allowed the carving out of ever stronger property rights from the public domain to protect industrial products derived from them.

In the case of patent law, the state and certain interest groups certainly collaborate quite closely and have done so for much of the past hundred years. But this relationship arose and persists not because certain non-state interest groups have been brought into government (as in the corporatist model) or because they have themselves taken over the system (as in the regulatory capture concept): the reality is that economically powerful interest groups and the regulators are, or at least consider themselves to be, dependent on each other. In the case of the former this dependence is real. For the regulators the situation is a little more complex owing to the nature of the system. The ideological glue that binds them often seems to be a story propagated by the patent community, adopted for convenience by interest groups and accepted by the regulators. This story then becomes the conventional wisdom of the period.

It must be conceded that interpretive custody over the patent system can never be absolute or permanent. Judiciaries do not always follow a proprietarian line vis-à-vis patents, while ideological control over the patent system has its limits. For instance, the European Court of Justice has sometimes prioritized internal market freedom over strong IP rights where the exercise of these rights has restricted movement of goods within the European Union in contravention of the Treaty of Rome. Moreover, as this chapter will show, concerns about these historical trends have coalesced into a very powerful backlash in the form of movements comprising individuals and civil society organizations. Against the odds, these have had some successes.

The Backlash

Until recently, intellectual property was a subject for specialists, and was considered to have little if anything to do with, for example, biodiversity conservation, the rights of indigenous peoples and poor farmers in developing countries, human rights (except for author's moral rights) or spiritual values, or with the interests of consumers, patients or librarians, to name just a few. Therefore, IP lawyers and commercial intellectual property user groups were the only ones assumed to have a legitimate interest in IP regulation and the only 'experts' able to offer rational and objective technical advice to regulators (which of course was regarded as the only kind of advice they really needed). Consequently, the national patent systems of most developed countries were securely in the interpretive custody of the patent community and those elements of the business community that were most effectively represented. The pharmaceutical industry has become one of the most influential of these elements.

The same may be said of the World Intellectual Property Organization. WIPO has always had a rather restricted view of what intellectual property experts look like, and has built up close relationships over many years with pro-strong IP interests such as the AIPPI, FICPI and the ICC that date as far back as the early days of BIRPI.

In recent years this state of affairs is being challenged. National intellectual property offices and politicians are beginning to listen to alternative voices. These are much more critical of the excessive influence of the rather closed network of IP experts and interest groups, and are more sceptical that stronger rights are in the best interests of the national population or, in the case of organizations like Third World Network and Oxfam, the developing world. The patent and business communities tend to be rather dismissive of these alternative voices on the grounds that they do not really understand IP law and misrepresent it in oversimplistic or even dishonest ways, and that they selectively deploy facts and figures of dubious validity for propaganda purposes. While some of the critical literature does indeed invite such disdain, most of it does not. Besides, the whole idea that interest groups favouring ever-stronger rights are above such behaviour themselves is simply untrue. After all, they have many more years' experience in propagandizing and political lobbying than their opponents, and of course are much better funded.

Several civil society organizations have actively sought to reverse the IP-strengthening trends of recent years. In the developed world, apart from holding up the EU Directive on biotechnological inventions and temporarily blocking the patenting of plants, opposition movements have been too weak to get very far.

Public awareness is still lacking and it is hard to convince members of the public that patents have any effect on their lives. At the international level and in a few developing countries like India, things have been much more eventful. Campaigns have involved such activities as lobbying governments to prevent the passage of strong IP legislation, publicly disclosing what they portray as especially egregious cases of 'biopiracy', legally challenging particularly controversial patents (such as the oncomouse patent, and patents relating to turmeric and neem tree seeds), inventing new terms and concepts such as 'biopiracy', 'farmers' rights',[5] and 'traditional resource rights',[6] and drafting and promoting model legislation to prevent biopiracy. The groups include Genetic Resources Action International, Institute for Agriculture and Trade Policy, Rural Advancement Foundation International (renamed ETC Group in 2001), Third World Network, Gaia Foundation, Research Foundation for Science, Technology and Ecology, Greenpeace and ActionAid. Many of these groups are themselves transnational organizations with branches and associate organizations or individuals in several countries. They are also highly skilled and motivated networkers. They disseminate information and organize their campaigns through websites, newsletters, media and e-mail alerts, sign-on declarations and letters circulated on the Internet, parallel sessions to intergovernmental conferences and attention-seeking stunts. Of all campaigns, the access to medicines campaign has probably been the most successful, involving as it did the Nobel Peace Prize-winning Médecins Sans Frontières, Health Action International, Oxfam and several other organizations, and drawing on the technical expertise not just of their own staff but of independent individuals, including some eminent academics. It seems likely that these counter-experts – counterparts to people like Eric Smith and Jacques Gorlin – will increasingly be used in such campaigns.

As we will see, the backlash (insofar as it relates specifically to the life science industries) actually began in the early 1980s and was focused on plant genetic resources for food and agriculture. By the end of the century, the resistance had advanced considerably and become transformed into a global network of campaigners working at the intergovernmental, national and local level on a broader range of interrelated issues. In their contest for the hearts and minds of the public, IP regulators and intergovernmental forums, words and ideas were their only weapons. After all, propaganda and forum shifting (albeit to a limited degree) are the only strategies available to underfunded participants. The other side of course can deploy a third, which is coercion.

While the resistance is certainly not winning the war, it has won some battles along the way. One of its successes is that international policy making and diplomacy increasingly treat intellectual property relating to biological and genetic material and the regulation of biodiversity control, access, use and exchange as interrelated topics for negotiation. This is in spite of the opposition to such a linkage by some of the technology-rich but biological resource-poor countries, most notably the USA. The result is that deliberations taking place at the Conference of the

Parties (COP) to the Convention on Biological Diversity (CBD), the Commission on Plant Genetic Resources for Food and Agriculture of the FAO, WIPO and the WTO tend often to cover the same ground and sometimes adopt agendas that most developed countries oppose.[7]

Knowledge Diplomacy as Biodiplomacy: the Convention on Biological Diversity and the FAO International Treaty

Two international forums, ostensibly dealing with non-IP issues, have become important arenas where non-business civil society organizations opposing IP rights relating to life forms and genetic material have been able to express their views directly to governmental representatives of developing countries, and have managed to become very influential. Delegates from these countries frequently take critical positions on IP which echo these views and that hardly suggest enthusiasm for the standards that TRIPS requires these same governments to attain. These are the aforementioned Conference of the Parties (COP) to the Convention on Biological Diversity (CBD), and the Commission on Plant Genetic Resources for Food and Agriculture of the FAO, which has for several years held negotiations relating to an agreement known as the International Undertaking on Plant Genetic Resources that culminated in November 2001 in the adoption of a legally binding international treaty. In both cases – and in contrast to TRIPS – civil society organizations not only played a major role in encouraging governments to agree on the need for international legal instruments to regulate the conservation of biodiversity and the use of plant genetic resources for food and agriculture, but had quite a lot of influence on the actual texts of both agreements. Critical perspectives on intellectual property are frequently expressed in these forums. Needless to say, though, most developed countries strongly defend IP rights in these forums, and since high-technology industrial users of genetic resources are important users of IP rights, life science corporations are major stakeholders and behind-the-scenes actors here as elsewhere.

The Convention on Biological Diversity

The CBD came into force in 1993 and now has 182 contracting parties.[8] Initially, there was little expectation that negotiations would become as politicized as they did. The USA had initially proposed to the Governing Council of the United Nations Environment Programme that there be a convention on biological diversity in 1987. By this time, the International Union for the Conservation of Nature (IUCN), a major international environmental NGO, had already begun drafting a convention on the in situ conservation of biological diversity. The Council adopted a resolution supporting IUCN's efforts, and requesting that UNEP's executive director 'establish an ad hoc working group ... to establish the desirability and possible form of an umbrella convention to rationalise current activities in this field' (cited in Burhenne, 1994: x). Two years later, the Governing Council followed up by authorizing the executive director to establish 'an ad hoc working group of legal and technical experts with a mandate to negotiate an international legal instrument for the conservation of the biological diversity of the planet' (ibid.: xi). Neither the US government nor IUCN envisaged that their efforts would spawn an agreement dealing not only with conservation but also with biotechnology, technology transfer and intellectual property rights. In fact, the USA would hardly have proposed it if it could have foreseen the outcome.

Agreeing a text acceptable to governments of the biodiversity-poor industrialized world and of the biodiversity-rich developing countries turned into an unexpectedly long, difficult and contentious process. Some developing countries, initially Malaysia and India, complained that it was unfair for influential conservation organizations (like IUCN) and developed country governments to expect them to protect their forests and forgo the economic benefits from selling timber or converting them to other uses. These countries argued vociferously that a quid pro quo for biodiversity preservation was fair and necessary. Realizing the potential economic value of their biodiversity wealth, and needing to improve their scientific, technological and financial capacities to exploit it, their position was that they had the right to set conditions on those seeking *their* resources, including the fair and equitable sharing of benefits such as the transfer of technology. Needless to say, perhaps, developed countries and transnational corporations wanted as few restrictions as possible on access to biological resources.

Intellectual property came up in the negotiations mainly in the context of technology transfer. Article 16 on access to and transfer of technology requires parties to the Convention to undertake to provide and/or facilitate access and transfer of technologies to other parties under fair and most favourable terms. The only technology referred to is biotechnology, but Article 16 is concerned with any technologies 'that are relevant to the conservation and sustainable use of biological diversity or make use of genetic resources and do not cause significant damage to the environment'. Recognizing that technologies are sometimes subject to patents and other IP rights, access to such technologies must be 'on terms which recognize and are consistent with the adequate and effective protection of intellectual property rights' (Article 16.2). Clearly, this is nothing for the life science industries to feel too concerned about. Indeed, the clause beginning 'adequate and effective protection' was specifically to establish a link with the draft TRIPS Agreement, which also used this language, as did the final version.

Paragraph 16.5 is a little more controversial, requiring the parties to cooperate to ensure that patents and other IP rights 'are supportive of and do not run counter to' the CBD's objectives. This reflects the profound disagreement during the negotiations between those who believed that IP rights conflict with the CBD's objectives and others that saw no contradiction. While the language is not particularly threatening, life science firms in the USA were nonetheless unhappy with the CBD's coverage of IP and with the Convention more generally, and persuaded President Bush that it was not in America's best interests to sign it. Although the USA did so a few years later, it remains one of the few countries in the world not to have ratified it.

To review implementation of the CBD, the Conference of the Parties (composed of all contracting parties) meets periodically (usually biannually). IP rights are most frequently discussed in deliberations on such topics as access to genetic resources, benefit sharing, technology transfer and the knowledge innovations and practices of indigenous and local communities. Perhaps the strongest criticisms of TRIPS and IP rights in general have arisen from debates falling within the latter topic.

The COP has become a forum in which TRIPS and IP rights are debated, critiqued (and defended) in a fairly open way. There are two reasons for this. First, the national delegations consist largely of civil servants from environment ministries. They tend to be concerned mostly about conservation, sustainable development and food security, and often have little contact with their trade ministry counterparts. Second, there are close links between many of the national delegations and well-organized networks of highly articulate and politically astute activists representing international civil society organizations that attend virtually all intergovernmental meetings relating to the CBD. The openness of the CBD forums (not just the COP, but also the Experts' Panel on Access and Benefit-Sharing, and the Ad hoc Open-ended Inter-sessional Working Group on Article 8(*j*)[9] and Related Provisions) has made the building of such links easier. Sometimes activists are even invited onto the official delegations. 'Biopiracy', a word coined by Pat Mooney, a well-known activist, is frequently invoked by developing country delegations to condemn transnational corporations, evidencing the extent to which the term has served to inspire critical perspectives and political activism relating to the role of IP rights in determining the skewed distribution of benefits from the commercial use of biogenetic resources.

Nevertheless, it is difficult to envisage the COP, even without the USA, ever adopting a protocol to the CBD that would require parties to reform their patent or PBR systems to give effect to certain CBD provisions such as those dealing with benefit sharing. Even if it did, many developed countries would simply refuse to ratify it. On the other hand, several developing countries have already introduced measures regulating IP rights to support the CBD's objectives that may in fact conflict with TRIPS, and more are likely to do so in the next few years. These include Costa Rica and the Andean Community countries. It is also noteworthy that Recital 55 of the EU Directive on the Legal Protection of Biotechnological Inventions requires member states to 'give particular weight to Article 3 and Article 8(*j*), the second sentence of Article 16(2) and Article 16(5) of the Convention [on Biological Diversity] when bringing into force the laws, regulations and administrative provisions necessary to comply with this Directive'. Nonetheless, civil society organizations had lobbied for much stronger language on bringing EU patent regulation into line with the CBD provisions on national sovereignty, traditional knowledge and IP rights and have criticized the language adopted for being toothless.

The FAO International Treaty on Plant Genetic Resources for Food and Agriculture

Cary Fowler and Pat Mooney, two political activists who were among the first to denounce the extension of IP rights to life forms in the USA and internationally, decided that forum shifting was a game that the weak could also play. In the early 1980s, they identified the Food and Agriculture Organization of the United Nations (FAO) as the most promising arena. They had done some consultancy work for the Mexican government on the scientific and political aspects of genetic resource control and erosion, sparking off a period of close collaboration between Mexican officials in Rome and civil society organizations. Mooney, who had already made quite an impact through a book called *Seeds of the Earth* (published in 1979) that took a critical stance on IP rights, played an important awareness-raising role, mobilizing a great many developing countries to take an active and united stand. The consequence was that the FAO became the principal battleground of what became popularly known as 'the seed wars', and with the advantage point held this time by the developing countries thanks to their strength in numbers and the fact that they had taken the initiative.

The main bone of contention was that the free exchange principle was being abused by the developed countries in two ways. First, most of the world base crop collections were held in the developed world even though most of the accessions had come from the developing world. Second, while folk varieties were treated as being the common heritage of humankind, plant breeders in the developed countries were securing IP protection for their own varieties. Again according to Fowler (1994: 181–2),

> To a certain extent this shift in arenas marked the first time NGOs, or opponents of plant patenting, had taken the initiative with their own proposals. Moving the debate to FAO allowed for this to happen because it shifted the power base from American to Third World interests. Furthermore, it extended the debate beyond patenting in the narrow sense, and thus moved the debate onto territory NGOs are most comfortable with – the connections between patenting and genetic conservation, and between these and development issues.

At the 1981 FAO Conference, a resolution called for the drafting of a legal convention against the vehement opposition of developed countries (especially the USA, the United Kingdom and Australia) and the seed industry. Two years later, the demand for a convention was replaced by a call for a non-binding 'undertaking', and for the creation of a new FAO Commission on Plant Genetic Resources (CPGR) where governments could meet for discussion and monitor what became known as the International Undertaking on Plant Genetic Resources. By the mid-1980s, over 100 countries agreed to the IUPGR, including many developed countries that would not have signed a binding convention. The first meeting of the CPGR took place in 1985. In spite of attempts by the USA to boycott the commission, 93 countries were represented. It is now the largest FAO commission, with 161 members plus the European Union.

The objectives of the IUPGR were 'to ensure the safe conservation and promote the unrestricted availability and sustainable utilization of plant genetic resources for present and future generations, by providing a flexible framework for sharing the benefits and burdens'. Controversially, the IUPGR treated all plant germplasm as part of the common heritage of mankind, including not just the folk varieties of traditional farmers but also commercial breeding lines. This explains much of the hostility from some developed countries towards the IUPGR.

However, a compromise was reached in 1989. At the insistence of some of the developed countries, IPR-protected plant varieties were excepted from application of the common heritage principle, while developing countries won a concession in the form of Farmers' Rights, a concept proposed by Mooney as a means of acknowledging 'the contribution farmers have made to the conservation and development of plant genetic resources, which constitute the basis of plant production throughout the world'. Farmers' Rights is not an IP right as such, but it is frequently suggested as a principle that could be introduced into an IP system for plant varieties as some form of compensation or benefit-sharing mechanism. Resolution 5/89 defined the concept as

> rights arising from the past, present and future contributions of farmers in conserving, improving and making available plant genetic resources particularly those in the centres of origin/diversity. Those rights are vested in the international community, as trustees for present and future generations of farmers, and supporting the continuation of their contributions as well as the attainment of overall purposes of the International Undertaking.

In May 1992, the Conference for the Adoption of the Agreed Text of the Convention on Biological Diversity (Nairobi Final Act) adopted Resolution 3 on The Interrelationship Between the Convention on Biological Diversity and the Promotion of Sustainable Agriculture. This recognized the need 'to seek solutions to outstanding matters concerning plant genetic resources within the Global System for the Conservation and Sustainable Use of Plant Genetic Resources for Food and Sustainable Agriculture, in particular: (a) Access to ex situ collections not acquired in accordance with this Convention; and (b) The question of farmers' rights' (FAO, 1993).

The following year, CPGR Resolution 93/1 called for the IUPGR to be revised in harmony with the CBD. To this end, the Commission, now called the Commission on Genetic Resources for Food and Agriculture (CGRFA), held a series of negotiations to revise the International Undertaking. Protracted discussions progressed, albeit slowly, at several extraordinary sessions of the CGRFA, and at a series of contact group meetings convened by the chair of the CGRFA.

Many of the most heated debates concerned the proposed multilateral system of exchange for crop genetic resources that the revised IUPGR would regulate. Although most governments favoured such a system, disagreements persisted about which crop species should be included in the system. The role of IP rights is a still more contentious issue. Developing countries were particularly concerned that the patenting of genes and plants based on material acquired from other countries through the system would effectively remove genetic material from an arrangement that is supposed to benefit all participating countries. Therefore many of them argued either that such patenting should not be allowed or that, if it is allowed, the patent owners should pay compensation. Interestingly, the seed industry was somewhat sympathetic to such concerns. In the light of Chapter 7, we should not be at all surprised by this. It is possible that the active engagement of the seed industry, which could easily see the advantages of a multilateral system of exchange and played a much more constructive role in discussions than the life science corporations, helped to make final agreement possible.

In November 2001, a revised IUPGR was not only agreed upon, but was turned into a legally binding agreement known as the International Treaty on Plant Genetic Resources for Food and Agriculture. Recognizing both the sovereign rights and the interdependence of countries over their plant genetic resources, the International Treaty established a multilateral system to facilitate access and benefit sharing (ABS). ABS is to be regulated principally by means of a standard material transfer agreement (MTA), a kind of contract, which will apply also to transfers to third parties and to all subsequent transfers.

One of the most controversial parts of the treaty is Article 12.3(*d*), which states that 'recipients shall not claim any intellectual property or other rights that limit the facilitated access to the plant genetic resources for food and agriculture, or their genetic parts and components, in the form received from the Multilateral System'. Such an undertaking will be provided in the standard MTA adopted to regulate the facilitated access. Japan and the USA both opposed this language and abstained from the vote on the adoption of the Treaty.

What exactly is the issue here? As has been shown, the developed countries allow the patenting of DNA sequences and chemical substances that have been isolated from plant material without any structural modification. Therefore a holder of such a patent could restrict – subject to possible research exemptions – use of the protected sequence or compound by others, and even access if the patent covers the method of isolation. To many developing countries (and even some developed countries), such patenting legitimizes misappropriation of resources to which they have sovereign rights, and is contrary to the spirit of an international agreement that emphasizes exchange rather than appropriation. Naturally, such sentiments are not shared by the USA and Japan, and these two countries were not alone in raising concerns about the IP-related parts of the treaty.

The treaty does not define Farmers' Rights. Article 9 states that national governments are responsible for realizing these rights as they see fit, and the treaty refers to three measures that governments should take to protect and promote them:

> (a) protection of traditional knowledge relevant to plant genetic resources for food and agriculture; (b) the right to equitably participate in sharing benefits arising from the utilization of plant genetic resources for food and agriculture; and (c) the right to participate in making decisions, at the national level, on matters related to the conservation and sustainable use of plant genetic resources for food and agriculture.

While none of these is necessarily IP-related, the last paragraph of Article 9 points out that 'nothing in this Article shall be interpreted to limit any rights that farmers have to save, use, exchange and sell farm-saved seed/propagating material, subject to national law and as appropriate'. Since many countries have not yet extended IP protection to plants or plant varieties, governments might decide to follow the example of India, whose recently passed PBR legislation upholds these latter rights to the full.

The International Treaty is definitely a small victory for the opponents of strong patent protection in the area of plant genetic resources. It is unlikely to lead to any substantial changes to the patent systems of the developed countries, but there is every possibility that developing countries will use the treaty as a source of principles as they implement Article 27.3(*b*) of TRIPS.

Biodiplomacy as Knowledge Diplomacy: WIPO and the WTO

The World Intellectual Property Organization

WIPO is hardly a forum of resistance. After all, its main raison d'être is to promote intellectual property rights worldwide. But since the coming into force of TRIPS, WIPO has sought to move into new areas and to modify its role somewhat. At the same time, WIPO has continued to be a site for negotiations pitting those favouring ever-stronger rights for industry against sceptical developing country representatives (though it must be said that these delegates, coming as they often do from IP offices, tend to be less sceptical than those attending TRIPS Council and FAO CGRFA meetings). So, while WIPO's activities may merely reinforce existing trends in international IP regulation, it is also conceivable (albeit unlikely at this stage) that some of them will not, and might even have the opposite effect.

In early 1998, shortly after Kamil Idris of Sudan had become the new director-general, WIPO established a new unit called the Global Intellectual Property Issues Division (GIPID). Its purpose was to identify and respond to the new challenges for the IP system of globalization and rapid technological change. As part of this mandate, the Division sought to identify potential new beneficiaries of IP rights, including traditional peoples and communities. The Division's mandate is to carry out research and explore the following issues: biotechnology and biodiversity, intellectual property and development, protection of traditional knowledge, innovations and creativity, and protection of folklore.

During 1998 and 1999, WIPO embarked on nine fact-finding missions in various parts of the world on traditional knowledge (TK), innovations and culture to investigate the needs and expectations of TK holders, bearing in mind the possible use of existing IP rights to protect their knowledge, innovations and culture (see WIPO, 2001). In addition, WIPO held four regional consultations on the protection of expressions of folklore, jointly with UNESCO. At three of these, recommendations were made that WIPO should establish a committee on folklore and TK to facilitate future work in this area.

Since 2001, GIPID (now called the Traditional Knowledge Division) has sought to go beyond identifying and investigating the issues involved and finding out the views of TK holders by addressing basic conceptual problems and testing practical solutions. The emphasis of its work has shifted towards such activities as pilot projects on the use of existing IP rights to protect TK, exploration of customary law and its relationship with the formal intellectual property system, and training and awareness-raising programmes for the benefit of TK holders. Not surprisingly, this work does not have the political support needed to achieve new legally binding norms. According to one commentator,

> GIPID's mandate is limited. American support for the new mandate was secured in return for the concession that GIPID was not 'on a norm setting track'; that is to say, that its work is not intended to feed into a process which would end with the creation of a treaty or recommendations. (Halewood, 1999: 986)

Nevertheless, some developing countries feel strongly enough about biopiracy to continue to raise the issue. In September 1999, WIPO's Standing Committee on the Law of Patents (SCP) held its third session, which was to be devoted mainly to discussing a draft Patent Law Treaty (PLT). The PLT was intended to harmonize certain patent procedures while steering clear of matters relating to substantive patent law. The Colombian delegation at the session submitted a brief document entitled 'Protection of biological and genetic resources'[10] that turned out to be quite controversial. The delegation proposed that the PLT include an article based on the two proposals that the document comprised. The first was that 'all industrial property protection shall guarantee the protection of the country's biological and genetic heritage. Consequently, the grant of patents or registrations that relate to elements of that heritage shall be subject to their having been acquired legally'. The second was that

> Every document shall specify the registration number of the contract affording access to genetic resources and a copy thereof where the goods or services for which protection is sought have been manufactured or developed from genetic resources, or products thereof, of which one of the member countries is the country of origin.

This idea of linking patent filing with access and benefit-sharing regulations gained the support of Bolivia, Paraguay, China, Namibia, Cameroon, Mexico, South Africa, Chile, Cuba, India, Kenya, Costa Rica and Barbados. Predictably, it did not go down well with some of the other delegations, including the USA, the European Community, Japan and Korea, all of which argued that the proposed article related to substantive patent law and therefore had no place in the Patent Law Treaty. As things turned out, Colombia's proposal did not fail completely, in that the concerns behind it were given other opportunities for expression within WIPO.

As a compromise, the SCP invited WIPO's International Bureau to do two things. The first was to include the issue of protection of biological and genetic resources on the agenda of that November's meeting of the Working Group on Biotechnological Inventions. The second was to arrange another meeting specifically on that issue. This Meeting on Intellectual Property and Genetic Resources took place in April 2000 and reached a consensus that 'WIPO should facilitate the continuation of consultations among Member States in coordination with the other concerned international organizations, through the conduct of appropriate legal and technical studies, and through the setting up of an appropriate forum within WIPO for future work.'[11]

Two months later, the Diplomatic Conference for the Adoption of the Patent Law Treaty took place. While the main purpose was of course to agree upon and formally adopt the PLT, there were also consultations on genetic resources. On the basis of these consultations, WIPO's director-general read out an agreed statement announcing that 'Member State discussions concerning genetic resources will continue at WIPO. The format of such discussions will be left to the Director General's discretion, in consultation with WIPO Member States.'[12] After the Conference, Idris continued to consult member states on how such discussions could continue.

For the 25th Session of WIPO's General Assembly, the secretariat prepared a document which invited member states to consider the establishment of an Intergovernmental Committee on Intellectual Property and Genetic Resources, Traditional Knowledge and Folklore (IGC). The WIPO Secretariat suggested that the IGC constitute a forum for members to discuss three themes that it had identified during the consultations. These were 'intellectual property issues that arise in the context of (i) access to genetic resources and benefit sharing; (ii) protection of traditional knowledge, whether or not associated with those resources; and (iii) the protection of expressions of folklore'.[13] This suggestion was enthusiastically supported by a large number of developing countries and was approved without formal opposition.

The first session of the IGC convened in April 2001, and the second took place the following December. Substantive discussion at the two meetings focused mainly on two subjects: operational principles for contractual agreements concerning access to genetic resources and benefit-sharing, and traditional knowledge as prior art. There was a clear division between those countries that favour the creation of new legal norms (mainly from Latin America and the African Group) and those against, including the USA and Canada. The latter group of countries – and industry representatives – considered that solutions should be sought within existing legal frameworks and, while willing to contemplate additional obligations, would prefer these to be non-binding.

The Committee also agreed that WIPO should continue its work to establish model IP clauses for contractual agreements regulating access and benefit sharing, possibly including the development of a database of such clauses to help guide negotiations. Approval was also given to continuation of WIPO's work on the IP aspects of documenting public domain traditional knowledge, the aim of which is to ensure that patent examiners are able to prevent cases where patents whose claims extend to traditional knowledge are improperly awarded. Towards the end of the meeting, several developing countries proposed, without objections from other participating countries, that WIPO should produce a document providing elements for model sui generis protection for traditional knowledge.

What are we to make of this? While the IGC may provide ideas and model provisions that countries might incorporate into their national legislation, it does not seem at all likely at this stage that any legally binding norms will be agreed upon at the international level that would in any way threaten the IP interests of the life science industries. It seems virtually certain that these industries and the patent community will take great pains to prevent any such outcome should it ever become a serious possibility.

The World Trade Organization

Like WIPO, it makes no sense at all to consider the WTO as a forum of resistance. Yet both have become battlegrounds, especially the WTO, and it is not a foregone conclusion that total victory will go to the rich and powerful. In fact, in future times, historians of trade law may point to 1999 as a year that marked a shift in the balance of power at the WTO. While the Quad countries (the USA, EU member states, Japan and Canada) were still disproportionately powerful, developing countries became more proactive and assertive. Developing countries have begun not only to complain in an organized fashion about TRIPS, but also to propose in a coordinated way. Thus, not only have developing countries actively opposed the raising of IP standards, but they have even proposed that TRIPS be revised in order to circumscribe certain rights, to maintain or even expand the exceptions, and to create new IP frameworks.

According to UNCTAD Secretary-General Rubens Ricupero, who had been strongly advocating a positive developing-country approach to trade negotiations, more than half of the 250 proposals submitted to the WTO General Council during the preparations for the Seattle Ministerial Conference came from developing countries (Ricupero, 2001: 40). Of these 250 proposals, 15 were on TRIPS and eight came from developing countries (UNCTAD, 2000: 13). And while many factors contributed to the collapse of the Seattle Conference, criticisms by many developing countries that they were being excluded from key negotiations probably contributed to its failure to launch a new trade round or even to agree on a declaration at all.

During the early stages of the 12-month period leading up to the Seattle Conference, a year when Article 27.3(*b*) of TRIPS was scheduled to be reviewed, it seemed that the USA, the EU and Japan were going to seek to raise the standards of protection. For its part, the USA, in a communication to the WTO General Council dated 19 November 1998, noted in reference to the 1999 review that the TRIPS Council is 'to consider whether it is desirable to modify the TRIPS Agreement by eliminating the exclusion from patentability of plants and animals and incorporating key provisions of the UPOV agreement regarding plant variety protection'.[14] This was presumptuous, given that an agenda for the review had not yet been decided upon.

A communication from the European Union to the General Council dated 2 June 1999,[15] while adopting a conciliatory tone, noted that 'it should of course be kept in mind that the TRIPS acquis is a basis from which to seek further improvements in the protection of IPR. There should therefore be no question, in future negotiations, of lowering of standards or granting of further transitional periods'. In similar vein, a submission from Japan to the General Council dated 6 July 1999[16] stated that

> Taking into account the nature of the TRIPS Agreement, that is, a minimum standard of intellectual property protection, we should not discuss the TRIPS Agreement with a view to reducing the current level of protection of intellectual property rights. To the contrary, the TRIPS Agreement should be improved properly in line with new technological development and social needs. For example, the TRIPS Agreement should deal with higher protection of intellectual property rights which has been achieved in other treaties or conventions in other fora appropriately.

Such statements were bound to provoke a reaction. As developing countries had their own grounds for dissatisfaction with TRIPS, they decided it was time to place their concerns on the negotiating table. In October 1999, 12 developing countries from Asia, Africa and Latin America submitted two joint papers to the General Council detailing the implementation issues to which they were seeking solutions.[17]

The two papers put forward several TRIPS-related proposals. One of these argued that TRIPS is incompatible with the CBD and sought a clear understanding that patents inconsistent with Article 15 of the CBD, which vests the authority to determine access to genetic resources in national governments, should not be granted. Several other proposals were directed to Article 27.3(*b*) and the review of its substantive provisions. Thus the 12 countries requested that the list of exceptions to patentability in Article 27.3(*b*) of the TRIPS Agreement should include the World Health Organization's list of essential drugs,[18] and also that the paragraph should be amended in light of the provisions of the CBD and the FAO International

Undertaking taking fully into account the conservation and sustainable use of biological diversity, the protection of the rights and knowledge of indigenous and local communities, and the promotion of farmers' rights. The review should also (i) clarify artificial distinctions between biological and microbiological organisms and processes; (ii) ensure the continuation of the traditional farming practices, including the right to save, exchange and save seeds, and sell their harvest; and (iii) prevent anti-competitive practices which will threaten food sovereignty of people in developing countries.

It is noteworthy, first, that most of the proposals were directed to the patents section of TRIPS, and especially the provision relating to biological and genetic resources. Second, they reflected a serious effort to harmonize positions held by the same governments at the CBD–COP and the FAO–CGRFA. Third, they incorporated positions that a certain number of influential northern and southern civil society organizations had been articulating for several years.

Traditional knowledge has become an especially important concern for many developing countries. On 6 August 1999, two important documents were submitted to the General Council. One of these, from the Permanent Mission of Venezuela,[19] proposed that the next review of TRIPS inter alia should 'establish on a mandatory basis within the TRIPS Agreement a system for the protection of intellectual property, with an ethical and economic content, applicable to the traditional knowledge of local and indigenous communities, together with recognition of the need to define the rights of collective holders'.[20]

The African Group of countries[21] proposed that, in the sentence on plant variety protection in Article 27.3(*b*), 'a footnote should be inserted stating that any sui generis law for plant variety protection can provide for [inter alia]: (i) the protection of the innovations of indigenous farming communities in developing countries, consistent with the Convention on Biological Diversity and the International Undertaking on Plant Genetic Resources'. This communication, which attracted considerable civil society organization support worldwide, also warned that, 'by mandating or enabling the patenting of seeds, plants and genetic and biological materials, Article 27.3(*b*) is likely to lead to appropriation of the knowledge and resources of indigenous and local communities'.

While Article 27.3(*b*) and traditional knowledge continue to be important areas of concern for many developing countries, at the century's end the need to resolve the access to medicines problem understandably became the most contentious TRIPS-related issue. This is of course mainly due to the current HIV/AIDS pandemic, which is the most serious public health crisis for many developing countries, especially in Africa. Millions of people throughout the world have already died and millions more infected people will do so in the next few years unless they can be treated with anti-retroviral drugs. Yet a tiny proportion of HIV/AIDS sufferers receives these extremely expensive treatments.

High prices for AIDS drugs are not the only factor limiting patients' access to them. Poor people often live far away from clinics and hospitals. Also many countries are short of medical practitioners trained to prescribe anti-AIDS drugs to patients in the appropriate combinations and dosages. Nonetheless, high prices obviously have a profound impact on the ability of poor people to acquire them, and patent monopolies place the companies holding them in a strong position to set prices at high levels.

Drug companies have come under heavy criticism for their patent and pricing policies in developing countries, and for using their political muscle to discourage developing countries from using a provision in TRIPS which permits compulsory licensing without prior negotiation 'in the case of a national emergency or other circumstances of extreme urgency or in cases of public non-commercial use' as long as the drugs so produced are 'predominantly for the supply of the domestic market'. Compulsory licensing is not necessarily a panacea,[22] but the very possibility of compulsory licensing tends to strengthen the bargaining position of governments, even if it is rarely used.

Some companies have offered voluntarily to sell their drugs at heavily reduced prices in some markets and even to donate them. But they are also determined to protect their monopolies and have actively pressured governments not to import drugs from countries producing generic versions. On occasions, they have managed to enlist the support of governments. The US and Swiss governments have been the most willing to back their companies in their disputes with desperate governments trying to respond to public health crises of a severity that is scarcely imaginable.

Consequently, developing countries have found themselves being bullied merely for interpreting TRIPS in ways that differed from those of powerful firms and governments yet were nonetheless legal. Perhaps the most egregious case of such bullying was when South Africa came under extremely heavy pressure both diplomatically and in the courts when it passed amendments to its Medicine and Related Substances Control Act. A recent World Bank report describes the legislation's contentious IP-related provisions:

> The amendments permit the health minister to revoke pharmaceutical patent rights in South Africa if he deems the associated medicines to be too expensive. They further empower the minister to order compulsory licensing if the patentee engages in abusive practices, defined basically as a failure to sell a drug in adequate amounts to meet demand, or a refusal to license the product on reasonable terms so that domestic firms may meet demand. They also permit parallel importation (imports of original or generic versions without the authorization of the South African patent holder) of drugs, and allow the health minister to override regulatory decisions concerning the safety and registration of medicines. The law requires pharmacists to employ generic substitution (prescribe generic versions of patented drugs) unless the doctor or patient forbids it, sets limits on pharmacy markup rates, and bans in-kind inducements from drug manufacturers to physicians. (World Bank 2001: 138)

According to the World Bank (ibid.: 138), 'while it may be a heavy dose of regulation, South Africa's law is probably consistent with TRIPS'. But this was not a view shared by the US government, which repeatedly demanded that the law be repealed. And in 1998, the Pharmaceutical Manufacturers Association of South Africa and 39 pharmaceutical corporations initiated legal proceedings against the national government to have the legislation overturned.

In early 2001, the case was dropped in the face of severe national and international condemnation that only the companies involved appeared not to have expected, and probably in the realization that they would have lost anyway. This episode was highly damaging for the image not only of the companies involved, but also of the TRIPS Agreement and the WTO. It reinforced the perception held by many people around the world that the rights of corporations have priority over the health needs of millions of dying poor people.

In April 2001, the Council for TRIPS accepted a request by a grouping of African countries known as 'the African Group' to hold a Special Discussion on Intellectual Property and Access to Medicines. This was held the following June. Prior to the Discussion, the African Group and 16 other developing countries prepared a paper which affirmed that 'nothing in the TRIPS Agreement should prevent Members from taking measures to protect public health'.[23] This was submitted at the Discussion along with another African Group paper proposing that WTO members issue a special declaration at the forthcoming Doha Ministerial Conference including the same language. This proposal was endorsed at the Discussion by Tanzania on behalf of the least-developed WTO members.[24] The USA, the European Union and Switzerland found such unity difficult to resist and accepted that a declaration was inevitable. Consequently, their aim was not to prevent it but to ensure that the strong rights provided by TRIPS would not be weakened.

In the lead-up to the November 2001 Doha conference, the propaganda war took some interesting turns. The USTR Office and the international research-based pharmaceutical industry lobby group thought they had won a propaganda victory with the publication the previous month in a respected US medical journal of a study by Amir Attaran of Harvard University and Lee Gillespie-White of the International Intellectual Property Institute, a pro-industry Washington-based organization headed by former PTO Commissioner and Business Software Alliance lobbyist Bruce Lehman (Attaran and Gillespie-White 2001). The paper provided data on the extent of patent protection throughout Africa of 15 anti-AIDS drugs, which showed that few of these were patented all that widely anywhere in the continent except a few countries such as South Africa. This finding suggested to the authors that 'patents and patent law are not a major barrier to treatment access in and of themselves'. This was of course very convenient for the industry and for the US government, whose chief TRIPS negotiator had apparently received the (officially embargoed) paper before its publication and was able to use the data at a meeting of the TRIPS Council in September 2001 in which the access to medicines issue was being debated.

The response from the public health activist was swift and effective. Five organizations, Consumer Project on Technology, Essential Action, Oxfam, Treatment Action Campaign and Health Gap, distributed a joint statement rebutting the Attaran and Gillespie-White paper and several other campaigners added criticisms of their own which were distributed on an email news service called IP Health which is managed by well-known IP activist James Love, who is director of the Consumer Project on Technology, and is subscribed to by many Geneva-based diplomats and officials (CPT *et al.*, 2001). Another response was circulated by the South African activist group Treatment Action Campaign. These critiques convincingly countered that, while the study's data are probably accurate as far they go, they fail to make a convincing case that patents do not obstruct treatment access in Africa.

There were three main criticisms. First, anti-retroviral (ARV) drug patent coverage tends to be quite comprehensive in countries that have high populations and/or relatively high incomes, *and* large numbers of HIV/AIDS sufferers. These include South Africa, Kenya and Zimbabwe. According to the above-mentioned rebuttal statement,

> The 23 countries in Sub-Saharan Africa that have 4 or more ARV products on patent have 53 per cent of the HIV+ patients and 68 per cent of the Region's GDP. The 20 Sub-Saharan countries that have patents on 6 or more ARV products have 46 per cent of the patients and 56 per cent of the region's GDP.

Second, effective treatment is based on the use of combinations of drugs. If only one ingredient in the cocktail is protected and sold at a monopoly price, the whole regime will be too expensive for most patients. Third, generic producers need to make profits like any other business. If they cannot sell in the major national markets or are only allowed to make one or two components of a combination therapy regime, they cannot easily achieve the economies of scale to make a profit. So it seems more than likely that, while the effects of patents will vary throughout the continent, patents *do* constitute a factor affecting access to medicines in Africa.

Another rather more unexpected development was the mysterious posting to addresses in the USA of mail carrying anthrax spores that resulted in the deaths of a number of unfortunate individuals. Following soon after the notorious September 11 attacks, there was understandable alarm that this might be a precursor to full-scale biological warfare. Consequently, the government decided to stockpile vast quantities of Bayer's ciprofloxacin (Cipro), which it considered to be the most effective drug for anthrax. The aim was to ensure that up to 10 million people could receive immediate treatment should the need arise. The government was concerned not only about whether it was possible to acquire so much Cipro at short notice but about the cost of doing so. In fact, Tommy Thompson, the Secretary of Health and Human Services, threatened Bayer that if they did not halve the price he would simply acquire the drug from other sources. At one stage he even raised the possibility of asking Congress to pass legislation exempting the government from compensating Bayer for ignoring its patent (Bradsher, 2001). This tough approach worked. Thompson successfully negotiated a large discount. But, by threatening to override the patent, the US government, which was at the same time pressuring developing-country governments not to issue compulsory licences to generic drug producers, looked hypocritical. To some critics, the main issue was not that the government had acted tough with Bayer but that it had in the end respected the company's patent. James Love, for example, accused the government of 'cutting corners on public health to protect [the US] negotiating position in the Doha WTO meeting' (Blustein, 2001).

So when representatives of the WTO member states gathered in Doha, while the most immediate concern on their minds was the possibility of terrorist attacks from Bin Laden's Al-Qaeda network, when it came to TRIPS the access to medicines issue was the only one that anybody was interested in. So while all three documents that came out of the Conference (the Ministerial Declaration, the Decision on Implementation-related Issues and Concerns, and the Declaration on the TRIPS Agreement and Public Health) had things to say about intellectual property, the substantive negotiations on TRIPS were devoted solely to access to medicines and specifically the text of the public health declaration.

In the event, the Doha conference adopted the Declaration on the TRIPS Agreement and Public Health, incorporating very similar language to that proposed by the developing countries (in fact, it states that 'the TRIPS Agreement does not and should not prevent Members from taking measures to protect public health'). The declaration consists of seven paragraphs, the most important of which is probably the fifth, which clarifies the freedoms all WTO members have with respect to compulsory licensing, their determination of what constitutes a national emergency or other circumstances of extreme urgency, and exhaustion of rights. Thus the declaration reaffirms the right to use to the full the provisions in TRIPS allowing each member 'to grant compulsory licences and the freedom to determine the grounds upon which such licences are granted'. The declaration explicitly mentions that public health crises 'relating to HIV/AIDS, tuberculosis, malaria and other epidemics, can represent a national emergency or other circumstances of extreme urgency'. Moreover, WTO members are free to establish their own regime for exhaustion of intellectual property rights. This is important because it means that, if national laws indicate that patent rights over drugs are exhausted by their first legitimate sale, countries can then import drugs legally purchased in countries where they are sold at a lower price.

In spite of its imperfections, the process of developing and negotiating the declaration has been a valuable experience for developing countries in Africa and elsewhere. The process was a unique collaborative effort involving trade negotiators, NGOs working in the areas of health and development, and academics that reflects an enhanced capacity to negotiate on important but technically complex issues in a united, effective and informed manner. The determination of the developing countries to have a meaningful declaration was such that last-minute attempts to dilute the text were headed off, ensuring that the outcome was a balanced document that was nonetheless fully compliant with TRIPS. But the fact that the research-based pharmaceutical industry has officially welcomed the declaration suggests they are not too concerned that it will lead to any significant weakening of IP standards throughout the world, least of all in their home countries.

The United Nations Commission on Human Rights: a New Front?

In August 2000, the Sub-Commission on the Promotion and Protection of Human Rights of the United Nations Commission on Human Rights adopted a resolution on 'Intellectual Property Rights and Human Rights', which was partly spurred by the initiative of the World Intellectual Property Organization to hold a panel discussion on Intellectual Property and Human Rights in 1998.[25] While the resolution has no legal status, it has attracted a great deal of attention to this issue. The 'actual or potential conflicts' referred to in the resolution are (i) impediments resulting from the application of IP rights to the transfer of technology to developing countries; (ii) the consequences of plant breeders' rights and the patenting of genetically modified organisms for the enjoyment of the basic right to food; (iii) the reduction of control by communities (especially indigenous communities) over their own genetic and natural resources and cultural values, leading to accusations of 'biopiracy'; and (iv) restrictions on access to patented pharmaceuticals and the implications for the enjoyment of a basic right to health. The resolution requested that the WTO take fully into account the obligations of member states under the international human rights conventions to which they are parties during its current review of TRIPS.

The WTO had not been consulted on this initiative and was apparently more than a little displeased that such a resolution could have been adopted in a forum not exactly noted for its interest or expertise in IP rights.[26] (Indeed, it would be fair to say that the resolution is not well written in places, or even completely accurate.) But matters did not rest there. In August 2001, the Sub-Commission considered two official reports on the relationship between intellectual property rights and human rights in general, and on the impact of TRIPS on human rights.[27] In response, another resolution was adopted which essentially reiterated the Sub-Commission's view that actual or potential conflict exists between the implementation of the TRIPS Agreement and the realization of economic, social and cultural rights. It requested that the UN High Commissioner for Human Rights seek observer status with the WTO for the current review of TRIPS. The resolution also stressed the need for adequate protection of the traditional knowledge and cultural values of indigenous peoples, and emphasized the Sub-Commission's concern for the protection of the heritage of indigenous peoples.[28]

According to the Sub-Commission, human rights obligations should take priority over economic agreements. Is this likely in the case of TRIPS? One must be doubtful that TRIPS will be revised in any way to accommodate human rights concerns. Nonetheless, several developing-country representatives at the June 2001 TRIPS Council Special Discussion on Intellectual Property and Access to Medicines invoked the human right to health in expressing their views,[29] and the demand of these countries for a Declaration on the TRIPS Agreement and Public Health was of course successful. This suggests that, in the battle for ideas, the human rights connection may prove to be a genuinely subversive weapon.

Is the Tide Turning?

The previous chapter explained how proponents of ever-higher levels of intellectual property protection for discoveries and innovations arising from the applied life sciences and biotechnology succeeded in getting their demands accepted by national policy makers and subsequently adopted globally. The present chapter has shown that, in spite of the extreme asymmetries in power, demanders of strong IP protection have lost some battles along the way. The FAO International Treaty represents one such small defeat, as does the Doha Declaration on TRIPS and Public Health. The UN Sub-Commission's resolutions and studies are probably no more than an irritation, although this particular way of framing IP issues could well inspire some creative thinking that may translate into effective campaigning. Apart from the CBD text itself, which does not threaten the intellectual property interests of the life science industries, the CBD forums have extended legitimacy to opponents of biotechnology patents and provided a venue for them to exchange ideas and develop strategies. In addition, a number of governments have been inspired by the CBD to adopt an idea, mooted originally by civil society organizations, that inventors claiming patents relating to biological or genetic material should be required to provide documentary evidence that the material was acquired in accordance with biodiversity access and benefit sharing regulations.[30] Previous chapters also showed that biotechnology patenting in developed countries has provoked organized opposition right from the start. It has also been pointed out that not all businesses have the same views on the scope of patent rights. For example, some pharmaceutical and life science corporations are antithetical to patents on DNA sequences (even though they may still consider it necessary to claim ownership of DNA themselves).

But does all this constitute convincing evidence that the tide is turning, and that proponents of strong IP standards have run into an increasingly irresistible force? As the next part of this chapter will suggest, this looks unlikely.

The Counter-resistance: Bilateralism and Harmonization

'The New Bilateralism'[31]

TRIPS is of course unfinished business. Developed countries would like to see the standards progressively raised, as would the life science TNCs (among others). While some developing countries accept the agreement as it is and seek to construe its rules as creatively as possible, others are actively trying to weaken the standards. In both cases, many of them share an interest in being able to extend the transitional periods without having to answer for their inaction to a WTO dispute settlement panel.

On the positive side, developed countries have softened their stance and have decided to focus for the time being on implementation of the existing standards rather than seeking to raise them further. And while many developing countries have failed to meet the built-in implementation deadlines, such as the requirement to provide protection for plant varieties by 2000, they are not being challenged at the WTO for this. Their counter-proposals and generally more proactive stance have forced the developed countries temporarily onto the back foot.

But it seems that the USA and the European Union are simply changing their strategies, including some more forum shifting, a tactic that, as we have seen, can be highly effective. While remaining engaged in Geneva, they are also sidestepping the WTO and directly pressing developing countries to raise their IP standards beyond those required by TRIPS, using sticks such as threats to remove trade concessions, and carrots like bilateral IP and free trade agreements. These agreements require developing country partners to undertake such commitments as to introduce TRIPS standards before the expiry of the transitional periods, to provide higher standards of protection than TRIPS requires and to extend the subject matter of IP protection in ways that TRIPS may not necessarily require. One such bilateral agreement, whose IP provisions are considered a model for others to follow by IP lobbyists and by Joseph Papovich, assistant US trade representative for intellectual property (BNA, 2001), is the 2000 'Agreement Between the United States of America and the Hashemite Kingdom of Jordan on the Establishment of a Free Trade Area'. The Agreement requires patents to be available for any invention in all fields of technology without including the exceptions contained in Article 27.3(*b*) of TRIPS. Jordan must also join UPOV. The number of these kinds of agreement is rapidly increasing, and many have provisions relating to biotechnology and plant breeding (see GRAIN, 2001).

This situation is grossly unfair. The problem facing developing countries is that, if they lack a clear idea of how – and even whether – biotechnology can benefit their economies and improve the lives of their citizens, they are in no position to design an IP system to promote welfare-enhancing biotechnological innovation. Moreover, many of these countries have no biotechnology industries to speak of, and there is every reason to be highly sceptical that such businesses will spring up just because life forms and microbiological processes can be patented. To make matters worse, their patent offices are likely to have to deal with large numbers of lengthy and highly technical patent applications. To give some idea of the potential difficulties here, in 2000, the US Patent and Trademark Office received a biotech patent application that was the equivalent of 400 000 pages long! And courts having the knowledge and experience to adjudicate disputes between different patent holders and to determine the appropriate scope of a biotech patent may simply not exist.

Harmonization

Harmonization entails making the patent system of countries more like each other in terms of administrative procedures and rules, enforcement standards and substantive law. TRIPS is not really about harmonization yet it is making the world's national and regional patent systems more similar to each other. Nonetheless, important differences remain. Apart from bilateralism, international harmonization initiatives by WIPO and a small number of important patent offices seem likely also to raise IP standards of protection around the globe above those strictly required by TRIPS.

One of the earliest calls for the harmonization of substantive patent law came from the USA in 1966, where the President's Commission on the Patent System declared:

> The ultimate goal in the protection of inventions should be the establishment of a universal patent, respected throughout the world, issued in the light of, and inventive over, all of the prior art of the world, and obtained quickly and inexpensively on a single application, but only in return for a genuine contribution to the progress of the useful arts. (Quoted in Rogan, 2002)

The Commission did not expect this to happen overnight. Consequently, initial demands for harmonization were directed mainly at procedural matters and aimed to reduce the duplication of effort caused by different patent offices examining applications for the same invention and to reduce costs for the applicants. The US, European and Japanese patent offices have been in close contact since 1983 and are cooperating in a number of areas to coordinate their approaches to searches, examinations and other procedures.

From 1985, WIPO held negotiations on patent law harmonization including administrative formalities and substantive law elements, and a Diplomatic Conference took place in 1991 at which WIPO presented a draft Patent Law Treaty (Uemura, 2000: 265). The Conference resulted in deadlock, for two reasons. The first was the determination of the US Congress to stick to first-to-invent in response to lobbying by independent inventor groups. The second was that industrial concerns in some European countries objected to having an international grace period for novelty (Bardehle, 1999: 304–5).[32] Clearly, some of the elements of harmonization are not to every business's taste. WIPO was requested to lower its ambitions, and in consequence the Patent Law Treaty adopted in 2000 dealt only with procedural matters.

Nonetheless, there is considerable interest in harmonizing substantive patent law, and efforts to do so are now moving apace. Japan is one of the most ambitious countries in this respect. A commission set up to advise the JPO that consisted almost entirely of industrialists and academics recommended in 1997 that the country take the lead in promoting a global patent system (see Commission on

Intellectual Property Rights, 1997). Needless to say, this would have to be consistent with its own extremely high levels of protection. This is somewhat ironic given that, just a few decades ago, the government's technology licensing policy was quite aggressive and foreign companies often felt short-changed by the patent system.[33]

WIPO has recently drafted a Substantive Patent Law Treaty that the organization's Standing Committee on the Law of Patents is currently debating. While such initiatives may never go much further than defining key terms such as prior art, novelty and inventive step, Shozo Uemura, WIPO's deputy director-general, recently suggested as a future possibility 'the establishment of basic principles regulating an ideal global patent system, according to which a patent granted in a civil procedure would have effect in different countries, and it would co-exist with existing national patent systems' (2000: 268). Obviously, any such system would have to provide agreed standards on the scope of patentable subject matter. And, as recent history shows, what the USA, EU and Japan agree upon the world will surely have to accept.

Towards a More Democratic Patent System

If the twenty-first century situation continues as it has begun, the regulatory spaces described in this book are likely to become ever more crowded with individuals and groups muscling in to influence IP policy as best they can. But who is going to win the competition for influence? And what difference will it make anyway? New institutionalism and historical experience seem to support the view that those with the most power and the best ideas will always win the war, but those with less power but better ideas can win some of the battles. It also seems that the victories are not always clear cut and a certain amount of ground has often to be ceded to the other side, especially when the powerful are unable to agree amongst themselves.

This suggests that, as the patent and PBR systems continue to evolve, the life science industries will be among the most effective drivers of change and will also benefit more than most. In consequence, it seems unlikely that there will be any rolling back of the proprietarian trends evident in the past few decades. At best, opponents may occasionally succeed in delaying or reducing the extent of the changes. But it is unlikely that they will be able to prevent them. Another plausible scenario, though, is that the exclusive rights sought by industry may become more effectively protected through technological means than through patents, just as hybridization has for decades made IP protection (except trade secrets) unnecessary for breeders using such methods of producing new plant varieties. Similarly, the so-called 'terminator technology', which causes harvested seeds to be sterile, could conceivably make IP rights unnecessary for plants and plant varieties if it ever sees the light of day. And advanced encryption technologies could likewise protect digital works in a more secure way than copyright ever can. So new technologies could result in patents and PBRs – and perhaps other IP rights too – withering away because nobody finds them useful any more. However, most indications are that patents and PBRs are here to stay for the foreseeable future, and many of the debates taking place over the past 100 years will continue for years to come.

As to whether all this actually matters, it is contended here that it is extremely important. For far too long, business and the patent community have been allowed to take interpretive custody of the patent system, with the result that we have an unbalanced system. We have given them the benefit of the doubt that their interpretations and prescriptions are technically sound, rational and in the interests of society as a whole. While the book has not attempted to prove that the system is unbalanced by failing adequately to meet wider interests than those of the people and businesses that profit directly from the system, it provides enough evidence to suggest this may well be the case. There is an urgent need for greater public participation in IP regulatory processes. They ought to be more democratic than they are. This chapter has shown that IP rights are getting a great deal of attention and one must hope that in the coming years this will translate into a movement that seeks to ensure that the patent system of the twenty-first century is much more democratic than that of the twentieth.

Notes

1 Fowler (1994: 180).
2 And currently heading another pro-business organization, the International Intellectual Property Institute.
3 Cited in G. Aharonian, Internet Patent News Service, 17 November 1996 [*patent-news@europe.std.com*].
4 Conversely, a century and a half ago, as Penrose reports (1951: 40), a connection between communism and the *pro-patent position* was made in a well-known publication: 'The London Economist (Feb. 1, 1851, p.114) said that for the legislature to take unto itself the power to distribute the fruits of discovery by providing for patents is to substitute "communism for property" and if it does in this case "why not in every case?"'
5 Both coined by Pat Mooney.
6 Coined by ethnobiologist and indigenous rights campaigner Darrell Posey.
7 Scandinavian countries sometimes break ranks and adopt developing-country positions, and this can help developing countries to overcome the reluctance of developed countries and pursue discussions on issues that concern them.
8 As of 7 January 2002. This includes the European Union.
9 Article 8(*j*) of the CBD requires contracting parties to 'respect, preserve and maintain knowledge, innovations and practices of indigenous and local communities embodying traditional lifestyles relevant for the conservation and sustainable use of biological diversity and promote their wider application with the approval and involvement of the holders of such knowledge, innovations and practices and encourage the equitable sharing of the benefits arising from the utilization of such knowledge, innovations and practices'.

10 WIPO Standing Committee on the Law of Patents (1999).
11 In WIPO (2000).
12 Ibid.
13 Ibid.
14 WTO General Council (1998).
15 WTO General Council (1999a).
16 WTO General Council (1999b).
17 See WTO General Council (1999c); also WTO General Council (1999d).
18 This is not a particularly ambitious demand, since 95 per cent of drugs on the WHO list of essential medicines are already off-patent. In fact, it is partly the relative cheapness of the drugs listed (due in large part to their patent-free status) that makes them 'essential' and thus worthy of inclusion.
19 WTO General Council (1999e).
20 A more detailed proposal for a legal framework on TK was submitted two months later to the General Council by the governments of Bolivia, Colombia, Ecuador, Nicaragua and Peru. See WTO General Council (1999f).
21 WTO General Council (1999g).
22 In cases where prior authorization from the patent owner is required (as is normally the case), negotiations can be complicated and take a long time to conclude. Second, the patent specification may not provide sufficient information to enable copying of the drug. In fact, with some drugs, the most efficient manufacturing process is protected by a separate patent, which may even be owned by a different company. Third, many countries may lack chemists who can do the copying, and licensees may not necessarily be able profitably to sell the drug at a much lower price than that of the patent-holding firm.
23 WTO TRIPS Council (2001a).
24 See WTO TRIPS Council (2001b).
25 UNHCR – Sub-Commission on the Promotion and Protection of Human Rights (2000).
26 As it was, the WTO was already annoyed about a Sub-Commission study on the issue of globalization and its impact on the full enjoyment of all human rights that referred to the WTO as a 'veritable nightmare' for 'certain sectors of humanity'.
27 UNCHR, Sub-Commission on the Promotion and Protection of Human Rights (2001a, 2001b).
28 UNHCR, Sub-Commission on the Promotion and Protection of Human Rights (2001c).
29 WTO TRIPS Council (2001b).
30 This idea appears first to have been suggested by Frédéric Hendrickx, Veit Koester (who was very much involved in the CBD negotiations) and Christian Prip in some articles, the first of which was published in 1993 (see Hendrickx *et al.*, 1993). But the proposal was taken up and further elaborated by others, most notably by Brendan Tobin, who was at the time working for the Peruvian Society for Environmental Law (see Tobin, 1997). Activists sought unsuccessfully to have the EU biotechnology inventions directive incorporate such a principle.
31 The term 'the new bilateralism' was coined by Drahos (see Drahos, 2001).
32 This was a defeat for AIPPI and FICPI, both of which have supported the international grace period over the years (Bardehle, 1999: 305).
33 Chalmers Johnson described a particularly notorious case that seems amply to justify foreign discontent with the Japanese patent system of the not so distant past (1995: 74–5):

On February 6, 1960, Texas Instruments filed an application for a Japanese patent protecting Jack Kilby and Robert Noyce's invention in 1959 of the integrated circuit. Some 29 years later, on October 30, 1989, the Japanese Patent Office, which is an integral part of MITI [Ministry of International Trade and Industry], granted the patent. It will run through November 27, 2001. Texas Instruments stands to make significant royalties during the 1990s from Japanese semiconductor manufacturers but, needless to say, the company was unable to protect its property during the almost 30 years when its Japanese competitors took over 90 percent of the Japanese market and 80 percent of the American market for computer semiconductors.

Chapter 10

Epilogue: the Life Science Industries in a Patent-free World

The privileges granted to inventions by patent laws are prohibitions on other men …. The privileges have stifled more inventions than they have promoted, and have caused more brilliant schemes to be set aside than the want of them could ever have induced men to conceal. Each patent is a prohibition against improvements in a particular direction, except by the patentee, for a certain number of years; and, however beneficial that may be to him who receives the privilege, the community cannot be benefited by it. (*The Economist*, 1 February 1851)[1]

What does this history of intellectual property rights and the life science industries tell us that has present-day relevance? Undoubtedly, the evolution of the international patent system reflects the development of new technologies, the growth of industrial sectors that use them, and the increased importance of patents to world trade. But these three factors do not tell the whole story. Ever since the late nineteenth century (and earlier in a few countries) patent-owning firms have been politically active in patent regulation in every economically advanced country, as have other groups such as lawyers and organizations representing pro-patent business interests. By and large, they have been quite successful in capturing – or at least closely collaborating with – state and regional regulatory agencies dealing with international commerce and industrial policy, to the point that the national interest is often treated as being identical to the demands of corporations. Legislatures then tend to fall under the influence of these expert patent communities, with the result that patents and other IP rights are reformed in ways that increasingly prioritize the interests of corporations over those of the general public.

In response, the general trend during the past century was for patent rights to become stronger, to extend to all and every field of technology (as is required by TRIPS), and to contain fewer exceptions. Many developing countries that had not introduced similar reforms earlier are doing so now. Whether the changes came as a direct result of new legislation, revisions to existing laws, court decisions or new patent office rules and procedures, the influence of organized interests was usually present. As a highly technical area of the law, these interests rarely encountered strong opposition and their interpretive custody over the various regulatory spaces, while far from absolutely secure, was sufficient to ensure that the patent system was usually friendliest to the wealthiest and best-organized domestic interest groups in

237

the developed countries for most of the past 120 years. This situation continues to this day.

The development of PBR systems followed a similar pattern to that of patents, except that their very creation was a consequence of the organized activities of people and groups representing an industrial sector whose corporate members were the intended beneficiaries. They did not seek to adapt a legal system which dates back to the Renaissance (as with patents); rather, they opted for the creation of an entirely new system which borrowed certain features from other IP rights but was fundamentally original.

As for the development implications of the rapid expansion of patentable subject matter and technological fields, this does not seem to suit the interests of the poor nations of the world. For example, India does not enjoy a comparative advantage in the supply of innovative pharmaceutical products, but it does in the manufacture and export of copied drugs. Many other poor countries cannot even make copied drugs and simply desire to gain access to foreign-made medicines at affordable prices. According to Michael Trebilcock of the University of Toronto and Robert Howse of the University of Michigan (1999: 314), 'a country would have little or no interest in protecting intellectual property rights in products of which it is solely an imitator and intends to remain so – here the national interest is above all consumer welfare, i.e. sourcing the product as cheaply as possible'. Past exceptions in Europe were undoubtedly based on such calculations of national self-interest. Similarly, many if not most developing countries would be better off not allowing medicines to be patented. If this is indeed the case, any 'legal straitjacket' that binds countries so tightly that they can no longer make such decisions should be avoided. Undeniably, TRIPS and the new bilateralism together form such a legal straitjacket which harmonization and inappropriate TRIPS-plus technical assistance from organizations like WIPO will tighten still further.

Having briefly summarized the role of the life science industries and their allies in driving the development of the patent and PBR systems, and suggested some general implications, it is fitting that this book should close with some reflections on the role of patents and PBRs in driving the development of the life sciences and the business sectors based upon them. Readers who have reached this stage of the book must surely wonder what difference patents and PBRs actually made to the life sciences, and in what ways things would be different today if the twentieth century had run its course without them, or at least with patent systems as they were before the century began. These final pages, then, shed a little light on the question of how far patents and PBRs were truly responsible for driving the scientific and technological advancements described in the book, for the discovery and development of welfare-enhancing applications such as medicines and plant varieties, or – to look from a more negative perspective – for the relative lack of new medicines and biotechnological innovations compared to a world without patents.

Going back to the beginning, there is undoubtedly a strong temporal correlation between the modernization of patent law and the adoption of in-house research and development. This is unlikely to be coincidental. But while industry clearly benefited wherever it was able to help design the patent system (as in Germany), it is far from certain that decisions to commit to expensive research and development programmes were made as a consequence of there being a patent system. For Britain and France, the product patent regime was actually quite unhelpful, while in Switzerland, the chemical industry could not take out patents even if it wanted to (which apparently it did not), yet it progressed rapidly nonetheless. The patent system probably did encourage firms in Germany to invest in research and development, but one must qualify this point by noting that some of the patent practices of those German chemical firms first to establish themselves as market leaders probably restricted research and development opportunities for other German and foreign firms. This should remind us of two things that a new institutionalist approach leads us to expect. First, changes in property rights structures can never make winners out of everybody. Second, the differences between the gains for some and the losses for others are bound to be great when the biggest right holders have, as they so often do, such a firm grip on the regulatory system to the partial or total exclusion of other holders, users and those representing consumer interests.

Dealing more generally with the scientific and technological advances described throughout the book, in all probability most of these would have developed pretty much as they did with or without patents or PBRs. Many, if not most, of the truly significant discoveries took place in universities and government research institutions. This is true for Perkin's accidental production of aniline, for Banting, Best and Collip's isolation of insulin, Fleming and Waksman's discoveries of penicillin and streptomycin, and Hensch's discovery of cortisone's anti-inflammatory action. It is also true for some of the most important techniques underpinning the new biotechnologies such as recombinant DNA and DNA sequencing. Indeed, it seems quite reasonable to argue that major breakthroughs are more likely to be achieved in universities than in companies because of the different ways that research is done in each kind of institution. In companies, the pursuit of profit tends to encourage research with obvious commercial applications. This is of course how business should do its research. Yet this is not how all research should be done. Unexpected but extremely significant discoveries often come out of research programmes that are not intended to make money, as well as the curiosity of individual scientists whose freedom is not constrained by having to demonstrate the economic value of their work. Admittedly, exceptions exist, such as the development of synthetic alizarin and indigo, and the discovery of the sulphonamides and of PCR. It is also true that product development is incredibly expensive and business bears much of the cost (even if not as much as some companies like to claim). This is why the advances just mentioned were built upon by the private sector, which invested money in the research and development needed to get these products to market and then to discover related products, many of which vastly improved the quality of life of many people. As for PBRs, the underlying science of breeding plant varieties was not affected by the new rights. To be fair, this was not its intent. The number of new varieties entering the market certainly changed. The basic methods of producing them employed by those using the PBR system did not.

But it is difficult to believe that the life science industries would have developed as they did in the absence of patents. Patents are probably more important for the fine chemical, pharmaceutical and biotechnological enterprises than for any other industrial sectors. But does this mean that drugs today would be lower in quantity if patent systems had remained as they were a century ago? It is impossible to do more than speculate. It seems plausible that, without the incentive effect of strong patent rights, fewer new drugs would have entered the market. If so, for developed countries at least, where price is not such an important issue as in poor countries, a plausible case could be made for arguing that we are better off, on balance, with the changes that have taken place than without them. But because so many abusive and anti-competitive practices have been allowed to persist, we should not be satisfied at all with the way things are. We still need to have a much more balanced system.

But it is also possible that the abandonment of working requirements, the restriction of compulsory licensing, the lifting of the bar on product patents and acceptance that a purified and/or isolated natural substance may constitute a patentable invention did not spur greater innovation than there would have been without these changes. Moreover, for many years now, the number of drug-related patents has vastly exceeded the quantity of drugs on the market or in development. Many of these patents are intended to extend existing monopolies. One can understand the desire of companies to seek to protect their investments as securely as possible. Patent protection *does* give companies the security they need to invest in research and development. But so many patents artificially increase the cost of doing research and by raising barriers to entry probably have inhibiting effects on innovation that may outweigh the stimulating effects that undoubtedly exist as well. One might add, too, that if the previous rules restricting patent rights had been retained, those drugs available would probably be cheaper because patent holders would be in a weaker position to eliminate competition. Admittedly, profit margins would in consequence be lower right across the industry, and this would presumably mean less money not just for marketing and advertising (see below) but also for research.

While much of the current debate on pharmaceutical patenting has to do with differences about where to strike the balance to ensure that protection is effective but not excessive, some critics have proposed that we would be better of by dispensing entirely with patents. In a well-known article published around the time of the Kefauver Committee hearings, Henry Steele argued that the elimination of patents would benefit the public as it would increase price competition and encourage research by non-corporate institutions, where most of the genuinely innovative pharmaceutical research (in his opinion) was carried out anyway (Steele, 1962: 162).

Can this be right? Convincing evidence either way is hard to come by. The experience of Italy during the 1950s and 1960s suggests that lack or absence of patent protection encourages imitative rather than truly innovative pharmaceutical research (Taylor and Silberston, 1973: 262–3). However, the introduction of product patent protection there has made little difference in terms of research and development expenditure and the development of innovative new products by domestic firms (Scherer and Weisburst, 1995). Therefore, just as critics who wish to use the Italian case to demonstrate that patents are unnecessary for pharmaceutical innovation need to explain the pre-patent era, those who wish to cite Italy as proof of the opposite must somehow explain the post-1978 situation.

We know that the industry did not spawn two of the three therapeutic revolutions described in Chapter 5 or the biotechnology revolution covered in Chapter 6. Yet the private sector has probably been responsible for the discovery and development of many if not most of the therapeutically significant drugs of the twentieth century. While this is a hotly disputed point, Duncan Reekie and Michael Weber reviewed several studies addressing this issue and found that every one showed beyond reasonable doubt that industry was responsible for discovering the vast majority of drugs introduced in the United States during the 1950s and 1960s (Reekie and Weber, 1979: 8–11).

On the other hand, universities have been and continue to be important sources of pharmaceutical innovation. Along with foundations, hospital research laboratories and public sector research agencies, they have been responsible for discovering *and* funding many of the most innovative and welfare-enhancing drugs. Reekie and Weber's study is of course rather old. A more recent finding is that the NIH, whose annual research budget is now around $23 billion, played a significant role in the development of all five best-selling drugs in 1995.[2] So perhaps we would be better off without having a pharmaceutical industry of the kind we have whose characteristics are (i) that it is dominated by a small number of giant corporations with an oligopolistic grip on many key therapeutic areas, (ii) that it generates very large returns by comparison with almost any other industrial sector, (iii) that it invests heavily in research and development, and (iv) that, despite all this, it is not so very self-sufficient when it comes to discovering and developing genuinely new medicines all by itself. And with it should go the patent system which has caused the industry to develop in the way it has done.

Or perhaps not. Taylor and Silberston's classic study on the economic impacts of the patent system on different industrial sectors provides a difference perspective. According to these authors, a weakening of the British patent system would probably result in reduced research and development outlays but massively increased expenditures on advertising and marketing, and on the promotion of brand names and minor product differentiation (1973: 266).

Yet things could hardly be worse in this respect than they are now. The so-called 'research-based industry' spends far more on advertising and marketing than it does on research. By way of illustration, a study by researchers at Boston University

School of Health found that the American brand-name drug sector increased its marketing staff from a total of 55 348 people in 1995 to 87 810 in 2000. In the same years the number of researchers actually fell, from 49 409 people to 48 527. One of the authors caustically remarked:

> These staffing patterns call into question the brand-name drug makers' self-definition as 'research-based' companies ... Since they now employ nearly 40,000 more people in marketing than in research, they might more appropriately call themselves 'America's marketing-based pharmaceutical companies'. Their priority today does not seem to be developing new treatments but defining and selling their brands. (Sager and Socolar, 2001)

But would a more efficient patent system, or perhaps no patent system at all, encourage the industry to spend less on sales promotion and more on research? Clearly, we should be sceptical of claims by industry that they compete purely on the basis of innovation and not also on marketing acumen or advertising expenditure. But there is no easy answer to the question. It is not at all certain that a job created in promotion is a job lost in research, or that, if we discouraged companies from spending so much on advertising, they would simply reallocate the unspent money to research. There again, it is certainly possible that companies would invest more in research to better differentiate their products from those of rivals if they could not do this through advertising. But how much more depends on a range of factors that go beyond the patent system. Nonetheless, we can hardly be satisfied with a situation whereby the patent incentive fails so badly to induce a greater commitment to research and development than it does when so much money is being spent on marketing. Probably, the only way to clarify the patenting–research–marketing connections would be to restrict marketing and advertising and then see where the companies divert their funds. Somehow, it is difficult to imagine the industry agreeing to put this to the test!

Two further complaints are made about the patent system which are important to consider. First, too much corporate research and development has been aimed at molecular manipulation that can be profitable but not very creative and not necessarily all that beneficial for patients. Patents are accused of failing to stimulate truly original research. Second, patents are blamed for distorting research priorities by encouraging research on treatments for relatively trivial ailments like baldness, on dealing with diet-related health concerns of affluent societies such as obesity and high cholesterol, and on chronic problems such as high blood pressure that do not cure patients but that need to be taken continually for many years. The criticism is not that companies should not do such research, but that there is a severe lack of spending on diseases that disproportionately affect the poor, such as malaria and tuberculosis (see MSF and DND Working Group, 2001). This is not just of academic interest. James Orbinski, President of the International Council of Médecins Sans Frontières, has pointed out, for example, that while 95 per cent of active TB cases occur in developing countries, no new drugs for the disease have been developed since 1967 (2001: 230–31). And the World Health Organization (1996) has estimated that only 4·3 per cent of pharmaceutical research and development expenditure is aimed at those health problems mainly concerning low- and middle-income countries.

Taking the first complaint, it is fair to point out that 'me-tooism' is not always a bad thing. The critical view, as expressed by Leigh Hancher, is that 'the patent system ... can exacerbate these problems [of investing mostly in the development of therapeutically identical products] by sheltering socially worthless but privately profitable research' (Hancher, 1990: 51). John Braithwaite concurs, citing a former employee of Squibb who when giving evidence to the Kefauver Committee explained that, during his tenure there, 25 per cent of the research budget went to 'worthwhile' projects, while the rest went on molecular manipulation. But he concedes that 'me-too research has occasionally stumbled upon significant therapeutic advances' (Braithwaite, 1984: 164). Even so, the industry's output in recent years has undeniably been disappointing with respect not only to the quantity of new drugs but, especially, to their quality. The lack of genuinely original products entering the market is a matter for serious concern. But is the patent system responsible? It is difficult to say whether a patent-free world would encourage more original research and less molecular manipulation, or the opposite. Even so, it may be true that the patent system is making the situation worse by encouraging the wrong kind of research. The possibility is certainly something that we ought to look into.

As for the second complaint, it is rather difficult to say whether patents are directly responsible for this. With or without patents, the profit motive of capitalism is in any case bound to encourage pharmaceutical research to be aimed at areas where the most money can be made. But this does not let patents completely off the hook. One could argue that if patents are meant to serve the public interest then they should encourage research where public needs are greatest.

Nevertheless, the situation is not very satisfactory and the patent system must carry some of the blame. In addition, the questionable practices the industry has resorted to over the years with the help of the patent system, such as price fixing, evergreening and collusion with generic producers, also suggest that the public has not benefited as much as it should from the balance struck by the law between their interests, and those of the industry, not forgetting in this case the interests also of others who end up paying the bills, such as health insurance companies. A rebalancing is necessary, including a complete rethink about how incentive structures could be changed to encourage more and better research by the industry that furthers public health priorities including, not just diseases commonly afflicting the affluent, but those affecting poorer people, and also rare diseases that cannot be treated because the market is too small to encourage drug development.[3]

As for the patenting of biotechnological inventions, while the pace of innovation has been quite rapid, the number of products entering the market is rather disappointing when measured against the initial expectations. To what extent can explanations be found in the recent changes to the patent system? It is in fact highly unlikely that innovation would have been slower if we had never allowed genes or DNA sequences to be patented, and might even have been faster. As for other isolated and purified natural substances, it is difficult to understand why these should still be patentable, or how we as members of the public can possibly benefit. Admittedly, DBFs need to get funds somehow and patents do play a role in attracting financial support. Moreover, without patents there is likely to be even more secrecy than there already is. But with a patent system that is less imperialistic as to subject matter, with a broader research exemption (or if patent law borrowed the fair dealing concept from copyright law), and which applied the criteria of novelty, inventive step and industrial application more rigorously than it seems to do today, genuinely innovative companies should still attract funds and there would likely be more of such businesses. Anyway, sooner or later investors will become better at differentiating between those DBFs doing useful research and those that are merely – in the words of a life science corporation patent lawyer the present author discussed this issue with – 'selling wind'. As for plants and animals, it is early days. Patenting has probably encouraged the development of new biotechnology products, especially plants. But apart from increasing the profits of the life science corporations and satisfying some but not all farmers, there are some reasonable doubts that the first wave of products coming out of this research is much better than the more conventionally developed existing ones or that such products do not have drawbacks of their own. Moreover, as with pharmaceuticals and health genomics, agrobiotechnology patenting is plagued by the same anti-commons problems. This is detrimental to innovation. It is difficult not to conclude that public expenditure on the life sciences, in this area as in many others, is likely to have spurred innovation over the years far more than the existence of patents.

Recent reports indicate that several European life science corporations are moving some of their research and development operations to the United States. Apart from the size of the US market and the existence of such an active DBF sector, a recent *Financial Times* story points out that the main attraction is the size of the public research infrastructure which these companies can tap into. This is the result of massive government expenditure on medical research which is now 'at least five times' greater than the European Union countries combined. The patent system does not appear to be a significant factor in these corporate decisions, at least in any direct sense (Dyer, 2002: 13).

A few words should be said about plant breeding and the seed industry. How would these have fared in a PBR-free world? In answering the question, one must first say that PBRs had nothing to do with the vast sums of money invested in the breeding of hybrids, which have from the start been the most profitable varieties. In fact, studies on the impacts of PBRs are few in number (see Rangnekar, 2002) and those which exist vary in their conclusions from the positive to the highly sceptical. One study on the US Plant Variety Protection Act, which lay somewhere between these extremes, revealed that, while research investment and the number of research programmes both increased, such research tended to focus mostly on those crops likely to offer the highest profits, which were soya and wheat (Butler and Marion, 1985). Lesser and Masson's (1983) study on the same legislation was unsurprisingly – given its American Seed Trade Association sponsorship – rather more favourable. But however positive or critical the findings are, it is not always easy to separate the incentive effect of PBRs from other factors that influence decisions on where a company should direct its research, such as increased industrial or consumer demand for certain crops and reduced demand for others. It is generally agreed that, because of PBRs, the number of varieties introduced into European and Northern markets is greater than it would otherwise have been. However, Dwijen Rangnekar (2000: 1) has suggested that, while this is probably true, PBRs encourage breeders to adopt strategies of planned obsolescence 'to reduce the durability of plant varieties so as to induce regular replacement purchases by farmers'. He claims some empirical evidence that UK wheat breeders do adopt such strategies. If this is correct, farmers may well benefit far less from PBRs than their proponents claim. Existing seed companies have almost certainly gained from the existence of PBRs, at least in the USA and Europe, as pharmaceutical companies and DBFs have from patents. The difference is that, as we saw in Chapter 7, PBRs have not enabled seed companies to maintain their independence. To sum up, PBRs are likely to have been beneficial on balance. But, if Rangnekar is right, we need to reflect on whether the right incentives are necessarily being created, and if they are not, how the system can be modified to encourage breeders to shift their research in more farmer-friendly directions.

If the rather negative view of patents held by *The Economist* in 1851 was and remains an accurate one, we would indeed be better off without patents. But the analytical tools to prove it either way do not exist. Doubtless there are serious limits to the reliability of economic analyses of the patent and PBR systems whatever methodology is adopted. The same goes for counter-factual speculation when directed to economic regulation over a long time scale. In the face of so many inevitable 'ifs', 'buts', 'on the other hands' and 'there agains', it really is difficult to be certain either way. Yet the story told here and the analytical approach chosen both strongly discourage any expectation that patents and PBRs (albeit to a less problematical extent) finely balance the interests of existing owners, potential owners, users and the public while optimally inducing welfare-enhancing innovation, or could ever do so. Such systems exist only in the minds of economists that do not factor interest group politics into their equations. More's the pity. The best we can do is reduce the built-in inequities and imbalances. It is extremely doubtful that we can remove them completely. Nonetheless, we should not give up trying.

Notes

1 In Machlup and Penrose (1950: 24).
2 As reported on ABC News on 29 May 2002 (*http://abcnews.go.com/onair/ ABCNEWSSpecials/pharmaceuticals_020529_pjr_feature.html*).
3 Admittedly, it can be very difficult to create positive incentives without inadvertently generating perverse incentives that unscrupulous companies will take advantage of. A United Nations Industrial Development Organization study describes an example from the USA to illustrate the difficulty facing policy makers in this regard:

> In 1983 the United States Congress passed a law granting tax breaks and a seven-year monopoly to companies producing orphan drugs. The drugs were defined as having annual sales of less than $5 million and a potential market of fewer than 200 000 patients. The law has had its successes, such as a treatment for porphyria – a painful and debilitating disease that afflicts only 100 people. It has also proved to have shortcomings. Some companies make use of their monopoly position to extract exorbitant prices. Others use particularly narrow definitions of the disease to ensure that the potential market is extremely small. A few companies have achieved orphan drug status through a 'salami technique': submitting multiple applications for the same drug by specifying different groups of symptoms, each of which affects fewer than 200 000 people (Ballance *et al.*, 1992: 18).

Bibliography

Academic Works

Abbott, F.M. (2002), 'The TRIPS Agreement, access to medicines, and the WTO Doha Ministerial Conference', *Journal of World Intellectual Property* 5 (1): 15–52.

Abraham, J. (2002), 'The political economy of medicines regulation in Europe', in H. Lawton-Smith (ed.), *The Regulation of Science and Technology*, Basingstoke: Palgrave.

Acharya, R. (1999), *The Emergence and Growth of Biotechnology: Experiences in Industrialised and Developing Countries*, Cheltenham, UK and Northampton, MA, USA: Edward Elgar.

Achilladelis, B. (1993), 'The dynamics of technological innovation: the sector of antibacterial medicines', *Research Policy* 22: 279–308.

Aftalion, F. (1991), *A History of the Chemical Industry*, Philadelphia: University of Pennsylvania Press.

Alford, W.P. (1993), 'Don't stop thinking about ... yesterday: why there was no indigenous counterpart to intellectual property law in imperial China', *Journal of Chinese Law* 7: 3–20.

Allyn, R.S. (1933a), 'More about plant patents', *Journal of the Patent Office Society* 15 (12): 963–70.

Allyn, R.S. (1933b), 'Plant patent queries', *Journal of the Patent Office Society* 15 (3): 180–86.

Almeida, P.R. de (1995), 'The political economy of intellectual property protection: technological protectionism and the transfer of revenue among nations', *International Journal of Technology Management* 10 (2/3): 214–29.

Anderfelt, U. (1971), *International Patent Legislation and Developing Countries*, The Hague: Martinus Nijhoff.

Arrow, K.J. (1962), 'Economic welfare and the allocation of resources in invention', in NBER (ed.), *The Rate and Direction of Innovative Activity*, Princeton: Princeton University Press.

Attaran, A. and L. Gillespie-White (2001), 'Do patents for antiretroviral drugs constrain access to AIDS treatment in Africa?', *Journal of the American Medical Association* 286 (15): 1886–92.

Baldwin, R., C. Scott and C. Hood (1998), 'Introduction', in R. Baldwin, C. Scott and C. Hood (eds), *A Reader on Regulation*, Oxford: Oxford University Press.

Ballance, R., J. Pogány and H. Forstner (1992), *The World's Pharmaceutical Industries: An International Perspective on Innovation, Competition and Policy. Prepared for the United Nations Industrial Development Organization*, Aldershot: Edward Elgar.

Barbanti, P., A. Gambardella and L. Orsenigo (1999), 'The evolution of collaborative relationships among firms in biotechnology', *International Journal of Biotechnology* 1 (1): 10–29.

Bardehle, H. (1999), 'A new approach to worldwide harmonization of patent law', *Journal of the Patent and Trademark Office Society* 81 (4): 303–10.

Barton, J.H. (1991), 'Patenting life', *Scientific American* 264 (3): 40–46.

Baumann, M., J. Bell, F. Koechlin and M. Pimbert (eds) (1996), *The Life Industry: Biodiversity, People and Profits*, London: Intermediate Technology Publications.

Beier, F.-K. (1981), 'The European patent system', *Vanderbilt Journal of Transnational Law* 14 (1): 1–15.

Beier, F.-K. (1984), 'One hundred years of international cooperation: the role of the Paris Convention in the past, present and future', *International Review of Industrial Property and Copyright Law* 15 (1): 1–20.

Beier, F.-K. (1986), 'The inventive step in its historical development', *International Review of Industrial Property and Copyright Law* 17 (3): 301.

Belt, H. van den (1992), 'Why monopoly failed: the rise and fall of Société La Fuschine', *British Journal for the History of Science* 25: 45–63.

Belt, H. van den and A. Rip (1989), 'The Nelson–Winter–Dosi model and synthetic dye chemistry', in W.E. Bijker, T.P. Hughes and T. Pinch (eds), *The Social Construction of Technological Systems*, Cambridge: MIT Press.

Benjamin, G. (1936), 'Plant patents in Germany', *Journal of the Patent Office Society* 18 (6): 462–3.

Bensaude-Vincent, B. and I. Stengers (1996), *A History of Chemistry*, Cambridge and London: Harvard University Press.

Bent, S.A., R.L. Schwaab, D.G. Conlin and D.D. Jeffery (1987), *Intellectual Property Rights in Biotechnology Worldwide*, Basingstoke: Macmillan.

Bently, L. and B. Sherman (2001), *Intellectual Property Law*, Oxford: Oxford University Press.

Bercovitz-Rodriguez, A. (1990), 'Historical trends in protection of technology in developed countries and their relevance for developing countries', Geneva: United Nations Conference on Trade and Development.

Berg, M. and K. Bruland (1998), 'Culture, institutions and technological transitions', in M. Berg and K. Bruland (eds), *Technological Revolutions in Europe: Historical Perspectives*, Cheltenham, UK and Northampton, MA, USA: Edward Elgar.

Berlan, J.-P. and R.C. Lewontin (1998), 'Cashing in on life – operation terminator', *Le Monde Diplomatique*, December (*http://www.monde-diplomatique.fr/inside/1998/12/02gen.html*).

Beyleveld, D. and R. Brownsword (1993), *Mice, Morality and Patents*, London: Common Law Institute of Intellectual Property.

Bhagwati, J. (1998), *A Stream of Windows: Unsettling Reflections on Trade, Immigration and Democracy*, Cambridge: MIT Press.

Bijman, J. (1999), 'Life science companies: can they combine seeds, agrochemicals and pharmaceuticals?', *Biotechnology and Development Monitor* (40): 14–19.

Black, J. (1997), 'New institutionalism and naturalism in socio-legal analysis: institutionalist approaches to regulatory decision making', *Law and Policy* 19 (1): 51–93.

Blakeney, M. (1996), *Trade Related Aspects of Intellectual Property Rights: A Concise Guide to the TRIPs Agreement*, London: Sweet and Maxwell.

Bliss, F.A. (1989), 'Plant breeding, crop cultivars, and the nature of genetic variability', in Crop Science Society of America, American Society of Agronomy and Soil Science Society of America (eds), *Intellectual Property Rights Associated with Plants*, Madison: CSSA, ASA and SSSA.

Bliss, M. (1982), *The Discovery of Insulin*, Toronto: McLelland and Stewart.

Borson, D.B. (1995), 'The Human Genome Project: patenting human genes and biotechnology. Is the human genome patentable?', *IDEA – The Journal of Law and Technology* 35 (4): 461–96.

Boyle, J. (1996), *Shamans, Software, and Spleens: Law and the Construction of the Information Society*, Cambridge and London: Harvard University Press.

Bozicevic, K. (1987), 'Distinguishing "products of nature" from products derived from nature', *Journal of the Patent and Trademark Office Society* 69 (8): 415–26.

Braithwaite, J. (1984), *Corporate Crime in the Pharmaceutical Industry*, London: Routledge and Kegan Paul.

Braithwaite, J. and P. Drahos (2000), *Global Business Regulation*, Cambridge: Cambridge University Press.

Breedveld, F.C. (2000), 'Therapeutic monoclonal antibodies', *The Lancet* 355: 735–40.

Bruce, D. and A. Bruce (1998), *Engineering Genesis – The Ethics of Genetic Engineering in Non-human Species*, London: Earthscan.

Brush, S.B. (1993), 'Indigenous knowledge of biological resources and intellectual property rights: the role of anthropology', *American Anthropologist* 95 (3): 653–86.

Brush, S.B. and D. Stabinsky (eds) (1996), *Valuing Local Knowledge: Indigenous People and Intellectual Property Rights*, Washington, DC and Covelo: Island Press.

Bud, R. (1993), *The Uses of Life: A History of Biotechnology*, Cambridge: Cambridge University Press.

Bugos, G.E. and D.J. Kevles (1992), 'Plants as intellectual property: American practice, law, and policy in a world context', *Osiris* 7: 75–104.

Burhenne, W.E. (1994), 'Foreword', in V. Sánchez and C. Juma (eds), *Biodiplomacy: Genetic Resources and International Relations*, Nairobi: African Centre for Technology Studies.

Burkitt, D. (2001), 'Copyrighting culture – the history and cultural specificity of the western model of copyright', *Intellectual Property Quarterly* (2): 146–86.

Butler, L.J. and B.W. Marion (1985), *The Impacts of Patent Protection on the US Seed Industry and Public Breeding*, Madison: University of Wisconsin-Madison.

Buttel, F.H. and J. Belsky (1987), 'Biotechnology, plant breeding, and intellectual property: social and ethical dimensions', *Science, Technology, and Human Values* 12 (1): 31–49.

Bynum, W.E. (1994), *Science and the Practice of Medicine in the Nineteenth Century*, Cambridge: Cambridge University Press.

Chandler, A.D. Jr. (1990), *Scale and Scope: The Dynamics of Industrial Capitalism*, Cambridge and London: Belknap Press.

Commons, J.R. (1934), *Institutional Economics: Its Place in Political Economy*, New York: Macmillan.

Cook, R.C. (1932), 'The first plant patent', *Journal of the Patent Office Society* 14 (5): 398–403.

Cook, R.C. (1937), 'The first plant patent decision', *Journal of the Patent Office Society* 19 (3): 187–92.

Cook-Deegan, R. (1994), *The Gene Wars: Science, Politics, and the Human Genome*, New York: W.W. Norton.

Coombe, R.J. (1998), *Cultural Life of Intellectual Properties: Authorship, Appropriation, and the Law*, Durham: Duke University Press.

Cooper, M.H. (1966), *Prices and Profits in the Pharmaceutical Industry*, Oxford and London: Pergamon Press.

Cornish, W.R. (1993), 'The international relations of intellectual property', *Cambridge Law Journal* 52 (1): 46–63.

Cornish, W.R. (1999), *Intellectual Property: Patents, Copyright, Trade Marks and Allied Rights*, 4th edn, London: Sweet and Maxwell.

Correa, C.M. (2000), *Intellectual Property Rights, the WTO and Developing Countries: The TRIPS Agreement and Policy Options*, London, New York and Penang: Zed Books and Third World Network.

Correa, C.M. (2001a), *Trends in Drug Patenting: Case Studies*, Buenos Aires: Corregidor.

Correa, C.M. (2001b), 'Public health and patent legislation in developing countries', *Tulane Journal of Technology and Intellectual Property* 3: 1–53.

Coulter, M. (1991), *Property in Ideas: The Patent Question in Mid-Victorian Britain*, Kirksville: The Thomas Jefferson University Press at Northeast Missouri State University.

Cragg, G.M., D.J. Newman and K.M. Snader (1997), 'Natural products in drug discovery and development', *Journal of Natural Products* 60 (1): 52–60.

The Crucible Group (1994), *People, Plants and Patents: The Impact of Intellectual Property on Trade, Plant Biodiversity, and Rural Society*, Ottawa: International Development Research Centre.

David, P. (1993), 'Intellectual property institutions and the panda's thumb: patents, copyrights, and trade secrets in economic theory and history', in M.B. Wallerstein, R.A. Schoen and M.E. Mogee (eds), *Global Dimensions of*

Intellectual Property Rights in Science and Technology, Washington, DC: National Academy Press.

Davies, K. (2001), *The Sequence: Inside the Race for the Human Genome*, London: Weidenfeld and Nicolson.

Demsetz, H. (1967), 'Toward a theory of property rights', *American Economic Review* 57: 347–59.

Dessemontet, F. (2000), *Intellectual Property Law in Switzerland*, The Hague, London and Berne: Kluwer Law International and Stämpfli.

Dicken, P. (1998), *Global Shift: Transforming the Global Economy*, 3rd edn, London: Paul Chapman Publishing.

Dienner, J.A. (1950), 'Patents and nationalism: a patent lawyer looks at the problem of European recovery', *Journal of the Patent Office Society* 32 (8): 615–28.

Djerassi, C. (2001), *The Man's Pill: Reflections on the 50th Birthday of the Pill*, Oxford: Oxford University Press.

Doern, G.B. (1999), *Global Change and Intellectual Property Agencies*, London and New York: Pinter.

Doll, J. (1998), 'Biotechnology: the patenting of DNA', *Science* 280: 689–90.

Doremus, P.N. (1996), 'The externalization of domestic regulation: intellectual property rights reform in a global era', *Global Legal Studies Journal* 3 (2): 341–74.

Drahos, P. (1996), *A Philosophy of Intellectual Property*, Aldershot, UK and Brookfield, US: Dartmouth.

Drahos, P. (1997), 'States and intellectual property: the past, the present and the future', in D. Saunders and B. Sherman (eds), *From Berne to Geneva: Recent Developments in Copyright and Neighbouring Rights*, Brisbane: Australian Key Centre for Cultural and Media Policy and Impart Corporation.

Drahos, P. (1999a), 'Biotechnology patents, markets and morality', *European Intellectual Property Review* 21 (9): 441–9.

Drahos, P. (1999b), 'Designing institutions in the information society', in S. Macdonald and J. Nightingale (eds), *Information and Organisation: A Tribute to the Work of Don Lamberton*, Amsterdam: Elsevier Science.

Drahos, P. (1999c), 'Introduction', in P. Drahos (ed.), *Intellectual Property Law. International Library of Essays in Law and Legal Theory, Volume 2*, Aldershot: Dartmouth.

Drahos, P. (2001), 'BITs and BIPs: bilateralism in intellectual property', *Journal of World Intellectual Property* 4 (6): 791–808.

D'Silva, J.E. (1989), 'Patenting of animals: a welfare viewpoint', in International Coalition for Development Action (ed.), *Patenting Life Forms in Europe. Proceedings of an International Conference at the European Parliament, Brussels, 7–8 February 1989*, Barcelona: ICDA Seeds Campaign.

Duessing, J.H. (1989), 'Patent protection for inventions from agricultural biotechnology', in International Coalition for Development Action (ed.), *Patenting Life Forms in Europe. Proceedings of an International Conference at* the European Parliament, Brussels, 7–8 February 1989, Barcelona: ICDA Seeds Campaign.

Duffin, J. (1999), *History of Medicine: A Scandalously Short Introduction*, Toronto: University of Toronto Press.

Dutfield, G. (2000), *Intellectual Property Rights, Trade and Biodiversity: Seeds and Plant Varieties*, London: Earthscan Books.

Dutton, H.I. (1984), *The Patent System and Inventive Activity during the Industrial Revolution, 1750–1852*, Manchester: Manchester University Press.

Eggertsson, T. (1990), *Economic Behaviour and Institutions*, Cambridge: Cambridge University Press.

Ely, J.W. Jr. (1992), *The Guardian of Every Other Right*, New York and Oxford: Oxford University Press.

Empel, M. van (1975), *The Granting of European Patents: Introduction to the Convention on the Grant of European Patents, Munich, October 5, 1973*, Leyden: A.W. Sijthoff.

Engelberg, A.B. (1999), 'Special patent provisions for pharmaceuticals: have they outlived their usefulness? A political, legislative and legal history of US law and observations for the future', *IDEA, The Journal of Law and Technology* 39 (3): 389–425.

Enyart, J.R. (1990), 'A GATT intellectual property code', *Les Nouvelles* (June): 53–6.

Ernst, D., L.K. Mytelka and T. Ganiatsos (1998), 'Technological capabilities in the context of export-led growth: a conceptual framework', in D. Ernst, T. Ganiatsos and L.K. Mytelka (eds), *Technological Dynamism and Export Success in Asia*, London: Routledge.

Evans, G.E. (1996), 'The principle of national treatment and the international protection of industrial property', *European Intellectual Property Review* 18 (3): 149–60.

Fairley, P. (1978), *The Conquest of Pain*, London: Michael Joseph.

Farnsworth, N. (1988), 'Screening plants for new medicines', in E.O. Wilson (ed.), *BioDiversity*, Washington, DC: National Academy Press.

Farrar, W.V. (1974), 'Synthetic dyes before 1860', *Endeavour* 33: 149–55.

Fishbein, M. (1937), 'Are patents on medicinal discoveries and on foods in the public interest?', *Journal of the Patent Office Society* 19 (12): 891–904.

Food and Agriculture Organization of the United Nations (1993), *Convention on Biological Diversity and Related Resolutions*, Commission on Plant Genetic Resources, Fifth session, Rome, 19–23 April 1993 [CPGR/93/Inf.3].

Fowler, C. (1994), *Unnatural Selection: Technology, Politics, and Plant Evolution*, Yverdon: Gordon and Breach.

Fransman, M. and S. Tanaka (1999), 'Visions of future technologies: government, globalisation, and universities in Japanese biotechnology', in M. Fransman (ed.), *Visions of Innovation: The Firm and Japan*, Oxford: Oxford University Press.

Freeman, C. and L. Soete. (1997), *The Economics of Industrial Innovation*, London: Pinter.

Frost, G.E. (1963), 'The case against drug patent compulsory licensing', *The Patent, Trademark and Copyright Journal of Research and Education* 7 (1): 84–102.

Funder, J. (1999), 'Rethinking patents for plant innovation', *European Intellectual Property Review* 21 (11): 551–7.

Gallochat, A. (2002), 'The criteria for patentability: where are the boundaries?', prepared for the WIPO Conference on the International Patent System, 25–7 March, Geneva.

Gaultier, G. (1997), 'The history of AIPPI', in General Secretariat of AIPPI (ed.), *AIPPI – 1897–1997 Centennial Edition: AIPPI and the Development of Industrial Property Protection 1897–1997*, Basle: AIPPI Foundation.

Geroski, P. (1995), 'Markets for technology: knowledge, innovation and appropriability', in P. Stoneman (ed.), *Handbook of the Economics of Innovation and Technological Change*, Oxford and Malden: Blackwell.

Gervais, D. (1998), *The TRIPS Agreement: A Negotiating History*, London: Sweet and Maxwell.

Gispen, K. (1989), *New Profession, Old Order: Engineers and German Society, 1815–1914*, Cambridge: Cambridge University Press.

Goodin, R.E. (1996), 'Institutions and their design', in R.E. Goodin (ed.), *The Theory of Institutional Design*, Cambridge: Cambridge University Press.

Goodman, J. and V. Walsh (2001), *The Story of Taxol: Nature and Politics in the Pursuit of an Anti-cancer Drug*, Cambridge: Cambridge University Press.

Graff, G. (2002), 'The sources of biological innovation for agriculture', PhD thesis, Department of Agricultural and Resource Economics, University of California, Berkeley.

Granstrand, O. (1999), *The Economics and Management of Intellectual Property: Towards Intellectual Capitalism*, Cheltenham, UK and Northampton, MA, USA: Edward Elgar.

Greaves, T. (ed.) (1994), *Intellectual Property Rights for Indigenous Peoples: A Sourcebook*, Oklahoma City: Society for Applied Anthropology.

Green, A.G. (1915 [1901]), 'The relative progress of the coal-tar colour industry in England and Germany during the past fifteen years', in W.M. Gardner (ed.), *The British Coal-Tar Industry: Its Origin, Development and Decline*, London: Williams and Norgate.

Greenberg, A.S. (1926), 'The lesson of the German-owned US chemical patents', *Journal of the Patent Office Society* 9 (1): 19–35.

Greengrass, B. (1989), 'UPOV and the protection of plant breeders – past developments, future perspectives', *International Review of Industrial Property and Copyright Law* 20 (5): 622–36.

Groves, P., A. Martino, C. Miskin and J. Richards (1993), *Intellectual Property and the Internal Market of the European Community*, London, Dordrecht, Boston: Graham and Trotman.

Grubb, P.W. (1999), *Patents for Chemicals, Pharmaceuticals and Biotechnology*, Oxford: Clarendon Press.

Haas, P. (1999), 'Social constructivism and the evolution of multilateral environmental governance', in J. Hart and A. Prakash (eds), *Globalization and Governance*, London: Routledge.

Haber, L.F. (1958), *The Chemical Industry during the Nineteenth Century: A Study of the Economic Aspect of Applied Chemistry in Europe and North America*, Oxford: Clarendon Press.

Hale, R.J. (1923), 'Coercion and distribution in a supposedly non-coercive state', *Political Science Quarterly* 38 (3): 470–94.

Halewood, M. (1997), 'Regulating patent holders: local working requirements and compulsory licences at international law', *Osgoode Hall Law Journal* 35 (2): 243–87.

Halewood, M. (1999), 'Indigenous and local knowledge in international law: a preface to sui generis intellectual property protection', *McGill Law Journal* 44: 953–96.

Hall, B.H. and R.M. Ham (1999), 'The determinants of patenting in the US semiconductor industry, 1980–1994', presented at the NBER Patent System and Innovation Conference, January, Santa Barbara, California.

Hancher, L. (1990), *Regulating for Competition: Government, Law, and the Pharmaceutical Industry in the United Kingdom and France*, Oxford: Clarendon Press.

Hancher, L. and M. Moran (1998), 'Organizing regulatory space', in R. Baldwin, C. Scott and C. Hood (eds), *A Reader on Regulation*, Oxford: Oxford University Press.

Harrison, B. (1997), *Lean and Mean: The Changing Landscape of Corporate Power in the Age of Flexibility*, New York and London: Guilford Press.

Haynes, W. (1945), *American Chemical Industry. Volume 2, The World War Period: 1912–22*, New York: Van Nostrand.

Hayward, P.A. (1987), *Hayward's Patent Cases 1600–1883. A Compilation of the English Patent Cases for those Years. Volume 1*, Abingdon: Professional Books Ltd.

Heitz, A. (1987), 'The history of plant variety protection', in UPOV (ed.), *The First Twenty-five Years of the International Convention for the Protection of New Varieties of Plants*, Geneva: International Union for the Protection of New Varieties of Plants.

Heller, M.A. and R.S. Eisenberg (1998), 'Can patents deter innovation? The anticommons in biomedical research', *Science* 280: 698–701.

Hendrickx, F., V. Koester and C. Prip (1993), 'Access to genetic resources: a legal analysis', *Environmental Policy and Law* 23 (6): 250–58.

Hobbelink, H. (1991), *Biotechnology and the Future of World Agriculture*, London and Atlantic Highlands: Zed Books.

Hobsbawm, E. (1995), *The Age of Extremes: The Short Twentieth Century 1914–1991*, London: Abacus.

Homburg, E. (1992), 'The emergence of research laboratories in the dyestuffs industry, 1870–1900', *British Journal for the History of Science* 25: 91–111.

Hornix, W.J. (1992), 'From process to plant: innovation in the early artificial dye industry', *British Journal for the History of Science* 25: 65–90.

Horstmeyer, M. (1998), 'The industry evolves within a political, social, and public policy context: a brief look at Britain, Germany, Japan, and the United States', in A. Arora, R. Landau and N. Rosenberg, *Chemicals and Long-term Economic Growth: Insights from the Chemical Industry*, New York, Chichester, Weinheim, Brisbane, Singapore and Toronto: John Wiley and Sons.

Howells, J. and I. Neary (1995), *Intervention and Technological Innovation: Government and the Pharmaceutical Industry in the UK and Japan*, Basingstoke and London: Macmillan.

International Human Genome Sequencing Consortium (2001), 'Initial sequencing and analysis of the human genome', *Nature* 409: 860–921.

Jackson, J.H. (1997), *The World Trading System: Law and Policy of International Economic Relations*, 2nd edn, Cambridge and London: The MIT Press.

Johnson, C. (1995), *Japan: Who Governs? The Rise of the Developmental State*, New York and London: W.W. Norton and Company.

Johnson, J.A. (1992), 'Hofmann's role in reshaping the academic–industrial alliance in German chemistry', in C. Meinel and H. Scholz (eds), *Die Allianz von Wissenschaft und Industrie August Wilhelm Hofmann (1818–1892)*, Weinheim, New York, Cambridge and Basle: VCH.

Joly, P.-B. (1999), 'Introduction: innovations and networks in biotechnology', *International Journal of Biotechnology* 1 (1): 1–9.

Jones, E. (2001), *The Business of Medicine: The Extraordinary History of Glaxo, a Baby Food Producer, Which Became One of the World's Most Successful Pharmaceutical Companies*, London: Profile Books.

Judson, H.F. (1996), *The Eighth Day of Creation: Makers of the Revolution in Biology*, expanded edn, Plainview: Cold Spring Harbor Laboratory Press.

Kaitin, K.I. (2000), *Don't Turn Back the Clock on Drug Regulatory Reform*, Boston: Tufts Center for the Study of Drug Development.

Kate, K. ten and S.A. Laird (1999), *The Commercial Use of Biodiversity: Access to Genetic Resources and Benefit Sharing*, London: Earthscan.

Kaufer, E. (1980), *The Economics of the Patent System*, Chur: Harwood Academic Publishers.

Kay, L.E. (1993), *The Molecular Vision of Life: Caltech, the Rockefeller Foundation, and the Rise of the New Biology*, New York and Oxford: Oxford University Press.

Kay, L.E. (2000), *Who Wrote the Book of Life? A History of the Genetic Code*, Stanford: Stanford University Press.

Kefauver, E., with the assistance of I. Till (1966), *In a Few Hands: Monopoly Power in America*, Harmondsworth: Penguin Books.

Kemman, H.A. (1961), 'Foreign patent relations: abstruse or simple?', *Journal of the Patent Office Society* 43 (11): 735–42.

Kenney, M. (1986), *Biotechnology: The University-Industrial Complex*, New Haven: Yale University Press.

Kenwood, A.G. and A.L. Lougheed (1999), *The Growth of the International Economy: 1820–2000*, 4th edn, London and New York: Routledge.

Kevles, D.J. (1994), 'Ananda Chakrabarty wins a patent: biotechnology, law, and society, 1972–1980', *Historical Studies in the Physical and Biological Sciences* 25 (1): 111–35.

Kevles, D.J. (2001), 'Patenting life: a historical overview of law, interests, and ethics', prepared for the Legal Theory Workshop, 20 December, Yale Law School.

Khan, B.Z. (2002), *Intellectual Property and Economic Development: Lessons from American and European History*, London: Commission on Intellectual Property Rights.

Khan, B.Z. and K.L. Sokoloff (1998), 'Patent institutions, industrial organization and early technological change: Britain and the United States, 1790–1850', in M. Berg and K. Bruland (eds), *Technological Revolutions in Europe: Historical Perspectives*, Cheltenham, UK and Northampton, MA, USA: Edward Elgar.

Klauer, G. (1936), 'The new German Patent Law', *Journal of the Patent Office Society* 18 (8): 481–500.

Kloppenburg, J. Jr. (1988), *First the Seed: The Political Economy of Plant Biotechnology*, Cambridge: Cambridge University Press.

Kornberg, A. (1995), *The Golden Helix: Inside Biotech Ventures*, Sausalito: University Science Books.

Kronstein, H. and I. Till (1947), 'A reevaluation of the international patent convention', *Law and Contemporary Problems* 12: 765–81.

Krosin, K. (1985), 'Are plants patentable under the Utility Patent Act?', *Journal of the Patent and Trademark Office Society* 67 (5): 220–38.

Kryder, R.D., S.P. Kowalski and A.F. Krattiger (2000), 'The intellectual and technical property components of pro-Vitamin A rice (GoldenRice™)' (ISAAA Brief 20), International Society for the Acquisition of Agri-biotech Applications, Ithaca.

Ladas, S. (1930), *The International Protection of Industrial Property. Volume 1*, Cambridge: Harvard University Press.

Ladas, S.P. (1975), *Patents, Trademarks, and Related Rights: National and International Protection. Volume 1*, Cambridge: Harvard University Press.

Lane, J.E. (1995), *The Public Sector: Concepts, Models and Approaches*, 2nd edn, London, Newbury Park and New Delhi: Sage Publications.

Lange, P. (1997), 'The non-patentability of plant varieties. The Decision of the Technical Board of Appeal 3.3.4 of February 21, 1995-T 356/93', *Plant Variety Protection* (83): 25–33.

Lederer, F. (1999), 'Equivalence of chemical product patents', *International Review of Industrial Property and Copyright Law* 30 (3): 275–84.

Le Fanu, J. (1999), *The Rise and Fall of Modern Medicine*, London: Little, Brown and Co.

Lesser, W.H. and R.T. Masson (1983), *An Economic Analysis of the Plant Variety Protection Act*, Washington, DC: American Seed Trade Association.

Lessig, L. (2001), *The Future of Ideas: The Fate of the Commons in a Connected World*, New York: Random House.

Levin, R.C., A.K. Klevorick, R.R. Nelson and S.G. Winter (1987), 'Appropriating the returns from industrial research and development', *Brookings Papers on Economic Activity*: 783–820.

Lewers, A.M. (1922), 'Composition of matter', *Journal of the Patent Office Society* 4 (11): 530–53.

Liebenau, J. (1984), 'Industrial R&D in pharmaceutical firms in the twentieth century', *Business History* 26 (3): 329–46.

Litman, J. (2001), *Digital Copyright*, Amherst: Prometheus Books.

Llewelyn, M. (1995), 'Article 53 revisited: Greenpeace v. Plant Genetic Systems NV', *European Intellectual Property Review* 17 (10): 506–11.

Llewelyn, M. (2000), 'The patentability of biological material: continuing contradiction and confusion', *European Intellectual Property Review* 22 (5): 191–7.

Long, C. (1999), 'Patents and innovation in biotechnology and genomics', in N. Imparato (ed.), *Capital for our Time: The Economic, Legal, and Management Challenges of Intellectual Capital*, Stanford: Hoover Institution Press.

Lynfield, H.G. (1969), 'The new French patent law', *IDEA* 13 (2): 201–10.

Macdonald, S. (2001), 'Exploring the hidden costs of patents' (QUNO Occasional Paper No. 4), Quaker United Nations Office, Geneva.

Machlup, F. and E. Penrose (1950), 'The Patent Controversy in the Nineteenth Century', *Journal of Economic History* 10 (1): 1–29.

MacLeod, C. (1988), *Inventing the Industrial Revolution: The English Patent System, 1660–1800*, Cambridge: Cambridge University Press.

MacLeod, C. (1991), 'The paradoxes of patenting: invention and its diffusion in 18th and 19th century Britain, France, and North America', *Technology and Culture* 32 (4): 885–911.

Majone, G. (1996), *Regulating Europe*, London and New York: Routledge.

Makkai, T. and J. Braithwaite (1998), 'In and out of the revolving door: making sense of regulatory capture', in R. Baldwin, C. Scott and C. Hood (eds), *A Reader on Regulation*, Oxford: Oxford University Press.

Mann, C.C. and M.L. Plummer (1991), *The Aspirin Wars: Money, Medicine, and 100 Years of Rampant Competition*, Cambridge: Harvard Business School Publications.

Mann, J. (1999), *The Elusive Magic Bullet: The Search for the Perfect Drug*, Oxford: Oxford University Press.

Mansfield, E. (1986), 'Patents and innovation: an empirical study', *Management Science* 32(2): 173–81.

March, J.G. and J.P. Olson (1984), 'The new institutionalism: organizational factors in political life', *American Political Science Review* 78: 738–49.

Maskus, K.E. (1998), 'The role of intellectual property rights in encouraging foreign direct investment and technology transfer', *Duke Journal of Comparative and International Law* 9 (1): 109–61.

May, C. (2000), *A Global Economy of Intellectual Property Rights: The New Enclosures*, London: Routledge.

McGrath, M. (1996), 'The patent provisions in TRIPS: protecting reasonable remuneration for services rendered – or the latest development in Western colonialism?', *European Intellectual Property Review* 18 (7): 398–403.

McKelvey, M. (1996), *Evolutionary Innovations: The Business of Biotechnology*, Oxford: Oxford University Press.

Menell, P.S. (1994), 'The challenges of reforming intellectual property protection for computer software', *Columbia Law Review* 94 (8): 2644–54.

Mercuro, N. and S.G. Medema (1997), *Economics and the Law: From Posner to Post-modernism*, Princeton: Princeton University Press.

Merges, R.P. (1996), 'Contracting into liability rules: intellectual property rights and collective rights organizations', *California Law Review* 84 (5): 1293–1386.

Merges, R.P. (1997), *Patent Law and Policy: Cases and Materials*, 2nd edn, Charlottesville: Michie Law Publishers.

Merges, R.P. (2000), 'Intellectual property rights and the new institutional economics', *Vanderbilt Law Review* 53 (6): 1857–77.

Merges, R.P. and R.R. Nelson (1990), 'On the complex economics of patent scope', *Columbia Law Review* 90: 839–916.

Meyer-Thurow, G. (1982), 'The industrialization of invention: a case study from the German chemical industry', *ISIS* 73: 363–81.

Millstone, E. (2002), 'The globalisation of environmental and consumer protection regulation: resources and accountability', in H. Lawton-Smith (ed.), *The Regulation of Science and Technology*, Basingstoke: Palgrave.

Moody, G. (2002), *Rebel Code: Linux and the Open Source Revolution*, London: Penguin Books.

Mooney, P.R. (1979), *Seeds of the Earth: Private or Public Resource?*, Ottawa: Canadian Council for International Cooperation and International Coalition for Development Action.

Mooney, P.R. (1996), *The Parts of Life: Agricultural Biodiversity, Indigenous Knowledge, and the Role of the Third System. Development Dialogue. Special Issue (1996:1–2)*, Dag Hammarskjöld Foundation, Uppsala.

Morange, M. (1998), *A History of Molecular Biology*, Cambridge: Harvard University Press.

Moufang, R. (1998), 'The concept of "ordre public" and morality in patent law', in G. van Overwalle (ed.), *Octrooirecht, Ethiek en Biotechnologie/Patent Law, Ethics and Biotechnology/Droit des Brevets, Ethique et Biotechnologie*, Brussels: Bruylant.

Mowery, D.C. and N. Rosenberg (1998), *Paths of Innovation: Technological Change in 20th Century America*, Cambridge: Cambridge University Press.

Mundo, P.A. (1999), *National Politics in a Global Economy: The Domestic Sources of US Trade Policy*, Washington, DC: Georgetown University Press.

Murmann, J.P. and R. Landau (1998), 'On the making of competitive advantage: the development of the chemical industries of Britain and Germany since 1850', in A. Arora, R. Landau and N. Rosenberg (eds), *Chemicals and Long-term Economic Growth: Insights from the Chemical Industry*, New York: John Wiley and Sons.

Mytelka, L.K. and T. Tesfachew (1998), 'The role of policy in promoting enterprise learning during early industrialization: lessons for African countries', UNCTAD, Geneva.

Nastelski, K. (1984), 'Product protection for chemical inventions in Germany', *International Review of Industrial Property and Copyright Law* 3 (3): 267–94.

Nicolai, T.R. (1972), 'First-to-file vs. first-to-invent: a comparative study based on German and United States patent law', *International Review of Industrial Property and Copyright Law* 3 (2): 103–39.

Noble, D.F. (1977), *America by Design: Science, Technology, and the Rise of Corporate Capitalism*, New York: Alfred A. Knopf.

North, D.C. (1990), *Institutions, Institutional Change and Economic Performance*, Cambridge: Cambridge University Press.

North, D.C. (1991), 'Institutions', *Journal of Economic Perspectives* 5 (1): 97–112.

Orbinski, J. (2001), 'Health, equity, and trade: a failure in global governance', in G.P. Sampson (ed.), *The Role of the World Trade Organization in Global Governance*, Tokyo: United Nations University.

Overwalle, G. van (1999), 'Patent protection for plants: a comparison of American and European approaches', *IDEA – The Journal of Law and Technology* 39 (2): 143–93.

Owen, B.M. and R. Braeutigam (1978), *The Regulation Game: Strategic Use of the Administrative Process*, Cambridge: Ballinger Publishing.

Owen, G. (1999), *From Empire to Europe: The Decline and Revival of British Industry Since the Second World War*, London: HarperCollins.

Owens, L. (1991), 'Patents, the "frontiers" of American invention, and the Monopoly Committee of 1939: anatomy of a discourse', *Technology and Culture* 32 (4): 1076–93.

Patel, P. and K. Pavitt (1995), 'Patterns of technological activity: their measurement and interpretation', in P. Stoneman (ed.), *Handbook of the Economics of Innovation and Technological Change*, Oxford and Malden: Blackwell.

Patel, S. (1989), 'Intellectual property rights in the Uruguay Round: A disaster for the South?', *Economic and Political Weekly* 24: 978–93.

Paterson, G. (2002), 'The creation of harmonised patent protection in Europe', in H. Lawton-Smith (ed.), *The Regulation of Science and Technology*, Basingstoke: Palgrave.

Penrose, E.T. (1951), *The Economics of the International Patent System*, Baltimore: Johns Hopkins University Press.

Perkin, W.H. (1915), 'The position of the organic chemical industry', in W.M. Gardner (ed.), *The British Coal-Tar Industry: Its Origin, Development and Decline*, London: Williams and Norgate.

Peters, B.G. (1999), *Institutional Theory in Political Science: The 'New Institutionalism'*, London and New York: Pinter.

Pistorius, R. and J. van Wijk (1999), *The Exploitation of Plant Genetic Information: Political Strategies in Crop Development*, Wallingford and New York: CABI Publishing.

Playfair, L. (1852), *Industrial Instruction on the Continent*, London: George E. Eyre and William Spottiswoode.

Plotkin, M.J. (2000), *Medicine Quest: In Search of Nature's Healing Secrets*, New York: Viking Penguin.

Pope, W.J. (1917), 'The national importance of chemistry', in A.C. Seward (ed.), *Science and the Nation*, Cambridge: Cambridge University Press.

Porter, R. (1997), *The Greatest Benefit to Mankind: A Medical History of Humanity from Antiquity to the Present*, London: HarperCollins.

Posey, D.A. (1990), 'Intellectual property rights: what is the position of ethnobiology?', *Journal of Ethnobiology* 10: 93–8.

Posey, D.A. and G. Dutfield (1996), *Beyond Intellectual Property: Toward Traditional Resource Rights for Indigenous Peoples and Local Communities*, Ottawa: International Development Research Centre.

Powell, W.W. (1999), 'The social construction of an organizational field: the case of biotechnology', *International Journal of Biotechnology* 1 (1): 42–66.

Principe, P. (1998), 'Economics and medicinal plants', in T.R. Tomlinson and O. Olayiwola Akerele (eds), *Medicinal Plants: Their Role in Health and Biodiversity*, Philadelphia: University of Pennsylvania Press.

Rabinow, P. (1996), *Making PCR: A Story of Biotechnology*, Chicago: University of Chicago Press.

Rai, A.K. (1999), 'Intellectual property rights in biotechnology: addressing new technology', *Wake Forest Law Review* 34: 827–47.

Rangnekar, D. (2000), 'Planned obsolescence and plant breeding: empirical evidence from wheat breeding in the UK (1965–1995)' (Economics Discussion Paper 00/8), Faculty of Human Sciences, Kingston University, Kingston upon Thames.

Rangnekar, D. (2002), 'Access to genetic resources, gene-based inventions and agriculture', Commission on Intellectual Property Rights, London.

Rapp, R.T. and R.P. Rozek (1990), 'Benefits and costs of intellectual property protection in developing countries', *Journal of World Trade* 24 (5): 75–102.

Reed, P. (1992), 'The British chemical industry and the indigo trade', *British Journal for the History of Science* 25: 113–25.

Reekie, W.D. and M.H. Weber (1979), *Profits, Politics and Drugs*, London: Macmillan.

Ricupero, R. (2001), 'Rebuilding confidence in the multilateral trading system: closing the "legitimacy gap"', in G.P. Sampson (ed.), *The Role of the World Trade Organization in Global Governance*, Tokyo: United Nations University.

Rivette, K.G. and D. Kline (2000), 'Discovering new value in intellectual property', *Harvard Business Review* (Jan.–Feb.): 54–66.

Robbins, L.J. (1961), 'The proposed new European patent', *The Patent, Trademark, and Copyright Journal of Research and Education* 5 (3): 217–32.

Robbins-Roth, C. (2000), *From Alchemy to IPO: The Business of Biotechnology*, Cambridge: Perseus Publishing.

Roe, J.E. (1943), 'War measures, the alien property custodian and patents', *Journal of the Patent Office Society* 25 (10): 692–728.

Roffe, P. (2000), 'The political economy of intellectual property rights – an historical perspective', in J. Faundez, M.E. Footer and J.J. Norton (eds), *Governance, Development and Globalization: A Tribute to Lawrence Tshuma*, London, Blackstone Press.

Rogan, J.E. (2002), 'The global recognition of patents: an agenda for the 21st century', prepared for the WIPO Conference on the International Patent System, 25–27 March, Geneva (*http://www.us-mission.ch/press2002/0326rogan.htm*).

Rollins, A.D. (1983), 'Novelty of metabolic product', *Journal of the Patent Office Society* 65 (7): 403–7.

Rories, C.C.P. (2001), 'Does the USPTO have authority to grant patents for novel varieties of sexually reproducing plants?', *Journal of the Patent and Trademark Office Society* 83 (10): 737–58.

Rose, M. (1993), *Authors and Owners: The Invention of Copyright*, Cambridge and London: Harvard University Press.

Rossman, J. (1931), 'Plant patents', *Journal of the Patent Office Society* 13 (1): 7–21.

Roy, W.G. (1997), *Socializing Capital: The Rise of the Large Industrial Corporation in America*, Princeton: Princeton University Press.

Ryan, M.P. (1998), *Knowledge Diplomacy: Global Competition and the Politics of Intellectual Property*, Washington, DC: Brookings Institution Press.

Sager, A. and D. Socolar (2001), 'Study of job data reveals drug makers' priorities – drug industry marketing staff soars while research staffing stagnates', Boston University School of Public Health, Boston.

Satchell, R.D. (1970), 'Chemical product patent practice in the United Kingdom', *International Review of Industrial Property and Copyright Law* 1 (2): 179–89.

Scherer, F.M. and S. Weisburst (1995), 'Economic effects of strengthening pharmaceutical patent protection in Italy', *International Review of Industrial Property and Copyright Law* 26 (6): 1009–24.

Schiff, E. (1971), *Industrialization without Patents: The Netherlands, 1869–1912, Switzerland, 1850–1907*, Princeton: Princeton University Press.

Schumpeter, J.A. (1983[1934]), *The Theory of Economic Development: An Inquiry into Profits, Capital, Credit, Interest, and the Business Cycle*, New Brunswick: Transaction Publishers.

Scotchmer, S. (1991), 'Standing on the shoulders of giants: cumulative research and the patent law', *Journal of Economic Perspectives* 5 (1): 29–41.

Scott, W.R. (1995), *Institutions and Organizations*, Thousand Oaks, London and New Delhi: Sage Publications.

Sehgal, S. (1996), 'IPR driven restructuring of the seed industry', *Biotechnology and Development Monitor*, December (29): 18–21.

Sell, S.K. (1998), *Power and Ideas: North–South Politics of Intellectual Property and Antitrust, Suny Series in Global Politics*, Albany: State University of New York Press.

Sell, S.K. (1999), 'Multinational corporations as agents of change: the globalization of intellectual property rights', in A.C. Cutler, V. Haufler and T. Porter (eds), *Private Authority and International Affairs*, Albany: State University of New York Press.

Senker, J. (1998), *Biotechnology and Competitive Advantage: Europe's Firms and the US Challenge*, Cheltenham, UK and Northampton, MA, USA: Edward Elgar.

Senker, J. and P. van Zwanenberg (2001), 'Final report: European biotechnology innovation systems', European Commission, Brussels (*http://www.sussex.ac.uk/spru/biotechnology/ebis/ebisfinalreport.pdf*).

Sherman, B. and L. Bently (1999), *The Making of Modern Intellectual Property Law: The British Experience, 1760–1911*, Cambridge: Cambridge University Press.

Shiva, V. (1996), 'Agricultural biodiversity, intellectual property rights and farmers' rights', *Economic and Political Weekly* 31: 1621–31.

Silverman, A. (1990), 'Intellectual property law and the venture capital process', *High Technology Law Journal* 5 (1): 157–92.

Simon, C. (1998), 'The rise of the Swiss chemical industry reconsidered', in E. Homburg, A.S. Travis and H.G. Schröter (eds), *The Chemical Industry in Europe, 1850–1914: Industrial Growth, Pollution, and Professionalization*, Dordrecht and Norwell: Kluwer Academic.

Slinn, J. (1995), 'Research and development in the UK pharmaceutical industry from the nineteenth century to the 1960s', in R. Porter and M. Teich (eds), *Drugs and Narcotics in History*, Cambridge: Cambridge University Press.

Sneader, W. (1985), *Drug Discovery: The Evolution of Modern Medicines*, Chichester, New York, Brisbane, Toronto, Singapore: John Wiley and Sons.

Spooner, L. (1971 [1855]), 'The law of intellectual property; or an essay on the right of authors and inventors to a perpetual property in their ideas', in C. Shively (ed.), *The Collected Works of Lysander Spooner. Volume 1*, Weston: M&S Press.

Spooner, L. (1884), 'A letter to scientists and inventors on the science of justice, and their rights of perpetual property in their discoveries and inventions', Cupples, Upham and Co., Boston.

Steele, H. (1962), 'Monopoly and competition in the ethical drugs market', *Journal of Law and Economics* 5: 131–64.

Steen, K. (1995), 'Confiscated commerce: American importers of German organic chemicals, 1914–1929', *History and Technology* 12: 261–84.

Stein, E. (1964), 'Assimilation of national laws as a function of European integration', *American Journal of International Law* 58: 1–40.

Sterckx, S. (ed.) (1997), *Biotechnology, Morality and Patents*, Aldershot: Ashgate.

Stigler, G. (1971), 'The Theory of Economic Regulation', *Bell Journal of Economics and Management Science* 2: 1–21.

Stolz, R. and R. Schwaiberger (1987), 'The correlation between dye chemistry and pharmacy in creating the modern chemotherapy', *History and Technology* 3: 193–203.

Stone, T. and G. Darlington (2000), *Pills, Potions and Poisons: How Drugs Work*, Oxford: Oxford University Press.

Strathern, M. (1999), *Property, Substance and Effect: Anthropological Essays on Persons and Things*, London and Brunswick: Athlone Press.

Straus, J. (1987), 'The relationship between plant variety protection and patent protection for biotechnological inventions from an international viewpoint', *International Review of Industrial Property and Copyright Law* 18 (6): 723–37.

Straus, J. (1998), 'The Rio Biodiversity Convention and intellectual property', *International Review of Industrial Property and Copyright Law* 29 (5): 602–15.

Sung, L.M. and D.J. Pelto (1998), 'The biotechnology patent landscape in the United States as we enter the new millennium', *Journal of World Intellectual Property* 1 (6): 889–901.

Taylor, C.T. and Z.A. Silberston (1973), *The Economic Impact of the Patent System: The British Experience*, Cambridge: Cambridge University Press.

Temin, P. (1979), 'Technology, regulation, and market structure in the modern pharmaceutical industry', *The Bell Journal of Economics* 10: 429–46.

Thomas, L.G. (1994), 'Implicit industrial policy: the triumph of Britain and the failure of France in global pharmaceuticals', *Industrial and Corporate Change* 3 (2): 451–89.

Thornström, C.-G. and U. Hossfeld (2002), 'Instant appropriation – Heinz Brücher and the SS botanical collecting commando to Russia 1943', *Plant Genetic Resources Newsletter* (129): 39–42.

Tobin, B. (1997), 'Certificates of origin: a role for IPR regimes in securing prior informed consent', in J. Mugabe, C.V. Barber, G. Henne, L. Glowka and A. La Viña (eds), *Access to Genetic Resources: Strategies for Sharing Benefits*, Nairobi: ACTS Press.

Travis, A.S. (1993), *The Rainbow Makers: Origins of the Synthetic Dyestuffs Industry in Western Europe*, Lehigh, PA: Lehigh University Press.

Trebilcock, M.J. and R. Howse (1999), *The Regulation of International Trade*, 2nd edn, London and New York: Routledge.

Tudge, C. (2000), *In Mendel's Footnotes: An Introduction to the Science and Technologies of Genes and Genetics from the Nineteenth Century to the Twenty-Second*, London: Jonathan Cape.

Tufts Center for the Study of Drug Development (2001), 'Backgrounder: a methodology for counting costs for pharmaceutical R&D', Tufts Center for the Study of Drug Development, Boston.

Tunzelman, G.N. von (1995), *Technology and Industrial Progress: Foundations for Economic Growth*, Cheltenham, UK and Lyme, US: Edward Elgar.

Uemura, S. (2000), 'WIPO update: patent law harmonization and the grace period', *CASRIP Publication Series: Rethinking Intellectual Property* 6: 263–70.

Varma, A. and D. Abraham (1996), 'DNA is different: legal obviousness and the balance between biotech inventors and the market', *Harvard Journal of Law and Technology* 9: 53–85.

Vaughan, F.L. (1951), 'Important differences in US and UK patent systems', *Journal of the Patent Office Society* 33 (11): 779–99.

Veblen, T. (1923), *Absentee Ownership and Business Enterprise in Recent Times*, New York: Huebsch.

Vellvé, R. (1992), *Saving the Seed: Genetic Diversity and European Agriculture*, London: Earthscan.

Venter, J.C. *et al.* (2001), 'The sequence of the human genome', *Science* 291: 1304–51.

Verma, S.K. (1995), 'TRIPS and plant variety protection in developing countries', *European Intellectual Property Review* 17 (6): 281–9.

Vojáček, J. (1936), *A Survey of the Principal National Patent Systems*, London: Sir Isaac Pitman and Sons.

Warren-Jones, A. (2001), *Patenting rDNA: Human and Animal Biotechnology in the United Kingdom and Europe*, Witney: Lawtext Publishing.

Watal, J. (2001), *Intellectual Property Rights in the WTO and Developing Countries*, New Delhi: Oxford University Press.

Watson, J.D. and F.H.C. Crick (1953), 'A structure for deoxyribose nucleic acid', *Nature* 171: 737–8.

Weatherall, M. (1990), *In Search of a Cure: A History of Pharmaceutical Discovery*, Oxford: Oxford University Press.

Webster, T. (1844), *Reports and Notes of Cases on Letters Patent for Inventions*, London: Thomas Blenkarn.

Wegner, H. (1993), *Patent Harmonization*, London: Sweet and Maxwell.

Weiner, C. (1989), 'Patenting and academic research: historical case studies', in V. Weil and J.W. Snapper (eds), *Owning Scientific and Technical Information*, New Brunswick and London: Rutgers University Press.

Wengenroth, U. (1997), 'Germany: competition abroad – cooperation at home, 1870–1900', in A.D. Chandler, F. Amatori and T. Hikino (eds), *Big Business and the Wealth of Nations*, Cambridge: Cambridge University Press.

Werth, B. (1994), *The Billion-dollar Molecule: One Company's Quest for the Perfect Drug*, New York: Touchstone.

Wijk, J. van, J.I. Cohen and J. Komen (1993), 'Intellectual Property Rights for Agricultural Biotechnology: Options and Implications for Developing Countries', ISNAR Research Report No. 3. International Centre for National Agricultural Research, The Hague.

Wilmut, I., K. Campbell and C. Tudge (2000), *The Second Creation: The Age of Biological Control by the Scientists Who Cloned Dolly*, London: Headline Book Publishing.

Wimmer, W. (1998), 'Innovation in the German pharmaceutical industry, 1880 to 1920', in E. Homburg, A.S. Travis and H.G. Schröter, *The Chemical Industry in Europe, 1850–1914: Industrial Growth, Pollution, and Professionalization*, Dordrecht and Norwell: Kluwer Academic.

Winter, G. (1992), 'Patent law policy in biotechnology', *Journal of Environmental Law* 4 (2): 167–87.

Wuesthoff, F. (1957), 'Patenting of plants', *Industrial Property Quarterly* (2): 12–30.

Žigić, K. (2000), 'Strategic trade policy, intellectual property rights protection, and North–South trade', *Journal of Development Economics* 61: 27–60.

Corporate and Interest Group Documents

American Pharmaceutical Association (1919), 'Report of the Committee on Patents and Trademarks of the American Pharmaceutical Association, August 1919', *Journal of the Patent Office Society* 2 (1): 76–82.

Association Internationale pour la Protection de la Propriété Industrielle (AIPPI) (1988), *Annuaire 1988/II – Comité Exécutif, Conseil des Présidents de Sydney 1988 (10–15 Avril 1988)*, Basle: AIPPI.

Bristol-Myers Squibb (2001), *Annual Report, 2000* (*http://www.bms.com/annual/2000ar/annual_site/fiancials/data/financial.html*).

Chartered Institute of Patent Agents (CIPA) (1998), 'Briefing paper – patenting in the pharmaceutical industry – Supplementary Protection Certificates', CIPA, London.

European Federation of Pharmaceutical Industries and Associations (EFPIA) (1998), *The Pharmaceutical Industry in Figures. 1998 Edition*, Brussels: EFPIA.

European Federation of Pharmaceutical Industries and Associations (EFPIA) (1999), 'Position paper – WTO Millennium Round', EFPIA, Brussels.

Pharmaceutical Research and Manufacturers of America (PhRMA) (1998), *Industry Profile. 1998 Edition*, Washington: PhRMA.

Pharmaceutical Research and Manufacturers of America (PhRMA) (1999), *Annual Report 1999–2000*, Washington: PhRMA.

Stewart, F.C. (1919), 'Letter to M.H. Coulston, President of the Patent Office Society', *Journal of the Patent Office Society* 2 (1): 73–5.

Wuesthoff, F. and F. Wuesthoff (1952), 'Protection of new varieties of cultivated plants. Vienna Congress 1952 of the International Association for the Protection of Industrial Property. Report in the name of the German Group'.

Civil Society Organization Documents

Cameron, J. and Z. Makuch (1995), *The UN Biodiversity Convention and the WTO TRIPS Agreement: Recommendations to Avoid Conflict and Promote Sustainable Development*, Gland: World Wide Fund For Nature.

Consumer Project on Technology, Essential Action, Oxfam, Treatment Access Campaign and Health Gap (2001), 'Comment on the Attaran/Gillespie-White and PhRMA surveys of patents on antiretroviral drugs in Africa' (*http://www.cptech.org/ip/health/africa/dopatentsmatterinafrica.html*).

ETC Group (2001), 'Globalization, Inc. concentration in corporate power: the unmentioned agenda', *ETC Group Communiqué* (71).

Genetic Resources Action International (GRAIN) (2001), '"TRIPS-plus" through the back door: how bilateral treaties impose much stronger rules for IPRs on life than the WTO', GRAIN, Barcelona.

Hunt, M. (2002), *Changing Patterns of Pharmaceutical Innovation*, Washington, DC: National Institute of Health Care Management Research and Educational Foundation.

Médecins Sans Frontières (MSF) and Drugs for Neglected Diseases (DND) Working Group (2001), *Fatal Imbalance: The Crisis in Research and Development for Drugs for Neglected Diseases*, Geneva: MSF and DND Working Group.

National Consumer Council (NCC) (1991), 'Intellectual Property: The Consumer View of Patents, Copyright, Trade Marks and Allied Rights' (International Trade and the Consumer Working Paper No. 6), NCC, London.

Nuffield Council on Bioethics (1999), *Genetically Modified Crops: The Ethical and Social Issues*, London: Nuffield Council on Bioethics.

Oxfam (2001), *Patent Injustice: How World Trade Rules Threaten the Health of the Poor*, Oxford: Oxfam.

Public Citizen (2001), *Rx R&D Myths: The Case Against the Drug Industry's 'R&D Scare Card'*, Washington, DC: Public Citizen.

Society, Religion and Technology Project of the Church of Scotland (1997), 'Ethical concerns about patenting in relation to living organisms: a summary of a submission to the European Commission and the European Parliament on the EC draft Patenting Directive', SRT Project, Edinburgh.

Tansey, G. (1999), *Trade, Intellectual Property, Food and Biodiversity: Key Issues and Options for the 1999 Review of Article 27.3(b) of the TRIPS Agreement*, London: Quaker Peace and Service.

Yamin, F. (1995), *The Biodiversity Convention and Intellectual Property Rights*, Gland: World Wide Fund for Nature.

Government Documents

Commission on Intellectual Property Rights (1997), *Towards the Era of Intellectual Creation: Challenges for Breakthrough. The Report of the Commission on Intellectual Property Rights in the Twenty-first Century*, Tokyo: JPO (*http://www.jpo.go.jp/tousie/21cene.htm*).

Japan Patent Office (2000), *Examination Guidelines for Patent and Utility Model*, Tokyo: JPO (*http://www.jpo.go.jp/infoe/1312-002_e.htm*).

Office of Technology Assessment of the United States Congress (OTA) (1989), *New Developments in Biotechnology: Patenting Life – Special Report*, Washington, DC: US Government Printing Office.

Quigg, D.J. (1987), 'Animals – patentability', *Journal of the Patent and Trademark Office Society* 69 (6): 328.

United Kingdom Board of Trade (1901), *Report of the Committee Appointed by the Board of Trade to Inquire into the Working of the Patents Acts on Certain Specified Questions ('The Fry Committee')*, London: HMSO.

United Kingdom Board of Trade (1931), *Report of the Departmental Commission on the Patents and Designs Acts and Practice of the Patent Office ('The Sargant Committee')*, London: HMSO.

United Kingdom Board of Trade (1947), *Patents and Designs Acts. Final Report of the Departmental Committee ('The Swan Committee')*, London: HMSO.

United Kingdom Board of Trade (1970), *The British Patent System: Report of the Committee to Examine the Patent System and Patent Law ('The Banks Committee')*, London: HMSO.

United Kingdom Department of Health (2001), *Pharmaceutical Industry Competitiveness Task Force. Final Report – March 2001*, London: Department of Health.

United Kingdom Ministry of Health (1967), *Report of the Committee of Enquiry into the Relationship of the Pharmaceutical Industry with the National Health Service, 1954–1967 ('The Sainsbury Committee')*, London: HMSO.

United States Patent and Trademark Office (2001), 'Utility examination guidelines', *Federal Register* 66 (4): 1092–99 (*http://www.uspto.gov/web/offices/com/sol/notices/utilexmguide.pdf*).

Intergovernmental Organization Documents

Bureaux Internationaux Réunis de la Protection de la Propriété Intellectuelle (BIRPI) (1958), *Documents de la Conférence de Lisbonne. Documents Anglais Nos. 201–323*.

Organization for Economic Cooperation and Development (OECD) (1996), *National Accounts 1960–1994. Vol. 2, Detailed Tables*, Paris: OECD.

United Nations Commission on Human Rights – Sub-Commission on the Promotion and Protection of Human Rights (2000), 'Intellectual property and human rights' – Resolution 2001/21. [E/CN.4/Sub.2/RES/2000/7].

United Nations Commission on Human Rights – Sub-Commission on the Promotion and Protection of Human Rights (2001a), 'Intellectual property rights and human rights. Report of the Secretary-General' [E/CN.4/Sub.2/2001/12].

United Nations Commission on Human Rights, Sub-Commission on the Promotion and Protection of Human Rights (2001b), 'The impact of the Agreement on Trade-Related Aspects of Intellectual Property Rights on human rights. Report of the High Commissioner' [E/CN.4/Sub.2/2001/13].

United Nations Commission on Human Rights, Sub-Commission on the Promotion and Protection of Human Rights (2001c), 'Intellectual property and human rights' – Resolution 2001/21 [E/CN.4/Sub.2/RES/2001/21].

United Nations Conference on Trade and Development (1974), 'The role of the patent system in the transfer of technology to developing countries', UNCTAD, Geneva.

United Nations Conference on Trade and Development (1975), 'The international patent system as an instrument for national development', UNCTAD, Geneva.

United Nations Conference on Trade and Development (2000), 'Elements of a positive agenda', in UNCTAD (ed.), *Positive Trade Agenda for Developing Countries: Issues for Future Trade Negotiations*, Geneva: UNCTAD.

United Nations Development Programme (1999), *Human Development Report 1999*, New York and Oxford: UNDP and Oxford University Press.

The World Bank (2001), *Global Economic Prospects and the Developing Countries 2002: Making Trade Work for the World's Poor*, Washington, DC: The World Bank.

World Health Organization (1996), 'Investing in health research and development: report of the ad hoc committee on health research relating to future intervention options', WHO, Geneva.

World Intellectual Property Organization (2000), 'Matters concerning intellectual property and genetic resources, traditional knowledge and folklore. Document prepared by the Secretariat' [WO/GA/26/6].

World Intellectual Property Organization (2001), *Intellectual Property Needs and Expectations of Traditional Knowledge Holders. WIPO Report on Fact-finding Missions on Intellectual Property and Traditional Knowledge 1998–1999*, Geneva: WIPO.

World Intellectual Property Organization (2002), 'Elements of a sui generis system for the protection of traditional knowledge. Document prepared by the Secretariat' [WIPO/GRTKF/IC/3/8].

World Intellectual Property Organization – Standing Committee on the Law of Patents (1999), 'Protection of biological and genetic resources. Proposal by the Delegation of Colombia' [SCP/3/10].

World Trade Organization – General Council (1998), 'Preparations for the 1999 Ministerial Conference. General Council discussion on mandated negotiations and the built-in agenda, 23 November 1998. Communication from the United States' [WT/GC/W/115].

World Trade Organization – General Council (1999a), 'Preparations for the 1999 Ministerial Conference. EC approach to trade-related aspects of intellectual property in the new round. Communication from the European Communities' [WT/GC/W/193].

World Trade Organization – General Council (1999b), 'Preparations for the 1999 Ministerial Conference. Proposal on trade-related aspects of intellectual property. Communication from Japan' [WT/GC/W/242].

World Trade Organization – General Council (1999c), 'Preparations for the 1999 Ministerial Conference. Implementation issues to be addressed before/at Seattle. Communication from Cuba, Dominican Republic, Egypt, El Salvador, Honduras, India, Indonesia, Malaysia, Nigeria, Pakistan, Sri Lanka and Uganda' [WT/GC/W/354].

World Trade Organization – General Council (1999d), 'Preparations for the 1999 Ministerial Conference. Implementation issues to be addressed in the first year of negotiations. Communication from Cuba, Dominican Republic, Egypt, El Salvador, Honduras, India, Indonesia, Malaysia, Nigeria, Pakistan, Sri Lanka and Uganda' [WT/GC/W/355].

World Trade Organization – General Council (1999e), 'Preparations for the 1999 Ministerial Conference. Proposals regarding the TRIPS Agreement (Paragraph 9(*a*)(ii) of the Geneva Ministerial Declaration). Communication from Venezuela' [WT/GC/W/282].

World Trade Organization – General Council (1999f), 'Preparations for the 1999 Ministerial Conference. Proposal on protection of the intellectual property rights relating to the traditional knowledge of local and indigenous communities. Communication from Bolivia, Colombia, Ecuador, Nicaragua and Peru' [WT/GC/W/362].

World Trade Organization – General Council (1999g), 'Preparations for the 1999 Ministerial Conference. The TRIPS Agreement. Communication from Kenya on behalf of the African Group' [WT/GC/W/302].

World Trade Organization – TRIPS Council (2001a), 'TRIPS and public health. Submission by the Africa Group, Barbados, Bolivia, Brazil, Dominican Republic, Ecuador, Honduras, India, Indonesia, Jamaica, Pakistan, Paraguay, Philippines, Peru, Sri Lanka, Thailand and Venezuela' [IP/C/W/296].

World Trade Organization – TRIPS Council (2001b), 'Special discussion on intellectual property and access to medicines' [IP/C/M/31].

World Trade Organization – Working Group on Trade and Transfer of Technology (2002), Trade and transfer of technology. Background note by the Secretariat' [WT/WGTTT/W/1].

Newspaper and Magazine Articles

Aldhous, P. (1996), 'Patent battle could hold up tests for cancer gene', *New Scientist* 13 January: 8.

Austin, M. (2001), 'Colo. AG sues 3 firms over drug', *Denver Post* 28 September (*http://www.denverpost.com/Stories/0,1002,33%257E161679,00.html*).

Blustein, P. (2001), 'Drug patent dispute poses trade threat – generics fight could derail WTO accord', *Washington Post* 26 October: E01.

Bradsher, K. (2001), 'Bayer agrees to charge government a lower price for anthrax medicine', *New York Times* 25 October.

Bureau of National Affairs (BNA) (2001), 'Cooperation, enforcement, TRIPs case will help protect IP rights, leader says', *BNA Daily Report for Executives* 1 October: A-20.

Coghlan, A. (1994), 'Applications for gene patents "thrown on bonfire"', *New Scientist* 19 February: 4–5.

Cookson, C. (2001), 'UK scientists responsible for third of genome project', *Financial Times*, 13 February: 2.

Drug and Market Development (1998), 'Monoclonal antibody therapy for leukemia and lymphoma', *Drug and Market Development* 9 (100): 264.

Dyer, G. (2002), 'Seeking freedom in New England', *Financial Times* 8 May: 13.

Guardian (various authors) (2000), 'Patenting life – special report' (special supplement), *Guardian* 15 November.

Kleiner, K. (2002), 'Bad for your health: are gene patents stopping patients getting the latest tests?', *New Scientist* 23 March: 6.

National Biological Impact Assessment Program/Information Systems for Biotechnology (NBIAP/ISB) (1994), 'Transgenic cotton patent under pressure', NBIAP/ISB website (*http://www.nbiap.vt.edu*).

National Biological Impact Assessment Program/Information Systems for Biotechnology (NBIAP/ISB) (1995), 'Patent office cancels broad patent on transgenic cotton', NBIAP/ISB website (*http://www.nbiap.vt.edu*).

Nature (editorial) (1995), 'Names for hijacking', *Nature* 373: 370.

Picard, A. (2002), 'Diabetics demand insulin safety probe', *The Globe and Mail* 6 February: 1.

Regalado, A. (2001), 'MIT researcher fueled genome-decoding race', *The Asian Wall Street Journal* 13 February: N4.

Reuters (2001a), 'AstraZeneca holds off rivals as US patent on world's top drug dies', 6 October (*http://www.economictimes.com/today/06worl11.htm*).

Reuters (2001b), 'Bayer says US Cipro patent "beyond doubt"', 26 October (*http://biz.yahoo.com/rf/011026/l26516703_1.html*).

Stix, G. (2001), 'Staking claims' (interview with Greg Aharonian), *Scientific American* 285 (6): 22.

Stokes, G. (2001), 'Patenting of genetic sequences: on the up and up', *IP Matters* April (*http://www.derwent.com/ipmatters/2001_01/genetics.html*).

Trudel, J.D. (1995), 'The great patent sellout', *Upside Magazine* November (http://www.upside.com/texis/mvm/story?id=34712c11c).

USA Today (2001), 'Cipro saga exposes how drugmakers protect profits', 29 October: 14A (*http://cgi.usatoday.com/usatonline/20011029/3574904s.htm*).

Washburn, J. (2001), 'Undue influence', *The American Prospect* 12(14) (http://www.prospect.org/print/V12/14/washburn-j.html).

Watkins, K. (1992), 'Battle for the rights to life', *Guardian* 7 February: 29.

Name Index

Abbott, F.M. 111
Abraham, D. 169
Abraham, J. 104, 123, 124
Acharya, R. 135, 143
Achilladelis, B. 94, 100, 102, 118, 133
Aftalion, F. 85
Aharonian, G. 35, 233
Albert, Prince 55
Aldhous, P. 144
Alford, W.P. 71
Allyn, R.S. 183, 193
Almeida, P.R. de 58
Alverstone, Lord 84
Anderfelt, U. 54
Anell, L. 203
Arnheim, N. 144
Arrow, K.J. 27
Attaran, A. 132, 225–6
Austin, M. 110
Avery, O. 137

Baekeland, L. 82
Baldwin, R. 26
Bale, H. 203
Ballance, R. 246
Banting, F. 117, 239
Barbanti, P. 172
Bardehle, H. 231, 234
Barton, J.H. 158
Baumann, M. 22
Baumgarten, J. 198
Beier, F.-K. 55, 57, 61, 87
Belsky, J. 22, 149
Belt, H. van den 81, 86
Benjamin, G. 184
Bensaude-Vincent, B. 74, 86, 87, 91
Bent, S.A. 62, 186
Bently, L. 10, 128

Bercovitz-Rodriguez, A. 78, 82
Berg, M. 70
Berlan, J.-P. 177
Best, C. 132, 239
Beyleveld, D. 22
Bhagwati, J. 22, 58, 204
Bijman, J. 148
Bin Laden, O. 227
Bismarck, Chancellor O. von 50, 77
Black, J. 26
Black, Sir J. 94
Blakeney, M. 202
Bliss, F.A. 176
Bliss, M. 117
Blustein, P. 227
Borson, D.B. 158
Bosenberg, H. 182–3
Botstein, D. 139
Boyer, H. 138, 143, 147, 150, 158, 168
Boyle, J. 17
Bozicevic, K. 155
Bradsher, K. 226
Braeutigam, R 31
Braithwaite, J. 30, 31, 45, 47, 71, 119, 197,
    198, 201, 203, 243
Breedveld, F.C. 138
Brownsword, R. 22
Bruce, A. 22
Bruce, D. 22
Bruland, K. 70
Brüning, A. 78
Brush, S.B. 22
Bud, R.   135, 152
Bugos, G.E. 178, 182, 183, 184, 186
Burbank, L. 182, 183
Burhenne, W.E. 213
Burkitt, D. 71
Bush, President G. 214

273

Subject Index

279